THE VINTAGE BOOK OF

CONTEMPORARY AMERICAN POETRY

THE VINTAGE BOOK OF
CONTEMPORARY AMERICAN POETRY

Edited and with an Introduction by

J. D. McCLATCHY

VINTAGE BOOKS

A Division of Random House, Inc.

NEW YORK

A Vintage Original, November 1990
First Edition

Copyright © 1990 by J. D. McClatchy

All rights reserved under International and Pan-American Copyright
Conventions. Published in the United States by Vintage Books, a division of
Random House, Inc., New York, and simultaneously in Canada by Random
House of Canada Limited, Toronto.

Library of Congress Cataloging-in-Publication Data
The Vintage book of contemporary American poetry / edited and with an
   introduction by J.D. McClatchy. — 1st ed.
     p. cm.
   "A Vintage original"—T.p. verso.
   ISBN 0-679-72858-9
     1. American poetry—20th century. I. McClatchy, J.D., 1945– .
PS615.V46 1990
811'.508—dc20   90-12246
                        CIP

Book design by Kathleen Carey

Manufactured in the United States of America
10 9

CONTENTS

INTRODUCTION

There is no need for any anthology to choose sides. No critic has to deploy our poets into opposing battle lines with names like Paleface and Redskin, or Academic and Avant-Garde. Best just to duck: the field echoes with sniper fire from the poets themselves. Whitman complained he couldn't stomach Poe's "lurid dreams." Dickinson wouldn't read Whitman at all; she had been told he was "disgraceful." William Carlos Williams railed at T. S. Eliot's *Waste Land* for having "wiped out our world as if an atom bomb had been dropped upon it." At one of their chilly meetings in Key West, Wallace Stevens told Robert Frost, "The trouble with you is you write about things." To which Frost retorted, "The trouble with you is you write about bric-a-brac." Even praise can sound surly, as when Robert Lowell wrote to Theodore Roethke about some new poems: "One of the things I marvel at in your poems is the impression they give of having been worked on an extra half day."

But these potshots are merely sibling rivalries and territorial imperatives. Styles, like personalities, can rub each other the wrong way. Though angry ideologies have been built of such flimsy stuff, it's usually done not by poets but by their dull readers. Poets themselves are the best readers of each other, and quick to see past stylistic differences. A poet's style or subject matter, after all, is not the end of his or her art. "Art," said Emerson, "is the path of a creator to his work." That *work*—the ambitious struggle with experience and language—only continues on the page what started behind the scenes. And when vanity drops its guard, poets often acknowledge secret affinities with their rivals, thefts from and homages to their masters. The general public might think, say, of Allen Ginsberg and Robert Lowell, the Beat and the patrician, as poetic adversaries. But Lowell gratefully acknowledged Ginsberg as a crucial influence on his pivotal *Life Studies,* and Ginsberg has called Lowell "America's leading poet." Mark Strand and James Merrill each write a poetry distinctly different from the other's, but both claim to have modeled their work on Elizabeth Bishop's—which resembles neither. Beneath the landscape of trends and schools and movements run underground streams of sympathy and influence.

From the start our tradition contained multitudes. From the engendering parents of the American line, Walt Whitman and Emily Dickinson, we inherited a set of extremes between which our poets have shifted. The soulful sprawl of Whitman's visionary descriptions, the fastidious measures of Dickinson's eerie hymns to unbelief—these remain strong stylistic impulses in American art. But the similar *work* of both these poets was something still more ambitious and accomplished, and altogether more influential. It seems Emerson, who first and best defined the American imagination, called that work into being. Our literature, he wrote, is "a platform whence we may command a view of our present life, a purchase by which we may move it." On that platform stands the poet, our representative, empowered to hold us steady to a truth until we can make it our own. If poets are liberating gods, that is because they free us from old habits and fixed ideas. Mere talent frolics and juggles; genius realizes and adds. The true poet's "meter-making argument"—that is to say, the *work* as distinct from the *art*—is with his or her own power to see words and things, birth and death, all as emblems of "the great and constant fact of Life."

In 1840, about the same time Emerson was writing his essay "The Poet," Alexis de Tocqueville completed *Democracy in America,* his shrewd portrait of the American character. In his travels around the fledgling nation, he found no worthy art, but he predicted great things. Americans had, he said, "the freedom and the knowledge acquired by their forefathers and the passions which are their own." There was, he discovered, no pioneer's hut without its copy of Shakespeare. (Tocqueville himself first read *Henry V* in a log cabin.) But Americans had not yet—or not until Whitman—learned how to write of their own passions. As for an eventual American style, Tocqueville presumed it would be "fantastic, incorrect, overburdened, and loose, almost always vehement and bold . . . with more wit than erudition, more imagination than profundity. The object of authors will be to astonish rather than please, and to stir the passions more than to charm the taste." He also predicted that the subject of an American poetry would be not history (Americans had none), not nature (only a mirror we hold up to ourselves), but the *self*. Americans, wrote Tocqueville, are "excited in reality only by a survey of themselves," and "each man instantly sees all his fellows when he surveys himself." Passions and ideas would be the poet's arena, and "the inner soul" the poet's pursuit. "I have only to look at myself," wrote Tocqueville fifteen years before the publication of *Leaves of Grass,* in order to "enlarge and to throw light on some of the obscurer recesses of the human heart" and thereby discover the high themes of American poetry—our passions, our doubts, our rare prosperities and inconceivable wretchedness. The true American poet—raucous or demure, passionate or reflective, traditional or experimental—touches what Tocqueville called "the hidden nerve."

For poetry in English, this has been the American century. Americans remade and dominated the art; they raised the stakes and named the terms. The heroic generation who made poetry modern—T. S. Eliot, Ezra Pound, William Carlos Williams, Marianne Moore, Hart Crane, Wallace Stevens—was followed by a generation who labored under giant shadows but who brought our poetry further forward by refining earlier experiments and refreshing older traditions. In fact, now that we are in a position to look back over the poetry of almost the entire twentieth century, the second half can be seen as a period even richer, though less convulsive, than the first. Poetry from World War II until the present—the scope of this anthology—has proved diverse, intrepid, spirited, and surprising. Three generations of poets are represented in this book; each has set about difficult tasks, engaged elegant, challenging possibilities. Each has touched the hidden nerve.

All this has occurred at a time when the fortunes of poetry seem to have simultaneously retreated and advanced. There is no doubt that poetry has, since 1950, lost its proprietary sway in the culture. The collaboration of major modernist poets in the decades following 1920 had cloaked the art in a hieratic obscurity and difficulty that lost it a General Public. Robert Frost kept one, but his example only made the more widespread isolation of other poets more poignant. Competing in a glutted marketplace of images, poetry came for many to seem a quaint anachronism. But at the same time, contemporary poetry became part of the university curriculum. New audiences and presses, more readers and subsidies, and certainly more poets than ever before crowded onto the scene. Public readings, workshops, programs, organizations, and opportunities boomed. All along, the debates, by now at least a century old, continued between highbrow and lowbrow. All along, critics puffed and scolded. And because we have no single literary capital—no London or Paris—but a patchwork of regional centers, competitive energies flourished.

But beyond the neglect and controversies, the quiet work of individual poets continued. What they continued, first of all, were the projects of their immediate predecessors. The example of T. S. Eliot spilling his private agonies into *The Waste Land* echoes through the searing confessions of Robert Lowell's *Life Studies,* just as the solemn brooding of Eliot's *Four Quartets* is resumed in Lowell's long sequence called *History*—or in the religious sensibility of poems by Gjertrud Schnackenberg. The canny accents of Robert Frost's backcountry monologues can be heard in Randall Jarrell's character studies, just as Frost's dark moral power haunts those narratives by Elizabeth Bishop that dramatize our "awful but cheerful" efforts to domesticate the world. The brilliant, scattered fragments of Ezra Pound's imagism are reassembled in the poems of James Wright, or of Charles Wright and Jorie Graham. Because Americans, for all their practicality, are essentially a thinking people, having first made themselves up out of ideas of freedom and equality, it is no surprise to find the historical inquiry that dominates the mythologies of Hart Crane and William Carlos Williams become the pulse in poems by Robert Penn Warren, or by Amy Clampitt, Jay Wright, and Robert Pinsky. (It was Warren who may have been speaking for that wing of American poetry which uses or usurps history when he said, "Historical sense and poetic sense should not, in the end, be contradictory, for if poetry is the little myth we make, history is the big myth we live, and in our living, constantly remake.") The rapturous metaphysical inquiries that

Wallace Stevens made of the imagination's dealings with reality can be subsequently traced in the work of James Merrill or Robert Duncan or John Hollander.

But for all these continuities, for all the innovations and diversity of contemporary poetry, it is still true that "the hidden nerve" provoked the best work of the period. In 1950 this would have been hard to see or predict. By then the lessons of the modernist masters—not their example so much as their tastes—had been thoroughly absorbed. The official style of the day called for a poised, ironic tone that flattered the mind it celebrated—its powers and limits. Poets sought an "impersonal" manner that could brood over spiritual conditions rather than emotional instants. The self was subsumed by a poem's "voice." Both the overwrought complexities of early Robert Lowell and the mild luxuries of early Richard Wilbur were typical. And rebellion was inevitable. The instinctive restlessness of individual poets would have assured changes, but there were larger forces at work as well. Ever since William Carlos Williams, American poets had felt the force of plain speaking—of the colloquial, the commonplace, a naturalistic aesthetic that was free from design or pretense. Many poets by the end of the 1950s had grown suspicious of form as a repressive, distorting medium. They saw its tone and shapes as a projection of worn-out traditional views onto experience that is feverish, rapid, unique. They wanted a free verse that, in D. H. Lawrence's terms, was "direct utterance from the instant, whole man," spontaneous and flexible as a flame.

For instance, Charles Olson's "open field" theories—of line lengths determined by the poet's breathing and fragments that leap kinetically down the page—looked back to Whitman's sense of a poem as an ensemble, and ahead to the spontaneity of the Beats and the New York School, for whom the poem is a chronicle of the creative act that produces it. This impulse for the "lifelike" can be seen as well in Theodore Roethke's plunge into the preconscious, or in the dreamwork of John Berryman's poems, even in the muted psychologizing of Randall Jarrell's monologues. It's apparent too in the whole confessional movement, with which W. D. Snodgrass, Robert Lowell, Anne Sexton, and Sylvia Plath are most strongly identified. The intimate and harrowing details of their accounts of betrayals and breakdowns, self-defeat and longing are an effort to admit into poetry what had been forbidden, suppressed. Taken together, all their efforts to reach what Tocqueville called "the obscurer recesses of the human heart" have helped keep the hazards of the self as the primary focus of contemporary poetry.

Along with Allen Ginsberg's *Howl,* Robert Lowell's *Life Studies,* published in 1959, is often taken as a turning point in American poetry. Lowell, who had learned from the Beats and from William Carlos Williams the value of a heightened immediacy, had also studied the prose of Flaubert and Chekhov in his effort to get a new rhythm and energy into his work. Other poets looked elsewhere. Some used drugs or Zen or the wilderness or radical politics—all of them rituals of concentration. Others sought the magical power beyond rationalism that myths and folklore promise. Several important poets—among them James Wright and W. S. Merwin—adopted the techniques of surrealism to create uncanny perspectives on experience. Like many others in the 1960s, they turned to foreign poets, both old and new, in Europe and Latin America, as a resource for their own work; they discovered not just matters of technique but ways of knowing.

There has always been a doughty isolationist strain in our culture, a homespun pride in what Whitman called our "indigenous" poetry. Part of Whitman's bravado—the part that has been heeded by the best of our contemporaries—is his genuine call to innovation. And part is blinders, a deep American fear of seeming traditional or cultivated. "No one will get at my verses," boasted Whitman, "who insists on viewing them as a literary performance." But that boast was made by a poet who had steeped himself in the Hebrew bible, in Hindu epics, Dante, and the Italian opera. During his young manhood, he would go to the long, bare shores of Coney Island and "declaim Homer and Shakespeare to the surf and sea-gulls by the hour." The wonder, he knew, was that he was not "overwhelmed by those mighty masters." (He thought it likely he was saved by having read them outdoors!) What he did not need to acknowledge was that he had been created by them. And it is often the case that our characteristically "indigenous" poets have drawn on Elsewhere. It is hard to think of Elizabeth Bishop's early work without its wash of Parisian surrealism, or her later without its Brazilian sketches. Such assimilations continue to be crucial to many of our poets, and encourage in them a turn of mind—this is quintessentially American—at once skeptical and open, yielding and withheld.

Suspicions about the "literary performance," however, have remained a habit during the past few decades, not least among some of our most literary poets. Richard Howard once astutely suggested that our postwar poets had deliberately gone about losing their Midas touch: unschooled themselves, roughened or loosened the golden nets of their verse, preferred the impression to the idea, a tentative flux to any ideal order. It is also true that, as they get older, poets (like other kinds of artists) often adopt a leaner, bonier style, more exposed to risk, assertion, wisdomwork, or confession. Still, one thinks of Frost's ovenbird who knew "in singing not to sing." Many poets have been—or been made—wary of the Privileged Moment. James Wright, for instance, in his famous poem "A Blessing," leads us up to an epiphany, but an altogether unexpected one. In John Ashbery's work such epiphanies are deflected or forgone; his poems slide among possibilities, distrustful of intensity or flourishes. This too is part of contemporary poetry's concern to rearrange the conventions of reading, to challenge and freshen our expectations.

The anthology that History eventually assembles from the poetry of this period will be a shorter book than this. But I'd have preferred to make this one still longer. The choices were rich and wide. But both the space and budget were limited. In making this selection I have naturally been led by my own tastes, but often led to the difficulty of deciding between favorites. Like the American imagination, this book is pluralistic. It draws on the California of Gary Snyder and Robert Hass, on the Pacific Northwest of David Wagoner and Carolyn Kizer, on the Midwest of Philip Levine and Richard Hugo, on the South of Charles Wright and Dave Smith, on the New York of Frank O'Hara, Irving Feldman, and Audre Lorde, on the New England of Louise Glück and Richard Wilbur. It is Wilbur, in fact, who can provide the best metaphor for my selection. In his poem "A Wall in the Woods," he describes coming upon an old stone wall and marveling at its odd balance, how such differently shaped rocks were made to hold together: "Look how with shims they made the stones weigh inward, / Binding the water-rounded with the flat.''

It is my hope that the poems in this anthology—and any anthology is finally a gathering of poems rather than of poets—*weigh inward.* There are poems here that look out at the world, and poems that are trained soulward. There are poems of political engagement and of pastoral withdrawal. Poems of intellectual poise, of emotional anguish. There are discursive poems that bristle with argument and explanation. There are epigrams and narratives and koans. There are poems that ramble genially, and poems in crisply rhyming quatrains that have disciplined themselves to nervy encounters with the sublime. All of them have put the private life on public view. Of the claims made that new literary movements—black, feminist, gay—have emerged, it would be better to say that new audiences have developed; weaker poets play to them, stronger poets (I have included several in this book) attend to their art and work to complicate the issues. And it is clear that, despite the claims of other genres, the lyric has continued to dominate our poetry. Whether stretched by Allen Ginsberg and James Merrill, or compressed by Robert Creeley and Edgar Bowers, the lyric poem—the song of the self—best captures the mind in collaboration with the heart, the psyche with the rhythms of verse; best isolates aspects of the individual in history, best joins the human with intimations of the divine.

I have begun this book with Robert Lowell and Elizabeth Bishop. They are placed slightly out of chronological order, and more generously represented than other poets. That is because I think they were—and remain—the strongest poets of their generation and have continued as towering models. (By the word *contemporary* in this book's title, I mean, of course, poets of this period—some of them now dead—whose work still lives with us and looks over the shoulders of today's readers and writers as a vital resource.) The embattled grandeur of Lowell's poems, the moral gravity of their historical inquiries, the often tender boldness with which he bore witness to his own turmoil and that of his times—these mark Lowell as an archetypal figure of the age, both its troubled conscience and its noble elegist. Elizabeth Bishop's modest career and reputation as a poet's poet may at one time have limited a true appreciation of her power. But over the past decade her work has come to seem unrivaled for its ability to estrange the familiar, to describe the space between moments, the textures of lives and places, the homely paradoxes and human reversals that go on under our light regard. Her mysteriously confidential tone of voice, the way she shuffled the orders of dream and reality, flesh and spirit, memory and loss—these are the terms of her mastery. What Randall Jarrell once wrote about Robert Frost could as well be said of Bishop: "The limits which existence approaches and falls back from have seldom been stated with such bare composure."

Lowell's febrile ambition and Bishop's uncanny composure stand out boldly, even against remarkable performances by their peers. In the two generations succeeding theirs, talent was more lavishly and equally spread around. By whatever historical accident, a group of formidable poets was born between 1925 and 1930. In 1926 alone, A. R. Ammons, Robert Creeley, Allen Ginsberg, James Merrill, Frank O'Hara, W. D. Snodgrass, and David Wagoner; in 1927, John Ashbery, Galway Kinnell, W. S. Merwin, and James Wright. This is the generation of poets who grew up during the Depression and a world war, apprenticed themselves to both poetry and its New Critical orthodoxies during the fifties and established their careers in the sixties—by which time they were restlessly seeking new channels of figural energy, new methods or refinements. By the eighties they'd become grand masters. And a new generation, born between 1940 and 1945, has now established its prominence. This group of poets, raised amidst a clamor of competing styles, a confusion of freedoms, has carefully but confidently rejected empty choices in order to discover and complete the hard tasks.

To represent these poets, I have not necessarily chosen poems merely to stand in for the various stages of their careers. If I have favored more recent work, that is because it is stronger; if I have preferred longer to shorter poems, that is because a poet's characteristic gifts—of voice and range, of description and argument, of insight and sympathy—are often best displayed when she or he has more, and more complex, material to work with.

The composer John Cage once told the painter Philip Guston, "When you start working, everybody is in your studio—the past, your friends, enemies, the art world, and above all, your own ideas—all are there. But as you continue, they start leaving one by one, and you are left completely alone." This anthology visits sixty-five men and women, the best poets of our time, alone with their art, with their passions, with the truth they would hold us steady to until we can make it our own.

THE VINTAGE BOOK OF

CONTEMPORARY
AMERICAN
POETRY

ROBERT LOWELL
(1917–1977)

Volume by volume, the books of Robert Lowell revealed the age in
which he lived, both drawing its portrait and animating its conscience.
At the time of his death, Lowell was the most prominent, influential,
and honored American poet of his generation. Born in Boston, the
heir to a patrician New England family, he was instinctively
rebellious; he dropped out of Harvard (preferring to study at Kenyon
College with John Crowe Ransom), converted to Catholicism, and
served time in jail as a conscientious objector during World War II.
His troubled family history, broken marriages, and manic-depressive
episodes later became the subjects of his poems, beginning with the
celebrated *Life Studies* in 1959, a book that also marked a shift away
from the dense symbolic rhetoric of his early work toward a more
open, febrile style. His preference for existential narrative, his
calculated use of surreal imagery, his deployment of historical
allusion, and his confessional method—these were constant during his
career, as were themes of will, authority, breakdown, and recrimination
in history and his own life. Lowell was active as a teacher, translator,
and playwright; he twice won the Pulitzer Prize (in 1947 and 1974), in ad-
dition to the National Book Award (1960), the Bollingen Prize (1962),
the National Book Critics Circle Award (1978), and many others.

The Quaker Graveyard in Nantucket

for Warren Winslow, Dead at Sea

Let man have dominion over the fishes of the sea and the
fowls of the air and the beasts of the whole earth, and every
creeping creature that moveth upon the earth.

I

A brackish reach of shoal off Madaket—
The sea was still breaking violently and night

Had steamed into our North Atlantic Fleet,
When the drowned sailor clutched the drag-net. Light
Flashed from his matted head and marble feet,
He grappled at the net
With the coiled, hurdling muscles of his thighs:
The corpse was bloodless, a botch of reds and whites,
Its open, staring eyes
Were lustreless dead-lights
Or cabin-windows on a stranded hulk
Heavy with sand. We weight the body, close
Its eyes and heave it seaward whence it came,
Where the heel-headed dogfish barks its nose
On Ahab's void and forehead; and the name
Is blocked in yellow chalk.
Sailors, who pitch this portent at the sea
Where dreadnaughts shall confess
Its hell-bent deity,
When you are powerless
To sand-bag this Atlantic bulwark, faced
By the earth-shaker, green, unwearied, chaste
In his steel scales: ask for no Orphean lute
To pluck life back. The guns of the steeled fleet
Recoil and then repeat
The hoarse salute.

I I

Whenever winds are moving and their breath
Heaves at the roped-in bulwarks of this pier,
The terns and sea-gulls tremble at your death
In these home waters. Sailor, can you hear
The Pequod's sea wings, beating landward, fall
Headlong and break on our Atlantic wall
Off 'Sconset, where the yawing S-boats splash
The bellbuoy, with ballooning spinnakers,
As the entangled, screeching mainsheet clears
The blocks: off Madaket, where lubbers lash
The heavy surf and throw their long lead squids
For blue-fish? Sea-gulls blink their heavy lids

Seaward. The winds' wings beat upon the stones,
Cousin, and scream for you and the claws rush
At the sea's throat and wring it in the slush
Of this old Quaker graveyard where the bones
Cry out in the long night for the hurt beast
Bobbing by Ahab's whaleboats in the East.

III

All you recovered from Poseidon died
With you, my cousin, and the harrowed brine
Is fruitless on the blue beard of the god,
Stretching beyond us to the castles in Spain,
Nantucket's westward haven. To Cape Cod
Guns, cradled on the tide,
Blast the eelgrass about a waterclock
Of bilge and backwash, roil the salt and sand
Lashing earth's scaffold, rock
Our warships in the hand
Of the great God, where time's contrition blues
Whatever it was these Quaker sailors lost
In the mad scramble of their lives. They died
When time was open-eyed,
Wooden and childish; only bones abide
There, in the nowhere, where their boats were tossed
Sky-high, where mariners had fabled news
Of IS, the whited monster. What it cost
Them is their secret. In the sperm-whale's slick
I see the Quakers drown and hear their cry:
"If God himself had not been on our side,
If God himself had not been on our side,
When the Atlantic rose against us, why,
Then it had swallowed us up quick."

IV

This is the end of the whaleroad and the whale
Who spewed Nantucket bones on the thrashed swell
And stirred the troubled waters to whirlpools
To send the Pequod packing off to hell:

This is the end of them, three-quarters fools,
Snatching at straws to sail
Seaward and seaward on the turntail whale,
Spouting out blood and water as it rolls,
Sick as a dog to these Atlantic shoals:
Clamavimus, O depths. Let the sea-gulls wail

For water, for the deep where the high tide
Mutters to its hurt self, mutters and ebbs.
Waves wallow in their wash, go out and out,
Leave only the death-rattle of the crabs,
The beach increasing, its enormous snout
Sucking the ocean's side.
This is the end of running on the waves;
We are poured out like water. Who will dance
The mast-lashed master of Leviathans
Up from this field of Quakers in their unstoned graves?

V

When the whale's viscera go and the roll
Of its corruption overruns this world
Beyond tree-swept Nantucket and Woods Hole
And Martha's Vineyard, Sailor, will your sword
Whistle and fall and sink into the fat?
In the great ash-pit of Jehoshaphat
The bones cry for the blood of the white whale,
The fat flukes arch and whack about its ears,
The death-lance churns into the sanctuary, tears
The gun-blue swingle, heaving like a flail,
And hacks the coiling life out: it works and drags
And rips the sperm-whale's midriff into rags,
Gobbets of blubber spill to wind and weather,
Sailor, and gulls go round the stoven timbers
Where the morning stars sing out together
And thunder shakes the white surf and dismembers
The red flag hammered in the mast-head. Hide,
Our steel, Jonas Messias, in Thy side.

V I

OUR LADY OF WALSINGHAM

There once the penitents took off their shoes
And then walked barefoot the remaining mile;
And the small trees, a stream and hedgerows file
Slowly along the munching English lane,
Like cows to the old shrine, until you lose
Track of your dragging pain.
The stream flows down under the druid tree,
Shiloah's whirlpools gurgle and make glad
The castle of God. Sailor, you were glad
And whistled Sion by that stream. But see:

Our Lady, too small for her canopy,
Sits near the altar. There's no comeliness
At all or charm in that expressionless
Face with its heavy eyelids. As before,
This face, for centuries a memory,
Non est species, neque decor,
Expressionless, expresses God: it goes
Past castled Sion. She knows what God knows,
Not Calvary's Cross nor crib at Bethlehem
Now, and the world shall come to Walsingham.

V I I

The empty winds are creaking and the oak
Splatters and splatters on the cenotaph,
The boughs are trembling and a gaff
Bobs on the untimely stroke
Of the greased wash exploding on a shoal-bell
In the old mouth of the Atlantic. It's well;
Atlantic, you are fouled with the blue sailors,
Sea-monsters, upward angel, downward fish:
Unmarried and corroding, spare of flesh
Mart once of supercilious, wing'd clippers,
Atlantic, where your bell-trap guts its spoil
You could cut the brackish winds with a knife

Here in Nantucket, and cast up the time
When the Lord God formed man from the sea's slime
And breathed into his face the breath of life,
And blue-lung'd combers lumbered to the kill.
The Lord survives the rainbow of His will.

Memories of West Street and Lepke

Only teaching on Tuesdays, book-worming
in pajamas fresh from the washer each morning,
I hog a whole house on Boston's
"hardly passionate Marlborough Street,"
where even the man
scavenging filth in the back alley trash cans,
has two children, a beach wagon, a helpmate,
and is a "young Republican."
I have a nine months' daughter,
young enough to be my granddaughter.
Like the sun she rises in her flame-flamingo infants' wear.

These are the tranquillized *Fifties*,
and I am forty. Ought I to regret my seedtime?
I was a fire-breathing Catholic C.O.,
and made my manic statement,
telling off the state and president, and then
sat waiting sentence in the bull pen
beside a Negro boy with curlicues
of marijuana in his hair.

Given a year,
I walked on the roof of the West Street Jail, a short
enclosure like my school soccer court,
and saw the Hudson River once a day
through sooty clothesline entanglements
and bleaching khaki tenements.

Strolling, I yammered metaphysics with Abramowitz,
a jaundice-yellow ("it's really tan")
and fly-weight pacifist,
so vegetarian,
he wore rope shoes and preferred fallen fruit.
He tried to convert Bioff and Brown,
the Hollywood pimps, to his diet.
Hairy, muscular, suburban,
wearing chocolate double-breasted suits,
they blew their tops and beat him black and blue.

I was so out of things, I'd never heard
of the Jehovah's Witnesses.
"Are you a C.O.?" I asked a fellow jailbird.
"No," he answered, "I'm a J.W."
He taught me the "hospital tuck,"
and pointed out the T-shirted back
of *Murder Incorporated's* Czar Lepke,
there piling towels on a rack,
or dawdling off to his little segregated cell full
of things forbidden the common man:
a portable radio, a dresser, two toy American
flags tied together with a ribbon of Easter palm.
Flabby, bald, lobotomized,
he drifted in a sheepish calm,
where no agonizing reappraisal
jarred his concentration on the electric chair—
hanging like an oasis in his air
of lost connections. . . .

Man and Wife

Tamed by *Miltown,* we lie on Mother's bed;
the rising sun in war paint dyes us red;
in broad daylight her gilded bed-posts shine,

abandoned, almost Dionysian.
At last the trees are green on Marlborough Street,
blossoms on our magnolia ignite
the morning with their murderous five days' white.
All night I've held your hand,
as if you had
a fourth time faced the kingdom of the mad—
its hackneyed speech, its homicidal eye—
and dragged me home alive. . . . Oh my *Petite,*
clearest of all God's creatures, still all air and nerve:
you were in your twenties, and I,
once hand on glass
and heart in mouth,
outdrank the Rahvs in the heat
of Greenwich Village, fainting at your feet—
too boiled and shy
and poker-faced to make a pass,
while the shrill verve
of your invective scorched the traditional South.

Now twelve years later, you turn your back.
Sleepless, you hold
your pillow to your hollows like a child;
your old-fashioned tirade—
loving, rapid, merciless—
breaks like the Atlantic Ocean on my head.

Skunk Hour

for Elizabeth Bishop

Nautilus Island's hermit
heiress still lives through winter in her Spartan cottage;
her sheep still graze above the sea.
Her son's a bishop. Her farmer

is first selectman in our village;
she's in her dotage.

Thirsting for
the hierarchic privacy
of Queen Victoria's century,
she buys up all
the eyesores facing her shore,
and lets them fall.

The season's ill—
we've lost our summer millionaire,
who seemed to leap from an L. L. Bean
catalogue. His nine-knot yawl
was auctioned off to lobstermen.
A red fox stain covers Blue Hill.

And now our fairy
decorator brightens his shop for fall;
his fishnet's filled with orange cork,
orange, his cobbler's bench and awl;
there is no money in his work,
he'd rather marry.

One dark night,
my Tudor Ford climbed the hill's skull;
I watched for love-cars. Lights turned down,
they lay together, hull to hull,
where the graveyard shelves on the town. . . .
My mind's not right.

A car radio bleats,
"Love, O careless Love. . . ." I hear
my ill-spirit sob in each blood cell,
as if my hand were at its throat. . . .
I myself am hell;
nobody's here—

only skunks, that search
in the moonlight for a bite to eat.
They march on their soles up Main Street:
white stripes, moonstruck eyes' red fire

under the chalk-dry and spar spire
of the Trinitarian Church.

I stand on top
of our back steps and breathe the rich air—
a mother skunk with her column of kittens swills the garbage
    pail.
She jabs her wedge-head in a cup
of sour cream, drops her ostrich tail,
and will not scare.

The Mouth of the Hudson

for Esther Brooks

A single man stands like a bird-watcher,
and scuffles the pepper and salt snow
from a discarded, gray
Westinghouse Electric cable drum.
He cannot discover America by counting
the chains of condemned freight-trains
from thirty states. They jolt and jar
and junk in the siding below him.
He has trouble with his balance.
His eyes drop,
and he drifts with the wild ice
ticking seaward down the Hudson,
like the blank sides of a jig-saw puzzle.

The ice ticks seaward like a clock.
A Negro toasts
wheat-seeds over the coke-fumes
of a punctured barrel.
Chemical air
sweeps in from New Jersey,
and smells of coffee.

Across the river
ledges of suburban factories tan
in the sulphur-yellow sun
of the unforgivable landscape.

For the Union Dead

"Relinquunt Omnia Servare Rem Publicam."

The old South Boston Aquarium stands
in a Sahara of snow now. Its broken windows are boarded.
The bronze weathervane cod has lost half its scales.
The airy tanks are dry.

Once my nose crawled like a snail on the glass;
my hand tingled
to burst the bubbles
drifting from the noses of the cowed, compliant fish.

My hand draws back. I often sigh still
for the dark downward and vegetating kingdom
of the fish and reptile. One morning last March,
I pressed against the new barbed and galvanized

fence on the Boston Common. Behind their cage,
yellow dinosaur steamshovels were grunting
as they cropped up tons of mush and grass
to gouge their underworld garage.

Parking spaces luxuriate like civic
sandpiles in the heart of Boston.
A girdle of orange, Puritan-pumpkin colored girders
braces the tingling Statehouse,

shaking over the excavations, as it faces Colonel Shaw
and his bell-cheeked Negro infantry

on St. Gaudens' shaking Civil War relief,
propped by a plank splint against the garage's earthquake.

Two months after marching through Boston,
half the regiment was dead;
at the dedication,
William James could almost hear the bronze Negroes breathe.

Their monument sticks like a fishbone
in the city's throat.
Its Colonel is as lean
as a compass-needle.

He has an angry wrenlike vigilance,
a greyhound's gentle tautness;
he seems to wince at pleasure,
and suffocate for privacy.

He is out of bounds now. He rejoices in man's lovely,
peculiar power to choose life and die—
when he leads his black soldiers to death,
he cannot bend his back.

On a thousand small town New England greens,
the old white churches hold their air
of sparse, sincere rebellion; frayed flags
quilt the graveyards of the Grand Army of the Republic.

The stone statues of the abstract Union Soldier
grow slimmer and younger each year—
wasp-waisted, they doze over muskets
and muse through their sideburns . . .

Shaw's father wanted no monument
except the ditch,
where his son's body was thrown
and lost with his "niggers."

The ditch is nearer.
There are no statutes for the last war here;
on Boylston Street, a commercial photograph
shows Hiroshima boiling

over a Mosler Safe, the "Rock of Ages"
that survived the blast. Space is nearer.
When I crouch to my television set,
the drained faces of Negro school-children rise like balloons.

Colonel Shaw
is riding on his bubble,
he waits
for the blessèd break.

The Aquarium is gone. Everywhere,
giant finned cars nose forward like fish;
a savage servility
slides by on grease.

Waking Early Sunday Morning

O to break loose, like the chinook
salmon jumping and falling back,
nosing up to the impossible
stone and bone-crushing waterfall—
raw-jawed, weak-fleshed there, stopped by ten
steps of the roaring ladder, and then
to clear the top on the last try,
alive enough to spawn and die.

Stop, back off. The salmon breaks
water, and now my body wakes
to feel the unpolluted joy
and criminal leisure of a boy—
no rainbow smashing a dry fly
in the white run is free as I,
here squatting like a dragon on
time's hoard before the day's begun!

Fierce, fireless mind, running downhill.
Look up and see the harbor fill:

business as usual in eclipse
goes down to the sea in ships—
wake of refuse, dacron rope,
bound for Bermuda or Good Hope,
all bright before the morning watch
the wine-dark hulls of yawl and ketch.

I watch a glass of water wet
with a fine fuzz of icy sweat,
silvery colors touched with sky,
serene in their neutrality—
yet if I shift, or change my mood,
I see some object made of wood,
background behind it of brown grain,
to darken it, but not to stain.

O that the spirit could remain
tinged but untarnished by its strain!
Better dressed and stacking birch,
or lost with the Faithful at Church—
anywhere, but somewhere else!
And now the new electric bells,
clearly chiming, "Faith of our fathers,"
and now the congregation gathers.

O Bible chopped and crucified
in hymns we hear but do not read,
none of the milder subtleties
of grace or art will sweeten these
stiff quatrains shoveled out four-square—
they sing of peace, and preach despair;
yet they gave darkness some control,
and left a loophole for the soul.

When will we see Him face to face?
Each day, He shines through darker glass.
In this small town where everything
is known, I see His vanishing
emblems, His white spire and flag-
pole sticking out above the fog,

like old white china doorknobs, sad,
slight, useless things to calm the mad.

Hammering military splendor,
top-heavy Goliath in full armor—
little redemption in the mass
liquidations of their brass,
elephant and phalanx moving
with the times and still improving,
when that kingdom hit the crash:
a million foreskins stacked like trash . . .

Sing softer! But what if a new
diminuendo brings no true
tenderness, only restlessness,
excess, the hunger for success,
sanity of self-deception
fixed and kicked by reckless caution,
while we listen to the bells—
anywhere, but somewhere else!

O to break loose. All life's grandeur
is something with a girl in summer . . .
elated as the President
girdled by his establishment
this Sunday morning, free to chaff
his own thoughts with his bear-cuffed staff,
swimming nude, unbuttoned, sick
of his ghost-written rhetoric!

No weekends for the gods now. Wars
flicker, earth licks its open sores,
fresh breakage, fresh promotions, chance
assassinations, no advance.
Only man thinning out his kind
sounds through the Sabbath noon, the blind
swipe of the pruner and his knife
busy about the tree of life . . .

Pity the planet, all joy gone
from this sweet volcanic cone;

peace to our children when they fall
in small war on the heels of small
war—until the end of time
to police the earth, a ghost
orbiting forever lost
in our monotonous sublime.

History

History has to live with what was here,
clutching and close to fumbling all we had—
it is so dull and gruesome how we die,
unlike writing, life never finishes.
Abel was finished; death is not remote,
a flash-in-the-pan electrifies the skeptic,
his cows crowding like skulls against high-voltage wire,
his baby crying all night like a new machine.
As in our Bibles, white-faced, predatory,
the beautiful, mist-drunken hunter's moon ascends—
a child could give it a face: two holes, two holes,
my eyes, my mouth, between them a skull's no-nose—
O there's a terrifying innocence in my face
drenched with the silver salvage of the mornfrost.

The Nihilist as Hero

"All our French poets can turn an inspired line;
who has written six passable in sequence?"
said Valéry. That was a happy day for Satan. . . .

I want words meat-hooked from the living steer,
but a cold flame of tinfoil licks the metal log,
beautiful unchanging fire of childhood
betraying a monotony of vision. . . .
Life by definition breeds on change,
each season we scrap new cars and wars and women.
But sometimes when I am ill or delicate,
the pinched flame of my match turns unchanging green,
a cornstalk in green tails and seeded tassel. . . .
A nihilist wants to live in the world as is,
and yet gaze the everlasting hills to rubble.

Reading Myself

Like thousands, I took just pride and more than just,
struck matches that brought my blood to a boil;
I memorized the tricks to set the river on fire—
somehow never wrote something to go back to.
Can I suppose I am finished with wax flowers
and have earned my grass on the minor slopes of
    Parnassus. . . .
No honeycomb is built without a bee
adding circle to circle, cell to cell,
the wax and honey of a mausoleum—
this round dome proves its maker is alive;
the corpse of the insect lives embalmed in honey,
prays that its perishable work live long
enough for the sweet-tooth bear to desecrate—
this open book . . . my open coffin.

Obit

Our love will not come back on fortune's wheel—

in the end it gets us, though a man know what he'd have:
old cars, old money, old undebased pre-Lyndon
silver, no copper rubbing through . . . old wives;
I could live such a too long time with mine.
In the end, every hypochondriac is his own prophet.
Before the final coming to rest, comes the rest
of all transcendence in a mode of being, hushing
all becoming. I'm for and with myself in my otherness,
in the eternal return of earth's fairer children,
the lily, the rose, the sun on brick at dusk,
the loved, the lover, and their fear of life,
their unconquered flux, insensate oneness, painful "It was. . . ."
After loving you so much, can I forget
you for eternity, and have no other choice?

Fishnet

Any clear thing that blinds us with surprise,
your wandering silences and bright trouvailles,
dolphin let loose to catch the flashing fish. . . .
saying too little, then too much.
Poets die adolescents, their beat embalms them,
the archetypal voices sing offkey;
the old actor cannot read his friends,
and nevertheless he reads himself aloud,
genius hums the auditorium dead.
The line must terminate.
Yet my heart rises, I know I've gladdened a lifetime
knotting, undoing a fishnet of tarred rope;

the net will hang on the wall when the fish are eaten,
nailed like illegible bronze on the futureless future.

Dolphin

My Dolphin, you only guide me by surprise,
captive as Racine, the man of craft,
drawn through his maze of iron composition
by the incomparable wandering voice of Phèdre.
When I was troubled in mind, you made for my body
caught in its hangman's-knot of sinking lines,
the glassy bowing and scraping of my will. . . .
I have sat and listened to too many
words of the collaborating muse,
and plotted perhaps too freely with my life,
not avoiding injury to others,
not avoiding injury to myself—
to ask compassion . . . this book, half fiction,
an eelnet made by man for the eel fighting—

my eyes have seen what my hand did.

Epilogue

Those blessèd structures, plot and rhyme—
why are they no help to me now
I want to make
something imagined, not recalled?
I hear the noise of my own voice:

The painter's vision is not a lens,
it trembles to caress the light.
But sometimes everything I write
with the threadbare art of my eye
seems a snapshot,
lurid, rapid, garish, grouped,
heightened from life,
yet paralyzed by fact.
All's misalliance.
Yet why not say what happened?
Pray for the grace of accuracy
Vermeer gave to the sun's illumination
stealing like the tide across a map
to his girl solid with yearning.
We are poor passing facts,
warned by that to give
each figure in the photograph
his living name.

ELIZABETH BISHOP
(1911–1979)

Although she wrote less than many of her peers, the evident mastery
of her poems secured for Elizabeth Bishop a leading position in her
generation. Her ingenuous style and reticent manner, forgoing strain
or pretension, led some critics to mistake her as merely agreeable.
Praised from the start for their clarity, wittily observed details, and
tonal control, the descriptive surfaces of Bishop's poems yield in
fact—through shifting scales and perspectives—to dark, abiding
mysteries. Her imagination, fascinated by travel, shuttled between
north and south—between the Nova Scotia of her childhood and the
Brazil of her adult life; between moral austerity and family, and the
languid estrangements of exile. She was born in Worcester,
Massachusetts. While she was still a child, her father died and her
mother was locked away in a mental asylum; Bishop was raised by
relatives in New England and Canada. She graduated from Vassar,
lived in New York City, France, Mexico, and Key West, then moved
to Brazil, where she lived for sixteen years before returning in 1970 to
teach at Harvard. She won the Pulitzer Prize in 1956 and
the National Book Award in 1970.

The Bight

On my birthday

At low tide like this how sheer the water is.
White, crumbling ribs of marl protrude and glare
and the boats are dry, the pilings dry as matches.
Absorbing, rather than being absorbed,
the water in the bight doesn't wet anything,
the color of the gas flame turned as low as possible.
One can smell it turning to gas; if one were Baudelaire
one could probably hear it turning to marimba music.
The little ocher dredge at work off the end of the dock

already plays the dry perfectly off-beat claves.
The birds are outsize. Pelicans crash
into this peculiar gas unnecessarily hard,
it seems to me, like pickaxes,
rarely coming up with anything to show for it,
and going off with humorous elbowings.
Black-and-white man-of-war birds soar
on impalpable drafts
and open their tails like scissors on the curves
or tense them like wishbones, till they tremble.
The frowsy sponge boats keep coming in
with the obliging air of retrievers,
bristling with jackstraw gaffs and hooks
and decorated with bobbles of sponges.
There is a fence of chicken wire along the dock
where, glinting like little plowshares,
the blue-gray shark tails are hung up to dry
for the Chinese-restaurant trade.
Some of the little white boats are still piled up
against each other, or lie on their sides, stove in,
and not yet salvaged, if they ever will be, from the last bad
     storm,
like torn-open, unanswered letters.
The bight is littered with old correspondences.
Click. Click. Goes the dredge,
and brings up a dripping jawful of marl.
All the untidy activity continues,
awful but cheerful.

Over 2,000 Illustrations and
a Complete Concordance

> Thus should have been our travels:
> serious, engravable.

The Seven Wonders of the World are tired
and a touch familiar, but the other scenes,
innumerable, though equally sad and still,
are foreign. Often the squatting Arab,
or group of Arabs, plotting, probably,
against our Christian Empire,
while one apart, with outstretched arm and hand
points to the Tomb, the Pit, the Sepulcher.
The branches of the date-palms look like files.
The cobbled courtyard, where the Well is dry,
is like a diagram, the brickwork conduits
are vast and obvious, the human figure
far gone in history or theology,
gone with its camel or its faithful horse.
Always the silence, the gesture, the specks of birds
suspended on invisible threads above the Site,
or the smoke rising solemnly, pulled by threads.
Granted a page alone or a page made up
of several scenes arranged in cattycornered rectangles
or circles set on stippled gray,
granted a grim lunette,
caught in the toils of an initial letter,
when dwelt upon, they all resolve themselves.
The eye drops, weighted, through the lines
the burin made, the lines that move apart
like ripples above sand,
dispersing storms, God's spreading fingerprint,
and painfully, finally, that ignite
in watery prismatic white-and-blue.

Entering the Narrows at St. Johns
the touching bleat of goats reached to the ship.
We glimpsed them, reddish, leaping up the cliffs
among the fog-soaked weeds and butter-and-eggs.
And at St. Peter's the wind blew and the sun shone madly.
Rapidly, purposefully, the Collegians marched in lines,
crisscrossing the great square with black, like ants.
In Mexico the dead man lay
in a blue arcade; the dead volcanoes

glistened like Easter lilies.
The jukebox went on playing "Ay, Jalisco!"
And at Volubilis there were beautiful poppies
splitting the mosaics; the fat old guide made eyes.
In Dingle harbor a golden length of evening
the rotting hulks held up their dripping plush.
The Englishwoman poured tea, informing us
that the Duchess was going to have a baby.
And in the brothels of Marrakesh
the little pockmarked prostitutes
balanced their tea-trays on their heads
and did their belly-dances; flung themselves
naked and giggling against our knees,
asking for cigarettes. It was somewhere near there
I saw what frightened me most of all:
A holy grave, not looking particularly holy,
one of a group under a keyhole-arched stone baldaquin
open to every wind from the pink desert.
An open, gritty, marble trough, carved solid
with exhortation, yellowed
as scattered cattle-teeth;
half-filled with dust, not even the dust
of the poor prophet paynim who once lay there.
In a smart burnoose Khadour looked on amused.

Everything only connected by "and" and "and."
Open the book. (The gilt rubs off the edges
of the pages and pollinates the fingertips.)
Open the heavy book. Why couldn't we have seen
this old Nativity while we were at it?
—the dark ajar, the rocks breaking with light,
an undisturbed, unbreathing flame,
colorless, sparkless, freely fed on straw,
and, lulled within, a family with pets,
—and looked and looked our infant sight away.

At the Fishhouses

Although it is a cold evening,
down by one of the fishhouses
an old man sits netting,
his net, in the gloaming almost invisible,
a dark purple-brown,
and his shuttle worn and polished.
The air smells so strong of codfish
it makes one's nose run and one's eyes water.
The five fishhouses have steeply peaked roofs
and narrow, cleated gangplanks slant up
to storerooms in the gables
for the wheelbarrows to be pushed up and down on.
All is silver: the heavy surface of the sea,
swelling slowly as if considering spilling over,
is opaque, but the silver of the benches,
the lobster pots, and masts, scattered
among the wild jagged rocks,
is of an apparent translucence
like the small old buildings with an emerald moss
growing on their shoreward walls.
The big fish tubs are completely lined
with layers of beautiful herring scales
and the wheelbarrows are similarly plastered
with creamy iridescent coats of mail,
with small iridescent flies crawling on them.
Up on the little slope behind the houses,
set in the sparse bright sprinkle of grass,
is an ancient wooden capstan,
cracked, with two long bleached handles
and some melancholy stains, like dried blood,
where the ironwork has rusted.
The old man accepts a Lucky Strike.
He was a friend of my grandfather.
We talk of the decline in the population
and of codfish and herring

while he waits for a herring boat to come in.
There are sequins on his vest and on his thumb.
He has scraped the scales, the principal beauty,
from unnumbered fish with that black old knife,
the blade of which is almost worn away.

Down at the water's edge, at the place
where they haul up the boats, up the long ramp
descending into the water, thin silver
tree trunks are laid horizontally
across the gray stones, down and down
at intervals of four or five feet.

Cold dark deep and absolutely clear,
element bearable to no mortal,
to fish and to seals . . . One seal particularly
I have seen here evening after evening.
He was curious about me. He was interested in music;
like me a believer in total immersion,
so I used to sing him Baptist hymns.
I also sang "A Mighty Fortress Is Our God."
He stood up in the water and regarded me
steadily, moving his head a little.
Then he would disappear, then suddenly emerge
almost in the same spot, with a sort of shrug
as if it were against his better judgment.
Cold dark deep and absolutely clear,
the clear gray icy water . . . Back, behind us,
the dignified tall firs begin.
Bluish, associating with their shadows,
a million Christmas trees stand
waiting for Christmas. The water seems suspended
above the rounded gray and blue-gray stones.
I have seen it over and over, the same sea, the same,
slightly, indifferently swinging above the stones,
icily free above the stones,
above the stones and then the world.
If you should dip your hand in,
your wrist would ache immediately,
your bones would begin to ache and your hand would burn

as if the water were a transmutation of fire
that feeds on stones and burns with a dark gray flame.
If you tasted it, it would first taste bitter,
then briny, then surely burn your tongue.
It is like what we imagine knowledge to be:
dark, salt, clear, moving, utterly free,
drawn from the cold hard mouth
of the world, derived from the rocky breasts
forever, flowing and drawn, and since
our knowledge is historical, flowing, and flown.

The Shampoo

The still explosions on the rocks,
the lichens, grow
by spreading, gray, concentric shocks.
They have arranged
to meet the rings around the moon, although
within our memories they have not changed.

And since the heavens will attend
as long on us,
you've been, dear friend,
precipitate and pragmatical;
and look what happens. For Time is
nothing if not amenable.

The shooting stars in your black hair
in bright formation
are flocking where,
so straight, so soon?
—Come, let me wash it in this big tin basin,
battered and shiny like the moon.

Brazil, January 1, 1502

. . . embroidered nature . . . tapestried landscape.

Landscape into Art, by Sir Kenneth Clark

Januaries, Nature greets our eyes
exactly as she must have greeted theirs:
every square inch filling in with foliage—
big leaves, little leaves, and giant leaves,
blue, blue-green, and olive,
with occasional lighter veins and edges,
or a satin underleaf turned over;
monster ferns
in silver-gray relief,
and flowers, too, like giant water lilies
up in the air—up, rather, in the leaves—
purple, yellow, two yellows, pink,
rust red and greenish white;
solid but airy; fresh as if just finished
and taken off the frame.

A blue-white sky, a simple web,
backing for feathery detail:
brief arcs, a pale-green broken wheel,
a few palms, swarthy, squat, but delicate;
and perching there in profile, beaks agape,
the big symbolic birds keep quiet,
each showing only half his puffed and padded,
pure-colored or spotted breast.
Still in the foreground there is Sin:
five sooty dragons near some massy rocks.
The rocks are worked with lichens, gray moonbursts
splattered and overlapping,
threatened from underneath by moss
in lovely hell-green flames,
attacked above
by scaling-ladder vines, oblique and neat,
"one leaf yes and one leaf no" (in Portuguese).

The lizards scarcely breathe; all eyes
are on the smaller, female one, back-to,
her wicked tail straight up and over,
red as a red-hot wire.

Just so the Christians, hard as nails,
tiny as nails, and glinting,
in creaking armor, came and found it all,
not unfamiliar:
no lovers' walks, no bowers,
no cherries to be picked, no lute music,
but corresponding, nevertheless,
to an old dream of wealth and luxury
already out of style when they left home—
wealth, plus a brand-new pleasure.
Directly after Mass, humming perhaps
L'Homme armé or some such tune,
they ripped away into the hanging fabric,
each out to catch an Indian for himself—
those maddening little women who kept calling,
calling to each other (or had the birds waked up?)
and retreating, always retreating, behind it.

Under the Window: Ouro Prêto

for Lilli Correia de Araújo

The conversations are simple: about food,
or, "When my mother combs my hair it hurts."
"Women." *"Women!"* Women in red dresses

and plastic sandals, carrying their almost
invisible babies—muffled to the eyes
in all the heat—unwrap them, lower them,

and give them drinks of water lovingly
from dirty hands, here where there used to be
a fountain, here where all the world still stops.

The water used to run out of the mouths
of three green soapstone faces. (One face laughed
and one face cried; the middle one just looked.

Patched up with plaster, they're in the museum.)
It runs now from a single iron pipe,
a strong and ropy stream. "Cold." "Cold as ice,"

all have agreed for several centuries.
Donkeys agree, and dogs, and the neat little
bottle-green swallows dare to dip and taste.

Here comes that old man with the stick and sack,
meandering again. He stops and fumbles.
He finally gets out his enamelled mug.

Here comes some laundry tied up in a sheet,
all on its own, three feet above the ground.
Oh, no—a small black boy is underneath.

Six donkeys come behind their "godmother"
—the one who wears a fringe of orange wool
with wooly balls above her eyes, and bells.

They veer toward the water as a matter
of course, until the drover's mare trots up,
her whiplash-blinded eye on the off side.

A big new truck, Mercedes-Benz, arrives
to overawe them all. The body's painted
with throbbing rosebuds and the bumper says

HERE AM I FOR WHOM YOU HAVE BEEN WAITING.
The driver and assistant driver wash
their faces, necks, and chests. They wash their feet,

their shoes, and put them back together again.
Meanwhile, another, older truck grinds up
in a blue cloud of burning oil. It has

a syphilitic nose. Nevertheless,
its gallant driver tells the passersby
NOT MUCH MONEY BUT IT IS AMUSING.

"She's been in labor now two days." "Transistors
cost much too much." "For lunch we took advantage
of the poor duck the dog decapitated."

The seven ages of man are talkative
and soiled and thirsty.
                            Oil has seeped into
the margins of the ditch of standing water

and flashes or looks upward brokenly,
like bits of mirror—no, more blue than that:
like tatters of the *Morpho* butterfly.

The Armadillo

for Robert Lowell

This is the time of year
when almost every night
the frail, illegal fire balloons appear.
Climbing the mountain height,

rising toward a saint
still honored in these parts,
the paper chambers flush and fill with light
that comes and goes, like hearts.

Once up against the sky it's hard
to tell them from the stars—
planets, that is—the tinted ones:
Venus going down, or Mars,

or the pale green one. With a wind,
they flare and falter, wobble and toss;

but if it's still they steer between
the kite sticks of the Southern Cross,

receding, dwindling, solemnly
and steadily forsaking us,
or, in the downdraft from a peak,
suddenly turning dangerous.

Last night another big one fell.
It splattered like an egg of fire
against the cliff behind the house.
The flame ran down. We saw the pair

of owls who nest there flying up
and up, their whirling black-and-white
stained bright pink underneath, until
they shrieked up out of sight.

The ancient owls' nest must have burned.
Hastily, all alone,
a glistening armadillo left the scene,
rose-flecked, head down, tail down,

and then a baby rabbit jumped out,
short- eared, to our surprise.
So soft!—a handful of intangible ash
with fixed, ignited eyes.

Too pretty, dreamlike mimicry!
O falling fire and piercing cry
and panic, and a weak mailed fist
clenched ignorant against the sky!

Filling Station

Oh, but it is dirty!
—this little filling station,
oil-soaked, oil-permeated
to a disturbing, over-all

black translucency.
Be careful with that match!

Father wears a dirty,
oil-soaked monkey suit
that cuts him under the arms,
and several quick and saucy
and greasy sons assist him
(it's a family filling station),
all quite thoroughly dirty.

Do they live in the station?
It has a cement porch
behind the pumps, and on it
a set of crushed and grease-
impregnated wickerwork;
on the wicker sofa
a dirty dog, quite comfy.

Some comic books provide
the only note of color—
of certain color. They lie
upon a big dim doily
draping a taboret
(part of the set), beside
a big hirsute begonia.

Why the extraneous plant?
Why the taboret?
Why, oh why, the doily?
(Embroidered in daisy stitch
with marguerites, I think,
and heavy with gray crochet.)

Somebody embroidered the doily.
Somebody waters the plant,
or oils it, maybe. Somebody
arranges the rows of cans
so that they softly say:
ESSO—SO—SO—SO
to high-strung automobiles.
Somebody loves us all.

In the Waiting Room

In Worcester, Massachusetts,
I went with Aunt Consuelo
to keep her dentist's appointment
and sat and waited for her
in the dentist's waiting room.
It was winter. It got dark
early. The waiting room
was full of grown-up people,
arctics and overcoats,
lamps and magazines.
My aunt was inside
what seemed like a long time
and while I waited I read
the *National Geographic*
(I could read) and carefully
studied the photographs:
the inside of a volcano,
black, and full of ashes;
then it was spilling over
in rivulets of fire.
Osa and Martin Johnson
dressed in riding breeches,
laced boots, and pith helmets.
A dead man slung on a pole
—"Long Pig," the caption said.
Babies with pointed heads
wound round and round with string;
black, naked women with necks
wound round and round with wire
like the necks of light bulbs.
Their breasts were horrifying.
I read it right straight through.
I was too shy to stop.
And then I looked at the cover:
the yellow margins, the date.

Suddenly, from inside,
came an *oh!* of pain
—Aunt Consuelo's voice—
not very loud or long.
I wasn't at all surprised;
even then I knew she was
a foolish, timid woman.
I might have been embarrassed,
but wasn't. What took me
completely by surprise
was that it was *me:*
my voice, in my mouth.
Without thinking at all
I was my foolish aunt,
I—we—were falling, falling,
our eyes glued to the cover
of the *National Geographic,*
February, 1918.

I said to myself: three days
and you'll be seven years old.
I was saying it to stop
the sensation of falling off
the round, turning world
into cold, blue-black space.
But I felt: you are an *I,*
you are an *Elizabeth,*
you are one of *them.*
Why should you be one, too?
I scarcely dared to look
to see what it was I was.
I gave a sidelong glance
—I couldn't look any higher—
at shadowy gray knees,
trousers and skirts and boots
and different pairs of hands
lying under the lamps.
I knew that nothing stranger
had ever happened, that nothing

stranger could ever happen.
Why should I be my aunt,
or me, or anyone?
What similarities—
boots, hands, the family voice
I felt in my throat, or even
the *National Geographic*
and those awful hanging breasts—
held us all together
or made us all just one?
How—I didn't know any
word for it—how "unlikely" . . .
How had I come to be here,
like them, and overhear
a cry of pain that could have
got loud and worse but hadn't?

The waiting room was bright
and too hot. It was sliding
beneath a big black wave,
another, and another.

Then I was back in it.
The War was on. Outside,
in Worcester, Massachusetts,
were night and slush and cold,
and it was still the fifth
of February, 1918.

One Art

The art of losing isn't hard to master;
so many things seem filled with the intent
to be lost that their loss is no disaster.

Lose something every day. Accept the fluster
of lost door keys, the hour badly spent.
The art of losing isn't hard to master.

Then practice losing farther, losing faster:
places, and names, and where it was you meant
to travel. None of these will bring disaster.

I lost my mother's watch. And look! my last, or
next-to-last, of three loved houses went.
The art of losing isn't hard to master.

I lost two cities, lovely ones. And, vaster,
some realms I owned, two rivers, a continent.
I miss them, but it wasn't a disaster.

—Even losing you (the joking voice, a gesture
I love) I shan't have lied. It's evident
the art of losing's not too hard to master
though it may look like (*Write* it!) like disaster.

Poem

About the size of an old-style dollar bill,
American or Canadian,
mostly the same whites, gray greens, and steel grays
—this little painting (a sketch for a larger one?)
has never earned any money in its life.
Useless and free, it has spent seventy years

as a minor family relic
handed along collaterally to owners
who looked at it sometimes, or didn't bother to.

It must be Nova Scotia; only there
does one see gabled wooden houses
painted that awful shade of brown.
The other houses, the bits that show, are white.
Elm trees, low hills, a thin church steeple
—that gray-blue wisp—or is it? In the foreground
a water meadow with some tiny cows,
two brushstrokes each, but confidently cows;
two minuscule white geese in the blue water,
back-to-back, feeding, and a slanting stick.
Up closer, a wild iris, white and yellow,
fresh-squiggled from the tube.
The air is fresh and cold; cold early spring
clear as gray glass; a half inch of blue sky
below the steel-gray storm clouds.
(They were the artist's specialty.)
A specklike bird is flying to the left.
Or is it a flyspeck looking like a bird?

Heavens, I recognize the place, I know it!
It's behind—I can almost remember the farmer's name.
His barn backed on that meadow. There it is,
titanium white, one dab. The hint of steeple,
filaments of brush-hairs, barely there,
must be the Presbyterian church.
Would that be Miss Gillespie's house?
Those particular geese and cows
are naturally before my time.

A sketch done in an hour, "in one breath,"
once taken from a trunk and handed over.
*Would you like this? I'll probably never
have room to hang these things again.
Your Uncle George, no, mine, my Uncle George,
he'd be your great-uncle, left them all with Mother*

when he went back to England.
You know, he was quite famous, an R.A. . . .

I never knew him. We both knew this place,
apparently, this literal small backwater,
looked at it long enough to memorize it,
our years apart. How strange. And it's still loved,
or its memory is (it must have changed a lot).
Our visions coincided—"visions" is
too serious a word—our looks, two looks:
art "copying from life" and life itself,
life and the memory of it so compressed
they've turned into each other. Which is which?
Life and the memory of it cramped,
dim, on a piece of Bristol board,
dim, but how live, how touching in detail
—the little that we get for free,
the little of our earthly trust. Not much.
About the size of our abidance
along with theirs: the munching cows,
the iris, crisp and shivering, the water
still standing from spring freshets,
the yet-to-be-dismantled elms, the geese.

THEODORE ROETHKE

(1908–1963)

Theodore Roethke once characterized the course of his career as the transformation of a self into a soul. His early work took its bearings from a childhood spent in the paradisal greenhouses of his father, who was a florist. Roethke's intimate evocations of nature's cycles of growth and decay led him next to attempt, in a series of long experimental poems, a "history of the psyche." His most private memories and preconscious desires were assembled into an account of emotional crisis that traces what he called "a slow spiritual progress."

His later work, more traditional in format, broadened from the minimal to the mystical, from "the terrible hunger for objects" to "the pure, sensuous form" of metaphysical vision. Roethke was born in Saginaw, Michigan, graduated from the University of Michigan, and was a teacher all his life. His courses at the University of Washington, where he taught from 1948 until his death, were famous and influential. He received the Pulitzer Prize in 1954, two National Book Awards (in 1959 and 1965), and the Bollingen Prize in 1958.

Cuttings

(later)

> This urge, wrestle, resurrection of dry sticks,
> Cut stems struggling to put down feet,
> What saint strained so much,
> Rose on such lopped limbs to a new life?
>
> I can hear, underground, that sucking and sobbing,
> In my veins, in my bones I feel it,—
> The small waters seeping upward,
> The tight grains parting at last.

When sprouts break out,
Slippery as fish,
I quail, lean to beginnings, sheath-wet.

Root Cellar

Nothing would sleep in that cellar, dank as a ditch,
Bulbs broke out of boxes hunting for chinks in the dark,
Shoots dangled and drooped,
Lolling obscenely from mildewed crates,
Hung down long yellow evil necks, like tropical snakes.
And what a congress of stinks!—
Roots ripe as old bait,
Pulpy stems, rank, silo-rich,
Leaf-mold, manure, lime, piled against slippery planks.
Nothing would give up life:
Even the dirt kept breathing a small breath.

The Shape of the Fire

1

What's this? A dish for fat lips.
Who says? A nameless stranger.
Is he a bird or a tree? Not everyone can tell.

Water recedes to the crying of spiders.
An old scow bumps over black rocks.
A cracked pod calls.

Mother me out of here. What more will the bones allow?
Will the sea give the wind suck? A toad folds into a stone.
These flowers are all fangs. Comfort me, fury.
Wake me, witch, we'll do the dance of rotten sticks.

Shale loosens. Marl reaches into the field. Small birds pass over
    water.
Spirit, come near. This is only the edge of whiteness.
I can't laugh at a procession of dogs.

    In the hour of ripeness the tree is barren.
    The she-bear mopes under the hill.
    Mother, mother, stir from your cave of sorrow.

A low mouth laps water. Weeds, weeds, how I love you.
The arbor is cooler. Farewell, farewell, fond worm.
The warm comes without sound.

2

    Where's the eye?
    The eye's in the sty.
    The ear's not here
    Beneath the hair.
    When I took off my clothes
    To find a nose,
    There was only one shoe
    For the waltz of To,
    The pinch of Where.

Time for the flat-headed man. I recognize that listener,
Him with the platitudes and rubber doughnuts,
Melting at the knees, a varicose horror.
Hello, hello. My nerves knew you, dear boy.
Have you come to unhinge my shadow?
Last night I slept in the pits of a tongue.
The silver fish ran in and out of my special bindings;
I grew tired of the ritual of names and the assistant keeper of
    the mollusks:
Up over a viaduct I came, to the snakes and sticks of another
    winter,

A two-legged dog hunting a new horizon of howls.
The wind sharpened itself on a rock;
A voice sang:

> Pleasure on ground
> Has no sound,
> Easily maddens
> The uneasy man.

> Who, careless, slips
> In coiling ooze
> Is trapped to the lips,
> Leaves more than shoes;

> Must pull off clothes
> To jerk like a frog
> On belly and nose
> From the sucking bog.

My meat eats me. Who waits at the gate?
Mother of quartz, your words writhe into my ear.
Renew the light, lewd whisper.

3

The wasp waits.
　　The edge cannot eat the center.
The grape glistens.
　　The path tells little to the serpent.
An eye comes out of the wave.
　　The journey from flesh is longest.
A rose sways least.
　　The redeemer comes a dark way.

4

Morning-fair, follow me further back
Into that minnowy world of weeds and ditches,
When the herons floated high over the white houses,
And the little crabs slipped into silvery craters.
When the sun for me glinted the sides of a sand grain,
And my intent stretched over the buds at their first trembling.

That air and shine: and the flicker's loud summer call:
The bearded boards in the stream and the all of apples;
The glad hen on the hill; and the trellis humming.
Death was not. I lived in a simple drowse:
Hands and hair moved through a dream of wakening blossoms.
Rain sweetened the cave and the dove still called;
The flowers leaned on themselves, the flowers in hollows;
And love, love sang toward.

5

To have the whole air!—
The light, the full sun
Coming down on the flowerheads,
The tendrils turning slowly,
A slow snail-lifting, liquescent;
To be by the rose
Rising slowly out of its bed,
Still as a child in its first loneliness;
To see cyclamen veins become clearer in early sunlight,
And mist lifting out of the brown cat-tails;
To stare into the after-light, the glitter left on the lake's
    surface,
When the sun has fallen behind a wooded island;
To follow the drops sliding from a lifted oar,
Held up, while the rower breathes, and the small boat drifts
    quietly shoreward;
To know that light falls and fills, often without our knowing,
As an opaque vase fills to the brim from a quick pouring,
Fills and trembles at the edge yet does not flow over,
Still holding and feeding the stem of the contained flower.

The Waking

I wake to sleep, and take my waking slow.
I feel my fate in what I cannot fear.
I learn by going where I have to go.

We think by feeling. What is there to know?
I hear my being dance from ear to ear.
I wake to sleep, and take my waking slow.

Of those so close beside me, which are you?
God bless the Ground! I shall walk softly there,
And learn by going where I have to go.

Light takes the Tree; but who can tell us how?
The lowly worm climbs up a winding stair;
I wake to sleep, and take my waking slow.

Great Nature has another thing to do
To you and me; so take the lively air,
And, lovely, learn by going where to go.

This shaking keeps me steady. I should know.
What falls away is always. And is near.
I wake to sleep, and take my waking slow.
I learn by going where I have to go.

I Knew a Woman

I knew a woman, lovely in her bones,
When small birds sighed, she would sigh back at them;
Ah, when she moved, she moved more ways than one:
The shapes a bright container can contain!
Of her choice virtues only gods should speak,

Or English poets who grew up on Greek
(I'd have them sing in chorus, cheek to cheek).

How well her wishes went! She stroked my chin,
She taught me Turn, and Counter-turn, and Stand;
She taught me Touch, that undulant white skin;
I nibbled meekly from her proffered hand;
She was the sickle; I, poor I, the rake,
Coming behind her for her pretty sake
(But what prodigious mowing we did make).

Love likes a gander, and adores a goose:
Her full lips pursed, the errant note to seize;
She played it quick, she played it light and loose;
My eyes, they dazzled at her flowing knees;
Her several parts could keep a pure repose,
Or one hip quiver with a mobile nose
(She moved in circles, and those circles moved).

Let seed be grass, and grass turn into hay:
I'm martyr to a motion not my own;
What's freedom for? To know eternity.
I swear she cast a shadow white as stone.
But who would count eternity in days?
These old bones live to learn her wanton ways:
(I measure time by how a body sways).

In a Dark Time

In a dark time, the eye begins to see,
I meet my shadow in the deepening shade;
I hear my echo in the echoing wood—
A lord of nature weeping to a tree.
I live between the heron and the wren,
Beasts of the hill and serpents of the den.

What's madness but nobility of soul
At odds with circumstance? The day's on fire!
I know the purity of pure despair,
My shadow pinned against a sweating wall.
That place among the rocks—is it a cave,
Or winding path? The edge is what I have.

A steady storm of correspondences!
A night flowing with birds, a ragged moon,
And in broad day the midnight come again!
A man goes far to find out what he is—
Death of the self in a long, tearless night,
All natural shapes blazing unnatural light.

Dark, dark my light, and darker my desire.
My soul, like some heat-maddened summer fly,
Keeps buzzing at the sill. Which I is *I*?
A fallen man, I climb out of my fear.
The mind enters itself, and God the mind,
And one is One, free in the tearing wind.

JOHN BERRYMAN
(1914–1972)

The early poetry of John Berryman is indebted to William Butler Yeats and W. H. Auden for its cerebral lyricism and scrupulous craft, for its presiding social and political concern of "the honourable and exhausted man." But with *Homage to Mistress Bradstreet* (1956), Berryman devised a new "self created" style, eccentric and edgy, which he next carried into the 385 *Dream Songs,* the major work of his career and a sequence that preoccupied him for a dozen years. It is a picaresque "Song of Myself," a montage of voices centered on Henry, Berryman's characterized version of himself; memories, guilts, fantasies, gossip, and grudges are juxtaposed in a tone that careens from the vulgar to the exalted, the manic to the depressed. "Loss, deaths, terror"—from the suicide of Berryman's father to the poet's own "horror of unlove"—are the poem's final subject. Berryman was born John Smith in McAlester, Oklahoma. Educated at Columbia and Cambridge, he had a distinguished career as teacher and scholar at Brown, Princeton, and the University of Minnesota. He received the Pulitzer Prize in 1965 and the National Book Award in 1969. He committed suicide by throwing himself off a bridge in Minneapolis.

The Moon and the Night and the Men

On the night of the Belgian surrender the moon rose
Late, a delayed moon, and a violent moon
For the English or the American beholder;
The French beholder. It was a cold night,
People put on their wraps, the troops were cold
No doubt, despite the calendar, no doubt
Numbers of refugees coughed, and the sight
Or sound of some killed others. A cold night.

On Outer Drive there was an accident:
A stupid well-intentioned man turned sharp

Right and abruptly he became an angel
Fingering an unfamiliar harp,
Or screamed in hell, or was nothing at all.
Do not imagine this is unimportant.
He was a part of the night, part of the land,
Part of the bitter and exhausted ground
Out of which memory grows.

                Michael and I
Stared at each other over chess, and spoke
As little as possible, and drank and played.
The chessmen caught in the European eye,
Neither of us I think had a free look
Although the game was fair. The move one made
It was difficult at last to keep one's mind on.
'Hurt and unhappy' said the man in London.
We said to each other, The time is coming near
When none shall have books or music, none his dear,
And only a fool will speak aloud his mind.
History is approaching a speechless end,
As Henry Adams said. Adams was right.

All this occurred on the night when Leopold
Fulfilled the treachery four years before
Begun—or was he well-intentioned, more
Roadmaker to hell than king? At any rate,
The moon came up late and the night was cold,
Many men died—although we know the fate
Of none, nor of anyone, and the war
Goes on, and the moon in the breast of man is cold.

F R O M **The Dream Songs**

1

Huffy Henry hid   the day,
unappeasable Henry sulked.
I see his point,—a trying to put things over.
It was the thought that they thought
they could *do* it made Henry wicked & away.
But he should have come out and talked.

All the world like a woolen lover
once did seem on Henry's side.
Then came a departure.
Thereafter nothing fell out as it might or ought.
I don't see how Henry, pried
open for all the world to see, survived.

What he has now to say is a long
wonder the world can bear & be.
Once in a sycamore I was glad
all at the top, and I sang.
Hard on the land wears the strong sea
and empty grows every bed.

4

Filling her compact & delicious body
with chicken páprika, she glanced at me
twice.
Fainting with interest, I hungered back
and only the fact of her husband & four other people
kept me from springing on her

or falling at her little feet and crying
'You are the hottest one for years of night

Henry's dazed eyes
have enjoyed, Brilliance.' I advanced upon
(despairing) my spumoni.—Sir Bones: is stuffed,
de world, wif feeding girls.

—Black hair, complexion Latin, jewelled eyes
downcast . . . The slob beside her   feasts . . . What wonders is
she sitting on, over there?
The restaurant buzzes. She might as well be on Mars.
Where did it all go wrong? There ought to be a law against
     Henry.
—Mr Bones: there is.

5

Henry sats in de bar & was odd,
off in the glass from the glass,
at odds wif de world & its god,
his wife is a complete nothing,
St Stephen
getting even.

Henry sats in de plane & was gay.
Careful Henry nothing said aloud
but where a Virgin out of cloud
to her Mountain dropt in light,
his thought made pockets & the plane buckt.
'Parm me, lady.' 'Orright.'

Henry lay in de netting, wild,
while the brainfever bird did scales;
Mr Heartbreak, the New Man,
come to farm a crazy land;
an image of the dead on the fingernail
of a newborn child.

14

Life, friends, is boring. We must not say so.
After all, the sky flashes, the great sea yearns,
we ourselves flash and yearn,
and moreover my mother told me as a boy
(repeatedly) 'Ever to confess you're bored
means you have no

Inner Resources.' I conclude now I have no
inner resources, because I am heavy bored.
Peoples bore me,
literature bores me, especially great literature,
Henry bores me, with his plights & gripes
as bad as achilles,

who loves people and valiant art, which bores me.
And the tranquil hills, & gin, look like a drag
and somehow a dog
has taken itself & its tail considerably away
into mountains or sea or sky, leaving
behind: me, wag.

29

There sat down, once, a thing on Henry's heart
só heavy, if he had a hundred years
& more, & weeping, sleepless, in all them time
Henry could not make good.
Starts again always in Henry's ears
the little cough somewhere, an odour, a chime.

And there is another thing he has in mind
like a grave Sienese face a thousand years
would fail to blur the still profiled reproach of. Ghastly,
with open eyes, he attends, blind.
All the bells say: too late. This is not for tears;
thinking.

But never did Henry, as he thought he did,
end anyone and hacks her body up

and hide the pieces, where they may be found.
He knows: he went over everyone, & nobody's missing.
Often he reckons, in the dawn, them up.
Nobody is ever missing.

46

I am, outside. Incredible panic rules.
People are blowing and beating each other without mercy.
Drinks are boiling. Iced
drinks are boiling. The worse anyone feels, the worse
treated he is. Fools elect fools.
A harmless man at an intersection said, under his breath:
    "Christ!"

That word, so spoken, affected the vision
of, when they trod to work next day, shopkeepers
who went & were fitted for glasses.
Enjoyed they then an appearance of love & law.
Millennia whift & waft—one, one—er, er . . .
Their glasses were taken from them, & they saw.

Man has undertaken the top job of all,
son fin. Good luck.
I myself walked at the funeral of tenderness.
Followed other deaths. Among the last,
like the memory of a lovely fuck,
was: *Do, ut des.*

76 HENRY'S CONFESSION

Nothin very bad happen to me lately.
How you explain that? —I explain that, Mr Bones,
terms o' your bafflin odd sobriety.
Sober as man can get, no girls, no telephones,
what could happen bad to Mr Bones?
—*If* life is a handkerchief sandwich,

in a modesty of death I join my father
who dared so long agone leave me.
A bullet on a concrete stoop
close by a smothering southern sea
spreadeagled on an island, by my knee.
—You is from hunger, Mr Bones,

I offers you this handkerchief, now set
your left foot by my right foot,
shoulder to shoulder, all that jazz,
arm in arm, by the beautiful sea,
hum a little, Mr Bones.
—I saw nobody coming, so I went instead.

77

Seedy Henry rose up shy in de world
& shaved & swung his barbells, duded Henry up
and p.a.'d poor thousands of persons on topics of grand
moment to Henry, ah to those less & none.
Wif a book of his in either hand
he is stript down to move on.

—Come away, Mr Bones.

—Henry is tired of the winter,
& haircuts, & a squeamish comfy   ruin-prone proud national
   mind,   & Spring (in the city so called).
Henry likes Fall.
Hé would be prepared to líve in a world of Fáll
for ever, impenitent Henry.
But the snows and summers grieve & dream;

thése fierce & airy occupations, and love,
raved away so many of Henry's years
it is a wonder that, with in each hand
one of his own mad books and all,
ancient fires for eyes, his head full
& his heart full, he's making ready to move on.

143

—That's enough of that, Mr Bones. *Some* lady you make.
Honour the burnt cork, be a vaudeville man,
I'll sing you now a song
the like of which may bring your heart to break:
he's gone! and we don't know where. When he began
taking the pistol out & along,

you was just a little; but gross fears
accompanied us along the beaches, pal.
My mother was scared almost to death.
He was going to swim out, with me, forevers,
and a swimmer strong he was in the phosphorescent   Gulf,
but he decided on lead.

That mad drive wiped out my childhood. I put him down
while all the same on forty years I love him
stashed in Oklahoma
besides his brother Will. Bite the nerve of the town
for anyone so desperate. I repeat: I love him
until *I* fall into coma.

257

The thunder & the flaw of their great quarrel
abased his pen. He could not likely think.
He took himself out of it,
both wrong & right, beyond well beyond moral,
in the groves of meaningless rage, which ache & stink
unlike old shit

which loses its power almost in an hour,
ours burgeons. When I trained my wives, I thought
now they'll be professional:
they became professional, at once wedlocks went sour
because they couldn't compete with Henry, who sought
their realizations. The J.P. coughed.

Married life is a boat
forever dubious, with the bilge stale.
There's no getting out of that.
Gongs & lightning crowd my returned throat,
I always wept at parades: I knew I'd fail:
Henry wandered back on stage & sat.

384

The marker slants, flowerless, day's almost done,
I stand above my father's grave with rage,
often, often before
I've made this awful pilgrimage to one
who cannot visit me, who tore his page
out: I come back for more,

I spit upon this dreadful banker's grave
who shot his heart out in a Florida dawn
O ho alas alas
When will indifference come, I moan & rave
I'd like to scrabble till I got right down
away down under the grass

and ax the casket open ha to see
just how he's taking it, which he sought so hard
we'll tear apart
the mouldering grave clothes ha & then Henry
will heft the ax once more, his final card,
and fell it on the start.

RANDALL JARRELL
(1914–1965)

Called by Robert Lowell "the most heartbreaking poet of his generation," Randall Jarrell was born in Nashville, Tennessee, and grew up in California. A graduate of Vanderbilt, he was later a professor at several colleges, but from 1947 until his death he taught primarily at the University of North Carolina at Greensboro. As a critic he was famous for his passionate advocacy and stinging dismissals. Some of Jarrell's best poems are about World War II; they portray war less as the destruction of others than as a brutalization of the self. Drawn to Germanic folklore and fairy tales, to the psychology of dreams and repression, Jarrell explored in his poems the "unknown unwanted life" as well as themes of transformation. The child, the aging woman, and the victim were favorite personae of his tender and subtle dramatic monologues. Though sometimes tinged with sentimentality, his poems are distinguished by their compassion and intelligence. He was given the National Book Award in 1961.

90 North

At home, in my flannel gown, like a bear to its floe,
I clambered to bed; up the globe's impossible sides
I sailed all night—till at last, with my black beard,
My furs and my dogs, I stood at the northern pole.

There in the childish night my companions lay frozen,
The stiff furs knocked at my starveling throat,
And I gave my great sigh: the flakes came huddling,
Were they really my end? In the darkness I turned to my rest.

—Here, the flag snaps in the glare and silence
Of the unbroken ice. I stand here,
The dogs bark, my beard is black, and I stare
At the North Pole . . .
           And now what? Why, go back.

Turn as I please, my step is to the south.
The world—my world spins on this final point
Of cold and wretchedness: all lines, all winds
End in this whirlpool I at last discover.

And it is meaningless. In the child's bed
After the night's voyage, in that warm world
Where people work and suffer for the end
That crowns the pain—in that Cloud-Cuckoo-Land

I reached my North and it had meaning.
Here at the actual pole of my existence,
Where all that I have done is meaningless,
Where I die or live by accident alone—

Where, living or dying, I am still alone;
Here where North, the night, the berg of death
Crowd me out of the ignorant darkness,
I see at last that all the knowledge

I wrung from the darkness—that the darkness flung me—
Is worthless as ignorance: nothing comes from nothing,
The darkness from the darkness. Pain comes from the darkness
And we call it wisdom. It is pain.

Eighth Air Force

If, in an odd angle of the hutment,
A puppy laps the water from a can
Of flowers, and the drunk sergeant shaving
Whistles *O Paradiso!*—shall I say that man
Is not as men have said: a wolf to man?

The other murderers troop in yawning;
Three of them play Pitch, one sleeps, and one
Lies counting missions, lies there sweating

Till even his heart beats: One; One; One.
O murderers! . . . Still, this is how it's done:

This is a war. . . . But since these play, before they die,
Like puppies with their puppy; since, a man,
I did as these have done, but did not die—
I will content the people as I can
And give up these to them: Behold the man!

I have suffered, in a dream, because of him,
Many things; for this last saviour, man,
I have lied as I lie now. But what is lying?
Men wash their hands, in blood, as best they can:
I find no fault in this just man.

The Death of the Ball Turret Gunner

From my mother's sleep I fell into the State,
And I hunched in its belly till my wet fur froze.
Six miles from earth, loosed from its dream of life,
I woke to black flak and the nightmare fighters.
When I died they washed me out of the turret with a hose.

The Woman at the Washington Zoo

The saris go by me from the embassies.

Cloth from the moon. Cloth from another planet.
They look back at the leopard like the leopard.

And I. . . .
                    this print of mine, that has kept its color

Alive through so many cleanings; this dull null
Navy I wear to work, and wear from work, and so
To my bed, so to my grave, with no
Complaints, no comment: neither from my chief,
The Deputy Chief Assistant, nor his chief—
Only I complain. . . . this serviceable
Body that no sunlight dyes, no hand suffuses
But, dome-shadowed, withering among columns,
Wavy beneath fountains—small, far-off, shining
In the eyes of animals, these beings trapped
As I am trapped but not, themselves, the trap,
Aging, but without knowledge of their age,
Kept safe here, knowing not of death, for death—
Oh, bars of my own body, open, open!

The world goes by my cage and never sees me.
And there come not to me, as come to these,
The wild beasts, sparrows pecking the llamas' grain,
Pigeons settling on the bears' bread, buzzards
Tearing the meat the flies have clouded. . . .
                                        Vulture,
When you come for the white rat that the foxes left,
Take off the red helmet of your head, the black
Wings that have shadowed me, and step to me as man:
The wild brother at whose feet the white wolves fawn,
To whose hand of power the great lioness
Stalks, purring. . . .
                    You know what I was,
You see what I am: change me, change me!

Cinderella

Her imaginary playmate was a grown-up
In sea-coal satin. The flame-blue glances,

The wings gauzy as the membrane that the ashes
Draw over an old ember—as the mother
In a jug of cider—were a comfort to her.
They sat by the fire and told each other stories.

"What men want. . . ." said the godmother softly—
How she went on it is hard for a man to say.
Their eyes, on their Father, were monumental marble.
Then they smiled like two old women, bussed each other,
Said, "Gossip, gossip"; and, lapped in each other's looks,
Mirror for mirror, drank a cup of tea.

Of cambric tea. But there is a reality
Under the good silk of the good sisters'
Good ball gowns. *She* knew. . . . Hard-breasted, naked-eyed,
She pushed her silk feet into glass, and rose within
A gown of imaginary gauze. The shy prince drank
A toast to her in champagne from her slipper

And breathed, "Bewitching!" Breathed, "I am bewitched!"
—She said to her godmother, "Men!"
And, later, looking down to see her flesh
Look back up from under lace, the ashy gauze
And pulsing marble of a bridal veil,
She wished it all a widow's coal-black weeds.

A sullen wife and a reluctant mother,
She sat all day in silence by the fire.
Better, later, to stare past her sons' sons,
Her daughters' daughters, and tell stories to the fire.
But best, dead, damned, to rock forever
Beside Hell's fireside—to see within the flames

The Heaven to whose gold-gauzed door there comes
A little dark old woman, the God's Mother,
And cries, "Come in, come in! My son's out now,
Out now, will be back soon, may be back never,
Who knows, eh? *We* know what they are—men, men!
But come, come in till then! Come in till then!"

Next Day

Moving from Cheer to Joy, from Joy to All,
I take a box
And add it to my wild rice, my Cornish game hens.
The slacked or shorted, basketed, identical
Food-gathering flocks
Are selves I overlook. Wisdom, said William James,

Is learning what to overlook. And I am wise
If that is wisdom.
Yet somehow, as I buy All from these shelves
And the boy takes it to my station wagon,
What I've become
Troubles me even if I shut my eyes.

When I was young and miserable and pretty
And poor, I'd wish
What all girls wish: to have a husband,
A house and children. Now that I'm old, my wish
Is womanish:
That the boy putting groceries in my car

See me. It bewilders me he doesn't see me.
For so many years
I was good enough to eat: the world looked at me
And its mouth watered. How often they have undressed me,
The eyes of strangers!
And, holding their flesh within my flesh, their vile

Imaginings within my imagining,
I too have taken
The chance of life. Now the boy pats my dog
And we start home. Now I am good.
The last mistaken,
Ecstatic, accidental bliss, the blind

Happiness that, bursting, leaves upon the palm
Some soap and water—
It was so long ago, back in some Gay

Twenties, Nineties, I don't know . . . Today I miss
My lovely daughter
Away at school, my sons away at school,

My husband away at work—I wish for them.
The dog, the maid,
And I go through the sure unvarying days
At home in them. As I look at my life,
I am afraid
Only that it will change, as I am changing:

I am afraid, this morning, of my face.
It looks at me
From the rear-view mirror, with the eyes I hate,
The smile I hate. Its plain, lined look
Of gray discovery
Repeats to me: "You're old." That's all, I'm old.

And yet I'm afraid, as I was at the funeral
I went to yesterday.
My friend's cold made-up face, granite among its flowers,
Her undressed, operated-on, dressed body
Were my face and body.
As I think of her I hear her telling me

How young I seem; I *am* exceptional;
I think of all I have.
But really no one is exceptional,
No one has anything, I'm anybody,
I stand beside my grave
Confused with my life, that is commonplace and solitary.

Well Water

What a girl called "the dailiness of life"
(Adding an errand to your errand. Saying,

"Since you're up . . ." Making you a means to
A means to a means to) is well water
Pumped from an old well at the bottom of the world.
The pump you pump the water from is rusty
And hard to move and absurd, a squirrel-wheel
A sick squirrel turns slowly, through the sunny
Inexorable hours. And yet sometimes
The wheel turns of its own weight, the rusty
Pump pumps over your sweating face the clear
Water, cold, so cold! you cup your hands
And gulp from them the dailiness of life.

ROBERT PENN WARREN

(1905–1989)

By the time he was named the nation's first official poet laureate in 1986, Robert Penn Warren had long been esteemed as the dean of American letters. As poet, novelist, playwright, critic, teacher, and editor, his achievements were varied and resplendent, his influence wide and profound. Warren was born in Guthrie, Kentucky, and educated at Vanderbilt, Berkeley, Yale, and Oxford. He taught at Louisiana State University, the University of Minnesota, and for many years at Yale. Honored with every possible prize, he is the only person to have received the Pulitzer Prize for both fiction (in 1947) and poetry (in 1958 and 1979). His early poems, written under the influence of John Crowe Ransom, deal in the delicate profundities of the metaphysical style. In midcareer he concentrated on novel writing, and when he returned to poetry in the 1950s, his work showed a new narrative vigor and thematic ambition. The poems of his last two decades are considered his best—craggy, surprising, and powerful. In them he employed moralized anecdotes, memories, and reveries as part of his restless inquiry into the nature of time and identity.

Masts at Dawn

Past second cock-crow yacht masts in the harbor go slowly
                                                white.

No light in the east yet, but the stars show a certain fatigue.
They withdraw into a new distance, have discovered our
                                unworthiness. It is long since

The owl, in the dark eucalyptus, dire and melodious, last
                                                called, and

Long since the moon sank and the English
Finished fornicating in their ketches. In the evening there
                                        was a strong swell.

Red died the sun, but at dark wind rose easterly, white sea
                        nagged the black harbor headland.

When there is a strong swell, you may, if you surrender to it,
                                        experience
A sense, in the act, of mystic unity with that rhythm. Your
                            peace is the sea's will.

But now no motion, the bay-face is glossy in darkness, like

An old window pane flat on black ground by the wall,
                        near the ash heap. It neither
Receives nor gives light. Now is the hour when the sea

Sinks into meditation. It doubts its own mission. The drowned
                                                cat
That on the evening swell had kept nudging the piles of the
                            pier and had seemed

To want to climb out and lick itself dry, now floats free. On
                that surface a slight convexity only, it is like

An eyelid, in darkness, closed. You must learn to accept the
                            kiss of fate, for

The masts go white slow, as light, like dew, from darkness
Condensed on them, on oiled wood, on metal. Dew whitens in
                                            darkness.

I lie in my bed and think how, in darkness, the masts go
                                    white.

The sound of the engine of the first fishing dory dies seaward.
                                        Soon
In the inland glen wakes the dawn-dove. We must try

To love so well the world that we may believe, in the end, in
                                    God.

Birth of Love

Season late, day late, sun just down, and the sky
Cold gunmetal but with a wash of live rose, and she,
From water the color of sky except where
Her motion has fractured it to shivering splinters of silver,
Rises. Stands on the raw grass. Against
The new-curdling night of spruces, nakedness
Glimmers and, at bosom and flank, drips
With fluent silver. The man,

Some ten strokes out, but now hanging
Motionless in the gunmetal water, feet
Cold with the coldness of depth, all
History dissolving from him, is
Nothing but an eye. Is an eye only. Sees

The body that is marked by his use, and Time's,
Rise, and in the abrupt and unsustaining element of air,
Sway, lean, grapple the pond-bank. Sees
How, with that posture of female awkwardness that is,
And is the stab of, suddenly perceived grace, breasts bulge
        down in
The pure curve of their weight and buttocks
Moon up and, in that swelling unity,
Are silver, and glimmer. Then

The body is erect, she is herself, whatever
Self she may be, and with an end of the towel grasped in each
        hand,
Slowly draws it back and forth across back and buttocks, but
With face lifted toward the high sky, where
The over-wash of rose color now fails. Fails, though no star
Yet throbs there. The towel, forgotten,
Does not move now. The gaze
Remains fixed on the sky. The body,

Profiled against the darkness of spruces, seems
To draw to itself, and condense in its whiteness, what light

In the sky yet lingers or, from
The metallic and abstract severity of water, lifts. The body,
With the towel now trailing loose from one hand, is
A white stalk from which the face flowers gravely toward the
    high sky.
This moment is non-sequential and absolute, and admits
Of no definition, for it
Subsumes all other, and sequential, moments, by which
Definition might be possible. The woman,

Face yet raised, wraps,
With a motion as though standing in sleep,
The towel about her body, under the breasts, and,
Holding it there, hieratic as lost Egypt and erect,
Moves up the path that, stair-steep, winds
Into the clamber and tangle of growth. Beyond
The lattice of dusk-dripping leaves, whiteness
Dimly glimmers, goes. Glimmers and is gone, and the man,

Suspended in his darkling medium, stares
Upward where, though not visible, he knows
She moves, and in his heart he cries out that, if only
He had such strength, he would put his hand forth
And maintain it over her to guard, in all
Her out-goings and in-comings, from whatever
Inclemency of sky or slur of the world's weather
Might ever be. In his heart
He cries out. Above

Height of the spruce-night and heave of the far mountain, he
    sees
The first star pulse into being. It gleams there.

I do not know what promise it makes to him.

Rattlesnake Country

for James Dickey

1

Arid that country and high, anger of sun on the mountains,
    but
One little patch of cool lawn:

                        Trucks
Had brought in rich loam. Stonework
Held it in place like a shelf, at one side backed
By the length of the house porch, at one end
By rock-fall. Above that, the mesquite, wolf-waiting. Its turn
Will, again, come.

                    Meanwhile, wicker chairs, all day,
Follow the shimmering shade of the lone cottonwood, the way
    that
Time, sadly seeking to know its own nature, follows
The shadow on a sun-dial. All day,
The sprinkler ejects its misty rainbow.

                                All day,
The sky shivers white with heat, the lake,
For its fifteen miles of distance, stretches
Tight under the white sky. It is stretched
Tight as a mystic drumhead. It glitters like neurosis.
You think it may scream, but nothing
Happens. Except that, bit by bit, the mountains
Get heavier all afternoon.

                        One day,
When some secret, high drift of air comes eastward over the
    lake,
Ash, gray, sifts minutely down on
Our lunch-time ice cream. Which is vanilla, and white.

There is a forest fire on Mount Ti-Po-Ki, which
Is at the western end of the lake.

2

If, after lunch, at God's hottest hour,
You make love, flesh, in that sweat-drench,
Slides on flesh slicker than grease. To grip
Is difficult.

        At drink-time,
The sun, over Ti-Po-Ki, sets
Lopsided, and redder than blood or bruised cinnabar,
    because of
The smoke there. Later,
If there is no moon, you can see the red eyes of fire
Wink at you from
The black mass that is the mountain.

At night, in the dark room, not able to sleep, you
May think of the red eyes of fire that
Are winking from blackness. You may,
As I once did, rise up and go from the house. But,
When I got out, the moon had emerged from cloud, and I
Entered the lake. Swam miles out,
Toward moonset. Motionless,
Awash, metaphysically undone in that silvered and
Unbreathing medium, and beyond
Prayer or desire, saw
The moon, slow, swag down, like an old woman's belly.

Going back to the house, I gave the now-dark lawn a wide
    berth.

At night the rattlers come out from the rock-fall.
They lie on the damp grass for coolness.

3

I-yee!—
    and the wranglers, they cry on the mountain, and
    waking
At dawn-streak, I hear it.

High on the mountain
I hear it, for snow-water there, snow long gone, yet seeps
 down
To green the raw edges and enclaves of forest
With a thin pasturage. The wranglers
Are driving our horses down, long before daylight, plunging
Through gloom of the pines, and in their joy
Cry out:

I-yee!

We ride this morning, and,
Now fumbling in shadow for *levis,* pulling my boots on, I hear
That thin cry of joy from the mountain, and what once I have,
Literally, seen, I now in my mind see, as I
Will, years later, in my mind, see it—the horsemen
Plunge through the pine-gloom, leaping
The deadfall—*I-yee!*—
Leaping the boulder—*I-yee!*—and their faces
Flee flickering white through the shadow—*I-yee!*—
And before them,
Down the trail and in dimness, the riderless horses,
Like quicksilver spilled in dark glimmer and roil, go
Pouring downward.

The wranglers cry out.

And nearer.

But,
Before I go for my quick coffee-scald and to the corral,
I hear, much nearer, not far from my open window, a croupy
Gargle of laughter.

It is Laughing Boy.

4

Laughing Boy is the name that my host—and friend—gives his
 yard-hand.
Laughing Boy is Indian, or half, and has a hare-lip.

Sometimes, before words come, he utters a sound like croupy
    laughter.
When he utters that sound his face twists. Hence the name.

Laughing Boy wakes up at dawn, for somebody
Has to make sure the rattlers are gone before
The nurse brings my host's twin baby daughters out to the
    lawn.
Laughing Boy, who does not like rattlers, keeps a tin can
Of gasoline covered with a saucer on an outer ledge of the
    porch.
Big kitchen matches are in the saucer. This
At the porch-end toward the rock-fall.

The idea is: Sneak soft-foot round the porch-end,
There between rattlers and rock-fall, and as one whips past,
Douse him. This with the left hand, and
At the same instant, with the nail of the right thumb,
Snap a match alight.

               The flame,
If timing is good, should, just as he makes his rock-hole,
Hit him.

The flame makes a sudden, soft, gaspy sound at
The hole-mouth, then dances there. The flame
Is spectral in sunlight, but flickers blue at its raw edge.

Laughing Boy has beautiful coordination, and sometimes
He gets a rattler. You are sure if
The soft, gasping sound and pale flame come before
The stub-buttoned tail has disappeared.

                  Whenever
Laughing Boy really gets a rattler, he makes that sound like
Croupy laughter. His face twists.

Once I get one myself. I see, actually, the stub-buttoned tail
Whip through pale flame down into earth-darkness.

"The son-of-a-bitch," I am yelling, "did you see me, I got
    him!"

I have gotten that stub-tailed son-of-a-bitch.

I look up at the sky. Already, that early, the sky shivers with
    whiteness.

5

What was *is* is now *was*. But
Is *was* but a word for wisdom, its price? Some from
That long-lost summer are dead now, two of the girls then
    young,
Now after their pain and delusions, worthy endeavors and lies,
    are,
Long since, dead.

          The third
Committed her first adultery the next year, her first lover
A creature odd for her choosing, he who
Liked poetry and had no ambition, and
She cried out in his arms, a new experience for her. But
There were the twins, and she had, of course,
Grown accustomed to money.

          Her second,
A man of high social position, who kept a score-card. With
    her,
Not from passion this time, just snobbery. After that,
From boredom. Forgot, finally,
The whole business, took up horse-breeding, which
Filled her time and even, I heard, made unneeded money,
    and in
The old news photo I see her putting her mount to the jump.
Her yet beautiful figure is poised forward, bent elbows
Neat to her tight waist, face
Thrust into the cleansing wind of her passage, the face
Yet smooth as a girl's, no doubt from the scalpel
Of the plastic surgeon as well as
From her essential incapacity
For experience.

The husband, my friend,
Would, by this time, be totally cynical. The children
Have been a disappointment. He would have heavy jowls.
Perhaps he is, by this time, dead.

As for Laughing Boy, he wound up in the pen. Twenty years.
This for murder. Indians
Just ought to leave whiskey to the white folks.

I can't remember the names of the others who came there,
The casual weekend-ers. But remember

What I remember, but do not
Know what it all means, unless the meaning inheres in
The compulsion to try to convert what now is *was*
Back into what was *is.*

                    I remember
The need to enter the night-lake and swim out toward
The distant moonset. Remember
The blue-tattered flick of white flame at the rock-hole
In the instant before I lifted up
My eyes to the high sky that shivered in its hot whiteness.

And sometimes—usually at dawn—I remember the cry on the
    mountain.

All I can do is to offer my testimony.

Evening Hawk

From plane of light to plane, wings dipping through
Geometries and orchids that the sunset builds,
Out of the peak's black angularity of shadow, riding
The last tumultuous avalanche of
Light above pines and the guttural gorge,
The hawk comes.

His wing
Scythes down another day, his motion
Is that of the honed steel-edge, we hear
The crashless fall of stalks of Time.

The head of each stalk is heavy with the gold of our error.

Look! Look! he is climbing the last light
Who knows neither Time nor error, and under
Whose eye, unforgiving, the world, unforgiven, swings
Into shadow.

Long now,
The last thrush is still, the last bat
Now cruises in his sharp hieroglyphics. His wisdom
Is ancient, too, and immense. The star
Is steady, like Plato, over the mountain.

If there were no wind we might, we think, hear
The earth grind on its axis, or history
Drip in darkness like a leaking pipe in the cellar.

CHARLES OLSON
(1910–1970)

"The work of each of us is to find out the true lineaments of
ourselves by facing up to the primal features of these founders who
lie buried in us," declared Charles Olson, who appropriately referred
to himself as an archaeologist. Especially in his lifelong epic *The
Maximus Poems,* he sought to create the myth of a place (his native
Gloucester, Massachusetts) by discovering the array of energies and
histories that constitute it. As a theoretician too Olson sought to
break through encrusted traditions. His influential 1950 manifesto
"Projective Verse" called for a poetry based on the breath rather than
the metrical line; for the page as a "composition by field," attracting
and discharging energies of intuition and allusion. Having studied at
Wesleyan, Yale, and Harvard, Olson taught at (and was eventually
rector of) Black Mountain College during its most excitingly
experimental years. Later teaching at the State University of
New York at Buffalo and the University of Connecticut, he was a
powerful force behind some of the changes that occurred in
postwar American poetry.

The Kingfishers

1

What does not change / is the will to change

He woke, fully clothed, in his bed. He
remembered only one thing, the birds, how
when he came in, he had gone around the rooms
and got them back in their cage, the green one first,
she with the bad leg, and then the blue,
the one they had hoped was a male

Otherwise? Yes, Fernand, who had talked lispingly of Albers &
    Angkor Vat.

He had left the party without a word. How he got up, got into
    his coat,
I do not know. When I saw him, he was at the door, but it did
    not matter,
he was already sliding along the wall of the night, losing
    himself
in some crack of the ruins. That it should have been he who
    said, "The kingfishers!
who cares
for their feathers
now?"

His last words had been, "The pool is slime." Suddenly
    everyone,
ceasing their talk, sat in a row around him, watched
they did not so much hear, or pay attention, they
wondered, looked at each other, smirked, but listened,
he repeated and repeated, could not go beyond his thought
"The pool   the kingfishers' feathers were wealth   why
did the export stop?"

It was then he left

2

I thought of the E on the stone, and of what Mao said
la lumière"
        but the kingfisher
de l'aurore"
        but the kingfisher flew west
est devant nous!
        he got the color of his breast
        from the heat of the setting sun!

The features are, the feebleness of the feet (syndactylism of
    the 3rd & 4th digit)
the bill, serrated, sometimes a pronounced beak, the wings
where the color is, short and round, the tail
inconspicuous.

But not these things were the factors. Not the birds.
The legends are

legends. Dead, hung up indoors, the kingfisher
will not indicate a favoring wind,
or avert the thunderbolt. Nor, by its nesting,
still the waters, with the new year, for seven days.
It is true, it does nest with the opening year, but not on the
    waters.
It nests at the end of a tunnel bored by itself in a bank. There,
six or eight white and translucent eggs are laid, on fishbones
not on bare clay, on bones thrown up in pellets by the birds.

                       On these rejectamenta
(as they accumulate they form a cup-shaped structure) the
    young are born.
And, as they are fed and grow, this nest of excrement and
    decayed fish becomes a dripping, fetid mass

Mao concluded:
              nous devons
                     nous lever
                            et agir!

3

When the attentions change / the jungle
leaps in
        even the stones are split
               they rive

Or,
enter
that other conqueror we more naturally recognize
he so resembles ourselves

But the E
cut so rudely on that oldest stone
sounded otherwise,
was differently heard

as, in another time, were treasures used:

(and, later, much later, a fine ear thought
a scarlet coat)

"of green feathers feet, beaks and eyes
of gold

"animals likewise,
resembling snails

"a large wheel, gold, with figures of unknown
four-foots,
and worked with tufts of leaves, weight
3800 ounces

"last, two birds, of thread and featherwork, the
quills
gold, the feet
gold, the two birds perched on two reeds

gold, the reeds arising from two embroidered
mounds,
one yellow, the other
white.

"And from each reed hung
seven feathered tassels.

In this instance, the priests
(in dark cotton robes, and dirty,
their dishevelled hair matted with blood, and flowing wildly
over their shoulders)
rush in among the people, calling on them
to protect their gods

And all now is war
where so lately there was peace,
and the sweet brotherhood, the use
of tilled fields.

4

Not one death but many,
not accumulation but change, the feed-back proves, the
feed-back is
the law

Into the same river no man steps twice
When fire dies air dies
No one remains, nor is, one

Around an appearance, one common model, we grow up
many. Else how is it,
if we remain the same,
we take pleasure now
in what we did not take pleasure before? love
contrary objects? admire and/or find fault? use
other words, feel other passions, have
nor figure, appearance, disposition, tissue
the same?
        To be in different states without a change
        is not a possibility

We can be precise. The factors are
in the animal and/or the machine the factors are
communication and/or control, both involve
the message. And what is the message? The message is
a discrete or continuous sequence of measurable events
        distributed in time

is the birth of air, is
the birth of water, is
a state between
the origin and
the end, between
birth and the beginning of
another fetid nest

is change, presents
no more than itself

And the too strong grasping of it,
when it is pressed together and condensed,
loses it

This very thing you are

I I

They buried their dead in a sitting posture
serpent   cane   razor   ray   of   the   sun

And she sprinkled water on the head of the child, crying
"Cioa-coatl! Cioa-coatl!"
with her face to the west

Where the bones are found, in each personal heap
with what each enjoyed, there is always
the Mongolian louse

The light is in the east. Yes. And we must rise, act. Yet
in the west, despite the apparent darkness (the whiteness
which covers all), if you look, if you can bear, if you can, long
    enough

            as long as it was necessary for him, my guide
            to look into the yellow of that longest-lasting
                rose

so you must, and, in that whiteness, into that face, with what
    candor, look

and, considering the dryness of the place
        the long absence of an adequate race

        (of the two who first came, each a conquistador, one
            healed, the other
        tore the eastern idols down, toppled
        the temple walls, which, says the excuser
        were black from human gore)

hear
hear, where the dry blood talks
    where the old appetite walks

                    la piu saporita et migliore
                    che si possa truovar al mondo

where it hides, look
in the eye how it runs
in the flesh / chalk

> but under these petals
> in the emptiness
> regard the light, contemplate
> the flower

whence it arose

> with what violence benevolence is bought
> what cost in gesture justice brings
> what wrongs domestic rights involve
> what stalks
> this silence

> what pudor pejorocracy affronts
> how awe, night-rest and neighborhood can rot
> what breeds where dirtiness is law
> what crawls
> below

III

I am no Greek, hath not th'advantage.
And of course, no Roman:
he can take no risk that matters,
the risk of beauty least of all.

But I have my kin, if for no other reason than
(as he said, next of kin) I commit myself, and,
given my freedom, I'd be a cad
if I didn't. Which is most true.

It works out this way, despite the disadvantage.
I offer, in explanation, a quote:
si j'ai du goût, ce n'est guères
que pour la terre et les pierres.

Despite the discrepancy (an ocean   courage   age)
this is also true: if I have any taste

it is only because I have interested myself
in what was slain in the sun

    I pose you your question:

shall you uncover honey / where maggots are?

    I hunt among stones

J . V . C U N N I N G H A M
(1911–1985)

James Vincent Cunningham was born in Maryland and educated at
Stanford. From 1952 until his retirement in 1980, he taught at
Brandeis and was active as a critic, translator, and editor. His
fastidious poems adopt cool, classical measures, and he was the
contemporary master of the epigram. Though small in bulk and scope,
Cunningham's work is honed to a mordant precision of style and
feeling. In it the contradictions of experience are reduced to moral
categories, then observed with a mature, sometimes embittered
wisdom that can sting while it instructs.

For My Contemporaries

How time reverses
The proud in heart!
I now make verses
Who aimed at art.

But I sleep well.
Ambitious boys
Whose big lines swell
With spiritual noise,

Despise me not,
And be not queasy
To praise somewhat:
Verse is not easy.

But rage who will.
Time that procured me
Good sense and skill
Of madness cured me.

To My Wife

And does the heart grow old? You know
In the indiscriminate green
Of summer or in earliest snow
A landscape is another scene,

Inchoate and anonymous,
And every rock and bush and drift
As our affections alter us
Will alter with the season's shift.

So love by love we come at last,
As through the exclusions of a rhyme,
Or the exactions of a past,
To the simplicity of time,

The antiquity of grace, where yet
We live in terror and delight
With love as quiet as regret
And love like anger in the night.

FROM A Century of Epigrams

29

HISTORY OF IDEAS

God is love. Then by conversion
Love is God, and sex conversion.

53

On a cold night I came through the cold rain
And false snow to the wind shrill on your pane

With no hope and no anger and no fear.
Who are you? and with whom do you sleep here?

55

I had gone broke, and got set to come back,
And lost, on a hot day and a fast track,
On a long shot at long odds, a black mare
By Hatred out of Envy by Despair.

62

You ask me how Contempt who claims to sleep
With every woman that has ever been
Can still maintain that women are skin deep?
They never let him any deeper in.

76

Good Fortune, when I hailed her recently,
Passed by me with the intimacy of shame
As one that in the dark had handled me
And could no longer recollect my name.

ROBERT HAYDEN
(1913–1980)

Robert Hayden was born in a Detroit ghetto called Paradise Valley.
He attended Detroit City College and did graduate work at the
University of Michigan, where he studied with W. H. Auden. He later
taught at Michigan and for many years at Fisk University. He served
as consultant in poetry to the Library of Congress from 1976 until
1978, and among his many honors was the grand prize for poetry at
the First World Festival of Negro Arts in Dakar. Although he'd been
fed the bread of bitterness and a "stangering" racism, Hayden was
adamant that he be considered an American poet rather than a black
poet. And although he was sometimes at odds with the "Black Arts"
movement, his finest poems focus on black history or draw on legends
from black folk culture. His best-known poem, "Middle Passage,"
turns on the 1839 *Amistad* mutiny, the toll of the slave trade, and the
heroism of Cinquez. Pivotal figures in the struggle for political and
human liberation—Nat Turner, Harriet Tubman, Frederick Douglass,
and Malcolm X among them—continued to fascinate Hayden and
elicited from him powerful meditations on the
malevolent or noble designs of history.

Night, Death, Mississippi

I

A quavering cry. Screech-owl?
Or one of them?
The old man in his reek
and gauntness laughs—

One of them, I bet—
and turns out the kitchen lamp,
limping to the porch to listen
in the windowless night.

Be there with Boy and the rest
if I was well again.
Time was. Time was.
White robes like moonlight

In the sweetgum dark.
Unbucked that one then
and him squealing bloody Jesus
as we cut it off.

Time was. A cry?
A cry all right.
He hawks and spits,
fevered as by groinfire.

Have us a bottle,
Boy and me—
he's earned him a bottle—
when he gets home.

I I

Then we beat them, he said,
beat them till our arms was tired
and the big old chains
messy and red.

O Jesus burning on the lily cross

Christ, it was better
than hunting bear
which don't know why
you want him dead.

O night, rawhead and bloodybones night

You kids fetch Paw
some water now so's he
can wash that blood
off him, she said.

O night betrayed by darkness not its own

Frederick Douglass

When it is finally ours, this freedom, this liberty, this beautiful
and terrible thing, needful to man as air,
usable as earth; when it belongs at last to all,
when it is truly instinct, brain matter, diastole, systole,
reflex action; when it is finally won; when it is more
than the gaudy mumbo jumbo of politicians:
this man, this Douglass, this former slave, this Negro
beaten to his knees, exiled, visioning a world
where none is lonely, none hunted, alien,
this man, superb in love and logic, this man
shall be remembered. Oh, not with statues' rhetoric,
not with legends and poems and wreaths of bronze alone,
but with the lives grown out of his life, the lives
fleshing his dream of the beautiful, needful thing.

Middle Passage

I

Jesús, Estrella, Esperanza, Mercy:

Sails flashing to the wind like weapons,
sharks following the moans the fever and the dying;
horror the corposant and compass rose.

Middle Passage:
voyage through death
to life upon these shores.

"10 April 1800—
Blacks rebellious. Crew uneasy. Our linguist says
their moaning is a prayer for death,

ours and their own. Some try to starve themselves.
Lost three this morning leaped with crazy laughter
to the waiting sharks, sang as they went under."

Desire, Adventure, Tartar, Ann:

Standing to America, bringing home
black gold, black ivory, black seed.

> *Deep in the festering hold thy father lies,*
> *of his bones New England pews are made,*
> *those are altar lights that were his eyes.*

Jesus   Saviour   Pilot   Me
Over   Life's   Tempestuous   Sea

We pray that Thou wilt grant, O Lord,
safe passage to our vessels bringing
heathen souls unto Thy chastening.

Jesus   Saviour

> "8 bells. I cannot sleep, for I am sick
> with fear, but writing eases fear a little
> since still my eyes can see these words take shape
> upon the page & so I write, as one
> would turn to exorcism. 4 days scudding,
> but now the sea is calm again. Misfortune
> follows in our wake like sharks (our grinning
> tutelary gods). Which one of us
> has killed an albatross? A plague among
> our blacks—Ophthalmia: blindness—& we
> have jettisoned the blind to no avail.
> It spreads, the terrifying sickness spreads.
> Its claws have scratched sight from the Capt.'s eyes
> & there is blindness in the fo'c'sle
> & we must sail 3 weeks before we come
> to port."

> *What port awaits us, Davy Jones'*
> *or home? I've heard of slavers drifting, drifting,*
> *playthings of wind and storm and chance, their crews*

gone blind, the jungle hatred
crawling up on deck.

Thou   Who   Walked   On   Galilee

"Deponent further sayeth *The Bella J*
left the Guinea Coast
with cargo of five hundred blacks and odd
for the barracoons of Florida:

"That there was hardly room 'tween-decks for half
the sweltering cattle stowed spoon-fashion there;
that some went mad of thirst and tore their flesh
and sucked the blood:

"That Crew and Captain lusted with the comeliest
of the savage girls kept naked in the cabins;
that there was one they called The Guinea Rose
and they cast lots and fought to lie with her:

"That when the Bo's'n piped all hands, the flames
spreading from starboard already were beyond
control, the negroes howling and their chains
entangled with the flames:

"That the burning blacks could not be reached,
that the Crew abandoned ship,
leaving their shrieking negresses behind,
that the Captain perished drunken with the wenches:

"Further Deponent sayeth not."

Pilot   Oh   Pilot   Me

I I

Aye, lad, and I have seen those factories,
Gambia, Rio Pongo, Calabar;
have watched the artful mongos baiting traps
of war wherein the victor and the vanquished

Were caught as prizes for our barracoons.
Have seen the nigger kings whose vanity

and greed turned wild black hides of Fellatah,
Mandingo, Ibo, Kru to gold for us.

And there was one—King Anthracite we named him—
fetish face beneath French parasols
of brass and orange velvet, impudent mouth
whose cups were carven skulls of enemies:

He'd honor us with drum and feast and conjo
and palm-oil-glistening wenches deft in love,
and for tin crowns that shone with paste,
red calico and German-silver trinkets

Would have the drums talk war and send
his warriors to burn the sleeping villages
and kill the sick and old and lead the young
in coffles to our factories.

Twenty years a trader, twenty years,
for there was wealth aplenty to be harvested
from those black fields, and I'd be trading still
but for the fevers melting down my bones.

III

Shuttles in the rocking loom of history,
the dark ships move, the dark ships move,
their bright ironical names
like jests of kindness on a murderer's mouth;
plough through thrashing glister toward
fata morgana's lucent melting shore,
weave toward New World littorals that are
mirage and myth and actual shore.

Voyage through death,
                    voyage whose chartings are unlove.

A charnel stench, effluvium of living death
spreads outward from the hold,
where the living and the dead, the horribly dying,
lie interlocked, lie foul with blood and excrement.

Deep in the festering hold thy father lies,
the corpse of mercy rots with him,
rats eat love's rotten gelid eyes.

But, oh, the living look at you
with human eyes whose suffering accuses you,
whose hatred reaches through the swill of dark
to strike you like a leper's claw.

You cannot stare that hatred down
or chain the fear that stalks the watches
and breathes on you its fetid scorching breath;
cannot kill the deep immortal human wish,
the timeless will.

"But for the storm that flung up barriers
of wind and wave, *The Amistad*, señores,
would have reached the port of Príncipe in two,
three days at most; but for the storm we should
have been prepared for what befell.
Swift as the puma's leap it came. There was
that interval of moonless calm filled only
with the water's and the rigging's usual sounds,
then sudden movement, blows and snarling cries
and they had fallen on us with machete
and marlinspike. It was as though the very
air, the night itself were striking us.
Exhausted by the rigors of the storm,
we were no match for them. Our men went down
before the murderous Africans. Our loyal
Celestino ran from below with gun
and lantern and I saw, before the cane-
knife's wounding flash, Cinquez,
that surly brute who calls himself a prince,
directing, urging on the ghastly work.
He hacked the poor mulatto down, and then
he turned on me. The decks were slippery
when daylight finally came. It sickens me
to think of what I saw, of how these apes

threw overboard the butchered bodies of
our men, true Christians all, like so much jetsam.
Enough, enough. The rest is quickly told:
Cinquez was forced to spare the two of us
you see to steer the ship to Africa,
and we like phantoms doomed to rove the sea
voyaged east by day and west by night,
deceiving them, hoping for rescue,
prisoners on our own vessel, till
at length we drifted to the shores of this
your land, America, where we were freed
from our unspeakable misery. Now we
demand, good sirs, the extradition of
Cinquez and his accomplices to La
Havana. And it distresses us to know
there are so many here who seem inclined
to justify the mutiny of these blacks.
We find it paradoxical indeed
that you whose wealth, whose tree of liberty
are rooted in the labor of your slaves
should suffer the august John Quincy Adams
to speak with so much passion of the right
of chattel slaves to kill their lawful masters
and with his Roman rhetoric weave a hero's
garland for Cinquez. I tell you that
we are determined to return to Cuba
with our slaves and there see justice done. Cinquez—
or let us say 'the Prince'—Cinquez shall die."

The deep immortal human wish,
the timeless will:

    Cinquez its deathless primaveral image,
    life that transfigures many lives.

Voyage through death
                 to life upon these shores.

JEAN GARRIGUE
(1912–1972)

"I prefer elaborate structures to functional slick ones," Jean Garrigue once told an interviewer. "Chopin, Keats, and Proust were early powerful influences. So were mountains and water." Although she could write plainer poems, most of her work exudes a romantic richness, intensely lyrical. Her refined extravagances encompassed as favorite subjects both travel (treated as an intimacy) and love (toured as a foreign place). Despite some archaisms and excess, her melodies are supple and her harmonies surprising. Garrigue was born in Evansville, Indiana, and studied at the University of Chicago and at Iowa. She later taught at many colleges, including Bard and Smith.

Amsterdam Letter

Brick distinguishes this country,
And broad windows—rather, rectangles
Of wide and glittering scope—
And cabbages.
Cattle a specialty, and cheese, storks—if they are not all dead
Or abandoned—and flowers, oh, flowers!
Some say as well, quick humor.
Is it a specimen of humor that a cabdriver proposes to marry
    me?
The speaking of English is at least general.
Also I have spoken a little Dutch with an old Frisian lady.
How affable she was, amusing and helpful!
(They *are* helpful and affable, and their far too occasional
    teams of horses
Wear rosettes by the ears.)
Aside from that, and above all, the dense, heavy, fragrant sky
And rich water, a further extension of color—
The sky a low window over this twining of green water and
    bridges—

And the sedate, gabled houses pressed closely together
And bicyclists, six abreast or more,
Skimming round corners like swallows.
How quiet they are! even the trolleys!
While the trains seem to glide like sleighs on runners
So that after those many places dedicated, it would seem, to
    clatter
The absence of it becomes an active delight in itself.

The delight is in part, of course, the lovely dividing of the city
By those ancient and ripe-green canals, and the mixed
    fragrance
Of the River Amstel and roasting coffee,
And the bravura of carved animal heads, the elegance of
    panels,
And those panes of violet and panes flushed yellow
That alternate the clear meaning of glass
With the blindness of shutters closed over warehouse
    windows,
And that Gothic German French sense of the arabesque and
    the scroll,
The urn and the garland of leaves.

As for that delicacy of manner, that responsiveness to many,
That prevalence of what seems self-possessed, contained, and
    easy—
I am speaking of those who went out of their way
To lead me to Rembrandt's house
(Which in his lifetime he lost),
Of the woman at the Cantine,
Of the Madame, too, in the Zeedjik,
Amiable conversationalists
Who did not make me feel stupid
Because I would never speak their language,
Who by a manner suggested
What I have no word for—
Unfeigned it is and unblighted,
That "generous, free disposition"
That so strongly confirms
A fitness of things,

As do also the upright geraniums,
All of which, by the elm-dark canals
(Where dogs on the loose loped up to me
With cold, wet noses
And ducks paddled under the Seven Arches
And the gilt swan rode on the crest of the fortified tower),
Offered some measurable glimpse of what
There, by the water beds
And the ancient, calmed passions of their reflections,
Informed me as the moon does,
Which was in part the pleasure of learning
Those words that I did from the old Frisian woman—
Horse, sky, cow, tree, thank you, I mean,
Beauty, and love.

Cracked Looking Glass

The tears, the firebursts and the vows,
The wild caprices and the bouts of pulse
The chills of sieged despairs, those flowers
Bought to match eyes and proffer aphrodisiacs
Of sighs and groans; the seizures.
World at the end of world when dusk falls slow
And all else but a taunting fast and loose.
Smooth skin, shut eyes and gliding limbs.

Love, I note you, stroke by stroke,
And show you how you play with shameless art
In the cracked looking glass that I hold up
What practice has made perfect, if it has.
The fits and starts, the going then to stay
The word, the gesture meant to take the heart
(If it be studied or be not)
Grand ceremonials of a play

By which we tried to live a passion out
By every nuance in a little room.
And cloistered so, tell out our stories
To pass the time until the moon rode high,
Improve upon the life we led,
Give gifts of praise, and so we did.
And if you postured in the looking glass
I made it for you, I held the witchery up
For you to see the secret life I guessed,
That more than improbable, celestial otherness.
And if you acted what I taught
Even as I learned it at your eyes
And your each ruse took on as if we borrowed
From every trick known to the over-wrought
And half-Platonic specialist,
We did it under moon craft or in twilight,
In all the half hours when the world becomes
All that imagination ever hoped it was.

My tear-quenched cost, I number half the ways
We chose a smoky vapor over fire
And tried to make a greater truth
Than what our contradictions could allow,
Exclaiming, as we breathed,
The true irrational.
And yet we were what we are.
And though the smoke is gone there is some fire
In saying so.

We made a play but not a discipline.
Love is the sternest master of the school.
But players tell a truth they cannot know.
They do not live it either, they enact
The fiery powers of instants in a light
Held up to them they cannot clarify.
Cease and be still. The pain is otherwise.
It's in the breaking face the clouds give to the moon
And in the flower that leans upon the air
Pouring its full life out into its scent.

After Reading *The Country of the Pointed Firs*

She was the one who lived up country
Half in the woods on a rain-washed road
With a well not near and a barn too far
And the fields ledgy and full of stones
That the crows cawed over and liked to walk in
And the hill and the hollow thick with fern
And in the swamp the cattails and rushes.

It was next to living in a town of birds
But she had hens and a row of bee hives.
When her mother died, and her girl, and Joel,
She told the bees so they'd not fly away
And hung black flags on the doors of the hives
Though they'd always go when they could to the woods
Or swarm on Sunday when she was at meeting.
For each who went she had told the bees.

Change and loss was what the brook cried
That she heard in the night—but she kept snug
With crow-wood for kindling, and the sun shone good
Through the tops of the pines, and her plants
Didn't fail her, and the rosebush always bloomed
By the gnawed fencepost—what the horse had done
When they had a horse and a cow and a dog.

O there had been many, and now was there none?
Lost at sea, they said, her son gone to sea
Lost at sea they said. But if he wasn't
And if he'd come back—so she'd stay till he came
Or whether or not.
Change and loss was what the brook cried
That she heard in the night when the clock whirred.

But when the fog from the southbank came through the firs
Till the air was like something made of cobwebs,
Thin as a cobweb, helpless as shadows
Swept here and there as the sea gulls mewed,
O then it seemed it was all one day
And no one gone and no one crossed over
Or when the rain gurgled in the eave spout
Or the wind walked on the roof like a boy.

Change and loss was what the brook cried
That she heard in the night when the clock whirred
Just before it clanged out its twelve heavy strokes
In the thick of the stillness, black as a crow,
But no scritching now with a scrawny great crackling,
And the rain not trickling, nothing to hark to,
Not even the tree at the north chamber window.

Till she routed it, horse and foot,
Thinking of walking to town through pastures
When the wood thrushes wept their notes
And the moss was thick on the cobbled stones
With the heron wading among the hummocks
Of the pursy meadow that went down to the sea.

And she had knitting and folks to visit,
Preserves to make, and cream tartar biscuit,
She knew where was elocamp, coltsfoot, lobelia,
And she'd make a good mess up for all as could use it,
And go to the well and let down the bucket
And see the sky there and herself in it
As the wind threw itself about in the bushes and shouted
And another day fresh as a cedar started.

MAY SWENSON
(1913–1989)

Born in Logan, Utah, May Swenson graduated with a science degree from Utah State University and in 1949 moved to New York City. For some years she worked as an editor at New Directions, but except for short stints as poet-in-residence she largely avoided the professional literary life. She received the Bollingen Prize in 1981 and was a chancellor of the Academy of American Poets. One critic called Swenson "the poet of the perceptible," and her best poems mark the convergence of inner and outer vision. With her instinctive curiosity—her subjects range from molecules to moon landings—she was aware that description is itself a moral commentary. She called her poems "things taking place," and her shaped poems ("iconographs" is her own term) are clever happenings. But all Swenson's work relies on wordplay, odd viewpoints, unexpected juxtapositions, and puzzling riddles.

Teleology

The eyes look front in humans.
Horse or dog could not shoot,

seeing two sides to everything.
Fish, who never shut their eyes,

can swim on their sides, and see
two worlds: blunt dark below;

above, the daggering light.
Round as a burr, the eye

its whole head, the housefly
sees in a whizzing circle.

Human double-barreled eyes,
in their narrow blind trained

forward, hope to shoot and hit
—if they can find it—

the backward-speeding hole
in the Cyclops face of the future.

Unconscious Came a Beauty

Unconscious
came a beauty to my
wrist
and stopped my pencil,
merged its shadow profile with
my hand's ghost
on the page:
Red Spotted Purple or else Mourning
Cloak,
paired thin-as-paper wings, near black,
were edged on the seam side poppy orange,
as were its spots.

I sat arrested, for its soot-haired
body's worm
shone in the sun.
It bent its tongue long as
a leg
black on my skin
and clung without my
feeling,
while its tomb-stained
duplicate parts of
a window opened.
And then I
moved.

Stone Gullets

Stone gullets among   Inrush Feed   Backsuck and
The boulders swallow   Outburst   Huge engorgements   Swallow
In gulps the sea   Tide crams jagged   Smacks snorts chuckups   Follow
In urgent thirst   Jaws the hollow   Insurge   Hollow
Gushing evacuations follow   Jetty it must   Outpush   Greed

Staying at Ed's Place

I like being in your apartment, and not disturbing anything.
As in the woods I wouldn't want to move a tree,
or change the play of sun and shadow on the ground.

The yellow kitchen stool belongs right there
against white plaster. I haven't used your purple towel
because I like the accidental cleft of shade you left in it.

At your small six-sided table, covered with mysterious
dents in the wood like a dartboard, I drink my coffee
from your brown mug. I look into the clearing

of your high front room, where sunlight slopes through bare
window squares. Your Afghanistan hammock, a man-sized
    cocoon
slung from wall to wall, your narrow desk and typewriter

are the only furniture. Each morning your light from the east
douses me where, with folded legs, I sit in your meadow,
a casual spread of brilliant carpets. Like a cat or dog

I take a roll, then, stretched out flat
in the center of color and pattern, I listen
to the remote growl of trucks over cobbles on Bethune Street
    below.

When I open my eyes I discover the peaceful blank
of the ceiling. Its old paint-layered surface is moonwhite
and trackless, like the Sea—of Tranquillity.

Strawberrying

My hands are murder-red. Many a plump head
drops on the heap in the basket. Or, ripe
to bursting, they might be hearts, matching
the blackbird's wing-fleck. Gripped to a reed
he shrieks his ko-ka-ree in the next field.
He's left his peck in some juicy cheeks, when
at first blush and mostly white, they showed
streaks of sweetness to the marauder.

We're picking near the shore, the morning
sunny, a slight wind moving rough-veined leaves
our hands rumple among. Fingers find by feel
the ready fruit in clusters. Here and there,
their squishy wounds. . . . Flesh was perfect
yesterday. . . . June was for gorging. . . .
sweet hearts young and firm before decay.

"Take only the biggest, and not too ripe,"
a mother calls to her girl and boy, barefoot
in the furrows. "Don't step on any. Don't
change rows. Don't eat too many." Mesmerized
by the largesse, the children squat and pull
and pick handfuls of rich scarlets, half
for the baskets, half for avid mouths.
Soon, whole faces are stained.

A crop this thick begs for plunder. Ripeness
wants to be ravished, as udders of cows when hard,
the blue-veined bags distended, ache to be stripped.

Hunkered in mud between the rows, sun burning
the backs of our necks, we grope for, and rip loose
soft nippled heads. If they bleed—too soft—
let them stay. Let them rot in the heat.

When, hidden away in a damp hollow under moldy
leaves, I come upon a clump of heart-shapes
once red, now spiderspit-gray, intact but empty,
still attached to their dead stems—
families smothered as at Pompeii—I rise
and stretch. I eat one more big ripe lopped
head. Red-handed, I leave the field.

ROBERT DUNCAN
(1919–1988)

Robert Duncan was born in Oakland, California. As an infant he was
adopted by theosophist foster parents on the basis of his astrological
chart, and he grew up steeped in hermetic myths and "sacred
presences." He later studied at Berkeley and, after sojourns abroad
and in New York, settled in San Francisco. He has been variously
associated with the Black Mountain poets (Duncan taught briefly at
Black Mountain College), the San Francisco Renaissance, and the
Beats. But his poetry turns on a different, more visionary axis than
any of theirs. Preoccupied with the "scales of the marvelous," he was
drawn to gnostic lore, natural mysteries, and dreamwork. He claimed
to "receive" his hieratic poems, each at once a "permission" or access
to magic and a copy or visible idea of the artist's original vision. Like
the universe, the poem is a field of correspondences, and to race
beyond the boundaries of convention, Duncan's poems use
incantatory murmur and inspired bursts.

A Poem Beginning with a Line
by Pindar

I

The light foot hears you and the brightness begins
god-step at the margins of thought,
        quick adulterous tread at the heart.
Who is it that goes there?
        Where I see your quick face
notes of an old music pace the air,
torso-reverberations of a Grecian lyre.

In Goya's canvas Cupid and Psyche
have a hurt voluptuous grace

bruised by redemption. The copper light
falling upon the brown boy's slight body
is carnal fate that sends the soul wailing
up from blind innocence, ensnared
    by dimness
into the deprivations of desiring sight.

But the eyes in Goya's painting are soft,
diffuse with rapture absorb the flame.
Their bodies yield out of strength.
    Waves of visual pleasure
wrap them in a sorrow previous to their impatience.

A bronze of yearning, a rose that burns
    the tips of their bodies, lips,
ends of fingers, nipples. He is not wingd.
His thighs are flesh, are clouds
    lit by the sun in its going down,
hot luminescence at the loins of the visible.

    But they are not in a landscape.
    They exist in an obscurity.

The wind spreading the sail serves them.
The two jealous sisters eager for her ruin
    serve them.
That she is ignorant, ignorant of what Love will be,
    serves them.

The dark serves them.
The oil scalding his shoulder serves them,
serves their story. Fate, spinning,
    knots the threads for Love.

Jealousy, ignorance, the hurt . . . serve them.

I I

This is magic. It is passionate dispersion.
What if they grow old? The gods
    would not allow it.
    Psyche is preserved.

In time we see a tragedy, a loss of beauty
    the glittering youth
of the god retains—but from this threshold
    it is age
that is beautiful. It is toward the old poets
    we go, to their faltering,
their unaltering wrongness that has style,
    their variable truth,
    the old faces,
words shed like tears from
a plenitude of powers time stores.

A stroke.   These little strokes.   A chill.
    The old man, feeble, does not recoil.
Recall. A phase so minute,
    only a part of the word in- jerrd.

    The Thundermakers descend,

damerging a nuv. A nerb.
    The present dented of the U
nighted stayd.   States.   The heavy clod?
    Cloud.   Invades the brain.   What
    if lilacs last in *this* dooryard bloomd?

Hoover, Roosevelt, Truman, Eisenhower—
where among these did the power reside
that moves the heart? What flower of the nation
bride-sweet broke to the whole rapture?
Hoover, Coolidge, Harding, Wilson
hear the factories of human misery turning out commodities.
For whom are the holy matins of the heart ringing?
Noble men in the quiet of morning hear
Indians singing the continent's violent requiem.
Harding, Wilson, Taft, Roosevelt,
idiots fumbling at the bride's door,
hear the cries of men in meaningless debt and war.
Where among these did the spirit reside
that restores the land to productive order?
McKinley, Cleveland, Harrison, Arthur,
Garfield, Hayes, Grant, Johnson,

dwell in the roots of the heart's rancor.
How sad "amid lanes and through old woods"
   echoes Whitman's love for Lincoln!

There is no continuity then. Only a few
   posts of the good remain. I too
that am a nation sustain the damage
   where smokes of continual ravage
obscure the flame.

            It is across great scars of wrong
  I reach toward the song of kindred men
  and strike again the naked string
old Whitman sang from. Glorious mistake!
  that cried:

  "The theme is creative and has vista."
  "He is the president of regulation."

I see always the under side turning,
fumes that injure the tender landscape.
  From which up break
lilac blossoms of courage in daily act
  striving to meet a natural measure.

III   *(for Charles Olson)*

          Psyche's tasks—the sorting of seeds
wheat   barley   oats   poppy   coriander
anise   beans   lentils   peas   —every grain
               in its right place
                        before nightfall;
gathering the gold wool from the cannibal sheep
(for the soul must weep
  and come near upon death);

harrowing Hell for a casket Proserpina keeps
                    that must not
  be opend . . . containing beauty?

no! Melancholy coild like a serpent
               that is deadly sleep

we are not permitted
                            to succumb to.

These are the old tasks.
You've heard them before.

They must be impossible. Psyche
must despair, be brought to her
                                insect instructor;
must obey the counsels of the green reed;
saved from suicide by a tower speaking,
    must follow to the letter
    freakish instructions.

In the story the ants help. The old man at Pisa
    mixd in whose mind
(to draw the sorts) are all seeds
            as a lone ant from a broken ant-hill
had part restored by an insect, was
    upheld by a lizard

                (to draw the sorts)
the wind is part of the process
                    defines a nation of the wind—

    father of many notions,
                    Who?
let the light into the dark?   began
the many movements of the passion?
                                West
from east   men push.
                    The islands are blessd
(cursed)   that swim below the sun,

    man upon whom the sun has gone down!

There is the hero who struggles east
widdershins to free the dawn and must
                    woo Night's daughter,
sorcery, black passionate rage, covetous queens,
so that the fleecy sun go   back from Troy,

Colchis, India . . . all the blazing armies
spent, he must struggle alone toward the pyres of Day.

                The light that is Love
rushes on toward passion. It verges upon dark.
    Roses and blood flood the clouds.
    Solitary first riders advance into legend.

  This land, where I stand, was all legend
in my grandfathers' time: cattle raiders,
    animal tribes, priests, gold.
It was the West. Its vistas painters saw
    in diffuse light, in melancholy,
in abysses left by glaciers as if they had been the sun
    primordial carving empty enormities
                out of the rock.

              Snakes lurkd
guarding secrets.   Those first ones
               survived solitude.

  Scientia
holding the lamp, driven by doubt;
Eros naked in foreknowledge
smiling in his sleep; and the light

spilld, burning his shoulder—the outrage
    that conquers legend—
passion, dismay, longing, search
    flooding up where
the Beloved is lost. Psyche travels
life after life, my life, station
    after station,
to be tried

    without break, without
news, knowing only—but what did she know?
    The oracle at Miletus had spoken
truth surely: that he was Serpent-Desire
    that flies thru the air,
a monster-husband. But she saw him fair

whom Apollo's mouthpiece said spread
  pain
beyond cure   to those
  wounded by his arrows.

Rilke torn by a rose thorn
blackend toward Eros. Cupidinous Death!
  that will not take no for an answer.

I V

  Oh yes!   Bless the footfall where
step by step   the boundary walker
(in Maverick Road   the snow
thud by thud   from the roof
circling the house—another tread)

  that foot   informd
by the weight of all things
  that can be elusive
no more than a nearness to the mind
  of a single image

  Oh yes!   this
most dear
  the catalyst force that renders clear
the days of a life from the surrounding medium!

  Yes, beautiful rare wilderness!
wildness that verifies strength of my tame mind,
  clearing held against indians,
health that prepared to meet death,
  the stubborn hymns going up
into the ramifications of the hostile air

  that, deceptive, gives way.

Who is there?   O, light the light!
  The Indians give way,   the clearing falls.
Great Death gives way   and unprepares us.
  Lust gives way.   The Moon gives way.
Night gives way.   Minutely,   the Day gains.

She saw the body of her beloved
    dismemberd in waking . . . or was it
in sight? *Finders Keepers* we sang
    when we were children or were taught to sing
before our histories began and we began
    who were beloved our animal life
toward the Beloved, sworn to be Keepers.

    On the hill before the wind came
the grass moved toward the one sea,
    blade after blade dancing in waves.

There the children turn the ring to the left.
There the children turn the ring to the right.
    Dancing . . . Dancing . . .

And the lonely psyche goes up thru the boy to the king
    that in the caves of history dreams.
Round and round the children turn.
    London Bridge that is a kingdom falls.

We have come so far that all the old stories
whisper once more.
Mount Segur, Mount Victoire, Mount Tamalpais . . .
    rise to adore the mystery of Love!

(An ode? Pindar's art, the editors tell us, was not a statue but
a mosaic, an accumulation of metaphor. But if he was archaic,
not classic, a survival of obsolete mode, there may have been
old voices in the survival that directed the heart. So, a line
from a hymn came in a novel I was reading to help me. Psyche,
poised to leap—and Pindar too, the editors write, goes too far,
topples over—listend to a tower that said, *Listen to me!* The
oracle had said, *Despair! The Gods themselves abhor his power.* And
then the virgin flower of the dark falls back flesh of our flesh
from which everywhere . . .

    the information flows
        that is yearning. A line of Pindar
    moves from the area of my lamp
        toward morning.

In the dawn that is nowhere
I have seen the willful children

clockwise and counter-clockwise turning.

Styx

And a tenth part of Okeanos is given to dark night
        a tithe of the pure water   under   earth
so that the clear fountains pour from rock face,
        tears stream from the caverns and clefts,
        down-running, carving woundrous ways in basalt resistance,
        cutting deep as they go into layers of time-layerd
            Gaia where She sleeps—

the cold water, the black rushing gleam, the
        moving down-rush, wash, gush out over
        bed-rock, toiling the boulders in flood,
        purling in deeps, broad flashing in falls—

And a tenth part of bright clear Okeanos
        his circulations— mists, rains, sheets, sheathes—
        lies in poisonous depths, the black water.

Styx   this carver of caverns beneath us is.
Styx   this black water,   this down-pouring.

The well is deep.   From its stillness
        the words our voices speak   echo.
        Resonance follows resonance.
        Waves of this sounding come up to us.

        We draw the black water, pure and cold.
        The light of day is not as bright
        as this crystal flowing.

Three thousand years we have recited its virtue
        out of Hesiod.

                          Is it twenty-five thousand
since the ice withdrew from the lands   and we
came forth from the realm of caverns where
the river beneath the earth   we knew
      we go back to.
Styx pouring down in the spring from its glacial remove,
      from the black ice.

Fifty million years—from the beginning of what we are—
      we knew the depth of this well to be.

      Fifty million years deep   —but our knowing deepens
          —time deepens—
                       this still water

we thirst for   in dreams we dread.

WILLIAM MEREDITH
(b. 1919)

William Meredith once praised W. H. Auden for having written down "the exact details of our plight" and for an "order revealed / by the closest looking." That sort of scrupulous moral attention has been the hallmark of Meredith's work as well, and he has acknowledged both Auden and Robert Frost as his models. His early poems seem embattled, pitting ideas of order against a world at war. Born in New York City and a graduate of Princeton, he served as a naval aviator in both the Second World War and the Korean War. His more mature poems, though troubled by dark forces in both society and the psyche, seek to affirm the common life. With their spare, cadenced grace—temperate, shrewd, meditative—they move easily between public issues and the private life, exploring the boundaries they share. Meredith taught for many years at Connecticut College and served as consultant in poetry to the Library of Congress from 1978 until 1980. He was awarded the Pulitzer Prize in 1988.

The Illiterate

Touching your goodness, I am like a man
Who turns a letter over in his hand
And you might think this was because the hand
Was unfamiliar but, truth is, the man
Has never had a letter from anyone;
And now he is both afraid of what it means
And ashamed because he has no other means
To find out what it says than to ask someone.

His uncle could have left the farm to him,
Or his parents died before he sent them word,
Or the dark girl changed and want him for beloved.
Afraid and letter-proud, he keeps it with him.

What would you call his feeling for the words
That keep him rich and orphaned and beloved?

Thoughts on One's Head

(in plaster, with a bronze wash)

A person is very self-conscious about his head.
It makes one nervous just to know it is cast
In enduring materials, and that when the real one is dead
The cast one, if nobody drops it or melts it down, will last.

We pay more attention to the front end, where the face is,
Than to the interesting and involute interior:
The Fissure of Rolando and such queer places
Are parks for the passions and fears and mild hysteria.

The things that go on there! Erotic movies are shown
To anyone not accompanied by an adult.
The marquee out front maintains a superior tone:
Documentaries on Sharks and The Japanese Tea Cult.

The fronts of some heads are extravagantly pretty.
These are the females. Men sometimes blow their tops
About them, launch triremes, sack a whole city.
The female head is mounted on rococo props.

Judgment is in the head somewhere; it keeps sums
Of pleasure and pain and gives belated warning;
This is the first place everybody comes
With bills, complaints, writs, summons, in the morning.

This particular head, to my certain knowledge
Has been taught to read and write, make love and money,
Operate cars and airplanes, teach in a college,
And tell involved jokes, some few extremely funny.

It was further taught to know and to eschew
Error and sin, which it does erratically.
This is the place the soul calls home just now.
One dislikes it of course: it is the seat of Me.

Consequences

i. of choice

Despair is big with friends I love,
Hydrogen and burning Jews.
I give them all the grief I have
But I tell them, friends, I choose, I choose,

Don't make me say against my glands
Or how the world has treated me.
Though gay and modest give offense
And people grieve pretentiously,

More than I hoped to do, I do
And more than I deserve I get;
What little I attend, I know
And it argues order more than not.

My desperate friends, I want to tell
Them, you take too delicate offense
At the stench of time and man's own smell,
It is only the smell of consequence.

ii. of love

People love each other and the light
Of love gilds but doesn't alter,
People don't change one another, can scarcely
By taking will and thought add a little
Now and then to their own statures

Which, praise them, they do,
So that here we are in all our sizes
Flooded in the impartial daylight sometimes,
Spotted sometimes in a light we make ourselves,
Human, the beams of attention
Of social animals at their work
Which is loving; and sometimes all dark.

The only correction is
By you of you, by me of me.
People are worth looking at in this light
And if you listen what they are saying is,
Love me sun out there whoever you are,
Chasing me from bed in the morning,
Spooking me all day with shadow,
Surprising me whenever you fall;
Make me conspicuous as I go here,
Spotted by however many beams,
Now light, finally dark. *I fear*
There is meant to be a lot of darkness,
You hear them say, but every last creature
Is the one it meant to be.

iii. my acts

The acts of my life swarm down the street like Puerto Rican
    kids,
Foreign but small and, except for one, unknived.
They do no harm though their voices slash like reeds;
All except one they have evidently been loved.

And down the hill where I've planted spruce and red pine
In a gang of spiked shadows they slouch at night.
I am reasonably brave. I have been, except on one occasion,
Myself: it is no good trying to be what you are not.

We live among gangs who seem to have no stake
In what we're trying to do, no sense of property or race,
Yet if you speak with authority they will halt and break
And sullenly, one by one, show you a local face.

I dreamt once that they caught me and, holding me down,
Burned my genitals with gasoline;
In my stupid terror I was telling them names
So my manhood kept and the rest went up in flames.

'Now, say the world is a fair place,' the biggest one said,
And because there was no face worse than my own there
I said it and got up. Quite a lot of me is charred.
By our code it is fair. We play fair. The world is fair.

Country Stars

The nearsighted child has taken off her glasses
and come downstairs to be kissed goodnight.
She blows on a black windowpane until it's white.
Over the apple trees a great bear passes
but she puts her own construction on the night.

Two cities, a chemical plant, and clotted cars
breathe our distrust of darkness on the air,
clouding the pane between us and the stars.
But have no fear, or only proper fear:
the bright watchers are still there.

The Jain Bird Hospital in Delhi

Outside the hotel window, unenlightened pigeons
weave and dive like Stukas on their prey,
apparently some tiny insect brother.
(In India, the attainment of non-violence

is considered a proper goal for human beings.)
If one of the pigeons should fly into the illusion

of my window and survive (the body is no illusion
when it's hurt) he could be taken across town to the bird-
hospital where Jains, skilled medical men,
repair the feathery sick and broken victims.
There, in reproof of violence
and of nothing else, live Mahavira's brothers and sisters.

To this small, gentle order of monks and nuns
it is bright Vishnu and dark Shiva who are illusion.
They trust in faith, cognition and non-violence
to release them from rebirth. They think that birds
and animals—like us, some predators, some prey—
should be ministered to no less than men and women.

The Jains who deal with creatures (and with laymen)
wear white, while their more enterprising hermit brothers
walk naked and are called *the sky-clad.* Jains pray
to no deity, human kindness being their sole illusion.
Mahavira and those twenty-three other airy creatures
who turned to saints with him, preached the doctrine of *ahimsa,*

which in our belligerent tongue becomes *non-violence.*
It's not a doctrine congenial to snarers and poultrymen,
who every day bring to market maimed pheasants.
Numbers of these are bought in by the Jain brothers
and brought, to grow back wing-tips and illusions,
to one of the hospitals succoring such small quarry.

When strong and feathered again, the lucky victims
get reborn on Sunday mornings to the world's violence,
released from the roofs of these temples to illusion.
It is hard for a westerner to speak about men and women
like these, who call the birds of the air *brothers.*
We recall the embarrassed fanfare for Francis and his flock.

We're poor forked sky-clad things ourselves
and God knows prey to illusion— *e.g.,* I claim these brothers
and sisters in India, stemming a little violence, among birds.

HOWARD NEMEROV
(b. 1920)

To "see in a thinking way" has been Howard Nemerov's ambition.
The variety of his work defeats easy classification. His darkly witty or
sardonic poems stand beside searchingly romantic ones. Lyrical,
observant metaphors give way to ironic, intellectual brooding. Above
all, like Robert Frost or W. H. Auden, Nemerov is a contemplative
poet, taking long, often skeptical views of modern society and
traditional values. He wants both to display and to test the power of
the mind as it threads a way through the maze of experience: "to
make some mind of what was only sense." Nemerov was born in New
York City and graduated from Harvard in 1941. During World War II
he served in the Royal Canadian Air Force and then the U.S. Army
Air Force. He has taught at Bennington, Brandeis, and since 1969 at
Washington University in St. Louis. In 1988 he was named the
nation's third poet laureate. In 1978 his *Collected Poems* was awarded
both the Pulitzer Prize and the National Book Award;
in 1981 he received the Bollingen Prize.

Storm Windows

People are putting up storm windows now,
Or were, this morning, until the heavy rain
Drove them indoors. So, coming home at noon,
I saw storm windows lying on the ground,
Frame-full of rain; through the water and glass
I saw the crushed grass, how it seemed to stream
Away in lines like seaweed on the tide
Or blades of wheat leaning under the wind.
The ripple and splash of rain on the blurred glass
Seemed that it briefly said, as I walked by,
Something I should have liked to say to you,
Something . . . the dry grass bent under the pane

Brimful of bouncing water . . . something of
A swaying clarity which blindly echoes
This lonely afternoon of memories
And missed desires, while the wintry rain
(Unspeakable, the distance in the mind!)
Runs on the standing windows and away.

Writing

The cursive crawl, the squared-off characters
these by themselves delight, even without
a meaning, in a foreign language, in
Chinese, for instance, or when skaters curve
all day across the lake, scoring their white
records in ice. Being intelligible,
these winding ways with their audacities
and delicate hesitations, they become
miraculous, so intimately, out there
at the pen's point or brush's tip, do world
and spirit wed. The small bones of the wrist
balance against great skeletons of stars
exactly; the blind bat surveys his way
by echo alone. Still, the point of style
is character. The universe induces
a different tremor in every hand, from the
check-forger's to that of the Emperor
Hui Tsung, who called his own calligraphy
the 'Slender Gold.' A nervous man
writes nervously of a nervous world, and so on.

Miraculous. It is as though the world
were a great writing. Having said so much,
let us allow there is more to the world
than writing: continental faults are not

bare convoluted fissures in the brain.
Not only must the skaters soon go home;
also the hard inscription of their skates
is scored across the open water, which long
remembers nothing, neither wind nor wake.

Money

AN INTRODUCTORY LECTURE

This morning we shall spend a few minutes
Upon the study of symbolism, which is basic
To the nature of money. I show you this nickel.
Icons and cryptograms are written all over
The nickel: one side shows a hunchbacked bison
Bending his head and curling his tail to accommodate
The circular nature of money. Over him arches
UNITED STATES OF AMERICA, and, squinched in
Between that and his rump, E PLURIBUS UNUM,
A Roman reminiscence that appears to mean
An indeterminately large number of things
All of which are the same. Under the bison
A straight line giving him a ground to stand on
Reads FIVE CENTS. And on the other side of our nickel
There is the profile of a man with long hair
And a couple of feathers in the hair; we know
Somehow that he is an American Indian, and
He wears the number nineteen-thirty-six.
Right in front of his eyes the word LIBERTY, bent
To conform with the curve of the rim, appears
To be falling out of the sky Y first; the Indian
Keeps his eyes downcast and does not notice this;
To notice it, indeed, would be shortsighted of him.
So much for the iconography of one of our nickels,

Which is now becoming a rarity and something of
A collectors' item: for as a matter of fact
There is almost nothing you can buy with a nickel,
The representative American Indian was destroyed
A hundred years or so ago, and his descendants'
Relations with liberty are maintained with reservations,
Or primitive concentration camps; while the bison,
Except for a few examples kept in cages,
Is now extinct. Something like that, I think,
Is what Keats must have meant in his celebrated
Ode on a Grecian Urn.
                          Notice, in conclusion,
A number of circumstances sometimes overlooked
Even by experts: (*a*) Indian and bison,
Confined to obverse and reverse of the coin,
Can never see each other; (*b*) they are looking
In opposite directions, the bison past
The Indian's feathers, the Indian past
The bison's tail; (*c*) they are upside down
To one another; (*d*) the bison has a human face
Somewhat resembling that of Jupiter Ammon.
I hope that our studies today will have shown you
Something of the import of symbolism
With respect to the understanding of what is symbolized.

The Dependencies

This morning, between two branches of a tree
Beside the door, epeira once again
Has spun and signed his tapestry and trap.
I test his early-warning system and
It works, he scrambles forth in sable with
The yellow hieroglyph that no one knows
The meaning of. And I remember now

How yesterday at dusk the nighthawks came
Back as they do about this time each year,
Grey squadrons with the slashes white on wings
Cruising for bugs beneath the bellied cloud.
Now soon the monarchs will be drifting south,
And then the geese will go, and then one day
The little garden birds will not be here.
See how many leaves already have
Withered and turned; a few have fallen, too.
Change is continuous on the seamless web,
Yet moments come like this one, when you feel
Upon your heart a signal to attend
The definite announcement of an end
Where one thing ceases and another starts;
When like the spider waiting on the web
You know the intricate dependencies
Spreading in secret through the fabric vast
Of heaven and earth, sending their messages
Ciphered in chemistry to all the kinds,
The whisper down the bloodstream: it is time.

Learning the Trees

Before you can learn the trees, you have to learn
The language of the trees. That's done indoors,
Out of a book, which now you think of it
Is one of the transformations of a tree.

The words themselves are a delight to learn,
You might be in a foreign land of terms
Like samara, capsule, drupe, legume and pome,
Where bark is papery, plated, warty or smooth.

But best of all are the words that shape the leaves—
Orbicular, cordate, cleft and reniform—

And their venation—palmate and parallel—
And tips—acute, truncate, auriculate.

Sufficiently provided, you may now
Go forth to the forests and the shady streets
To see how the chaos of experience
Answers to catalogue and category.

Confusedly. The leaves of a single tree
May differ among themselves more than they do
From other species, so you have to find,
All blandly says the book, "an average leaf."

Example, the catalpa in the book
Sprays out its leaves in whorls of three
Around the stem; the one in front of you
But rarely does, or somewhat, or almost;

Maybe it's not catalpa? Dreadful doubt.
It may be weeks before you see an elm
Fanlike in form, a spruce that pyramids,
A sweetgum spiring up in steeple shape.

Still, *pedetemtim* as Lucretius says,
Little by little, you do start to learn;
And learn as well, maybe, what language does
And how it does it, cutting across the world

Not always at the joints, competing with
Experience while cooperating with
Experience, and keeping an obstinate
Intransigence, uncanny, of its own.

Think finally about the secret will
Pretending obedience to Nature, but
Invidiously distinguishing everywhere,
Dividing up the world to conquer it,

And think also how funny knowledge is:
You may succeed in learning many trees
And calling off their names as you go by,
But their comprehensive silence stays the same.

Because You Asked about
the Line between Prose and Poetry

Sparrows were feeding in a freezing drizzle
That while you watched turned into pieces of snow
Riding a gradient invisible
From silver aslant to random, white, and slow.

There came a moment that you couldn't tell.
And then they clearly flew instead of fell.

The War in the Air

For a saving grace, we didn't see our dead,
Who rarely bothered coming home to die
But simply stayed away out there
In the clean war, the war in the air.

Seldom the ghosts came back bearing their tales
Of hitting the earth, the incompressible sea,
But stayed up there in the relative wind,
Shades fading in the mind,

Who had no graves but only epitaphs
Where never so many spoke for never so few:
Per ardua, said the partisans of Mars,
Per aspera, to the stars.

That was the good war, the war we won
As if there were no death, for goodness' sake,
With the help of the losers we left out there
In the air, in the empty air.

RICHARD WILBUR

(b. 1921)

The son of a portrait painter, Richard Wilbur was born in New York City. After graduating from Amherst, he served overseas in the army during World War II, then returned to Harvard, where he earned a master's degree in 1947. He has taught at Wellesley, Wesleyan, and Smith and been acclaimed as a translator, Broadway lyricist, and editor. He has been awarded the Pulitzer Prize (in 1957 and 1989), the Bollingen Prize (as translator in 1963 and as poet in 1971), the National Book Award in 1957, and many other honors. In 1987 he was named the nation's second poet laureate. From the start of his prodigious career, Wilbur's technical mastery, as well as the clarity, grace, and compassion of his poems, has been recognized. He writes a stately poetry of ideas that depends on ironic wit and intellectual poise. But his sacramental imagination is grounded in a detailed observation of the natural world; Randall Jarrell once singled out Wilbur's "lyric calling-to-life of the things of this world."

A Baroque Wall-Fountain in the Villa Sciarra

for Dore and Adja

Under the bronze crown
Too big for the head of the stone cherub whose feet
    A serpent has begun to eat,
Sweet water brims a cockle and braids down

    Past spattered mosses, breaks
On the tipped edge of a second shell, and fills
    The massive third below. It spills
In threads then from the scalloped rim, and makes

A scrim or summery tent
For a faun-ménage and their familiar goose.
 Happy in all that ragged, loose
Collapse of water, its effortless descent

 And flatteries of spray,
The stocky god upholds the shell with ease,
 Watching, about his shaggy knees,
The goatish innocence of his babes at play;

 His fauness all the while
Leans forward, slightly, into a clambering mesh
 Of water-lights, her sparkling flesh
In a saecular ecstasy, her blinded smile

 Bent on the sand floor
Of the trefoil pool, where ripple-shadows come
 And go in swift reticulum,
More addling to the eye than wine, and more

 Interminable to thought
Than pleasure's calculus. Yet since this all
 Is pleasure, flash, and waterfall,
Must it not be too simple? Are we not

 More intricately expressed
In the plain fountains that Maderna set
 Before St. Peter's—the main jet
Struggling aloft until it seems at rest

 In the act of rising, until
The very wish of water is reversed,
 That heaviness borne up to burst
In a clear, high, cavorting head, to fill

 With blaze, and then in gauze
Delays, in a gnatlike shimmering, in a fine
 Illumined version of itself, decline,
And patter on the stones its own applause?

 If that is what men are
Or should be, if those water-saints display
 The pattern of our areté,
What of these showered fauns in their bizarre,

Spangled, and plunging house?
They are at rest in fulness of desire
    For what is given, they do not tire
Of the smart of the sun, the pleasant water-douse

    And riddled pool below,
Reproving our disgust and our ennui
    With humble insatiety.
Francis, perhaps, who lay in sister snow

    Before the wealthy gate
Freezing and praising, might have seen in this
    No trifle, but a shade of bliss—
That land of tolerable flowers, that state

    As near and far as grass
Where eyes become the sunlight, and the hand
    Is worthy of water: the dreamt land
Toward which all hungers leap, all pleasures pass.

Looking into History

I

Five soldiers fixed by Mathew Brady's eye
Stand in a land subdued beyond belief.
Belief might lend them life again. I try
Like orphaned Hamlet working up his grief

To see my spellbound fathers in these men
Who, breathless in their amber atmosphere,
Show but the postures men affected then
And the hermit faces of a finished year.

The guns and gear and all are strange until
Beyond the tents I glimpse a file of trees
Verging a road that struggles up a hill.

They're sycamores.
               The long-abated breeze

Flares in those boughs I know, and hauls the sound
Of guns and a great forest in distress.
Fathers, I know my cause, and we are bound
Beyond that hill to fight at Wilderness.

I I

But trick your eyes with Birnam Wood, or think
How fire-cast shadows of the bankside trees
Rode on the back of Simois to sink
In the wide waters. Reflect how history's

Changes are like the sea's, which mauls and mulls
Its salvage of the world in shifty waves,
Shrouding in evergreen the oldest hulls
And yielding views of its confounded graves

To the new moon, the sun, or any eye
That in its shallow shoreward version sees
The pebbles charging with a deathless cry
And carageen memorials of trees.

I I I

Now, old man of the sea,
I start to understand:
The will will find no stillness
Back in a stilled land.

The dead give no command
And shall not find their voice
Till they be mustered by
Some present fatal choice.

Let me now rejoice
In all impostures, take
The shape of lion or leopard,
Boar, or watery snake,

Or like the comber break,
Yet in the end stand fast
And by some fervent fraud
Father the waiting past,

Resembling at the last
The self-established tree
That draws all waters toward
Its live formality.

Love Calls Us to the Things of This World

The eyes open to a cry of pulleys,
And spirited from sleep, the astounded soul
Hangs for a moment bodiless and simple
As false dawn.
        Outside the open window
The morning air is all awash with angels.

   Some are in bed-sheets, some are in blouses,
Some are in smocks: but truly there they are.
Now they are rising together in calm swells
Of halcyon feeling, filling whatever they wear
With the deep joy of their impersonal breathing;

   Now they are flying in place, conveying
The terrible speed of their omnipresence, moving
And staying like white water; and now of a sudden
They swoon down into so rapt a quiet
That nobody seems to be there.
        The soul shrinks

   From all that it is about to remember,
From the punctual rape of every blessèd day,
And cries,

"Oh, let there be nothing on
earth but laundry,
Nothing but rosy hands in the rising steam
And clear dances done in the sight of heaven."

Yet, as the sun acknowledges
With a warm look the world's hunks and colors,
The soul descends once more in bitter love
To accept the waking body, saying now
In a changed voice as the man yawns and rises,

"Bring them down from their ruddy gallows;
Let there be clean linen for the backs of thieves;
Let lovers go fresh and sweet to be undone,
And the heaviest nuns walk in a pure floating
Of dark habits,
keeping their difficult balance."

Mind

Mind in its purest play is like some bat
That beats about in caverns all alone,
Contriving by a kind of senseless wit
Not to conclude against a wall of stone.

It has no need to falter or explore;
Darkly it knows what obstacles are there,
And so may weave and flitter, dip and soar
In perfect courses through the blackest air.

And has this simile a like perfection?
The mind is like a bat. Precisely. Save
That in the very happiest intellection
A graceful error may correct the cave.

Advice to a Prophet

When you come, as you soon must, to the streets of our city,
Mad-eyed from stating the obvious,
Not proclaiming our fall but begging us
In God's name to have self-pity,

Spare us all word of the weapons, their force and range,
The long numbers that rocket the mind;
Our slow, unreckoning hearts will be left behind,
Unable to fear what is too strange.

Nor shall you scare us with talk of the death of the race.
How should we dream of this place without us?—
The sun mere fire, the leaves untroubled about us,
A stone look on the stone's face?

Speak of the world's own change. Though we cannot conceive
Of an undreamt thing, we know to our cost
How the dreamt cloud crumbles, the vines are blackened
      by frost,
How the view alters. We could believe,

If you told us so, that the white-tailed deer will slip
Into perfect shade, grown perfectly shy,
The lark avoid the reaches of our eye,
The jack-pine lose its knuckled grip

On the cold ledge, and every torrent burn
As Xanthus once, its gliding trout
Stunned in a twinkling. What should we be without
The dolphin's arc, the dove's return,

These things in which we have seen ourselves and spoken?
Ask us, prophet, how we shall call
Our natures forth when that live tongue is all
Dispelled, that glass obscured or broken

In which we have said the rose of our love and the clean
Horse of our courage, in which beheld

The singing locust of the soul unshelled,
And all we mean or wish to mean.

Ask us, ask us whether with the worldless rose
Our hearts shall fail us; come demanding
Whether there shall be lofty or long standing
When the bronze annals of the oak-tree close.

Walking to Sleep

As a queen sits down, knowing that a chair will be there,
Or a general raises his hand and is given the field-glasses,
Step off assuredly into the blank of your mind.
Something will come to you. Although at first
You nod through nothing like a fogbound prow,
Gravel will breed in the margins of your gaze,
Perhaps with tussocks or a dusty flower,
And, humped like dolphins playing in the bow-wave,
Hills will suggest themselves. All such suggestions
Are yours to take or leave, but hear this warning:
Let them not be too velvet green, the fields
Which the deft needle of your eye appoints,
Nor the old farm past which you make your way
Too shady-linteled, too instinct with home.
It is precisely from Potemkin barns
With their fresh-painted hex signs on the gables,
Their sparkling gloom within, their stanchion-rattle
And sweet breath of silage, that there comes
The trotting cat whose head is but a skull.
Try to remember this: what you project
Is what you will perceive; what you perceive
With any passion, be it love or terror,
May take on whims and powers of its own.
Therefore a numb and grudging circumspection
Will serve you best, unless you overdo it,

Watching your step too narrowly, refusing
To specify a world, shrinking your purview
To a tight vision of your inching shoes—
Which may, as soon you come to think, be crossing
An unseen gorge upon a rotten trestle.
What you must manage is to bring to mind
A landscape not worth looking at, some bleak
Champaign at dead November's end, its grass
As dry as lichen, and its lichens grey,
Such glumly simple country that a glance
Of flat indifference from time to time
Will stabilize it. Lifeless thus, and leafless,
The view should set at rest all thoughts of ambush.
Nevertheless, permit no roadside thickets
Which, as you pass, might shake with worse than wind;
Revoke all trees and other cover; blast
The upstart boulder which a flicking shape
Has stepped behind; above all, put a stop
To the known stranger up ahead, whose face
Half turns to mark you with a creased expression.
Here let me interject that steady trudging
Can make you drowsy, so that without transition,
As when an old film jumps in the projector,
You will be wading a dun hallway, rounding
A newel post, and starting up the stairs.
Should that occur, adjust to circumstances
And carry on, taking these few precautions:
Detach some portion of your thought to guard
The outside of the building; as you wind
From room to room, leave nothing at your back,
But slough all memories at every threshold;
Nor must you dream of opening any door
Until you have foreseen what lies beyond it.
Regardless of its seeming size, or what
May first impress you as its style or function,
The abrupt structure which involves you now
Will improvise like vapor. Groping down
The gritty cellar steps and past the fuse-box,
Brushing through sheeted lawn-chairs, you emerge

In some cathedral's pillared crypt, and thence,
Your brow alight with carbide, pick your way
To the main shaft through drifts and rubbly tunnels.
Promptly the hoist, ascending toward the pit-head,
Rolls downward past your gaze a dinted rock-face
Peppered with hacks and drill-holes, which acquire
Insensibly the look of hieroglyphics.
Whether to surface now within the vast
Stone tent where Cheops lay secure, or take
The proffered shed of corrugated iron
Which gives at once upon a vacant barracks,
Is up to you. Need I, at this point, tell you
What to avoid? Avoid the pleasant room
Where someone, smiling to herself, has placed
A bowl of yellow freesias. Do not let
The thought of her in yellow, lithe and sleek
As lemonwood, mislead you where the curtains,
Romping like spinnakers which taste the wind,
Bellying out and lifting till the sill
Has shipped a drench of sunlight, then subsiding,
Both warm and cool the love-bed. Your concern
Is not to be detained by dread, or by
Such dear acceptances as would entail it,
But to pursue an ever-dimming course
Of pure transition, treading as in water
Past crumbling tufa, down cloacal halls
Of boarded-up hotels, through attics full
Of glassy taxidermy, moping on
Like a drugged fire-inspector. What you hope for
Is that at some point of the pointless journey,
Indoors or out, and when you least expect it,
Right in the middle of your stride, like that,
So neatly that you never feel a thing,
The kind assassin Sleep will draw a bead
And blow your brains out.
                              What, are you still awake?
Then you must risk another tack and footing.
Forget what I have said. Open your eyes
To the good blackness not of your room alone

But of the sky you trust is over it,
Whose stars, though foundering in the time to come,
Bequeath us constantly a jetsam beauty.
Now with your knuckles rub your eyelids, seeing
The phosphenes caper like St. Elmo's fire,
And let your head heel over on the pillow
Like a flung skiff on wild Gennesaret.
Let all things storm your thought with the moiled flocking
Of startled rookeries, or flak in air,
Or blossom-fall, and out of that come striding
In the strong dream by which you have been chosen.
Are you upon the roads again? If so,
Be led past honeyed meadows which might tempt
A wolf to graze, and groves which are not you
But answer to your suppler self, that nature
Able to bear the thrush's quirky glee
In stands of chuted light, yet praise as well,
All leaves aside, the barren bark of winter.
When, as you may, you find yourself approaching
A crossroads and its laden gallows tree,
Do not with hooded eyes allow the shadow
Of a man moored in air to bruise your forehead,
But lift your gaze and stare your brother down,
Though the swart crows have pecked his sockets hollow.
As for what turn your travels then will take,
I cannot guess. Long errantry perhaps
Will arm you to be gentle, or the claws
Of nightmare flap you pathless God knows where,
As the crow flies, to meet your dearest horror.
Still, if you are in luck, you may be granted,
As, inland, one can sometimes smell the sea,
A moment's perfect carelessness, in which
To stumble a few steps and sink to sleep
In the same clearing where, in the old story,
A holy man discovered Vishnu sleeping,
Wrapped in his maya, dreaming by a pool
On whose calm face all images whatever
Lay clear, unfathomed, taken as they came.

Hamlen Brook

At the alder-darkened brink
Where the stream slows to a lucid jet
I lean to the water, dinting its top with sweat,
    And see, before I can drink,

A startled inchling trout
Of spotted near-transparency,
Trawling a shadow solider than he.
    He swerves now, darting out

To where, in a flicked slew
Of sparks and glittering silt, he weaves
Through stream-bed rocks, disturbing foundered leaves,
    And butts then out of view

Beneath a sliding glass
Crazed by the skimming of a brace
Of burnished dragon-flies across its face,
    In which deep cloudlets pass

And a white precipice
Of mirrored birch-trees plunges down
Toward where the azures of the zenith drown.
    How shall I drink all this?

Joy's trick is to supply
Dry lips with what can cool and slake,
Leaving them dumbstruck also with an ache
    Nothing can satisfy.

MONA VAN DUYN
(b. 1921)

Born and educated in Iowa, Mona Van Duyn has lived for many years
in St. Louis, where she taught at Washington University and with her
husband edited *Perspective*. In 1971 she won both the Bollingen Prize
and the National Book Award, and in 1991 she was awarded the
Pulitzer Prize. A canny realism underlies Van Duyn's views of art and
love, which usually start as pure vision and often end in something
more troubled, more domestic and human. But the very effort to
shape experience into a pattern, she has written, "assumes a caring
about other human beings, a caring which is a form of love." Her
intellectual balance, as well as her preferred narrative and formal
strategies, serve to heighten the ordinary (what she calls the "motley
and manifold"), and control the bizarre.

Homework

for Jim

Lest the fair cheeks begin their shrivelling
before a keeping eye has lit on their fairness,
I pluck from the stony world some that can't cling
to stone, for a homely, transparent form to bless.

Smothering Elbertas, if not Albertines,
in the thick, scalding sweetness of my care,
I add a touch of tart malice, some spicy scenes
and stirring, and screw the lid on love's breathless jar.

There in a frieze they stand, and there they can stay
until, in the fickle world's or the jaded heart's
hunger for freshness, they are consumed away.
Oh I know, I know that, great or humble, the arts

in their helplessness can save but a few selves
by such disguises from Time's hideous bite,

and yet, a sweating Proust of the pantry shelves,
I cupboard these pickled peaches in Time's despite.

Into Mexico

Past the angular maguey fields, a ride on the optic nerve,
we come to the first rest stop, and the visit begins.
It is what I have always wanted; to follow the first signs
in another language makes me weak with joy. I am brave
out back in a courtyard, by a shack that might be the toilet,
when bulging señoras bump me on the back and shoulder me.
If they look at me I do not know what they see,
since even metaphors are changed. Overhead in the heat
the skinned, outrageous body of some animal hangs from a
    line.
Is it rotting, or drying? I've never smelled its rawness before.
Yes, there is a stool in the shack, and soiled toilet paper
in a waist-high pile beside it. Water is in a can.

I touch the paper on the roll, it is rough, it is like . . . nothing
    else.
I am behind the eyes at last. It is as if one could by-pass
love, when the other eyes parry with a picture of one's own
    face,
and never arrive at marriage, either true or false,
when eyes glaze and minds are more private than ever,
but could stop in between at a point where no one
can stop. To be in one's first foreign country, in approximation,
is to be in you—or to feel what it must be like to be there.

Now it is one long agony of taking-in. From the bus
I can see inside the palings, or tin, or straw of a shelter,
and all pots, braziers and pallets are unfamiliar.
At the first market, walking in through the restless
yellow of bananas, I will go to such furnishings and handle
    them.

Country dogs here are yellow also, with a long body.
And all the time I have lived as if you were like me.
Now, here, I am released from that stratagem.

In the city I would never have expected a glassy hotel
to rise between little sheds of pink and orange cement,
nor men to pull down their pants and squat in the vacant
lot downtown. Sweet rolls—I am trying to taste them all,
but it will take weeks—are named for creatures and the parts
of creatures, Snails, Cheeks, Noses, Ears, Dogs.
What is that snarled bouquet of herbs a little boy drags
toward home, making a green sweep of the streets?
A woman kneels on the pavement all day to sell
six pyramids of seven cracked walnuts each.
I tongue a clay cup that tastes of dark and starch,
and buy eggs singly, since the price of one is marked on its
    shell.
Each noise, each name, is enchanted and necessary.
I drift in bed, astonished by faintness and nausea and chills.
I would never have felt this way—is this the way it feels?
Thousands of black beans shine near sweet potato candy.

One starves for this journey, I think, a simple sensing
    of what is
not thou, not it, but you—a visit behind the eyes
where the map bulges into belief, relief, presents sea,
mountains, macadam, presents a strange and willful country.

The Twins

My sweet-faced, tattle-tale brother was born blind,
but the colors drip in his head. He paints with his fingers.
All day with his pots and paper he follows me around
wherever I set up my easel, till I pinch his bat ears,

then before he goes he swears he didn't feel anything.
But he knows my feelings, sneaks them out of my skin.
The things he knows! Leaving me squeezed and sulking,
he pretends he felt them himself and tells everyone.

Nobody ever blames him. He's terribly talented.
The world, glimpsing itself through him, will grow
sick with self-love, it seems, and under his eyelid
lie down, in burning shame, with its own shadow,

whereas, on my canvas, it wears its gray and brown
like a fat beaver, and even as I sweat on my brush,
all forms, at its simple-minded toothy grin,
branches, limbs, trunks, topple in a watery backwash.

When he goes to sleep, he says, the world stays in his head
like a big spiderweb strung between ear and ear,
buzzing like telephone wires, and what he has heard
all night, next morning has happened, is true, is there.

Though it always comes back for me, thick, bathed, grateful,
everything has to be re-imagined each sunrise
when I crawl from my black comfort. But I can't make
    a phone call.
I have to talk to something in front of my eyes.

You'd never know we were close. When we meet strangers
they poke my round stomach and pat his long bare legs,
I gush, and he, or that's what it looks like, glares,
then he stomps on my oils and we fight like cats and dogs.

But when it rains sometimes, and he feels it and I hear it,
and he closes my eyes with his fingers to stop my raining,
and one tear falls before everything is quiet,
and his tear is the color of cinnamon on my tongue,

oh then we leave together and nobody can find us.
Not even our mother, if she came, could tell us apart.
Only the stars can see, who cluster around us,
my painted person crouched in his painted heart.

A View

You drive, the road aims for a mountain.
Down paving, toward the low basket of the sun,

a jackrabbit is dribbled by slaps of hot wind.
Hummocky, glazed, superficial, tanned

the landspread. I ride beside you, in the time
of life to note character, waiting for the sublime.

Enhancement of hills. Foisted up by their trite
avowals, we grow more close and hot.

Far ahead, something definite is about to occur.
The way goes flat, dusky. There they are,

the god, looming, and with him—but she is terrible!—
lying at his feet, his own foothill,

wrinkled, blue, balding, risen-above,
her back all sore from trails, child-ridden, shoved

to the ground in a dumpy heap, mined-out,
learned-on by the high one until that

moment he knew his own destiny, donned
a green-black cloak, rose up around

mid-life to stay with the stars, his face flint,
his eyes slatey and bland, and she went

into her change. Oh she was fanciful once,
garbed in dapples of yarrow, lupine and gentians,

silvery inside, always a-chatter
with rockchuck and nuthatch, point-breasted, and later

glad to be taken. Opened unmercifully,
she was used all over. Then, so accessible, she

was fair game for everyone. Even her shale
surfaces have been wrung out for oil.

He stands nearby, unmoved. He knows
how not to be. Even at sundown he flourishes.

He can sway in aspen and tender seedgrass
in his low meadows, wearing the disgrace

of his early delicacy still, where blue grouse,
calliope hummingbird, rosy finch rise

and fall in paintbrush, harebell, penstemon,
beeplant, columbine. Nothing is gone.

He shows without shame these young, soft
traces, having gone on to lift

into view rock ribs and evergreen
masculinity. He transcends every mine,

they are small scars in his potency, something
unearthly shocked, shook him and kept him ascending.

He grew rough, scrabbly, wore outlaw underbrush,
gray fox, bobcat and cougar, secret fish.

Then he was stale for a while, all bare bone, then reared
a feast of self in a head uncovered,

streaked gray and white, playing cool, leaning
on no shoulder, above raining,

oblivious of his past, in pride of escape.
Never down-hearted, he is wholly grown up.

You turn and ask how I am. I say
I'm admiring the scenery, and am O.K.

The Stream

for my mother

Four days with you, my father three months dead.
You can't tell months from years, but you feel sad,

and you hate the nursing home. I've arranged a lunch
for the two of us, and somehow you manage to pinch

the pin from Madrid I bought you closed at the neck
of your best red blouse, put on new slacks, and take

off your crocheted slippers to put on shiny shoes,
all by yourself. "I don't see how you could close

that pin. You look so nice!" "Well, I tried and tried,
and worked till I got it. They didn't come," you said.

"Mother, I'm sorry, this is the wrong day,
our lunch is tomorrow. Here's a big kiss anyway

for dressing up for me. The nurse will come in
tomorrow and help you put on your clothes and pin."

"These last few days her mind has certainly cleared.
Of course the memory's gone," your doctor said.

Next day they bathed you, fixed your hair and dressed
you up again, got a wheelchair and wheeled you past

the fat happy babbler of nonsense who rolled her chair
all day in the hall, the silent stroller who wore

a farmer's cap and bib overalls with rows
of safety pins on the bib, rooms of old babies

in cribs, past the dining hall, on down to a sunny
lounge in the other wing. "Where can I pee,

if I have to pee? I don't like it here, I'm afraid.
Where's my room? I'm going to faint," you said.

But they came with the lunch and card table and chairs
and bustled and soothed you and you forgot the fears

and began to eat. The white tablecloth, the separate
plate for salad, the silvery little coffee pot,

the covers for dishes must have made you feel
you were in a restaurant again after all

those shut-in years. (Dad would never spend the money,
but long ago you loved to eat out with me.)

You cleaned your soup bowl and dishes, one by one,
and kept saying, "This is fun! This is *fun!*"

The cake fell from your trembly fork, so I fed
it to you. "Do you want mine, too?" "Yes," you said,

"and I'll drink your milk if you don't want it." (You'd
lost twelve pounds already by refusing your food.)

I wheeled you back. "Well, I never did *that* before!
Thank you, Jane." "We'll do it again." "Way down *there,*"

you marveled. You thanked me twice more. My eyes were wet.
"You're welcome, Mother. You'll have a good nap now,
      I'll bet."

I arranged for your old companion, who came twice a day,
to bring you milkshakes, and reached the end of my stay.

On the last night I helped you undress. Flat dugs
like antimacassars lay on your chest, your legs

and arms beetle-thin swung from the swollen belly
(the body no more misshapen, no stranger to see,

after all, at the end than at the beloved beginning).
You chose your flowered nightgown as most becoming.

You stood at the dresser, put your teeth away,
washed your face, smoothed on Oil of Olay,

then Avon night cream, then put Vicks in your nose,
then lay on the bed. I sat beside your knees

to say goodbye for a month. "You know I'll call
every Sunday and write a lot. Try to eat well—"

Tears stopped my voice. With a girl's grace you sat up
and, as if you'd done it lifelong, reached out to cup

my face in both your hands, and, as easily
as if you'd said it lifelong, you said, "Don't cry,

don't cry. You'll never know how much I love you."
I kissed you and left, crying. It felt true.

I forgot to tell them that you always sneaked your meat,
you'd bragged, to the man who ate beside you. One night

at home, my heart ringing with what you'd said,
then morning, when the phone rang to say you were dead.

I see your loving look wherever I go.
What is love? Truly I do not know.

Sometimes, perhaps, instead of a great sea,
it is a narrow stream running urgently

far below ground, held down by rocky layers,
the deeds of mother and father, helpless sooth-sayers

of how our life is to be, weighted by clay,
the dense pressure of thwarted needs, the replay

of old misreadings, by hundreds of feet of soil,
the gifts and wounds of the genes, the short or tall

shape of our possibilities, seeking
and seeking a way to the top, while above, running

and stumbling this way and that on the clueless ground,
another seeker clutches a dowsing-wand

which bends, then lifts, dips, then straightens, everywhere,
saying to the dowser, it is there, it is not there,

and the untaught dowser believes, does not believe,
and finally simply stands on the ground above,

till a sliver of stream finds a crack and makes its way,
slowly, too slowly, through rock and earth and clay.

Here at my feet I see, after sixty years,
the welling water—to which I add these tears.

HOWARD MOSS

(1922–1987)

Quintessentially a New York poet—sophisticated, skeptical, witty—Howard Moss was born in New York City and lived there all his life. Though an occasional playwright, teacher, and critic, he was most closely identified with *The New Yorker*, where for nearly forty years he served as poetry editor. The poet always feels, he wrote, "the pull between speech and eloquence . . . how to speak in the name of something real without being merely commonplace." Moss's own manner of speaking was cultivated but subdued, attentive to happenstance and undertone, curious about the dreamlife of art and memory and the unconscious. The astringent lyricism of his early work darkened over the years into a melancholy, often elegiac, tone, sometimes disguised as clever satire. Despite his cosmopolitan style, the enduring cycles of nature—the seeds and seasons of growth and decay—were his standard, and Moss searched for his mysteries in the everyday. He won the National Book Award in 1972.

The Pruned Tree

As a torn paper might seal up its side,
Or a streak of water stitch itself to silk
And disappear, my wound has been my healing,
And I am made more beautiful by losses.
See the flat water in the distance nodding
Approval, the light that fell in love with statues,
Seeing me alive, turn its motion toward me.
Shorn, I rejoice in what was taken from me.

What can the moonlight do with my new shape
But trace and retrace its miracle of order?
I stand, waiting for the strange reaction
Of insects who knew me in my larger self,
Unkempt, in a naturalness I did not love.

Even the dog's voice rings with a new echo,
And all the little leaves I shed are singing,
Singing to the moon of shapely newness.

Somewhere what I lost I hope is springing
To life again. The roofs, astonished by me,
Are taking new bearings in the night, the owl
Is crying for a further wisdom, the lilac
Putting forth its strongest scent to find me.
Butterflies, like sails in grooves, are winging
Out of the water to wash me, wash me.
Now, I am stirring like a seed in China.

The Wars

How can I tell you of the terrible cries
Never sounded, of the nerves that fail,
Not in jungle warfare or a southern jail,
But in some botched affair where two people sit
Quite calmly under a blood-red lamp
In a Chinese restaurant, a ludicrous swamp
Of affection, fear drowning in the amber
Tea when no word comes to mind
To stand for the blood already spilled,
For rejection, denial, for all those years
Of damage done in the polite wars?

And what do I know of the terrible cries
That are really sounded on the real hill
Where the soldiers sweat in the Asian night
And the Asians sweat where the soldiers flail
The murderous grass, and the peasants reel
Back in a rain of gasoline,
And the shells come home and the bombs come down
Quite calmly under a blood-red moon

Not far from China, and the young are killed,
Mere numerals in the casualties
Of this year's war, and the war of years?

He stands with a knife in the Daily News.
They are snaking their way into the hills.
She is walking up Broadway to hurt again.
They are fleeing under a hail of shells.
He is taking her neck into his hands.
A human seed squats in the dark.
She is scalding the baby in the bath.
He feels the bullet enter his skin.
She spits in the face of the riot squad.
They are sitting down, they are opening wounds.

Ménage à Trois

Another sunset of scrambled eggs
And wine, Mars under the piano, laughing,
Venus at the door of the frigidaire,
Saying, "We're all out of blood again!"
How I deplore her use of the language!
You ask how we get along? Not well.
Temperamental discrepancies:
Her habit of saying nothing grandly,
His fake interest in the cause of things.
The food is dreadful. The weather worse.
So much for all the touted joys
Of the Riviera—or wherever we are.
The dullness of the nights is hard to believe,
Though, from outside, I gather we cause
A sensation. Who's sleeping with whom?
We keep them guessing: Nobody is.
The schedule goes something like this:

She works on her cookbook, "Venus Cooks,"
He works part time at the Peace Foundation.
And I start out—well, you know me:
I rip through the Debussy Preludes, shave,
Feel ashamed at detesting travel,
Read, write, go for a walk, and think—
Not that there's much here to think about.
Lunch, usually mushrooms picked
By the local mushroom maniac, whom
We trust, *ça va sans dire,* then back
To my desk for a note or two, more work,
He comes home, she *in* from the gazebo,
Where she writes—and then it's cocktail time!
Singapore slings served in jelly glasses,
Both à la mode in nineteen thirty-nine
(That's the year the Spanish War closed down).
To say I was bored would overstate the case.
I'm languid. They're worse. Desultory.

Of course, he's nineteen, and has fresh thoughts,
She *can* be amusing. At dusk, on the terrace,
I get myself up like a Chinese sage,
My bathrobe from Brooks dyed raven blue,
And we talk of our Oedipal strangulations—
Each so different and each the same.
Later, we provide pornography
(Mental) for the neighbors, who watch our blinds
As if they were about to disclose an orgy,
Something worthy of the TV sets
They hunch over like a herd of cattle.
Then, with a little citrus kiss goodnight,
We part, and so the days go by. . . .

We're followed to the market by a limousine,
Green, a Rolls, in which an assassin
Is discreetly invisible in the back seat.
So we say. It's probably the victim.
I have come to believe in loneliness,
Disguised as it is as an optical illusion.
Rumors are rife: something rose from the sea,

Somebody saw a stain of blood—
But, no matter what they say, the sun's the same.
This morning, I wrote, beginning a poem,
"That sedative, the sun"—but I couldn't go on.
They're at the door. Another game.
She: (Screaming) "Leave me *alone!*"
He: "Tonight, we'll really go to town."
You want my view of the whole situation?
It's old, inadequate, and flourishing.

Elegy for My Sister

1

Getting out of bed one day, you broke
Your leg simply by standing up,
The bones too frail, the marrow gone,
Melted into a kind of eggshell sawdust,
The Crab, and chemotherapy against it,
The cure as killing as the pain it cured . . .

Why torture myself? Or you?—sailed into
The port of Nothing or that Elysium
Of childish happiness the heart sets store by,
Which, for you, would be a house in Larchmont,
Or the first time you arrived in Paris. . . .

2

Now the vials have closed and all the druggists
Vanished into smoke, along what walks
Will the ghost of you appear in a summer nightgown,
Silvery as moonlight on a sill,
Supple as the girl you were, who, frowning,

Dazzled guests with showy piano pieces?
You never got the hang of it, never quite took in
The Bach Partitas or the Chopin Études,
Languishing always over "Clair de Lune"—
Moony on the upstairs porch and downcast,
Waiting for the phone to ring, or waiting
Simply for the end of waiting. Left in
My possession—the irony of phrases!—
Is a photograph of you posed on a pony
Somewhere in Maine—white cap, white coat—
And one from Lakewood. I remember going
Up by train once, dancing in the aisles
While the train sneaked through faint zebra woods of pine. . . .

3

That afternoon will come when the schoolgirl walking
Home from the classroom in the spring will feel
The first onslaught of the terror of seasons,
The blood of the hour a permanent imprint.
Approaching the bridge, will she be in her newness
The last straw just as the ship in the river

Appears and the jaws of the bridge fly open—
The drab barge below with its scruffy captain
Commanding the air with bleatings and whistles,
The smokestack's blunt, swift-moving cigar
Blurring the trees in a smudge of smoke,
The birds in the sky in a net, then not?

Above the run-down, oily garages
Of the Bronx—old brickwork, carwash rinses,
The abandoned piecemeal junk of the car lots—
A vapor trail goes into the workshop
Of the clouds, the spring comes on in the bushes,
Forsythia making its annual statement.

The bridge underneath is ever so slightly
Tearing a suture of itself in secret;
And what is most feared is about to happen:

The stage-set of a world taken for granted
Will drop from the sky, robots of ashes
In clouds grow solidly real, and murders

That always before occurred at a distance
Strangle the neck at home. How the small thing
Matters: the phones getting through, the cables
Never exhaling invisible, lethal
Fumes, the macadam keeping its bubbles
Of tar intact. . . . The bridge sways, opens,

And the cell is about to distort the message
Life had meant it to carry from the start,
Letting death's emperor through. The tiny
Deadly protein blossoms. The blossoms
Open to yellow, true yellow in the spring
Outside your Memorial Hospital window.

4

What errors you made you made in wanting
To be warm again or held or human
And not for the wolf of cash or the mean,
Sloe-eyed beauty of power or the game
Of the wily outwitting the unaware,
Or simulated pain used as a lure.
How stupid the endings of life can be!
Old age not seeing the sea at its foot,
Not hearing the music still to be heard.
Dead to all things but the shape of the self,
The violent tear out blood with their hands,
The insane hold up the cardboard pieces
Of a world they can no longer fit together,
And the cruel: the slack nurse, the greedy aide,
The doctor no longer aware of pain . . .

5

How all the terminals of the body
Ply their invisible servings and turnings,
The loading of freight, the slipping of cargo

Into the cell, the interior vision
Blind as the blood erasing the causeway
Connecting vital island to island.

What are ideas but architecture
Taking nature to heart and sustaining
Inviolable forms: the fleur-de-lis,

The subtle acanthus, the shell-like dominions
Of diamond accretions royal on coal,
The Gothic tower and the rabbit warren,

The fine interchange of matter and matter,
The natural and social shifting in the bonds
Of dialogues and elegies that rise from soil.

6

All the allowable days on circling
Boats turning inward toward the center
Of the circle of the water of the river
Have been disallowed by the squarely arriving
Tugboat from which a peg-legged captain
Smoking a panatela is lowered
Into a launch behind him his shadowy
Crew and now you see them advancing
Climbing the ropes toward the deck you're on
The smoke the river the trees going past you
Into the mist the birds growing weaker
Downriver somewhere there is connected
Song water falling rapids of birdcalls
Way off the cry of the throat of fever
The faintest releases of animal sound
The sky coming nearer, closer and closer,
The distances moving toward you and farther
Away the repeated echoes of names
Called across water   then it is over.

Rules of Sleep

In the sludge drawer of animals in arms,
Where the legs entwine to keep the body warm
Against the winter night, some cold seeps through—
It is the future: say, a square of stars
In the windowpane, suggesting the abstract
And large, or a sudden shift in position
That lets one body know the other's free to move
An inch away, and then a thousand miles,
And, after that, even intimacy
Is only another form of separation.

Einstein's Bathrobe

I wove myself of many delicious strands
Of violet islands and sugar-balls of thread
So faintly green a small white check between
Balanced the field's wide lawn, a plaid
Gathering in loose folds shaped around him
Those Princeton mornings, slowly stage-lit, when
The dawn took the horizon by surprise
And from the marsh long, crayoned birds
Rose up, ravens, maybe crows, or raw-voiced,
Spiteful grackles with their clothespin legs,
Black-winged gossips rising out of mud
And clattering into sleep. They woke my master
While, in the dark, I waited, knowing
Sooner or later he'd reach for me
And, half asleep, wriggle into my arms.
Then it seemed a moonish, oblique light
Would gradually illuminate the room,

The world turn on its axis at a different slant,
The furniture a shipwreck, the floor askew,
And, in old slippers, he'd bumble down the stairs.
Genius is human and wants its coffee hot—
I remember mornings when he'd sit
For hours at breakfast, dawdling over notes,
Juice and toast at hand, the world awake
To spring, the smell of honeysuckle
Filling the kitchen. A silent man,
Silence became him most. How gently
He softened the edges of a guessed-at impact
So no one would keel over from the blow—
A blow like soft snow falling on a lamb.
He'd fly down from the heights to tie his shoes
And cross the seas to get a glass of milk,
Bismarck with a harp, who'd doff his hat
(As if he ever wore one!) and softly land
On nimble feet so not to startle. He walked
In grandeur much too visible to be seen—
And how many versions crawled out of the Press!
A small pre-Raphaelite with too much hair;
A Frankenstein of test tubes; a "refugee"—
A shaman full of secrets who could touch
Physics with a wand and body forth
The universe's baby wrapped in stars.
From signs Phoenicians scratched into the sand
With sticks he drew the contraries of space:
Whirlwind Nothing and Volume in its rage
Of matter racing to undermine itself,
And when the planets sang, why, he sang back
The lieder black holes secretly adore.

At tea at Mercer Street every afternoon
His manners went beyond civility,
Kindness not having anything to learn;
I was completely charmed. And fooled.
What a false view of the universe *I* had!
The horsehair sofa, the sagging chairs,
A fire roaring behind the firescreen—

Imagine thinking Princeton was the world!
Yet I wore prescience like a second skin:
When Greenwich and Palomar saw eye to eye,
Time and space having found their rabbi,
I felt the dawn's black augurs gather force,
As if I knew in the New Jersey night
The downcast sky that was to clamp on Europe,
That Asia had its future in my pocket.

JAMES DICKEY
(b. 1923)

Born in Atlanta, Georgia, James Dickey was a high-school football star and a combat fighter pilot in World War II before graduating from Vanderbilt and starting a career in advertising. A Guggenheim Fellowship in 1961 and a year in Italy changed his course. Since then he has written and taught, notably at the University of South Carolina. He received the National Book Award in 1966 and served as consultant in poetry to the Library of Congress from 1966 until 1968. Dickey links the poetic imagination with "the emotional, half-animal, intuitive way in which we actually experience the world" and the exuberant way we possess and shape that world. With a burly bravura, his early poems are animated by dramatic or mythic encounters with primal forces, "the forfeited animal grace of human beings." He has called his fascination with violence and the grotesque a "country surrealism." In his later work Dickey has tried to walk the "razor's edge between sublimity and absurdity"; the sprawling, experimental format of his poems seeks to explore the energies of power and crisis.

The Heaven of Animals

Here they are. The soft eyes open.
If they have lived in a wood
It is a wood.
If they have lived on plains
It is grass rolling
Under their feet forever.

Having no souls, they have come,
Anyway, beyond their knowing.
Their instincts wholly bloom
And they rise.
The soft eyes open.

To match them, the landscape flowers,
Outdoing, desperately
Outdoing what is required:
The richest wood,
The deepest field.

For some of these,
It could not be the place
It is, without blood.
These hunt, as they have done,
But with claws and teeth grown perfect,

More deadly than they can believe.
They stalk more silently,
And crouch on the limbs of trees,
And their descent
Upon the bright backs of their prey

May take years
In a sovereign floating of joy.
And those that are hunted
Know this as their life,
Their reward: to walk

Under such trees in full knowledge
Of what is in glory above them,
And to feel no fear,
But acceptance, compliance.
Fulfilling themselves without pain

At the cycle's center,
They tremble, they walk
Under the tree,
They fall, they are torn,
They rise, they walk again.

The Hospital Window

I have just come down from my father.
Higher and higher he lies
Above me in a blue light
Shed by a tinted window.
I drop through six white floors
And then step out onto pavement.

Still feeling my father ascend,
I start to cross the firm street,
My shoulder blades shining with all
The glass the huge building can raise.
Now I must turn round and face it,
And know his one pane from the others.

Each window possesses the sun
As though it burned there on a wick.
I wave, like a man catching fire.
All the deep-dyed windowpanes flash,
And, behind them, all the white rooms
They turn to the color of Heaven.

Ceremoniously, gravely, and weakly,
Dozens of pale hands are waving
Back, from inside their flames.
Yet one pure pane among these
Is the bright, erased blankness of nothing.
I know that my father is there,

In the shape of his death still living.
The traffic increases around me
Like a madness called down on my head.
The horns blast at me like shotguns,
And drivers lean out, driven crazy—
But now my propped-up father

Lifts his arm out of stillness at last.
The light from the window strikes me
And I turn as blue as a soul,

As the moment when I was born.
I am not afraid for my father—
Look! He is grinning; he is not

Afraid for my life, either,
As the wild engines stand at my knees
Shredding their gears and roaring,
And I hold each car in its place
For miles, inciting its horn
To blow down the walls of the world

That the dying may float without fear
In the bold blue gaze of my father.
Slowly I move to the sidewalk
With my pin-tingling hand half dead
At the end of my bloodless arm.
I carry it off in amazement,

High, still higher, still waving,
My recognized face fully mortal,
Yet not; not at all, in the pale,
Drained, otherworldly, stricken,
Created hue of stained glass.
I have just come down from my father.

The Sheep Child

Farm boys wild to couple
With anything   with soft-wooded trees
With mounds of earth   mounds
Of pinestraw   will keep themselves off
Animals by legends of their own:
In the hay-tunnel dark
And dung of barns, they will
Say   I have heard tell

That in a museum in Atlanta
Way back in a corner somewhere
There's this thing that's only half
Sheep   like a woolly baby
Pickled in alcohol   because
Those things can't live   his eyes
Are open   but you can't stand to look
I heard from somebody who . . .

But this is now almost all
Gone. The boys have taken
Their own true wives in the city,
The sheep are safe in the west hill
Pasture   but we who were born there
Still are not sure. Are we,
Because we remember, remembered
In the terrible dust of museums?

Merely with his eyes, the sheep-child may

Be saying   saying

> I am here, in my father's house.
> I who am half of your world, came deeply
> To my mother in the long grass
> Of the west pasture, where she stood like moonlight
> Listening for foxes. It was something like love
> From another world that seized her
> From behind, and she gave, not lifting her head
> Out of dew, without ever looking, her best
> Self to that great need. Turned loose, she dipped her face
> Farther into the chill of the earth, and in a sound
> Of sobbing   of something stumbling
> Away, began, as she must do,
> To carry me. I woke, dying,
>
> In the summer sun of the hillside, with my eyes
> Far more than human. I saw for a blazing moment
> The great grassy world from both sides,
> Man and beast in the round of their need,
> And the hill wind stirred in my wool,

My hoof and my hand clasped each other,
I ate my one meal
Of milk, and died
Staring. From dark grass I came straight

To my father's house, whose dust
Whirls up in the halls for no reason
When no one comes   piling deep in a hellish mild
*   corner,*
And, through my immortal waters,
I meet the sun's grains eye
To eye, and they fail at my closet of glass.
Dead, I am most surely living
In the minds of farm boys: I am he who drives
Them like wolves from the hound bitch and calf
And from the chaste ewe in the wind.
They go into woods   into bean fields   they go
Deep into their known right hands. Dreaming of me,
They groan   they wait   they suffer
Themselves, they marry, they raise their kind.

The Strength of Fields

. . . a separation from the world,
a penetration to some source of power
and a life-enhancing return . . .
        Van Gennep: *Rites de Passage*

Moth-force a small town always has,

Given the night.

                What field-forms can be,
Outlying the small civic light-decisions over
      A man walking near home?
                Men are not where he is

Exactly now, but they are around him   around him like
the strength

Of fields.   The solar system floats on
Above him in town-moths.
Tell me, train-sound,
With all your long-lost grief,
what I can give.
Dear Lord of all the fields
what am I going to *do?*
Street-lights, blue-force and frail
As the homes of men, tell me how to do it   how
To withdraw   how to penetrate and find the source
Of the power you always had
light as a moth, and rising
With the level and moonlit expansion
Of the fields around, and the sleep of hoping men.

You?   I?   What difference is there?   We can all be
saved

By a secret blooming. Now as I walk
The night   and you walk with me   we know simplicity
Is close to the source that sleeping men
Search for in their home-deep beds.

We know that the sun is away   we know that the sun
can be conquered
By moths, in blue home-town air.
The stars splinter, pointed and wild. The dead lie
under
The pastures.   They look on and help.   Tell me, freight-train,
When there is no one else
To hear.   Tell me in a voice the sea
Would have, if it had not a better one: as it lifts,
Hundreds of miles away, its fumbling, deep-structured
roar
Like the profound, unstoppable craving
Of nations for their wish.
Hunger, time and the moon:

The moon lying on the brain

                   as on the excited sea   as on
    The strength of fields.   Lord, let me shake
  With purpose.   Wild hope can always spring
  From tended strength.   Everything is in that.
    That and nothing but kindness.   More kindness, dear
                                         Lord
Of the renewing green.   That is where it all has to start:
  With the simplest things.   More kindness will do nothing
                                              less
       Than save every sleeping one
        And night-walking one

Of us.
      My life belongs to the world. I will do what I can.

ANTHONY HECHT
(b. 1923)

Anthony Hecht was born in New York City and studied at Bard, Kenyon, and Columbia. He served overseas in the army during World War II and later began a teaching career, first at Bard and Smith, then at the University of Rochester, and since 1985 at Georgetown. He was awarded the Pulitzer Prize in 1968 and the Bollingen Prize in 1983. From 1982 until 1984 he served as consultant in poetry to the Library of Congress. From the start Hecht has persisted in a virtuosic formality; his poems are contained and dignified, but the natural nobility in their purposes and sympathies can break into broad humor or streetwise slang. Beneath their elegant surfaces his poems often manifest an unnerving intensity, which Hecht uses to explore the violence and baffled suffering in human history and the helpless isolation of the private life.

A Hill

In Italy, where this sort of thing can occur,
I had a vision once—though you understand
It was nothing at all like Dante's, or the visions of saints,
And perhaps not a vision at all. I was with some friends,
Picking my way through a warm sunlit piazza
In the early morning. A clear fretwork of shadows
From huge umbrellas littered the pavement and made
A sort of lucent shallows in which was moored
A small navy of carts. Books, coins, old maps,
Cheap landscapes and ugly religious prints
Were all on sale. The colors and noise
Like the flying hands were gestures of exultation,
So that even the bargaining
Rose to the ear like a voluble godliness.
And then, when it happened, the noises suddenly stopped,

And it got darker; pushcarts and people dissolved
And even the great Farnese Palace itself
Was gone, for all its marble; in its place
Was a hill, mole-colored and bare. It was very cold,
Close to freezing, with a promise of snow.
The trees were like old ironwork gathered for scrap
Outside a factory wall. There was no wind,
And the only sound for a while was the little click
Of ice as it broke in the mud under my feet.
I saw a piece of ribbon snagged on a hedge,
But no other sign of life. And then I heard
What seemed the crack of a rifle. A hunter, I guessed;
At least I was not alone. But just after that
Came the soft and papery crash
Of a great branch somewhere unseen falling to earth.

And that was all, except for the cold and silence
That promised to last forever, like the hill.

Then prices came through, and fingers, and I was restored
To the sunlight and my friends. But for more than a week
I was scared by the plain bitterness of what I had seen.
All this happened about ten years ago,
And it hasn't troubled me since, but at last, today,
I remembered that hill; it lies just to the left
Of the road north of Poughkeepsie; and as a boy
I stood before it for hours in wintertime.

Third Avenue in Sunlight

Third Avenue in sunlight. Nature's error.
Already the bars are filled and John is there.
Beneath a plentiful lady over the mirror
He tilts his glass in the mild mahogany air.

I think of him when he first got out of college,
Serious, thin, unlikely to succeed;
For several months he hung around the Village,
Boldly T-shirted, unfettered but unfreed.

Now he confides to a stranger, "I was first scout,
And kept my glimmers peeled till after dark.
Our outfit had as its sign a bloody knout,
We met behind the museum in Central Park.

Of course, we were kids." But still those savages,
War-painted, a flap of leather at the loins,
File silently against him. Hostages
Are never taken. One summer, in Des Moines,

They entered his hotel room, tomahawks
Flashing like barracuda. He tried to pray.
Three years of treatment. Occasionally he talks
About how he almost didn't get away.

Daily the prowling sunlight whets its knife
Along the sidewalk. We almost never meet.
In the Rembrandt dark he lifts his amber life.
My bar is somewhat further down the street.

"More Light! More Light!"

for Heinrich Blücher and Hannah Arendt

Composed in the Tower before his execution
These moving verses, and being brought at that time
Painfully to the stake, submitted, declaring thus:
"I implore my God to witness that I have made no crime."

Nor was he forsaken of courage, but the death was horrible,
The sack of gunpowder failing to ignite.
His legs were blistered sticks on which the black sap
Bubbled and burst as he howled for the Kindly Light.

And that was but one, and by no means one of the worst;
Permitted at least his pitiful dignity;
And such as were by made prayers in the name of Christ,
That shall judge all men, for his soul's tranquillity.

We move now to outside a German wood.
Three men are there commanded to dig a hole
In which the two Jews are ordered to lie down
And be buried alive by the third, who is a Pole.

Not light from the shrine at Weimar beyond the hill
Nor light from heaven appeared. But he did refuse.
A Lüger settled back deeply in its glove.
He was ordered to change places with the Jews.

Much casual death had drained away their souls.
The thick dirt mounted toward the quivering chin.
When only the head was exposed the order came
To dig him out again and to get back in.

No light, no light in the blue Polish eye.
When he finished a riding boot packed down the earth.
The Lüger hovered lightly in its glove.
He was shot in the belly and in three hours bled to death.

No prayers or incense rose up in those hours
Which grew to be years, and every day came mute
Ghosts from the ovens, sifting through crisp air,
And settled upon his eyes in a black soot.

Peripeteia

Of course, the familiar rustling of programs,
My hair mussed from behind by a grand gesture
Of mink. A little craning about to see
If anyone I know is in the audience,

And, as the house fills up,
A mild relief that no one there knows me.
A certain amount of getting up and down
From my aisle seat to let the others in.
Then my eyes wander briefly over the cast,
Management, stand-ins, make-up men, designers,
Perfume and liquor ads, and rise prayerlike
To the false heaven of rosetted lights,
The stucco lyres and emblems of high art
That promise, with crude Broadway honesty,
Something less than perfection:
Two bulbs are missing and Apollo's bored.

And then the cool, drawn-out anticipation,
Not of the play itself, but the false dusk
And equally false night when the houselights
Obey some planetary rheostat
And bring a stillness on. It is that stillness
I wait for.
                    Before it comes,
Whether we like it or not, we are a crowd,
Foul-breathed, gum-chewing, fat with arrogance,
Passion, opinion, and appetite for blood.
But in that instant, which the mind protracts,
From dim to dark before the curtain rises,
Each of us is miraculously alone
In calm, invulnerable isolation,
Neither a neighbor nor a fellow but,
As at the beginning and end, a single soul,
With all the sweet and sour of loneliness.
I, as a connoisseur of loneliness,
Savor it richly, and set it down
In an endless umber landscape, a stubble field
Under a lilac, electric, storm-flushed sky,
Where, in companionship with worthless stones,
Mica-flecked, or at best some rusty quartz,
I stood in childhood, waiting for things to mend.
A useful discipline, perhaps. One that might lead
To solitary, self-denying work

That issues in something harmless, like a poem,
Governed by laws that stand for other laws,
Both of which aim, through kindred disciplines,
At the soul's knowledge and habiliment.
In any case, in a self-granted freedom,
The mind, lone regent of itself, prolongs
The dark and silence; mirrors itself, delights
In consciousness of consciousness, alone,
Sufficient, nimble, touched with a small grace.

Then, as it must at last, the curtain rises,.
The play begins. Something by Shakespeare.
Framed in the arched proscenium, it seems
A dream, neither better nor worse
Than whatever I shall dream after I rise
With hat and coat, go home to bed, and dream.
If anything, more limited, more strict—
No one will fly or turn into a moose.
But acceptable, like a dream, because remote,
And there is, after all, a pretty girl.
Perhaps tonight she'll figure in the cast
I summon to my slumber and control
In vast arenas, limitless space, and time
That yield and sway in soft Einsteinian tides.
Who is she? Sylvia? Amelia Earhart?
Some creature that appears and disappears
From life, from reverie, a fugitive of dreams?
There on the stage, with awkward grace, the actors,
Beautifully costumed in Renaissance brocade,
Perform their duties, even as I must mine,
Though not, as I am, always free to smile.

Something is happening. Some consternation.
Are the knives out? Is someone's life in danger?
And can the magic cloak and book protect?
One has, of course, real confidence in Shakespeare.
And I relax in my plush seat, convinced
That prompt as dawn and genuine as a toothache
The dream will be accomplished, provisionally true

As anything else one cares to think about.
The players are aghast. Can it be the villain,
The outrageous drunks, plotting the coup d'état,
Are slyer than we thought? Or we more innocent?
Can it be that poems lie? As in a dream,
Leaving a stunned and gap-mouthed Ferdinand,
Father and faery pageant, she, even she,
Miraculous Miranda, steps from the stage,
Moves up the aisle to my seat, where she stops,
Smiles gently, seriously, and takes my hand
And leads me out of the theatre, into a night
As luminous as noon, more deeply real,
Simply because of her hand, than any dream
Shakespeare or I or anyone ever dreamed.

The Feast of Stephen

I

The coltish horseplay of the locker room,
Moist with the steam of the tiled shower stalls,
With shameless blends of civet, musk and sweat,
Loud with the cap-gun snapping of wet towels
Under the steel-ribbed cages of bare bulbs,
In some such setting of thick basement pipes
And janitorial realities
Boys for the first time frankly eye each other,
Inspect each others' bodies at close range,
And what they see is not so much another
As a strange, possible version of themselves,
And all the sparring dance, adrenal life,
Tense, jubilant nimbleness, is but a vague,
Busy, unfocused ballet of self-love.

I I

If the heart has its reasons, perhaps the body
Has its own lumbering sort of carnal spirit,
Felt in the tingling bruises of collision,
And known to captains as *esprit de corps.*
What is this brisk fraternity of timing,
Pivot and lobbing arc, or indirection,
Mens sana in men's sauna, in the flush
Of health and toilets, private and corporal glee,
These fleet caroms, *pliés* and genuflections
Before the salmon-leap, the leaping fountain
All sheathed in glistening light, flexed and alert?
From the vast echo-chamber of the gym,
Among the scumbled shouts and shrill of whistles,
The bounced basketball sound of a leather whip.

I I I

Think of those barren places where men gather
To act in the terrible name of rectitude,
Of acned shame, punk's pride, muscle or turf,
The bully's thin superiority.
Think of the *Sturm-Abteilungs Kommandant*
Who loves Beethoven and collects Degas,
Or the blond boys in jeans whose narrowed eyes
Are focussed by some hard and smothered lust,
Who lounge in a studied mimicry of ease,
Flick their live butts into the standing weeds,
And comb their hair in the mirror of cracked windows
Of an abandoned warehouse where they keep
In darkened readiness for their occasion
The rope, the chains, handcuffs and gasoline.

I V

Out in the rippled heat of a neighbor's field,
In the kilowatts of noon, they've got one cornered.
The bugs are jumping, and the burly youths
Strip to the waist for the hot work ahead.

They go to arm themselves at the dry-stone wall,
Having flung down their wet and salty garments
At the feet of a young man whose name is Saul.
He watches sharply these superbly tanned
Figures with a swimmer's chest and shoulders,
A miler's thighs, with their self-conscious grace,
And in between their sleek, converging bodies,
Brilliantly oiled and burnished by the sun,
He catches a brief glimpse of bloodied hair
And hears an unintelligible prayer.

JAMES SCHUYLER
(1923–1991)

"To me," James Schuyler said, "much of poetry is as concerned with
looking at things and trying to transcribe them as painting is." The
precise and vibrant colors of his poems—his still lifes and portrait
sketches—render both homely, random objects and passing fancies in
a style of seemingly casual charm. The whole pageant of the
quotidian—the gifts and griefs a life offers—passed before his regard.
But there is more here than meets the eye. Schuyler's is a poetry of
sensibility, relying on tone rather than shape or argument. By turns
whimsical or melancholy, he assembled collages of moods and objects
that heighten the solitude from which they were observed. His was a
transparent, *plein-air* style, open, digressive, genial, flush with "the
unexpectedness of nature." Schuyler was born in Chicago and came to
New York City in the late 1940s. He wrote novels, plays, and art
criticism; from 1955 until 1961 he was on the staff of the Museum of
Modern Art. He received the Pulitzer Prize in 1981.

The Crystal Lithium

The smell of snow, stinging in nostrils as the wind lifts it from
 a beach
Eye-shuttering, mixed with sand, or when snow lies under the
 street lamps and on all
And the air is emptied to an uplifting gassiness
That turns lungs to winter waterwings, buoying, and the bright
 white night
Freezes in sight a lapse of waves, balsamic, salty, unexpected:
Hours after swimming, sitting thinking biting at a hangnail
And the taste of the—to your eyes—invisible crystals irradiates
 the world
"The sea is salt"
"And so am I"

"Don't bite your nails"
                        and the metal flavor of a nail—are these
   brads?—
Taken with a slight spitting motion from between teeth and
   whanged into place
(Boards and sawdust) and the nail set is ridged with cold
Permanently as marble, always degrees cooler than the rooms
   of air it lies in
Felt as you lay your cheek upon the counter on which sits a
   blue-banded cup
A counter of condensed wintry exhalations glittering
   infinitesimally
A promise, late on a broiling day in late September, of the cold
   kiss
Of marble sheets to one who goes barefoot quickly in the
   snow and early
Only so far as the ashcan—bang, dump—and back and slams
   the door:
Too cold to get up though at the edges of the blinds the sky
Shows blue as flames that break on a red sea in which black
   coals float:
Pebbles in a pocket embed the seam with grains of sand
Which, as they will, have found their way into a pattern
   between foot and bedfoot
"A place for everything and everything in its place" how
   wasteful, how wrong
It seems when snow in fat, hand-stuffed flakes falls slow and
   steady in the sea
"Now you see it, now you don't" the waves growl as they
   grind ashore and roll out
At your feet (in boots) a Christmas tree naked of needles
Still wound with swags of tarnishing tinsel, faintly alarming as
   the thought
Of damp electricity or sluggish lightning and for your
   health-desiring pains
The wind awards: Chapped Lips: on which to rub Time's latest
   acquisition
Tinned, dowel-shaped and inappropriately flavored sheep wool
   fat

A greasy sense-eclipsing fog "I can't see
Without my glasses" "You certainly can't see with them all
    steamed up
Like that. Pull over, park and wipe them off." The thunder of
    a summer's day
Rolls down the shimmering blacktop and mowed grass juice
    thickens the air
Like "Stir until it coats the spoon, remove from heat, let cool
    and chill"
Like this, graying up for more snow, maybe, in which a small
    flock
Of—sparrows?—small, anyway, dust kitty-colored birds fly up
On a dotted diagonal and there, ah, is the answer:
Starlings, bullies of birdland, lousing up
The pecking order, respecters of no rights (what bird is)
    unloved (oh?)
Not so likeable as some: that's temperate enough and the
    temperature
Drops to rise to snowability of a softness even in its scent of
    roses
Made of untinted butter frosting: Happy Name Day, Blue Jay,
    staggering
On slow-up wings into the shrunk into itself from cold
    forsythia snarl
And above these thoughts there waves another tangle but one
    parched with heat
And not with cold although the heat is on because of cold
    settled all
About as though, swimming under water, in clearly fishy
    water, you
Inhaled and found one could and live and also found you
    altogether
Did not like it, January, laid out on a bed of ice, disgorging
February, shaped like a flounder, and March with her steel
    bead pocketbook,
And April, goofy and under-dressed and with a loud laugh,
    and May
Who will of course be voted Miss Best Liked (she expects it),
And June, with a toothpaste smile, fresh from her flea bath,
    and gross July,

Flexing itself, and steamy August, with thighs and eyes to
   match, and September
Diving into blue October, dour November, and deadly dull
   December which now
And then with a surprised blank look produces from its hand
   the ace of trumps
Or sets within the ice white hairline of a new moon the
   gibbous rest:
Global, blue, Columbian, a blue dull definite and thin as the
   first day
Of February when, in the steamed and freezing capital cash
   built
Without a plan to be its own best monument its skyline set in
   stacks
Like poker chips (signed, "Autodidact"), at the crux of a view
   there crosses
A flatcar-trailer piled with five of the cheaper sort of yachts,
   tarpaulined,
Plus one youth in purple pants, a maid in her uniform and an
   "It's not real
Anything" Cossack hat and coat, a bus one-quarter full of
   strangers and
The other familiar fixings of lengthening short days: "He's
   outgrown them
Before you can turn around" and see behind you the landscape
   of the past
Where beached boats bask and terraced cliffs are hung with
   oranges
Among dark star-gleaming leaves, and, descending the dizzying
   rough stairs
Littered with goat-turd beads—such packaging—you—he—
   she—
One—someone—stops to break off a bit of myrtle and recite
   all the lines
Of Goethe that come back, and those in French, *"Connais-
   tu . . . ?"* the air
Fills with chalk dust from banged erasers, behind the February
   dunes
Ice boats speed and among the reeds there winds a little frozen
   stream

Where kids in kapok ice-skate and play at Secret City as the
    sun
Sets before dinner, the snow on fields turns pink and under the
    hatched ice
The water slides darkly and over it a never before seen
    liquefaction of the sun
In a chemical yellow greener than sulphur a flash of petroleum
    by-product
Unbelievable, unwanted and as lovely as though someone you
    knew all your life
Said the one inconceivable thing and then went on washing
    dishes: the sky
Flows with impersonal passion and loosening jet trails (eyes
    tearing from the cold)
And on the beach, between foam frozen in a thick scalloped
    edging so like
Weird cheek-mottling pillowcase embroidery, on the
    water-darkened sand the waves
Keep free of frost, a gull strangles on a length of nylon fishline
    and the dog
Trots proudly off, tail held high, to bury a future dinner
    among cut grass on a dune:
The ice boats furl their sails and all pile into cars and go off to
    the super market
Its inviting foods and cleansers sold under tunes with sealed-in
    memory-flavor
"Hot House Rhubarb" "White Rock Girl" "Citrus Futures"
    "Cheap Bitter Beans" and
In its parking lot vast as the kiss to which is made the most
    complete surrender
In a setting of leaves, backs of stores, a house on a rise
    admired for being
Somewhat older than some others (prettier, too?) a man in a
    white apron embraces a car
Briefly in the cold with his eyes as one might hug oneself for
    warmth for love
—What a paint job, smooth as an eggplant; what a meaty
    chest, smooth as an eggplant
—Is it too much to ask your car to understand you? the
    converse isn't and the sky

Maps out new roads so that, driving at right angles to the
  wind, clouds in ranks
Contrive in diminishing perspective a part of a picture postcard
  of a painting
Over oak scrub where a filling station has: gas, a locked toilet
  (to keep dirt in)
A busted soda pop machine, no maps and "I couldn't tell you
  thet" so
The sky empties itself to a color, there, where yesterday's
  puddle
Offers its hospitality to people-trash and nature-trash in tans
  and silvers
And black grit like that in corners of a room in this or that
  cheap dump
Where the ceiling light burns night and day and we stare at or
  into each
Other's eyes in hope the other reads there what he reads:
  snow, wind
Lifted; black water, slashed with white; and that which is,
  which is beyond
Happiness or love or mixed with them or more than they or
  less, unchanging change,
"Look," the ocean said (it was tumbled, like our sheets), "look
  in my eyes"

Shimmer

The pear tree that last year
was heavy-laden this year
bears little fruit. Was
it that wet spring we had?
All the pear tree leaves
go shimmer, all at once. The
August sun blasts down
into the coolness from the

ocean. *The New York Times*
is on strike. My daily
fare! I'll starve! Not
quite. On my sill, balls
of twine wrapped up in
cellophane glitter. The
brown, the white and one
I think you'd call écru.
The sunlight falls partly
in a cup: it has a blue
transfer of two boys, a
dog and a duck and says,
"Come Away Pompey." I
like that cup, half
full of sunlight. Today
you could take up the
tattered shadows off
the grass. Roll them
and stow them. And collect
the shimmerings in a
cup, like the coffee
here at my right hand.

Korean Mums

beside me in this garden
are huge and daisy-like
(why not? are not
oxeye daisies a chrysanthemum?),
shrubby and thick-stalked,
the leaves pointing up
the stems from which
the flowers burst in
sunbursts. I love

this garden in all its moods,
even under its winter coat
of salt hay, or now,
in October, more than
half gone over: here
a rose, there a clump
of aconite. This morning
one of the dogs killed
a barn owl. Bob saw
it happen, tried to
intervene. The airedale
snapped its neck and left
it lying. Now the bird
lies buried by an apple
tree. Last evening
from the table we saw
the owl, huge in the dusk,
circling the field
on owl-silent wings.
The first one ever seen
here: now it's gone,
a dream you just remember.

The dogs are barking. In
the studio music plays
and Bob and Darragh paint.
I sit scribbling in a little
notebook at a garden table,
too hot in a heavy shirt
in the mid-October sun
into which the Korean mums
all face. There is a
dull book with me,
an apple core, cigarettes,
an ashtray. Behind me
the rue I gave Bob
flourishes. Light on leaves,
so much to see, and
all I really see is that

owl, its bulk troubling
the twilight. I'll
soon forget it: what
is there I have not forgot?
Or one day will forget:
this garden, the breeze
in stillness, even
the words, Korean mums.

DENISE LEVERTOV
(b. 1923)

"I believe in writing about what lies under the hand, in a sense,"
Denise Levertov maintains. "Not necessarily in the visual world—the
external world—it can be an inner experience—but it must be
something true." Her attention to inner experience may derive from
her heritage: she is descended on her father's side from a Hasidic
Russian rabbi and on her mother's side from a Welsh mystic. Levertov
was born in England and educated at home. She emigrated to the
United States in 1948 and came to ally herself with the aesthetics of
William Carlos Williams, Robert Duncan, and Robert Creeley. Political
causes have passionately engaged her, although in most of her work
she seeks what she has called "poems of an inner harmony in utter
contrast to the chaos in which they exist." City life, sexual turmoil,
the domestic rounds, the vivid and threatened natural world, the
mythic underpinnings of the ordinary—these are the recurrent subjects
of Levertov's spare, direct, surprising poems.

Clouds

The clouds as I see them, rising
urgently, roseate in the
mounting of somber power

surging in evening haste over
roofs and hermetic
grim walls—

Last night
As if death had lit a pale light
in your flesh, your flesh
was cold to my touch, or not cold
but cool, cooling, as if the last traces
of warmth were still fading in you.

My thigh burned in cold fear where
yours touched it.

But I forced to mind my vision of a sky
close and enclosed, unlike the space in which
     these clouds move—
a sky of gray mist it appeared—
and how looking intently at it we saw
its gray was not gray but a milky white
in which radiant traces of opal greens,
fiery blues, gleamed, faded, gleamed again,
and how only then, seeing the color in the gray,
a field sprang into sight, extending
between where we stood and the horizon,

a field of freshest deep spiring grass
starred with dandelions,
green and gold
gold and green alternating in closewoven
chords, madrigal field.

Is death's chill that visited our bed
other than what it seemed, is it
a gray to be watched keenly?

Wiping my glasses and leaning westward,
clearing my mind of the day's mist and leaning
into myself to see
the colors of truth

I watch the clouds as I see them
in pomp advancing, pursuing
the fallen sun.

The Ache of Marriage

The ache of marriage:

thigh and tongue, beloved,
are heavy with it,
it throbs in the teeth

We look for communion
and are turned away, beloved,
each and each

It is leviathan and we
in its belly
looking for joy, some joy
not to be known outside it

two by two in the ark of
the ache of it.

Intrusion

After I had cut off my hands
and grown new ones

something my former hands had longed for
came and asked to be rocked.

After my plucked out eyes
had withered, and new ones grown

something my former eyes had wept for
came asking to be pitied.

August, 1969

Seeing for a Moment

I thought I was growing wings—
it was a cocoon.

I thought, now is the time to step
into the fire—
it was deep water.

Eschatology is a word I learned
as a child: the study of Last Things;

facing my mirror—no longer young,
    the news—always of death,
        the dogs—rising from sleep and clamoring
           and howling, howling,

nevertheless
I see for a moment
that's not it: it is
the First Things.

Word after word
floats through the glass.
Towards me.

Prisoners

Though the road turn at last
to death's ordinary door,
and we knock there, ready
to enter and it opens
easily for us,
        yet
all the long journey

we shall have gone in chains,
fed on knowledge-apples
acrid and riddled with grubs.

We taste other food that life,
like a charitable farm-girl,
holds out to us as we pass—
but our mouths are puckered,
a taint of ash on the tongue.

It's not joy that we've lost—
wildfire, it flares
in dark or shine as it will.
What's gone
is common happiness,
plain bread we could eat
with the old apple of knowledge.

That old one—it griped us sometimes,
but it was firm, tart,
sometimes delectable . . .

The ashen apple of these days
grew from poisoned soil. We are prisoners
and must eat
our ration. All the long road
in chains, even if, after all,
we come to
death's ordinary door, with time
smiling its ordinary
long-ago smile.

RICHARD HUGO
(1923–1982)

Richard Hugo was born and educated in Seattle. He studied there
with Theodore Roethke, the strongest influence on his early work.
Having served as a bombardier in World War II, he worked for a
dozen years at the Boeing Co. before joining the faculty of the
University of Montana, where he taught until his death. The pulsing
lyric chant in his first book gave way to what he called his "harsh,
often/booming voice," alternately stern or tender about his patched
life and bruised feelings. The spirit of place—whether the American
West or the Scottish isles—animates his best work, which was often
triggered, he said, by "something, a small town or an abandoned
house, that I feel others would ignore." Montana's now deserted
mining towns, which Walt Whitman had envisioned as his fabled
"western settlement," were for Hugo deserted myths as well, and
counterparts to the self's diminishment.

Graves at Elkhorn

for Joe Ward

'Eighty-nine was bad. At least a hundred
children died, the ones with money planted
in this far spot from the town. The corn
etched in these stones was popular that year.
'Our dearest one is gone.' The poorer ones
used wood for markers. Their names
got weaker every winter. Now gray wood
offers a blank sacrifice to rot.

The yard and nearly every grave are fenced.
Something in this space must be defined—
where the lot you paid too much for ends
or where the body must not slide beyond.

The yard should have a limit like the town.
The last one buried here: 1938. The next
to last: 1911 from a long disease.

The fence around the yard is barbed, maintained
by men, around the graves, torn down
by pines. Some have pines for stones.
The yard is this far from the town because
when children die the mother should repeat
some form of labor, and a casual glance
would tell you there could be no silver here.

The Lady in Kicking Horse Reservoir

Not my hands but green across you now.
Green tons hold you down, and ten bass curve
teasing in your hair. Summer slime
will pile deep on your breast. Four months of ice
will keep you firm. I hope each spring
to find you tangled in those pads
pulled not quite loose by the spillway pour,
stars in dead reflection off your teeth.

Lie there lily still. The spillway's closed.
Two feet down most lakes are common gray.
This lake is dark from the black blue Mission range
climbing sky like music dying Indians once wailed.
On ocean beaches, mystery fish
are offered to the moon. Your jaws go blue.
Your hands start waving every wind.
Wave to the ocean where we crushed a mile of foam.

We still love there in thundering foam
and love. Whales fall in love with gulls
and tide reclaims the Dolly skeletons

gone with a blast of aching horns to China.
Landlocked in Montana here
the end is limited by light, the final note
will trail off at the farthest point we see,
already faded, lover, where you bloat.

All girls should be nicer. Arrows rain
above us in the Indian wind. My future
should be full of windy gems, my past
will stop this roaring in my dreams.
Sorry. Sorry. Sorry. But the arrows sing:
no way to float her up. The dead sink
from dead weight. The Mission range
turns this water black late afternoons.

One boy slapped the other. Hard.
The slapped boy talked until his dignity
dissolved, screamed a single 'stop'
and went down sobbing in the company pond.
I swam for him all night. My only suit
got wet and factory hands went home.
No one cared the coward disappeared.
Morning then: cold music I had never heard.

Loners like work best on second shift.
No one liked our product and the factory closed.
Off south, the bison multiply so fast
a slaughter's mandatory every spring
and every spring the creeks get fat
and Kicking Horse fills up. My hope is vague.
The far blur of your bones in May
may be nourished by the snow.

The spillway's open and you spill out
into weather, lover down the bright canal
and mother, irrigating crops
dead Indians forgot to plant.
I'm sailing west with arrows to dissolving foam
where waves strand naked Dollys.
Their eyes are white as oriental mountains
and their tongues are teasing oil from whales.

Degrees of Gray in Philipsburg

You might come here Sunday on a whim.
Say your life broke down. The last good kiss
you had was years ago. You walk these streets
laid out by the insane, past hotels
that didn't last, bars that did, the tortured try
of local drivers to accelerate their lives.
Only churches are kept up. The jail
turned 70 this year. The only prisoner
is always in, not knowing what he's done.

The principal supporting business now
is rage. Hatred of the various grays
the mountain sends, hatred of the mill,
The Silver Bill repeal, the best liked girls
who leave each year for Butte. One good
restaurant and bars can't wipe the boredom out.
The 1907 boom, eight going silver mines,
a dance floor built on springs—
all memory resolves itself in gaze,
in panoramic green you know the cattle eat
or two stacks high above the town,
two dead kilns, the huge mill in collapse
for fifty years that won't fall finally down.

Isn't this your life? That ancient kiss
still burning out your eyes? Isn't this defeat
so accurate, the church bell simply seems
a pure announcement: ring and no one comes?
Don't empty houses ring? Are magnesium
and scorn sufficient to support a town,
not just Philipsburg, but towns
of towering blondes, good jazz and booze
the world will never let you have
until the town you came from dies inside?

Say no to yourself. The old man, twenty
when the jail was built, still laughs

although his lips collapse. Someday soon,
he says, I'll go to sleep and not wake up.
You tell him no. You're talking to yourself.
The car that brought you here still runs.
The money you buy lunch with,
no matter where it's mined, is silver
and the girl who serves your food
is slender and her red hair lights the wall.

The River Now

Hardly a ghost left to talk with. The slavs moved on
or changed their names to something green. Greeks gave up
old dishes and slid into repose. Runs of salmon thin
and thin until a ripple in October might mean carp.
Huge mills bang and smoke. Day hangs thick with commerce
and my favorite home, always overgrown with roses,
collapsed like moral advice. Tugs still pound against
the outtide pour but real, running on some definite fuel.
I can't dream anything, not some lovely woman
murdered in a shack, not saw mills going broke,
not even wild wine and a landslide though I knew both well.
The blood still begs direction home. This river points
the way north to the blood, the blue stars certain
in their swing, their fix. I pass the backwash where
the cattails still lean north, familiar grebes pop up,
the windchill is the same. And it comes back with the odor
of the river, some way I know the lonely sources
of despair break down from too much love. No matter
how this water fragments in the reeds, it rejoins
the river and the bright bay north receives it all,
new salmon on their way to open ocean,
the easy tub returned.

EDGAR BOWERS
(b. 1924)

Edgar Bowers was born in Rome, Georgia. After army service he graduated from the University of North Carolina and took his doctorate at Stanford. Since 1958 he has taught at the University of California at Santa Barbara. In 1989 he won the Bollingen Prize. His mentor Yvor Winters once described Bowers as having "the temperament of the mystical Calvinist," and themes of the fallen man and "divine indifference" thread through all his work. Addressing his poems, Bowers once compared them to snow: "You are the flakes, and all the rest was I, / The sky, the landscape, and the freezing spell." His grave poems, from which everything inessential has been pared away, are stoic in the face of loss, self-possessed even when the poet has been undone.

An Afternoon at the Beach

I'll go among the dead to see my friend.
The place I leave is beautiful: the sea
Repeats the winds' far swell in its long sound,
And, there beside it, houses solemnly
Shine with the modest courage of the land,
While swimmers try the verge of what they see.

I cannot go, although I should pretend
Some final self whose phantom eye could see
Him who because he is not cannot change.
And yet the thought of going makes the sea,
The land, the swimmers, and myself seem strange,
Almost as strange as they will someday be.

Amor Vincit Omnia

Love is no more.
It died as the mind dies: the pure desire
Relinquishing the blissful form it wore,
The ample joy and clarity expire.

Regret is vain.
Then do not grieve for what you would efface,
The sudden failure of the past, the pain
Of its unwilling change, and the disgrace.

Leave innocence,
And modify your nature by the grief
Which poses to the will indifference
That no desire is permanent in sense.

Take leave of me.
What recompense, or pity, or deceit
Can cure, or what assumed serenity
Conceal the mortal loss which we repeat?

The mind will change, and change shall be relief.

FROM Autumn Shade

3

Awakened by some fear, I watch the sky.
Compelled as though by purposes they know,
The stars, in their blue distance, still affirm
The bond of heaven and earth, the ancient way.
This old assurance haunts small creatures, dazed
In icy mud, though cold may freeze them there
And leave them as they are all summer long.
I cannot sleep. Passion and consequence,

The brutal given, and all I have desired
Evade me, and the lucid majesty
That warmed the dull barbarian to life.
So I lie here, left with self-consciousness,
Enemy whom I love but whom his change
And his forgetfulness again compel,
Impassioned, toward my lost indifference,
Faithful, but to an absence. Who shares my bed?
Who lies beside me, certain of his waking,
Led sleeping, by his own dream, to the day?

6

Snow and then rain. The roads are wet. A car
Slips and strains in the mire, and I remember
Driving in France: weapons-carriers and jeeps;
Our clothes and bodies stiffened by mud; our minds
Diverted from fear. We labor. Overhead,
A plane, Berlin or Frankfurt, now New York.
The car pulls clear. My neighbor smiles. He is old.
Was this our wisdom, simply, in a chance,
In danger, to be mastered by a task,
Like groping round a chair, through a door, to bed?

8

I drive home with the books that I will read.
The streets are harsh with traffic. Where I once
Played as a boy amid old stands of pine,
Row after row of houses. Lined by the new
Debris of wealth and power, the broken road.
Then miles of red clay bank and frugal ground.
At last, in the minor hills, my father's place,
Where I can find my way as in a thought—
Gardens, the trees we planted, all we share.
A Cherokee trail runs north to summer hunting.
I see it, when I look up from the page.

9

In nameless warmth, sun light in every corner,
Bending my body over my glowing book,

I share the room. Is it with a voice or touch
Or look, as of an absence, learned by love,
Now, merely mine? Annunciation, specter
Of the worn out, lost, or broken, telling what future,
What vivid loss to come, you change the room
And him who reads here. Restless, he will stir,
Look round, and see the room renewed, and line,
Color, and shape as, in desire, they are,
Not shadows but substantial light, explicit,
Bright as glass, inexhaustible, and true.

CAROLYN KIZER
(b. 1925)

Carolyn Kizer was born in Spokane, Washington, graduated from
Sarah Lawrence, and studied further at Columbia and the University
of Washington. From 1966 until 1970 she was the first director of
literary programs at the National Endowment for the Arts, and since
then she has taught at colleges around the country. Her own teacher,
Theodore Roethke, once praised Kizer's willingness "to take chances
with unusual material." She is a versatile, full-throated, tough-minded
poet. Her early work dwelt on themes of love and nature, but her
later poems have engaged social and political issues. Long before it
became a literary fashion, Kizer's feminism was a passionate
argument. She ponders the domestic and emotional lives of women
but also explores the "whole wild, lost, betrayed and secret life" of
female creativity. Her fascination with mythologies has encouraged
her to construct new emblems of womanhood and to criticize old
attitudes in a tone that ranges from the learned through the sardonic
to the tender. She was awarded the Pulitzer Prize in 1985.

A Muse of Water

We who must act as handmaidens
To our own goddess, turn too fast,
Trip on our hems, to glimpse the muse
Gliding below her lake or sea,
Are left, long-staring after her,
Narcissists by necessity;

Or water-carriers of our young
Till waters burst, and white streams flow
Artesian, from the lifted breast:
Cup-bearers then, to tiny gods,
Imperious table-pounders, who
Are final arbiters of thirst.

Fasten the blouse, and mount the steps
From kitchen taps to Royal Barge,
Assume the trident, don the crown,
Command the Water Music now
That men bestow on Virgin Queens;
Or, goddessing above the waist,

Appear as swan on Thames or Charles
Where iridescent foam conceals
The paddle-stroke beneath the glide:
Immortal feathers preened in poems!
Not our true, intimate nature, stained
By labor, and the casual tide.

Masters of civilization, you
Who moved to river bank from cave,
Putting up tents, and deities,
Though every rivulet wander through
The final, unpolluted glades
To cinder-bank and culvert-lip,

And all the pretty chatterers
Still round the pebbles as they pass
Lightly over their watercourse,
And even the calm rivers flow,
We have, while springs and skies renew,
Dry wells, dead seas, and lingering drouth.

Water itself is not enough.
Harness her turbulence to work
For man: fill his reflecting pools.
Drained for his cofferdams, or stored
In reservoirs for his personal use:
Turn switches! Let the fountains play!

And yet these buccaneers still kneel
Trembling at the water's verge:
"Cool River-Goddess, sweet ravine,
Spirit of pool and shade, inspire!"
So he needs poultice for his flesh.
So he needs water for his fire.

We rose in mists and died in clouds
Or sank below the trammeled soil
To silent conduits underground,
Joining the blind-fish, and the mole.
A gleam of silver in the shale:
Lost murmur! Subterranean moan!

So flows in dark caves, dries away,
What would have brimmed from bank to bank,
Kissing the fields you turned to stone,
Under the boughs your axes broke.
And you blame streams for thinning out,
Plundered by man's insatiate want?

Rejoice when a faint music rises
Out of a brackish clump of weeds,
Out of the marsh at ocean-side,
Out of the oil-stained river's gleam,
By the long causeways and gray piers
Your civilizing lusts have made.

Discover the deserted beach
Where ghosts of curlews safely wade:
Here the warm shallows lave your feet
Like tawny hair of magdalens.
Here, if you care, and lie full-length,
Is water deep enough to drown.

Amusing Our Daughters

for Robert Creeley

We don't lack people here on the Northern coast,
But they are people one meets, not people one cares for.
So I bundle my daughters into the car
And with my brother poets, go to visit you, brother.

Here come your guests! A swarm of strangers and children;
But the strangers write verses, the children are daughters like
  yours.
We bed down on mattresses, cots, roll up on the floor:
Outside, burly old fruit trees in mist and rain;
In every room, bundles asleep like larvae.

We waken and count our daughters. Otherwise, nothing
  happens.
You feed them sweet rolls and melon, drive them all to the
  zoo;
Patiently, patiently, ever the father, you answer their
  questions.
Later we eat again, drink, listen to poems.
Nothing occurs, though we are aware you have three daughters
Who last year had four. But even death becomes part of our
  ease:
Poems, parenthood, sorrow, all we have learned
From these, of tenderness, holds us together
In the center of life, entertaining daughters
By firelight, with cake and songs.

You, my brother, are a good and violent drinker,
Good at reciting short-line or long-line poems.
In time we will lose all our daughters, you and I,
Be temperate, venerable, content to stay in one place,
Sending our messages over the mountains and waters.

FROM Pro Femina

I

From Sappho to myself, consider the fate of women.
How unwomanly to discuss it! Like a noose or an albatross
      necktie
The clinical sobriquet hangs us: cod-piece coveters.
Never mind these epithets; I myself have collected some
      honeys.
Juvenal set us apart in denouncing our vices
Which had grown, in part, from having been set apart:
Women abused their spouses, cuckolded them, even plotted
To poison them. Sensing, behind the violence of his manner—
"Think I'm crazy or drunk?"—his emotional stake in us,
As we forgive Strindberg and Nietzsche, we forgive all those
Who cannot forget us. We *are* hyenas. Yes, we admit it.

While men have politely debated free will, we have howled
      for it,
Howl still, pacing the centuries, tragedy heroines.
Some who sat quietly in the corner with their embroidery
Were Defarges, stabbing the wool with the names of their
      ancient
Oppressors, who ruled by the divine right of the male—
I'm impatient of interruptions! I'm aware there were millions
Of mutes for every Saint Joan or sainted Jane Austen,
Who, vague-eyed and acquiescent, worshiped God as a man.
I'm not concerned with those cabbageheads, not truly feminine
But neutered by labor. I mean real women, like *you* and
      like *me*.

Freed in fact, not in custom, lifted from furrow and scullery,
Not obliged, now, to be the pot for the annual chicken,
Have we begun to arrive in time? With our well-known
Respect for life because it hurts so much to come out with it;
Disdainful of "sovereignty," "national honor" and other
      abstractions;

We can say, like the ancient Chinese to successive waves of
    invaders,
"Relax, and let us absorb you. You can learn temperance
In a more temperate climate." Give us just a few decades

Of grace, to encourage the fine art of acquiescence
And we might save the race. Meanwhile, observe our creative
    chaos,
Flux, efflorescence—whatever you care to call it!

II

I take as my theme "The Independent Woman,"
Independent but maimed: observe the exigent neckties
Choking violet writers; the sad slacks of stipple-faced matrons;
Indigo intellectuals, crop-haired and callous-toed,
Cute spectacles, chewed cuticles, aced out by full-time beauties
In the race for a male. Retreating to drabness, bad manners
And sleeping with manuscripts. Forgive our transgressions
Of old gallantries as we hitch in chairs, light our own
    cigarettes,
Not expecting your care, having forfeited it by trying to get
    even.

But we need dependency, cosseting and well-treatment.
So do men sometimes. Why don't they admit it?
We will be cows for a while, because babies howl for us,
Be kittens or bitches, who want to eat grass now and then
For the sake of our health. But the role of pastoral heroine
Is not permanent, Jack. We want to get back to the meeting.

Knitting booties and brows, tartars or termagants, ancient
Fertility symbols, chained to our cycle, released
Only in part by devices of hygiene and personal daintiness,
Strapped into our girdles, held down, yet uplifted by man's
Ingenious constructions, holding coiffures in a breeze,
Hobbled and swathed in whimsey, tripping on feminine

Shoes with fool heels, losing our lipsticks, you, me,
In ephemeral stockings, clutching our handbags and packages.

Our masks, always in peril of smearing or cracking,
In need of continuous check in the mirror or silverware,
Keep us in thrall to ourselves, concerned with our surfaces.
Look at man's uniform drabness, his impersonal envelope!
Over chicken wrists or meek shoulders, a formal, hard-fibered
    assurance.
The drape of the male is designed to achieve self-forgetfulness.

So, Sister, forget yourself a few times and see where it gets
    you:
Up the creek, alone with your talent, sans everything else.
You can wait for the menopause, and catch up on your
    reading.
So primp, preen, prink, pluck and prize your flesh,
All posturings! All ravishment! All sensibility!
Meanwhile, have you used your mind today?
What pomegranate raised you from the dead,
Springing, full-grown, from your own head, Athena?

DONALD JUSTICE
(b. 1925)

Born in Miami and educated there (in part by the composer Carl
Ruggles), Donald Justice returned to his native state in 1982 as
professor of English at the University of Florida at Gainesville. For
many years, he had taught in the Iowa Writers Workshop. "I indulge
myself," says the speaker of one Justice poem, "in rich refusals." His
emblematic landscapes are filled with absences—with the faded, the
provisional, the emptied out, "a land of others and of silence"
shimmering with unsteady or vaguely menacing signs and wonders.
Beneath their reflective surfaces, his poems stir memories of an
innocence obscurely betrayed. Whether poetry can adequately reveal
or possibly redeem those memories is the question he has posed from
the start, for himself and his reader. The modesty of Justice's tone and
his fastidious craft hide from some the skill with which he can eerily
make the familiar strange. Justice's first book won the Lamont Prize in
1959; his *Selected Poems* won the Pulitzer Prize in 1980.

The Evening of the Mind

Now comes the evening of the mind.
Here are the fireflies twitching in the blood;
Here is the shadow moving down the page
Where you sit reading by the garden wall.
Now the dwarf peach trees, nailed to their trellises,
Shudder and droop. You know their voices now,
Faintly the martyred peaches crying out
Your name, the name nobody knows but you.
It is the aura and the coming on.
It is the thing descending, circling, here.
And now it puts a claw out and you take it.
Thankfully in your lap you take it, so.

You said you would not go away again,
You did not want to go away—and yet,

210   ·

It is as if you stood out on the dock
Watching a little boat drift out
Beyond the sawgrass shallows, the dead fish . . .
And you were in it, skimming past old snags,
Beyond, beyond, under a brazen sky
As soundless as a gong before it's struck—
Suspended how?—and now they strike it, now
The ether dream of five-years-old repeats, repeats,
And you must wake again to your own blood
And empty spaces in the throat.

Men at Forty

Men at forty
Learn to close softly
The doors to rooms they will not be
Coming back to.

At rest on a stair landing,
They feel it
Moving beneath them now like the deck of a ship,
Though the swell is gentle.

And deep in mirrors
They rediscover
The face of the boy as he practices tying
His father's tie there in secret

And the face of that father,
Still warm with the mystery of lather.
They are more fathers than sons themselves now.
Something is filling them, something

That is like the twilight sound
Of the crickets, immense,

Filling the woods at the foot of the slope
Behind their mortgaged houses.

The Tourist from Syracuse

One of those men who can be a car salesman
or a tourist from Syracuse or a hired assassin.
John D. MacDonald

You would not recognize me.
Mine is the face which blooms in
The dank mirrors of washrooms
As you grope for the light switch.

My eyes have the expression
Of the cold eyes of statues
Watching their pigeons return
From the feed you have scattered,

And I stand on my corner
With the same marble patience.
If I move at all, it is
At the same pace precisely

As the shade of the awning
Under which I stand waiting
And with whose blackness it seems
I am already blended.

I speak seldom, and always
In a murmur as quiet
As that of crowds which surround
The victims of accidents.

Shall I confess who I am?
My name is all names, or none.
I am the used-car salesman,
The tourist from Syracuse,

The hired assassin, waiting.
I will stand here forever
Like one who has missed his bus—
Familiar, anonymous—

On my usual corner,
The corner at which you turn
To approach that place where now
You must not hope to arrive.

Variations on a Text by Vallejo

Me moriré en París con aguacero . . .

I will die in Miami in the sun,
On a day when the sun is very bright,
A day like the days I remember, a day like other days,
A day that nobody knows or remembers yet,
And the sun will be bright then on the dark glasses of
    strangers
And in the eyes of a few friends from my childhood
And of the surviving cousins by the graveside,
While the diggers, standing apart, in the still shade of the
    palms,
Rest on their shovels, and smoke,
Speaking in Spanish softly, out of respect.

I think it will be on a Sunday like today,
Except that the sun will be out, the rain will have stopped,
And the wind that today made all the little shrubs kneel down;
And I think it will be a Sunday because today,
When I took out this paper and began to write,
Never before had anything looked so blank,
My life, these words, the paper, the gray Sunday;
And my dog, quivering under a table because of the storm,

Looked up at me, not understanding,
And my son read on without speaking, and my wife slept.

Donald Justice is dead. One Sunday the sun came out,
It shone on the bay, it shone on the white buildings,
The cars moved down the street slowly as always, so many,
Some with their headlights on in spite of the sun,
And after a while the diggers with their shovels
Walked back to the graveside through the sunlight,
And one of them put his blade into the earth
To lift a few clods of dirt, the black marl of Miami,
And scattered the dirt, and spat,
Turning away abruptly, out of respect.

The Assassination

It begins again, the nocturnal pulse.
It courses through the cables laid for it.
It mounts to the chandeliers and beats there, hotly.
We are too close. Too late, we would move back.
We are involved with the surge.

Now it bursts. Now it has been announced.
Now it is being soaked up by newspapers.
Now it is running through the streets.
The crowd has it. The woman selling carnations
And the man in the straw hat stand with it in their shoes.

Here is the red marquee it sheltered under,
Here is the ballroom, here
The sadly various orchestra led
By a single gesture. My arms open.
It enters. Look, we are dancing.

June 5, 1968

Mule Team and Poster

Two mules stand waiting in front of the brick wall of a
      warehouse,
         hitched to a shabby flatbed wagon.
Its spoked wheels resemble crude wooden flowers
         pulled recently from a deep and stubborn mud.

The rains have passed over for now
         and the sun is back,
Invisible, but everywhere present,
         and of a special brightness, like God.

The way the poster for the traveling show
         still clings to its section of the wall
It looks as though a huge door stood open
         or a terrible flap of brain had been peeled back,
             revealing

Someone's idea of heaven:
         seven dancing-girls, caught on the upkick,
All in fringed dresses and bobbed hair.
         One wears a Spanish comb and has an escort . . .

Meanwhile the mules crunch patiently the few cornshucks
         someone has thoughtfully scattered for them.
The poster is torn in places, slightly crumpled;
         a few bricks, here and there, show through.

And a long shadow—
         the last shade perhaps in all of Alabama—
Stretches beneath the wagon, crookedly,
         like a great scythe laid down there and forgotten.

                 on a photograph by Walker Evans (Alabama, 1936)

FRANK O'HARA
(1926–1966)

Frank O'Hara was born in Baltimore and raised in Massachusetts. After service in the navy he studied at Harvard and the University of Michigan, then moved to New York City as soon as he could. "I can't even enjoy a blade of grass," he once wrote, "unless I know there's a subway handy, or a record store or some other sign that people do not totally *regret* life." From 1952 until his untimely death, O'Hara was on the staff of the Museum of Modern Art. He was active in the art scene, continued as a playwright and critic, and was the epicenter of a circle of poets that came to be called the New York School. He struck off fresh-minted, ebullient poems that fed on the "rancid nourishment" of Manhattan, its hybrid of high and low cultures, and the rushing traffic of romance. "You just go on your nerve" was O'Hara's aesthetic motto for poems with an offhand, vertiginous immediacy that is sometimes campy, sometimes surreal.

To the Harbormaster

I wanted to be sure to reach you;
though my ship was on the way it got caught
in some moorings. I am always tying up
and then deciding to depart. In storms and
at sunset, with the metallic coils of the tide
around my fathomless arms, I am unable
to understand the forms of my vanity
or I am hard alee with my Polish rudder
in my hand and the sun sinking. To
you I offer my hull and the tattered cordage
of my will. The terrible channels where
the wind drives me against the brown lips
of the reeds are not all behind me. Yet
I trust the sanity of my vessel; and

if it sinks, it may well be in answer
to the reasoning of the eternal voices,
the waves which have kept me from reaching you.

A Step Away from Them

It's my lunch hour, so I go
for a walk among the hum-colored
cabs. First, down the sidewalk
where laborers feed their dirty
glistening torsos sandwiches
and Coca-Cola, with yellow helmets
on. They protect them from falling
bricks, I guess. Then onto the
avenue where skirts are flipping
above heels and blow up over
grates. The sun is hot, but the
cabs stir up the air. I look
at bargains in wristwatches. There
are cats playing in sawdust.
                            On
to Times Square, where the sign
blows smoke over my head, and higher
the waterfall pours lightly. A
Negro stands in a doorway with a
toothpick, languorously agitating.
A blonde chorus girl clicks: he
smiles and rubs his chin. Everything
suddenly honks: it is 12:40 of
a Thursday.
               Neon in daylight is a
great pleasure, as Edwin Denby would
write, as are light bulbs in daylight.
I stop for a cheeseburger at JULIET'S

CORNER. Giulietta Masina, wife of
Federico Fellini, *è bell' attrice.*
And chocolate malted. A lady in
foxes on such a day puts her poodle
in a cab.
         There are several Puerto
Ricans on the avenue today, which
makes it beautiful and warm. First
Bunny died, then John Latouche,
then Jackson Pollock. But is the
earth as full as life was full, of them?
And one has eaten and one walks,
past the magazines with nudes
and the posters for BULLFIGHT and
the Manhattan Storage Warehouse,
which they'll soon tear down. I
used to think they had the Armory
Show there.
         A glass of papaya juice
and back to work. My heart is in my
pocket, it is Poems by Pierre Reverdy.

Meditations in an Emergency

Am I to become profligate as if I were a blonde? Or religious as
if I were French?

    Each time my heart is broken it makes me feel more adventur-
ous (and how the same names keep recurring on that interminable
list!), but one of these days there'll be nothing left with which to
venture forth.

    Why should I share you? Why don't you get rid of someone
else for a change?

I am the least difficult of men. All I want is boundless love.

Even trees understand me! Good heavens, I lie under them, too, don't I? I'm just like a pile of leaves.

However, I have never clogged myself with the praises of pastoral life, nor with nostalgia for an innocent past of perverted acts in pastures. No. One need never leave the confines of New York to get all the greenery one wishes—I can't even enjoy a blade of grass unless I know there's a subway handy, or a record store or some other sign that people do not totally *regret* life. It is more important to affirm the least sincere; the clouds get enough attention as it is and even they continue to pass. Do they know what they're missing? Uh huh.

My eyes are vague blue, like the sky, and change all the time; they are indiscriminate but fleeting, entirely specific and disloyal, so that no one trusts me. I am always looking away. Or again at something after it has given me up. It makes me restless and that makes me unhappy, but I cannot keep them still. If only I had grey, green, black, brown, yellow eyes; I would stay at home and do something. It's not that I'm curious. On the contrary, I am bored but it's my duty to be attentive, I am needed by things as the sky must be above the earth. And lately, so great has *their* anxiety become, I can spare myself little sleep.

Now there is only one man I love to kiss when he is unshaven. Heterosexuality! you are inexorably approaching. (How discourage her?)

St. Serapion, I wrap myself in the robes of your whiteness which is like midnight in Dostoevsky. How am I to become a legend, my dear? I've tried love, but that hides you in the bosom of another and I am always springing forth from it like the lotus— the ecstasy of always bursting forth! (but one must not be distracted by it!) or like a hyacinth, "to keep the filth of life away," yes, there, even in the heart, where the filth is pumped in and slanders and pollutes and determines. I will my will, though I may become famous for a mysterious vacancy in that department, that greenhouse.

Destroy yourself, if you don't know!

It is easy to be beautiful; it is difficult to appear so. I admire you, beloved, for the trap you've set. It's like a final chapter no one reads because the plot is over.

"Fanny Brown is run away—scampered off with a Cornet of Horse; I do love that little Minx, & hope She may be happy, tho' She has vexed me by this Exploit a little too.—Poor silly Cecchina! or F:B: as we used to call her.—I wish She had a good Whipping and 10,000 pounds."—Mrs. Thrale.

I've got to get out of here. I choose a piece of shawl and my dirtiest suntans. I'll be back, I'll re-emerge, defeated, from the valley; you don't want me to go where you go, so I go where you don't want me to. It's only afternoon, there's a lot ahead. There won't be any mail downstairs. Turning, I spit in the lock and the knob turns.

Why I Am Not a Painter

I am not a painter, I am a poet.
Why? I think I would rather be
a painter, but I am not. Well,

for instance, Mike Goldberg
is starting a painting. I drop in.
"Sit down and have a drink" he
says. I drink; we drink. I look
up. "You have SARDINES in it."
"Yes, it needed something there."
"Oh." I go and the days go by
and I drop in again. The painting
is going on, and I go, and the days
go by. I drop in. The painting is
finished. "Where's SARDINES?"
All that's left is just
letters, "It was too much," Mike says.

But me? One day I am thinking of
a color: orange. I write a line
about orange. Pretty soon it is a
whole page of words, not lines.
Then another page. There should be
so much more, not of orange, of
words, of how terrible orange is
and life. Days go by. It is even in
prose, I am a real poet. My poem
is finished and I haven't mentioned
orange yet. It's twelve poems, I call
it ORANGES. And one day in a gallery
I see Mike's painting, called SARDINES.

The Day Lady Died

It is 12:20 in New York a Friday
three days after Bastille day, yes
it is 1959 and I go get a shoeshine
because I will get off the 4:19 in East Hampton
at 7:15 and then go straight to dinner
and I don't know the people who will feed me

I walk up the muggy street beginning to sun
and have a hamburger and a malted and buy
an ugly NEW WORLD WRITING to see what the poets
in Ghana are doing these days
                  I go on to the bank
and Miss Stillwagon (first name Linda I once heard)
doesn't even look up my balance for once in her life
and in the GOLDEN GRIFFIN I get a little Verlaine
for Patsy with drawings by Bonnard although I do
think of Hesiod, trans. Richmond Lattimore or
Brendan Behan's new play or *Le Balcon* or *Les Nègres*

of Genet, but I don't, I stick with Verlaine
after practically going to sleep with quandariness

and for Mike I just stroll into the PARK LANE
Liquor Store and ask for a bottle of Strega and
then I go back where I came from to 6th Avenue
and the tobacconist in the Ziegfeld Theatre and
casually ask for a carton of Gauloises and a carton
of Picayunes, and a NEW YORK POST with her face on it

and I am sweating a lot by now and thinking of
leaning on the john door in the 5 SPOT
while she whispered a song along the keyboard
to Mal Waldron and everyone and I stopped breathing

Having a Coke with You

is even more fun than going to San Sebastian, Irún, Hendaye,
    Biarritz, Bayonne
or being sick to my stomach on the Travesera de Gracia in
    Barcelona
partly because in your orange shirt you look like a better
    happier St. Sebastian
partly because of my love for you, partly because of your love
    for yoghurt
partly because of the fluorescent orange tulips around the
    birches
partly because of the secrecy our smiles take on before people
    and statuary
it is hard to believe when I'm with you that there can be
    anything as still
as solemn as unpleasantly definitive as statuary when right in
    front of it
in the warm New York 4 o'clock light we are drifting back and
    forth
between each other like a tree breathing through its spectacles

and the portrait show seems to have no faces in it at all, just
    paint
you suddenly wonder why in the world anyone ever did them
                                                                   I look
at you and I would rather look at you than all the portraits in
    the world
except possibly for the *Polish Rider* occasionally and anyway it's
    in the Frick
which thank heavens you haven't gone to yet so we can go
    together the first time
and the fact that you move so beautifully more or less takes
    care of Futurism
just as at home I never think of the *Nude Descending a Staircase* or
at a rehearsal a single drawing of Leonardo or Michelangelo
    that used to wow me
and what good does all the research of the Impressionists do
    them
when they never got the right person to stand near the tree
    when the sun sank
or for that matter Marino Marini when he didn't pick the rider
    as carefully
as the horse
                    it seems they were all cheated of some
marvellous experience
which is not going to go wasted on me which is why I'm
    telling you about it

Ave Maria

    Mothers of America
                       let your kids go to the movies!
      get them out of the house so they won't know what you're up to

it's true that fresh air is good for the body
                              but what about the soul
that grows in darkness, embossed by silvery images
and when you grow old as grow old you must
                                    they won't hate you
they won't criticize you they won't know
                              they'll be in some glamorous
                              country
they first saw on a Saturday afternoon or playing hookey
they may even be grateful to you
                        for their first sexual experience
which only cost you a quarter
                              and didn't upset the peaceful home
they will know where candy bars come from
                              and gratuitous bags of popcorn
as gratuitous as leaving the movie before it's over
with a pleasant stranger whose apartment is in the Heaven on Earth Bldg
near the Williamsburg Bridge
                        oh mothers you will have made the little tykes
so happy because if nobody does pick them up in the movies
they won't know the difference
                        and if somebody does it'll be sheer gravy
and they'll have been truly entertained either way
instead of hanging around the yard
                                    or up in their room
                                          hating you
prematurely since you won't have done anything horribly mean yet
except keeping them from the darker joys
                                    it's unforgivable the latter
so don't blame me if you won't take this advice
                              and the family breaks up
and your children grow old and blind in front of a TV set
                                          seeing
movies you wouldn't let them see when they were young

DAVID WAGONER
(b. 1926)

David Wagoner was born in Ohio and raised in Indiana. He graduated
from Pennsylvania State University and Indiana University. Drawn by
his teacher and friend Theodore Roethke, Wagoner went to teach at
the University of Washington in 1954 and has remained in Seattle
ever since. The landscape of the Pacific Northwest—its rain forests,
rivers, deserts, and coastline—have inspired much of his best poetry,
as have the legends of the Northwest Coast and Plateau Indians.
Wagoner's poetry has considerable range, and he is a prolific novelist
as well. His work is marked by stylistic dexterity, lyric grace, and
emotional and intellectual clarity. He can be mystical as well as
practical, witty as well as celebratory, and there is a distilled grandeur
to his vision of man's communion with the natural world.

The Best Slow Dancer

Under the sagging clotheslines of crepe paper
By the second string of teachers and wallflowers
In the school gym across the key through the glitter
Of mirrored light three-second rule forever
Suspended you danced with her the best slow dancer
Who stood on tiptoe who almost wasn't there
In your arms like music she knew just how to answer
The question mark of your spine your hand in hers
The other touching that place between her shoulders
Trembling your countless feet light-footed sure
To move as they wished wherever you might stagger
Without her she turned in time she knew where you were
In time she turned her body into yours
As you moved from thigh to secrets to breast yet never
Where you would be for all time never closer
Than your cheek against her temple her ear just under

Your lips that tried all evening long to tell her
You weren't the worst one not the boy whose mother
Had taught him to count to murmur over and over
One slide two slide three slide now no longer
The one in the hallway after class the scuffler
The double clubfoot gawker the mouth breather
With the wrong haircut who would never kiss her
But see her dancing off with someone or other
Older more clever smoother dreamier
Not waving a sister somebody else's partner
Lover while you went floating home through the air
To lie down lighter than air in a moonlit shimmer
Alone to whisper yourself to sleep remember.

The Naval Trainees Learn How
to Jump Overboard

The last trainees are climbing the diving tower
As slowly as they dare, their fingers trembling
On the wet rungs, bare feet reluctantly
Going one step higher, one more, too far
Above the water waiting to take them in.

They stand on top, knees slightly buckled, nowhere
To put their hands, all suddenly thinking how
Good it's always been to be braced up
By something, anything, but ready to be let down
By their loud instructor thirty feet below.

They are the last ones learning how to jump
Feet-first into the swimming pool, to windward
From an imagined ship (in case of drift or fire),
Their ankles crossed, their loose life jackets held
Down with one hand, their noses pinched with the other.

They pause at the edge. Only one second away
From their unsupported arches, the surface glitters,
Looking too solid, too jagged and broken,
A place strictly for sinking, no place to go.
Each has his last split-second second thoughts.

Others are treading water, hooting and whistling
Abandon Ship and General Alarm,
But these stare toward the emptiest of horizons.
Upright, blue-lipped, no longer breathing, already
Drowned, they commit their bodies to the deep.

The Excursion of the Speech
and Hearing Class

They had come to see the salmon lunging and leaping
Up the white spillway, but the water was empty.
Now one young girl lingers behind the others,
And slowly, her thin arms held out from her sides,
Alone on the riverbank, she begins to dance.

Her body moves as the salmon would have moved
In place, holding that place in a soundless calm
Under a soundless frenzy of surfaces
Against a current only she remembers
To welcome, to break through, to gather again.

The wind and the river pulse against her face
And under her feet. She listens to what they know
And moves her lips to find the mouth of the river
And the mouth of the slow wind against her mouth.
The source of the river and the source of the wind

Have taken her breath away. But the others come
Shaking their fingers, opening and closing
Their mouths, to take her back to another silence.

Five Dawn Skies in November

1

At the roots of clouds a cutworm hollowing
The night, its eyes moonblind.

2

On the sheen of a lake the moment before wind,
Before rain, a loon floating asleep.

3

As smoothly blurred as (seen through water) a marten
Rippling among marshgrass.

4

Deepening into winter, a bear at her burrow
At first light on the first light snow.

5

A salmon stranded on stones, its mouth still opening
And closing toward the river.

Making Camp

When their eyes opened, it was more than morning.
They lay by a fallen tree as if it had burned
All night for them, a backlog
Where the true burning came from red crest lichen
And the green blaze of star moss.

There was no other fire except among leaves
Overhead, among leaves beside them.

They had changed. They had been changed. They saw
As clearly as if the air had turned to light
Spineleaf moss and earthstar
Without moving their hands or their bodies,
Map lichen gleaming on rock, not saying where
They were, not saying where to go,
But to begin.

They began making their camp crosswind by water
Facing the southerly bent firebow
Of the sun. They gathered the dead
Branches that had kept the sky from falling
Before falling themselves.
They gathered boughs, a browse bed and a firebed
And, at the turning point, made fire.

The Source

Neither had said they were going to climb to it,
But they kept walking beside the stream
Under the high shade
Of fir trees, upslope, wading through ferns and leaves
As if through a living and dying current,
Through water itself
Whenever the sea-green walls of the creek bank
Steepened to overhangs where roots
Clung wrong-side up
And seedling firs lurched out from under a world
That dared them to survive one birth.
They shared smooth stones
With sandpipers and dippers, with gold-eyed frogs,

Shared low-slung branches with green herons,
With kingfishers,
Warblers, and winter wrens, who watched them pass
Songless to higher ground, to a light
Thinning out, a waterfall
Where the creek was rain and a sideways mist and past
The sidelong mouths of runnels and freshets
Glistening, as cold
To their fingers' touch as the promises of winter.
More shallow, its stones no longer softened
By white-water crowfoot and pale
Flowerless fountain moss, the creek seemed younger,
Hurrying, its surface quick, more hectic,
As if it felt no longing
Yet to have anything like the sea to turn to.
They climbed past thicker and smaller trees,
Past the half-dead
And the weathered barkless gray dead at the treeline,
Climbed toward spillways of snow on the mountain
Through avalanche lily, sorrel,
Through lupine, through snow, the light a snowfall,
A blue-white daylight the color of snowmelt
Shimmering by their feet,
Still only half persuaded not to be ice
But to give in to the full beginning
Of flowing. At the rim
Of a pond near the foot of steep snow-drifted talus,
Half-frozen, they knelt where the foot-wide creek
Was now being born
Again and again under their eyes. They drank
From the source, their blue lips going numb
At that strange kiss.
They kissed like strangers. They watched the creek spill over
Stones like first words: *Only*
Begin, and the rest will follow.

ROBERT CREELEY
(b. 1926)

Robert Creeley was born in Arlington, Massachusetts, attended Harvard, and was an ambulance driver, chicken farmer, expatriate, and publisher. He later taught at Black Mountain College, took an M.A. from the University of New Mexico, and since 1966 has taught at the State University of New York at Buffalo. Strongly influenced by William Carlos Williams, and later by Charles Olson and Robert Duncan, Creeley holds as his ideal a poem, as he says, whose "words are returned to an almost primal circumstance, by a technique that makes use of feedback, that is, a repetitive relocation of phrasing where words are returned to an almost objective state of presence so that they *speak* rather than someone speaking through them." Troubled by the problem of mediated utterance, Creeley strives for immediacy, for "a more resonant echo of the subconscious or inner experience." Terse and subdued, his poems seek to record pulses of feeling. Their tone is often vulnerable or celebratory: he is our contemporary cavalier poet.

I Know a Man

As I sd to my
friend, because I am
always talking,—John, I

sd, which was not his
name, the darkness sur-
rounds us, what

can we do against
it, or else, shall we &
why not, buy a goddamn big car,

drive, he sd, for
christ's sake, look
out where yr going.

The Rescue

The man sits in a timelessness
with the horse under him in time
to a movement of legs and hooves
upon a timeless sand.

Distance comes in from the foreground
present in the picture as time
he reads outward from
and comes from that beginning.

A wind blows in
and out and all about the man
as the horse ran
and runs to come in time.

A house is burning in the sand.
A man and horse are burning.
The wind is burning.
They are running to arrive.

Air: "The Love of a Woman"

The love of a woman
is the possibility which
surrounds her as hair
her head, as the love of her

follows and describes
her. But what if
they die, then there is
still the aura

left, left sadly, but
hovers in the air, surely,
where this had taken place?
Then sing, of her, of whom

it will be said, he
sang of her, it was the
song he made which made her
happy, so she lived.

For Friendship

For friendship
make a chain that holds,
to be bound to
others, two by two,

a walk, a garland,
handed by hands
that cannot move
unless they hold.

For Love

for Bobbie

Yesterday I wanted to
speak of it, that sense above
the others to me
important because all

that I know derives
from what it teaches me.
Today, what is it that
is finally so helpless,

different, despairs of its own
statement, wants to
turn away, endlessly
to turn away.

If the moon did not . . .
no, if you did not
I wouldn't either, but
what would I not

do, what prevention, what
thing so quickly stopped.
That is love yesterday
or tomorrow, not

now. Can I eat
what you give me. I
have not earned it. Must
I think of everything

as earned. Now love also
becomes a reward so
remote from me I have
only made it with my mind.

Here is tedium,
despair, a painful
sense of isolation and
whimsical if pompous

self-regard. But that image
is only of the mind's
vague structure, vague to me
because it is my own.

Love, what do I think
to say. I cannot say it.
What have you become to ask,
what have I made you into,

companion, good company,
crossed legs with skirt, or
soft body under
the bones of the bed.

Nothing says anything
but that which it wishes
would come true, fears
what else might happen in

some other place, some
other time not this one.
A voice in my place, an
echo of that only in yours.

Let me stumble into
not the confession but
the obsession I begin with
now. For you

also (also)
some time beyond place, or
place beyond time, no
mind left to

say anything at all,
that face gone, now.
Into the company of love
it all returns.

Again

One more day gone,
done, found in
the form of days.

It began, it
ended—was
forward, backward,

slow, fast, a
sun shone, clouds,
high in the air I was

for awhile with others,
then came down
on the ground again.

No moon. A room in
a hotel—to begin
again.

The World

I wanted so ably
to reassure you, I wanted
the man you took to be me,

to comfort you, and got
up, and went to the window,
pushed back, as you asked me to,

the curtain, to see
the outline of the trees
in the night outside.

The light, love,
the light we felt then,
greyly, was it, that

came in, on us, not
merely my hands or yours,
or a wetness so comfortable,

but in the dark then
as you slept, the grey
figure came so close

and leaned over,
between us, as you
slept, restless, and

my own face had to
see it, and be seen by it,
the man it was, your

grey lost tired bewildered
brother, unused, untaken—
hated by love, and dead,

but not dead, for an
instant, saw me, myself
the intruder, as he was not.

I tried to say, it is
all right, she is
happy, you are no longer

needed. I said,
he is dead, and he
went as you shifted

and woke, at first afraid,
then knew by my own knowing
what had happened—

and the light then
of the sun coming
for another morning
in the world.

ALLEN GINSBERG
(b. 1926)

For several decades now the best-known American poet of his
generation, Allen Ginsberg has been as much a social force as a
literary phenomenon. Born in Newark, New Jersey, and educated at
Columbia, he had become the leading figure of the Beat movement by
the late 1950s. His boldly passionate early poems, "Howl" and
"Kaddish," established him as a major voice and influence. A list of
phrases reminds one of Ginsberg's involvement with the
counterculture and political activism of the 1960s and 1970s: flower
power, be-in, LSD, mantra, peace march, gay rights, environmental
protest. In his journalistic, improvisatory, "thought-breath" poems,
Ginsberg became his own subject: the flux of his moods, opinions, and
sensations; his worldwide travels and drug trips; his homosexuality
and Buddhist views; his political grumblings, prophetic outcries, and
dark vision of America's sickened soul. Younger readers are
instinctively drawn to his exuberant dissent and experiment; older
readers see him in the line of Romantic bards; Ginsberg himself wants
to be remembered "as someone in the tradition of the oldtime
American transcendentalist individualism, from the old gnostic
tradition . . . Thoreau, Emerson, . . . Whitman . . .
just carrying it on into the 20th century."

FROM Howl

for Carl Solomon

I

I saw the best minds of my generation destroyed by madness,
    starving hysterical naked,

dragging themselves through the negro streets at dawn looking for
an angry fix,
angelheaded hipsters burning for the ancient heavenly connection
to the starry dynamo in the machinery of night,
who poverty and tatters and hollow-eyed and high sat up smoking
in the supernatural darkness of cold-water flats floating across
the tops of cities contemplating jazz,
who bared their brains to Heaven under the El and saw Mo-
hammedan angels staggering on tenement roofs illuminated,
who passed through universities with radiant cool eyes hallucinat-
ing Arkansas and Blake-light tragedy among the scholars of
war,
who were expelled from the academies for crazy & publishing
obscene odes on the windows of the skull,
who cowered in unshaven rooms in underwear, burning their
money in wastebaskets and listening to the Terror through
the wall,
who got busted in their pubic beards returning through Laredo
with a belt of marijuana for New York,
who ate fire in paint hotels or drank turpentine in Paradise Alley,
death, or purgatoried their torsos night after night
with dreams, with drugs, with waking nightmares, alcohol and
cock and endless balls,
incomparable blind streets of shuddering cloud and lightning in
the mind leaping toward poles of Canada & Paterson, il-
luminating all the motionless world of Time between,
Peyote solidities of halls, backyard green tree cemetery dawns,
wine drunkenness over the rooftops, storefront boroughs of
teahead joyride neon blinking traffic light, sun and moon and
tree vibrations in the roaring winter dusks of Brooklyn, ash-
can rantings and kind king light of mind,
who chained themselves to subways for the endless ride from
Battery to holy Bronx on benzedrine until the noise of wheels
and children brought them down shuddering mouth-wracked
and battered bleak of brain all drained of brilliance in the
drear light of Zoo,
who sank all night in submarine light of Bickford's floated out and
sat through the stale beer afternoon in desolate Fugazzi's,
listening to the crack of doom on the hydrogen jukebox,

who talked continuously seventy hours from park to pad to bar
to Bellevue to museum to the Brooklyn Bridge,
a lost battalion of platonic conversationalists jumping down the
stoops off fire escapes off windowsills off Empire State out of
the moon,
yacketayakking screaming vomiting whispering facts and memo-
ries and anecdotes and eyeball kicks and shocks of hospitals
and jails and wars,
whole intellects disgorged in total recall for seven days and nights
with brilliant eyes, meat for the Synagogue cast on the pave-
ment,
who vanished into nowhere Zen New Jersey leaving a trail of
ambiguous picture postcards of Atlantic City Hall,
suffering Eastern sweats and Tangerian bone-grindings and mi-
graines of China under junk-withdrawal in Newark's bleak
furnished room,
who wandered around and around at midnight in the railroad yard
wondering where to go, and went, leaving no broken hearts,
who lit cigarettes in boxcars boxcars boxcars racketing through
snow toward lonesome farms in grandfather night,
who studied Plotinus Poe St. John of the Cross telepathy and bop
kabbalah because the cosmos instinctively vibrated at their
feet in Kansas,
who loned it through the streets of Idaho seeking visionary indian
angels who were visionary indian angels,
who thought they were only mad when Baltimore gleamed in
supernatural ecstasy,
who jumped in limousines with the Chinaman of Oklahoma on
the impulse of winter midnight streetlight smalltown rain,
who lounged hungry and lonesome through Houston seeking jazz
or sex or soup, and followed the brilliant Spaniard to converse
about America and Eternity, a hopeless task, and so took ship
to Africa,
who disappeared into the volcanoes of Mexico leaving behind
nothing but the shadow of dungarees and the lava and ash of
poetry scattered in fireplace Chicago,
who reappeared on the West Coast investigating the FBI in beards
and shorts with big pacifist eyes sexy in their dark skin pass-
ing out incomprehensible leaflets,

who burned cigarette holes in their arms protesting the narcotic tobacco haze of Capitalism,

who distributed Supercommunist pamphlets in Union Square weeping and undressing while the sirens of Los Alamos wailed them down, and wailed down Wall, and the Staten Island ferry also wailed,

who broke down crying in white gymnasiums naked and trembling before the machinery of other skeletons,

who bit detectives in the neck and shrieked with delight in police-cars for committing no crime but their own wild cooking pederasty and intoxication,

who howled on their knees in the subway and were dragged off the roof waving genitals and manuscripts, [. . .]

who demanded sanity trials accusing the radio of hypnotism & were left with their insanity & their hands & a hung jury,

who threw potato salad at CCNY lecturers on Dadaism and subsequently presented themselves on the granite steps of the madhouse with shaven heads and harlequin speech of suicide, demanding instantaneous lobotomy,

and who were given instead the concrete void of insulin Metrazol electricity hydrotherapy psychotherapy occupational therapy pingpong & amnesia,

who in humorless protest overturned only one symbolic pingpong table, resting briefly in catatonia,

returning years later truly bald except for a wig of blood, and tears and fingers, to the visible madman doom of the wards of the madtowns of the East,

Pilgrim State's Rockland's and Greystone's foetid halls, bickering with the echoes of the soul, rocking and rolling in the midnight solitude-bench dolmen-realms of love, dream of life a nightmare, bodies turned to stone as heavy as the moon,

with mother finally ******, and the last fantastic book flung out of the tenement window, and the last door closed at 4 A.M. and the last telephone slammed at the wall in reply and the last furnished room emptied down to the last piece of mental furniture, a yellow paper rose twisted on a wire hanger in the closet, and even that imaginary, nothing but a hopeful little bit of hallucination—

ah, Carl, while you are not safe I am not safe, and now you're
  really in the total animal soup of time—
and who therefore ran through the icy streets obsessed with a
  sudden flash of the alchemy of the use of the ellipse the
  catalog the meter & the vibrating plane,
who dreamt and made incarnate gaps in Time & Space through
  images juxtaposed, and trapped the archangel of the soul
  between 2 visual images and joined the elemental verbs and
  set the noun and dash of consciousness together jumping with
  sensation of Pater Omnipotens Aeterna Deus
to recreate the syntax and measure of poor human prose and stand
  before you speechless and intelligent and shaking with
  shame, rejected yet confessing out the soul to conform to the
  rhythm of thought in his naked and endless head,
the madman bum and angel beat in Time, unknown, yet putting
  down here what might be left to say in time come after death,
and rose reincarnate in the ghostly clothes of jazz in the goldhorn
  shadow of the band and blew the suffering of America's
  naked mind for love into an eli eli lamma lamma sabacthani
  saxophone cry that shivered the cities down to the last radio
with the absolute heart of the poem of life butchered out of their
  own bodies good to eat a thousand years.

Sunflower Sutra

I walked on the banks of the tincan banana dock and sat down
  under the huge shade of a Southern Pacific locomotive to look
  at the sunset over the box house hills and cry.
Jack Kerouac sat beside me on a busted rusty iron pole, compan-
  ion, we thought the same thoughts of the soul, bleak and blue
  and sad-eyed, surrounded by the gnarled steel roots of trees
  of machinery.
The oily water on the river mirrored the red sky, sun sank on top
  of final Frisco peaks, no fish in that stream, no hermit in those
  mounts, just ourselves rheumy-eyed and hung-over like old
  bums on the river-bank, tired and wily.

Look at the Sunflower, he said, there was a dead gray shadow
　　against the sky, big as a man, sitting dry on top of a pile of
　　ancient sawdust—
—I rushed up enchanted—it was my first sunflower, memories of
　　Blake—my visions—Harlem
and Hells of the Eastern rivers, bridges clanking Joes Greasy Sand-
　　wiches, dead baby carriages, black treadless tires forgotten
　　and unretreaded, the poem of the riverbank, condoms & pots,
　　steel knives, nothing stainless, only the dank muck and the
　　razor-sharp artifacts passing into the past—
and the gray Sunflower poised against the sunset, crackly bleak
　　and dusty with the smut and smog and smoke of olden
　　locomotives in its eye—
corolla of bleary spikes pushed down and broken like a battered
　　crown, seeds fallen out of its face, soon-to-be-toothless
　　mouth of sunny air, sunrays obliterated on its hairy head like
　　a dried wire spiderweb,
leaves stuck out like arms out of the stem, gestures from the
　　sawdust root, broke pieces of plaster fallen out of the black
　　twigs, a dead fly in its ear,
Unholy battered old thing you were, my sunflower O my soul, I
　　loved you then!
The grime was no man's grime but death and human locomotives,
all that dress of dust, that veil of darkened railroad skin, that smog
　　of cheek, that eyelid of black mis'ry, that sooty hand or phal-
　　lus or protuberance of artificial worse-than-dirt—industrial—
　　modern—all that civilization spotting your crazy golden
　　crown—
and those blear thoughts of death and dusty loveless eyes and ends
　　and withered roots below, in the home-pile of sand and saw-
　　dust, rubber dollar bills, skin of machinery, the guts and
　　innards of the weeping coughing car, the empty lonely tincans
　　with their rusty tongues alack, what more could I name, the
　　smoked ashes of some cock cigar, the cunts of wheelbarrows
　　and the milky breasts of cars, wornout asses out of chairs &
　　sphincters of dynamos—all these
entangled in your mummied roots—and you there standing before
　　me in the sunset, all your glory in your form!
A perfect beauty of a sunflower! a perfect excellent lovely sun-

flower existence! a sweet natural eye to the new hip moon, woke up alive and excited grasping in the sunset shadow sunrise golden monthly breeze!

How many flies buzzed round you innocent of your grime, while you cursed the heavens of the railroad and your flower soul?

Poor dead flower? when did you forget you were a flower? when did you look at your skin and decide you were an impotent dirty old locomotive? the ghost of a locomotive? the specter and shade of a once powerful mad American locomotive?

You were never no locomotive, Sunflower, you were a sunflower!

And you Locomotive, you are a locomotive, forget me not!

So I grabbed up the skeleton thick sunflower and stuck it at my side like a scepter,

and deliver my sermon to my soul, and Jack's soul too, and anyone who'll listen,

—We're not our skin of grime, we're not our dread bleak dusty imageless locomotive, we're all golden sunflowers inside, blessed by our own seed & hairy naked accomplishment-bodies growing into mad black formal sunflowers in the sunset, spied on by our eyes under the shadow of the mad locomotive riverbank sunset Frisco hilly tincan evening sitdown vision.

Berkeley, 1955

My Sad Self

to Frank O'Hara

Sometimes when my eyes are red
I go up on top of the RCA Building
        and gaze at my world, Manhattan—
            my buildings, streets I've done feats in,
                lofts, beds, coldwater flats
        —on Fifth Ave below which I also bear in mind,

its ant cars, little yellow taxis, men
walking the size of specks of wool—
Panorama of the bridges, sunrise over Brooklyn machine,
sun go down over New Jersey where I was born
& Paterson where I played with ants—
my later loves on 15th Street,
my greater loves of Lower East Side,
my once fabulous amours in the Bronx
faraway—
paths crossing in these hidden streets,
my history summed up, my absences
and ecstasies in Harlem—
— sun shining down on all I own
in one eyeblink to the horizon
in my last eternity—
matter is water.

Sad,
I take the elevator and go
down, pondering,
and walk on the pavements staring into all man's
plateglass, faces,
questioning after who loves,
and stop, bemused
in front of an automobile shopwindow
standing lost in calm thought,
traffic moving up & down 5th Avenue blocks behind me
waiting for a moment when . . .

Time to go home & cook supper & listen to
the romantic war news on the radio
. . . all movement stops
& I walk in the timeless sadness of existence,
tenderness flowing thru the buildings,
my fingertips touching reality's face,
my own face streaked with tears in the mirror
of some window—at dusk—
where I have no desire—
for bonbons—or to own the dresses or Japanese
lampshades of intellection—

Confused by the spectacle around me,
    Man struggling up the street
    with packages, newspapers,
                ties, beautiful suits
    toward his desire
    Man, woman, streaming over the pavements
    red lights clocking hurried watches &
      movements at the curb—

And all these streets leading
    so crosswise, honking, lengthily,
      by avenues
    stalked by high buildings or crusted into slums
      thru such halting traffic
             screaming cars and engines
so painfully to this
    countryside, this graveyard
      this stillness
             on deathbed or mountain
  once seen
    never regained or desired
            in the mind to come
where all Manhattan that I've seen must disappear.

                New York, October 1958

Wales Visitation

White fog lifting & falling on mountain-brow
    Trees moving in rivers of wind
        The clouds arise
  as on a wave, gigantic eddy lifting mist
    above teeming ferns exquisitely swayed
              along a green crag
    glimpsed thru mullioned glass in valley raine—

Bardic, O Self, Visitacione, tell naught
    but what seen by one man in a vale in Albion,
        of the folk, whose physical sciences end in Ecology,
            the wisdom of earthly relations,
      of mouths & eyes interknit ten centuries visible
        orchards of mind language manifest human,
    of the satanic thistle that raises its horned symmetry
    flowering above sister grass-daisies' pink tiny
            bloomlets angelic as lightbulbs—

Remember 160 miles from London's symmetrical thorned
    tower
        & network of TV pictures flashing bearded your Self
the lambs on the tree-nooked hillside this day bleating
heard in Blake's old ear, & the silent thought of
    Wordsworth in eld
                           Stillness
    clouds passing through skeleton arches of Tintern Abbey—
        Bard Nameless as the Vast, babble to Vastness!

All the Valley quivered, one extended motion, wind
                undulating on mossy hills
    a giant wash that sank white fog delicately down red runnels
                on the mountainside
    whose leaf-branch tendrils moved asway
              in granitic undertow down—
and lifted the floating Nebulous upward, and lifted the arms of
    the trees
        and lifted the grasses an instant in balance
            and lifted the lambs to hold still
    and lifted the green of the hill, in one solemn wave

A solid mass of Heaven, mist-infused, ebbs thru the vale,
    a wavelet of Immensity, lapping gigantic through Llanthony
    Valley,
the length of all England, valley upon valley under Heaven's
    ocean
                      tonned with cloud-hang,
    —Heaven balanced on a grassblade.
Roar of the mountain wind slow, sigh of the body,

One Being on the mountainside stirring gently
　　Exquisite scales trembling everywhere in balance,
　one motion thru the cloudy sky-floor shifting on the million
　　feet of daisies,
one Majesty the motion that stirred wet grass quivering
　　to the farthest tendril of white fog poured down
　　　　　　through shivering flowers on the
　　　　　　mountain's head—

No imperfection in the budded mountain,
　　Valleys breathe, heaven and earth move together,
　　daisies push inches of yellow air, vegetables tremble,
　　　　　　grass shimmers green
sheep speckle the mountainside, revolving their jaws with
　　empty eyes,
　　　　　　　　horses dance in the warm rain,
　　tree-lined canals network live farmland,
　　　　　　blueberries fringe stone walls on hawthorn'd
　　　　　　hills,
　　pheasants croak on meadows haired with fern—
Out, out on the hillside, into the ocean sound, into delicate
　　gusts of wet air,
Fall on the ground, O great Wetness, O Mother, No harm on
　　your body!
Stare close, no imperfection in the grass,
　　　　each flower Buddha-eye, repeating the story,
　　　　　　myriad-formed—
Kneel before the foxglove raising green buds, mauve bells drooped
　　doubled down the stem trembling antennae,
　　& look in the eyes of the branded lambs that stare
　　breathing stockstill under dripping hawthorn—
I lay down mixing my beard with the wet hair of the mountainside,
　　smelling the brown vagina-moist ground, harmless,
　　　　tasting the violet thistle-hair, sweetness—
One being so balanced, so vast, that its softest breath
　　moves every floweret in the stillness on the valley floor,
　　trembles lamb-hair hung gossamer rain-beaded in the grass,
lifts trees on their roots, birds in the great draught
　　hiding their strength in the rain, bearing same weight,

Groan thru breast and neck, a great Oh! to earth heart
Calling our Presence together
The great secret is no secret
Senses fit the winds,
Visible is visible,
rain-mist curtains wave through the bearded vale,
gray atoms wet the wind's kabbala
Crosslegged on a rock in dusk rain,
rubber booted in soft grass, mind moveless,
breath trembles in white daisies by the roadside,
Heaven breath and my own symmetric
Airs wavering thru antlered green fern
drawn in my navel, same breath as breathes thru Capel-Y-Ffn,
Sounds of Aleph and Aum
through forests of gristle,
my skull and Lord Hereford's Knob equal,
All Albion one.

What did I notice? Particulars! The
vision of the great One is myriad—
smoke curls upward from ashtray,
house fire burned low,
The night, still wet & moody black heaven
starless
upward in motion with wet wind.

July 29, 1967 (LSD)—August 3, 1967 (London)

W. D. SNODGRASS

(b. 1926)

Born in Wilkinsburg, Pennsylvania, William DeWitt Snodgrass served in the navy and later studied at the University of Iowa while working as a hotel clerk and hospital aide. Since 1955 he has taught at various universities and is currently a professor at the University of Delaware.
His first book, *Heart's Needle,* won the Pulitzer Prize in 1960 and influenced the emerging more extreme confessional work of Robert Lowell and Anne Sexton. His lyrical accounts of the turmoil in his private life—divorces, betrayals, the purgatories of everyday life—catch up patterns of violence and failure familiar from Greek myths or Freudian case studies. His later work has gone on to study, in a series of dramatic monologues, the horrific psychology of Nazi leaders—and, by extension, those forces that move in "implacably to rule us, unaware." Snodgrass began by reacting against the elaborately obscure, symbolic poems favored in the 1950s. He wanted his own poems to be based in actual experience, and his charged sincerity gives them their intimacy and authority.

April Inventory

The green catalpa tree has turned
All white; the cherry blooms once more.
In one whole year I haven't learned
A blessed thing they pay you for.
The blossoms snow down in my hair;
The trees and I will soon be bare.

The trees have more than I to spare.
The sleek, expensive girls I teach,
Younger and pinker every year,
Bloom gradually out of reach.
The pear tree lets its petals drop
Like dandruff on a tabletop.

The girls have grown so young by now
I have to nudge myself to stare.
This year they smile and mind me how
My teeth are falling with my hair.
In thirty years I may not get
Younger, shrewder, or out of debt.

The tenth time, just a year ago,
I made myself a little list
Of all the things I'd ought to know,
Then told my parents, analyst,
And everyone who's trusted me
I'd be substantial, presently.

I haven't read one book about
A book or memorized one plot.
Or found a mind I did not doubt.
I learned one date. And then forgot.
And one by one the solid scholars
Get the degrees, the jobs, the dollars.

And smile above their starchy collars.
I taught my classes Whitehead's notions;
One lovely girl, a song of Mahler's.
Lacking a source-book or promotions,
I showed one child the colors of
A luna moth and how to love.

I taught myself to name my name,
To bark back, loosen love and crying;
To ease my woman so she came,
To ease an old man who was dying.
I have not learned how often I
Can win, can love, but choose to die.

I have not learned there is a lie
Love shall be blonder, slimmer, younger;
That my equivocating eye
Loves only by my body's hunger;
That I have forces, true to feel,
Or that the lovely world is real.

While scholars speak authority
And wear their ulcers on their sleeves,
My eyes in spectacles shall see
These trees procure and spend their leaves.
There is a value underneath
The gold and silver in my teeth.

Though trees turn bare and girls turn wives,
We shall afford our costly seasons;
There is a gentleness survives
That will outspeak and has its reasons.
There is a loveliness exists,
Preserves us, not for specialists.

FROM Heart's Needle

2

Late April and you are three; today
   We dug your garden in the yard.
To curb the damage of your play,
Strange dogs at night and the moles tunneling,
   Four slender sticks of lath stand guard
      Uplifting their thin string.

So you were the first to tramp it down.
   And after the earth was sifted close
You brought your watering can to drown
All earth *and* us. But these mixed seeds are pressed
   With light loam in their steadfast rows.
      Child, we've done our best.

Someone will have to weed and spread
   The young sprouts. Sprinkle them in the hour
When shadow falls across their bed.
You should try to look at them every day

Because when they come to full flower
   I will be away.

6

   Easter has come around
again; the river is rising
   over the thawed ground
and the banksides. When you come you bring
   an egg dyed lavender.
We shout along our bank to hear
our voices returning from the hills to meet us.
   We need the landscape to repeat us.

   You lived on this bank first.
While nine months filled your term, we knew
   how your lungs, immersed
in the womb, miraculously grew
   their useless folds till
the fierce, cold air rushed in to fill
them out like bushes thick with leaves. You took your hour,
   caught breath, and cried with your full lung power.

   Over the stagnant bight
we see the hungry bank swallow
   flaunting his free flight
still; we sink in mud to follow
   the killdeer from the grass
that hides her nest. That March there was
rain; the rivers rose; you could hear killdeers flying
   all night over the mudflats crying.

   You bring back how the red-
winged blackbird shrieked, slapping frail wings,
   diving at my head—
I saw where her tough nest, cradled, swings
   in tall reeds that must sway
with the winds blowing every way.
If you recall much, you recall this place. You still
   live nearby—on the opposite hill.

After the sharp windstorm
of July Fourth, all that summer
    through the gentle, warm
afternoons, we heard great chain saws chirr
    like iron locusts. Crews
of roughneck boys swarmed to cut loose
branches wrenched in the shattering wind, to hack free
    all the torn limbs that could sap the tree.

    In the debris lay
starlings, dead. Near the park's birdrun
    we surprised one day
a proud, tan-spatted, buff-brown pigeon.
    In my hands she flapped so
fearfully that I let her go.
Her keeper came. And we helped snarl her in a net.
    You bring things I'd as soon forget.

    You raise into my head
a Fall night that I came once more
    to sit on your bed;
sweat beads stood out on your arms and fore-
    head and you wheezed for breath,
for help, like some child caught beneath
its comfortable woolly blankets, drowning there.
    Your lungs caught and would not take the air.

    Of all things, only we
have power to choose that we should die;
    nothing else is free
in this world to refuse it. Yet I,
    who say this, could not raise
myself from bed how many days
to the thieving world. Child, I have another wife,
    another child. We try to choose our life.

Mementos, 1

Sorting out letters and piles of my old
   Canceled checks, old clippings, and yellow note cards
That meant something once, I happened to find
   Your picture. *That* picture. I stopped there cold,
Like a man raking piles of dead leaves in his yard
      Who has turned up a severed hand.

Still, that first second, I was glad: you stand
   Just as you stood—shy, delicate, slender,
In that long gown of green lace netting and daisies
   That you wore to our first dance. The sight of you stunned
Us all. Well, our needs were different, then,
      And our ideals came easy.

Then through the war and those two long years
   Overseas, the Japanese dead in their shacks
Among dishes, dolls, and lost shoes; I carried
   This glimpse of you, there, to choke down my fear,
Prove it had been, that it might come back.
      That was before we got married.

—Before we drained out one another's force
   With lies, self-denial, unspoken regret
And the sick eyes that blame; before the divorce
   And the treachery. Say it: before we met. Still,
I put back your picture. Someday, in due course,
      I will find that it's still there.

A Locked House

        As we drove back, crossing the hill,
        The house still

Hidden in the trees, I always thought—
A fool's fear—that it might have caught
Fire, someone could have broken in.
As if things must have been
Too good here. Still, we always found
It locked tight, safe and sound.

I mentioned that, once, as a joke;
No doubt we spoke
Of the absurdity
To fear some dour god's jealousy
Of our good fortune. From the farm
Next door, our neighbors saw no harm
Came to the things we cared for here.
What did we have to fear?

Maybe I should have thought: all
Such things rot, fall—
Barns, houses, furniture.
We two are stronger than we were
Apart; we've grown
Together. Everything we own
Can burn; we know what counts—some such
Idea. We said as much.

We'd watched friends driven to betray;
Felt that love drained away
Some self they need.
We'd said love, like a growth, can feed
On hate we turn in and disguise;
We warned ourselves. That you might despise
Me—hate all we both loved best—
None of us ever guessed.

The house still stands, locked, as it stood
Untouched a good
Two years after you went.
Some things passed in the settlement;
Some things slipped away. Enough's left
That I come back sometimes. The theft
And vandalism were our own.
Maybe we should have known.

JAMES MERRILL
(b. 1926)

Renowned for the witty elegance and humane complexity of his work,
and considered the leading lyric poet of his generation, James Merrill
was born in New York City, the son of a financier. He graduated from
Amherst in 1947. Since 1954 he has lived in Stonington, Connecticut,
although he has spent part of each year in Greece or Key West. His
various homes and the displacements and discoveries of his travels are
the subjects of many of his poems. Merrill has consistently written
within the traditions of formal verse—"form's what affirms," he
says—but he has inflected his poems with a distinctly urbane, allusive
voice. Merrill is an autobiographical poet who has written poignantly
about his domestic and romantic life ("chronicles of love and loss," he
calls these poems). His masterwork is *The Changing Light at Sandover,* an
epic poem on occult themes. He has been awarded the Pulitzer Prize
(1977), two National Book Awards (1967 and 1979), the Bollingen
Prize (1973), and the National Book Critics Circle Award (1984).

A Renewal

Having used every subterfuge
To shake you, lies, fatigue, or even that of passion,
Now I see no way but a clean break.
I add that I am willing to bear the guilt.

You nod assent. Autumn turns windy, huge,
A clear vase of dry leaves vibrating on and on.
We sit, watching. When I next speak
Love buries itself in me, up to the hilt.

Voices from the Other World

Presently at our touch the teacup stirred,
Then circled lazily about
From A to Z. The first voice heard
(If they are voices, these mute spellers-out)
Was that of an engineer

Originally from Cologne.
Dead in his 22nd year
Of cholera in Cairo, he had KNOWN
NO HAPPINESS. He once met Goethe, though.
Goethe had told him: PERSEVERE.

Our blind hound whined. With that, a horde
Of voices gathered above the Ouija board,
Some childish and, you might say, blurred
By sleep; one little boy
Named Will, reluctant possibly in a ruff

Like a large-lidded page out of El Greco, pulled
Back the arras for that next voice,
Cold and portentous: ALL IS LOST.
FLEE THIS HOUSE. OTTO VON THURN UND TAXIS.
OBEY. YOU HAVE NO CHOICE.

Frightened, we stopped; but tossed
Till sunrise striped the rumpled sheets with gold.
Each night since then, the moon waxes,
Small insects flit round a cold torch
We light, that sends them pattering to the porch . . .

But no real Sign. New voices come,
Dictate addresses, begging us to write;
Some warn of lives misspent, and all of doom
In ways that so exhilarate
We are sleeping sound of late.

Last night the teacup shattered in a rage.
Indeed, we have grown nonchalant

Towards the other world. In the gloom here,
Our elbows on the cleared
Table, we talk and smoke, pleased to be stirred

Rather by buzzings in the jasmine, by the drone
Of our own voices and poor blind Rover's wheeze,
Than by those clamoring overhead,
Obsessed or piteous, for a commitment
We still have wit to postpone

Because, once looked at lit
By the cold reflections of the dead
Risen extinct but irresistible,
Our lives have never seemed more full, more real,
Nor the full moon more quick to chill.

Days of 1964

Houses, an embassy, the hospital,
Our neighborhood sun-cured if trembling still
In pools of the night's rain . . .
Across the street that led to the center of town
A steep hill kept one company part way
Or could be climbed in twenty minutes
For some literally breathtaking views,
Framed by umbrella pines, of city and sea.
Underfoot, cyclamen, autumn crocus grew
Spangled as with fine sweat among the relics
Of good times had by all. If not Olympus,
An out-of-earshot, year-round hillside revel.

I brought home flowers from my climbs.
Kyria Kleo who cleaned for us
Put them in water, sighing *Virgin, Virgin.*
Her legs hurt. She wore brown, was fat, past fifty,

And looked like a Palmyra matron
Copied in lard and horsehair. How she loved
You, me, loved us all, the bird, the cat!
I think now she *was* love. She sighed and glistened
All day with it, or pain, or both.
(We did not notably communicate.)
She lived nearby with her pious mother
And wastrel son. She called me her real son.

I paid her generously, I dare say.
Love makes one generous. Look at us. We'd known
Each other so briefly that instead of sleeping
We lay whole nights, open, in the lamplight,
And gazed, or traded stories.

One hour comes back—you gasping in my arms
With love, or laughter, or both,
I having just remembered and told you
What I'd looked up to see on my way downtown at noon:
Poor old Kleo, her aching legs,
Trudging into the pines. I called,
Called three times before she turned.
Above a tight, skyblue sweater, her face
Was painted. Yes. Her face was painted
Clown-white, white of the moon by daylight,
Lidded with pearl, mouth a poinsettia leaf,
Eat me, pay me—the erotic mask
Worn the world over by illusion
To weddings of itself and simple need.

Startled mute, we had stared—was love illusion?—
And gone our ways. Next, I was crossing a square
In which a moveable outdoor market's
Vegetables, chickens, pottery kept materializing
Through a dream-press of hagglers each at heart
Leery lest he be taken, plucked,
The bird, the flower of that November mildness,
Self lost up soft clay paths, or found, foothold,
Where the bud throbs awake
The better to be nipped, self on its knees in mud—
Here I stopped cold, for both our sakes;

And calmer on my way home bought us fruit.

Forgive me if you read this. (And may Kyria Kleo,
Should someone ever put it into Greek
And read it aloud to her, forgive me, too.)
I had gone so long without loving,
I hardly knew what I was thinking.

Where I hid my face, your touch, quick, merciful,
Blindfolded me. A god breathed from my lips.
If that was illusion, I wanted it to last long;
To dwell, for its daily pittance, with us there,
Cleaning and watering, sighing with love or pain.
I hoped it would climb when it needed to the heights
Even of degradation, as I for one
Seemed, those days, to be always climbing
Into a world of wild
Flowers, feasting, tears—or was I falling, legs
Buckling, heights, depths,
Into a pool of each night's rain?
But you were everywhere beside me, masked,
As who was not, in laughter, pain, and love.

Willowware Cup

Mass hysteria, wave after breaking wave
Blueblooded Cantonese upon these shores

Left the gene pool Lux-opaque and smoking
With dimestore mutants. One turned up today.

Plum in bloom, pagoda, blue birds, plume of willow—
Almost the replica of a prewar pattern—

The same boat bearing the gnat-sized lovers away,
The old bridge now bent double where her father signals

Feebly, as from flypaper, minding less and less.
Two smaller retainers with lanterns light him home.

Is that a scroll he carries? He must by now be immensely
Wise, and have given up earthly attachments, and all that.

Soon, of these May mornings, rising in mist, he will ask
Only to blend—like ink in flesh, blue anchor

Needled upon drunkenness while its destroyer
Full steam departs, the stigma throbbing, intricate—

Only to blend into a crazing texture.
You are far away. The leaves tell what they tell.

But this lone, chipped vessel, if it fills,
Fills for you with something warm and clear.

Around its inner horizon the old odd designs
Crowd as before, and seem to concentrate on you.

They represent, I fancy, a version of heaven
In its day more trouble to mend than to replace:

Steep roofs aslant, minutely tiled;
Tilted honeycombs, thunderhead blue.

Lost in Translation

for Richard Howard

Diese Tage, die leer dir scheinen
und wertlos für das All,
haben Wurzeln zwischen den Steinen
und trinken dort überall.

    A card table in the library stands ready
    To receive the puzzle which keeps never coming.
    Daylight shines in or lamplight down

Upon the tense oasis of green felt.
Full of unfulfillment, life goes on,
Mirage arisen from time's trickling sands
Or fallen piecemeal into place:
German lesson, picnic, see-saw, walk
With the collie who "did everything but talk"—
Sour windfalls of the orchard back of us.
A summer without parents is the puzzle,
Or should be. But the boy, day after day,
Writes in his Line-a-Day *No puzzle.*

He's in love, at least. His French Mademoiselle,
In real life a widow since Verdun,
Is stout, plain, carrot-haired, devout.
She prays for him, as does a curé in Alsace,
Sews costumes for his marionettes,
Helps him to keep behind the scene
Whose sidelit goosegirl, speaking with his voice,
Plays Guinevere as well as Gunmoll Jean.
Or else at bedtime in his tight embrace
Tells him her own French hopes, her German fears,
Her—but what more is there to tell?
Having known grief and hardship, Mademoiselle
Knows little more. Her languages. Her place.
Noon coffee. Mail. The watch that also waited
Pinned to her heart, poor gold, throws up its hands—
No puzzle! Steaming bitterness
Her sugars draw pops back into his mouth, translated:
"Patience, chéri. Geduld, mein Schatz."
(Thus, reading Valéry the other evening
And seeming to recall a Rilke version of "Palme,"
That sunlit paradigm whereby the tree
Taps a sweet wellspring of authority,
The hour came back. Patience dans l'azur.
Geduld im . . . Himmelblau? Mademoiselle.)

Out of the blue, as promised, of a New York
Puzzle-rental shop the puzzle comes—
A superior one, containing a thousand hand-sawn,
Sandal-scented pieces. Many take

Shapes known already—the craftsman's repertoire
Nice in its limitation—from other puzzles:
Witch on broomstick, ostrich, hourglass,
Even (surely not just in retrospect)
An inchling, innocently branching palm.
These can be put aside, made stories of
While Mademoiselle spreads out the rest face-up,
Herself excited as a child; or questioned
Like incoherent faces in a crowd,
Each with its scrap of highly colored
Evidence the Law must piece together.
Sky-blue ostrich? Likely story.
Mauve of the witch's cloak white, severed fingers
Pluck? Detain her. The plot thickens
As all at once two pieces interlock.

Mademoiselle does borders—(Not so fast.
A London dusk, December last.
Chatter silenced in the library
This grown man reenters, wearing grey.
A medium. All except him have seen
Panel slid back, recess explored,
An object at once unique and common
Displayed, planted in a plain tole
Casket the subject now considers
Through shut eyes, saying in effect:
"Even as voices reach me vaguely
A dry saw-shriek drowns them out,
Some loud machinery—a lumber mill?
Far uphill in the fir forest
Trees tower, tense with shock,
Groaning and cracking as they crash groundward.
But hidden here is a freak fragment
Of a pattern complex in appearance only.
What it seems to show is superficial
Next to that long-term lamination
Of hazard and craft, the karma that has
Made it matter in the first place.
Plywood. Piece of a puzzle." Applause

Acknowledged by an opening of lids
Upon the thing itself. A sudden dread—
But to go back. All this lay years ahead.)

Mademoiselle does borders. Straight-edge pieces
Align themselves with earth or sky
In twos and threes, naive cosmogonists
Whose views clash. Nomad inlanders meanwhile
Begin to cluster where the totem
Of a certain vibrant egg-yolk yellow
Or pelt of what emerging animal
Acts on the straggler like a trumpet call
To form a more sophisticated unit.
By suppertime two ragged wooden clouds
Have formed. In one, a Sheik with beard
And flashing sword hilt (he is all but finished)
Steps forward on a tiger skin. A piece
Snaps shut, and fangs gnash out at us!
In the second cloud—they gaze from cloud to cloud
With marked if undecipherable feeling—
Most of a dark-eyed woman veiled in mauve
Is being helped down from her camel (kneeling)
By a small backward-looking slave or page-boy
(Her son, thinks Mademoiselle mistakenly)
Whose feet have not been found. But lucky finds
In the last minutes before bed
Anchor both factions to the scene's limits
And, by so doing, orient
Them eye to eye across the green abyss.
The yellow promises, oh bliss,
To be in time a sumptuous tent.

Puzzle begun I write in the day's space,
Then, while she bathes, peek at Mademoiselle's
Page to the curé: ". . . cette innocente mère,
Ce pauvre enfant, que deviendront-ils?"
Her azure script is curlicued like pieces
Of the puzzle she will be telling him about.
(Fearful incuriosity of childhood!
"Tu as l'accent allemand," said Dominique.

Indeed. Mademoiselle was only French by marriage.
Child of an English mother, a remote
Descendant of the great explorer Speke,
And Prussian father. No one knew. I heard it
Long afterwards from her nephew, a UN
Interpreter. His matter-of-fact account
Touched old strings. My poor Mademoiselle,
With 1939 about to shake
This world where "each was the enemy, each the friend"
To its foundations, kept, though signed in blood,
Her peace a shameful secret to the end.)
"Schlaf wohl, chéri." Her kiss. Her thumb
Crossing my brow against the dreams to come.

This World that shifts like sand, its unforeseen
Consolidations and elate routine,
Whose Potentate had lacked a retinue?
Lo! it assembles on the shrinking Green.

Gunmetal-skinned or pale, all plumes and scars,
Of Vassalage the noblest avatars—
The very coffee-bearer in his vair
Vest is a swart Highness, next to ours.

Kef easing Boredom, and iced syrups, thirst,
In guessed-at glooms old wives who know the worst
Outsweat that virile fiction of the New:
"Insh'Allah, he will tire—" "—or kill her first!"

(Hardly a proper subject for the Home,
Work of—dear Richard, I shall let *you* comb
Archives and learned journals for his name—
A minor lion attending on Gérôme.)

While, thick as Thebes whose presently complete
Gates close behind them, Houri and Afreet
Both claim the Page. He wonders whom to serve,
And what his duties are, and where his feet,

And if we'll find, as some before us did,
That piece of Distance deep in which lies hid

Your tiny apex sugary with sun,
Eternal Triangle, Great Pyramid!

Then Sky alone is left, a hundred blue
Fragments in revolution, with no clue
To where a Niche will open. Quite a task,
Putting together Heaven, yet we do.

It's done. Here under the table all along
Were those missing feet. It's done.

The dog's tail thumping. Mademoiselle sketching
Costumes for a coming harem drama
To star the goosegirl. All too soon the swift
Dismantling. Lifted by two corners,
The puzzle hung together—and did not.
Irresistibly a populace
Unstitched of its attachments, rattled down.
Power went to pieces as the witch
Slithered easily from Virtue's gown.
The blue held out for time, but crumbled, too.
The city had long fallen, and the tent,
A separating sauce mousseline,
Been swept away. Remained the green
On which the grown-ups gambled. A green dusk.
First lightning bugs. Last glow of west
Green in the false eyes of (coincidence)
Our mangy tiger safe on his bared hearth.

Before the puzzle was boxed and readdressed
To the puzzle shop in the mid-Sixties,
Something tells me that one piece contrived
To stay in the boy's pocket. How do I know?
I know because so many later puzzles
Had missing pieces—Maggie Teyte's high notes
Gone at the war's end, end of the vogue for collies,
A house torn down; and hadn't Mademoiselle
Kept back her pitiful bit of truth as well?
I've spent the last days, furthermore,
Ransacking Athens for that translation of "Palme."
Neither the Goethehaus nor the National Library

Seems able to unearth it. Yet I can't
Just be imagining. I've seen it. Know
How much of the sun-ripe original
Felicity Rilke made himself forego
(Who loved French words—verger, mûr, parfumer)
In order to render its underlying sense.
Know already in that tongue of his
What Pains, what monolithic Truths
Shadow stanza to stanza's symmetrical
Rhyme-rutted pavement. Know that ground plan left
Sublime and barren, where the warm Romance
Stone by stone faded, cooled; the fluted nouns
Made taller, lonelier than life
By leaf-carved capitals in the afterglow.
The owlet umlaut peeps and hoots
Above the open vowel. And after rain
A deep reverberation fills with stars.

Lost, is it, buried? One more missing piece?

But nothing's lost. Or else: all is translation
And every bit of us is lost in it
(Or found—I wander through the ruin of S
Now and then, wondering at the peacefulness)
And in that loss a self-effacing tree,
Color of context, imperceptibly
Rustling with its angel, turns the waste
To shade and fiber, milk and memory.

W . S . M E R W I N
(b. 1927)

William Stanley Merwin was born in New York City, the son of a minister, and raised in New Jersey and Pennsylvania. After graduating from Princeton, he moved to Europe and made his living by translating and writing. In 1968 he returned permanently to the United States but refused an academic career; he now lives in Hawaii.

A prolific writer, he has published many volumes of poems, translations, prose, and memoirs. He was awarded the Pulitzer Prize in 1971 and the Bollingen Prize in 1979. Merwin's early work absorbed the major traditions of English Romantic poetry; it is mythic or emblematic and richly rhetorical. By 1963, however, he had evolved a new style—austere, impersonal, disjunctive, often surrealistic. A poem, he wrote, should be "not a manipulable, more or less recurring pattern, but an unduplicatable resonance, something that would be like an echo except that it is repeating no sound." Beneath their oracular textures, Merwin's poems have an acute political conscience, troubled by "a society whose triumphs one after the other emerge as new symbols of death."

The Animals

All these years behind windows
With blind crosses sweeping the tables

And myself tracking over empty ground
Animals I never saw

I with no voice

Remembering names to invent for them
Will any come back will one

Saying yes

Saying look carefully yes
We will meet again

Some Last Questions

What is the head
    A. Ash
What are the eyes
    A. The wells have fallen in and have
       Inhabitants
What are the feet
    A. Thumbs left after the auction
No what are the feet
    A. Under them the impossible road is moving
       Down which the broken necked mice push
       Balls of blood with their noses
What is the tongue
    A. The black coat that fell off the wall
       With sleeves trying to say something
What are the hands
    A. Paid
No what are the hands
    A. Climbing back down the museum wall
       To their ancestors the extinct shrews that will
       Have left a message
What is the silence
    A. As though it had a right to more
Who are the compatriots
    A. They make the stars of bone

The River of Bees

In a dream I returned to the river of bees
Five orange trees by the bridge and
Beside two mills my house

Into whose courtyard a blind man followed
The goats and stood singing
Of what was older

Soon it will be fifteen years

He was old he will have fallen into his eyes

I took my eyes
A long way to the calendars
Room after room asking how shall I live

One of the ends is made of streets
One man processions carry through it
Empty bottles their
Image of hope
It was offered to me by name

Once once and once
In the same city I was born
Asking what shall I say

He will have fallen into his mouth
Men think they are better than grass

I return to his voice rising like a forkful of hay

He was old he is not real nothing is real
Nor the noise of death drawing water

We are the echo of the future

On the door it says what to do to survive
But we were not born to survive
Only to live

For the Anniversary of My Death

Every year without knowing it I have passed the day
When the last fires will wave to me
And the silence will set out

Tireless traveller
Like the beam of a lightless star

Then I will no longer
Find myself in life as in a strange garment
Surprised at the earth
And the love of one woman
And the shamelessness of men
As today writing after three days of rain
Hearing the wren sing and the falling cease
And bowing not knowing to what

The Asians Dying

When the forests have been destroyed their darkness remains
The ash the great walker follows the possessors
Forever
Nothing they will come to is real
Nor for long
Over the watercourses
Like ducks in the time of the ducks
The ghosts of the villages trail in the sky
Making a new twilight

Rain falls into the open eyes of the dead
Again again with its pointless sound
When the moon finds them they are the color of everything

The nights disappear like bruises but nothing is healed
The dead go away like bruises
The blood vanishes into the poisoned farmlands
Pain the horizon
Remains
Overhead the seasons rock
They are paper bells
Calling to nothing living

The possessors move everywhere under Death their star
Like columns of smoke they advance into the shadows
Like thin flames with no light
They with no past
And fire their only future

For a Coming Extinction

Gray whale
Now that we are sending you to The End
That great god
Tell him
That we who follow you invented forgiveness
And forgive nothing

I write as though you could understand
And I could say it
One must always pretend something
Among the dying
When you have left the seas nodding on their stalks
Empty of you
Tell him that we were made
On another day

The bewilderment will diminish like an echo
Winding along your inner mountains
Unheard by us
And find its way out
Leaving behind it the future
Dead
And ours

When you will not see again
The whale calves trying the light
Consider what you will find in the black garden

And its court
The sea cows the Great Auks the gorillas
The irreplaceable hosts ranged countless
And fore-ordaining as stars
Our sacrifices
Join your word to theirs
Tell him
That it is we who are important

The Night of the Shirts

Oh pile of white shirts who is coming
to breathe in your shapes to carry your numbers
to appear
what hearts
are moving toward their garments here
their days
what troubles beating between arms

you look upward through
each other saying nothing has happened
and it has gone away and is sleeping
having told the same story
and we exist from within
eyes of the gods

you lie on your backs
and the wounds are not made
the blood has not heard
the boat has not turned to stone
and the dark wires to the bulb
are full of the voice of the unborn

Bread

Each face in the street is a slice of bread
wandering on
searching

somewhere in the light the true hunger
appears to be passing them by
they clutch

have they forgotten the pale caves
they dreamed of hiding in
their own caves
full of the waiting of their footprints
hung with the hollow marks of their groping
full of their sleep and their hiding

have they forgotten the ragged tunnels
they dreamed of following in out of the light
to hear step after step
the heart of bread
to be sustained by its dark breath
and emerge

to find themselves alone
before a wheat field
raising its radiance to the moon

St Vincent's

Thinking of rain clouds that rose over the city
on the first day of the year

in the same month
I consider that I have lived daily and with

eyes open and ears to hear
these years across from St Vincent's Hospital
above whose roof those clouds rose

its bricks by day a French red under
cross facing south
blown-up neo-classic facades the tall
dark openings between columns at
the dawn of history
exploded into many windows
in a mortised face

inside it the ambulances have unloaded
after sirens' howling nearer through traffic on
Seventh Avenue long
ago I learned not to hear them
even when the sirens stop

they turn to back in
few passers-by stay to look
and neither do I

at night two long blue
windows and one short one on the top floor
burn all night
many nights when most of the others are out
on what floor do they have
anything

I have seen the building drift moonlit through geraniums
late at night when trucks were few
moon just past the full
upper windows parts of the sky
as long as I looked
I watched it at Christmas and New Year
early in the morning I have seen the nurses ray out through
arterial streets
in the evening have noticed internes blocks away
on doorsteps one foot in the door

I have come upon the men in gloves taking out
the garbage at all hours
piling up mountains of

plastic bags white strata with green intermingled and
black
I have seen one pile
catch fire and studied the cloud
at the ends of the jets of the hoses
the fire engines as near as that
red beacons and
machine-throb heard by the whole body
I have noticed molded containers stacked outside
a delivery entrance on Twelfth Street
whether meals from a meal factory made up with those
mummified for long journeys by plane
or specimens for laboratory
examination sealed at the prescribed temperatures
either way closed delivery

and approached faces staring from above
crutches or tubular clamps
out for tentative walks
have paused for turtling wheel-chairs
heard visitors talking in wind on each corner
while the lights changed and
hot dogs were handed over at the curb
in the middle of afternoon
mustard ketchup onions and relish
and police smelling of ether and laundry
were going back

and I have known them all less than the papers of our days
smoke rises from the chimneys do they have an incinerator
what for
how warm do they believe they have to maintain the air
in there
several of the windows appear
to be made of tin
but it may be the light reflected

I have imagined bees coming and going
on those sills though I have never seen them

who was St Vincent

A . R . AMMONS
(b. 1926)

Born on a farm in Whiteville, North Carolina, Archibald Randolph
Ammons studied chemistry at Wake Forest, and science has continued
to shape his thought and metaphors. He went on to graduate study in
English at Berkeley, but for the next decade worked for a biological
glass manufacturing company in New Jersey while he wrote poems in
obscurity. He published his first book at his own expense. Ammons
has been a prolific poet and has allied himself with the Transcendental
strain of American writing. Epigrammatic poems of natural
observation—briefings, they could be called—alternate in Ammons's
work with long rambles in verse that brood on abstract or visionary
matters. The seasons and energies of creation, from cell to cosmos, are
his emblematic texts. Since 1964 he has taught at Cornell, and his
work has been honored with the National Book Award (1973),
the Bollingen Prize (1975), and the National Book Critics
Circle Award (1982).

He Held Radical Light

He held radical light
as music in his skull: music
turned, as
over ridges immanences of evening light
rise, turned
back over the furrows of his brain
into the dark, shuddered,
shot out again
in long swaying swirls of sound:

reality had little weight in his transcendence
so he
had trouble keeping
his feet on the ground, was

terrified by that
and liked himself, and others, mostly
under roofs:
nevertheless, when the
light churned and changed

his head to music, nothing could keep him
off the mountains, his
head back, mouth working,
wrestling to say, to cut loose
from the high, unimaginable hook:
released, hidden from stars, he ate,
burped, said he was like any one
of us: demanded he
was like any one of us.

Gravelly Run

I don't know somehow it seems sufficient
to see and hear whatever coming and going is,
losing the self to the victory
    of stones and trees,
of bending sandpit lakes, crescent
round groves of dwarf pine:

for it is not so much to know the self
as to know it as it is known
    by galaxy and cedar cone,
as if birth had never found it
and death could never end it:

the swamp's slow water comes
down Gravelly Run fanning the long
    stone-held algal

hair and narrowing roils between
the shoulders of the highway bridge:

holly grows on the banks in the woods there,
and the cedars' gothic-clustered
    spires could make
green religion in winter bones:

so I look and reflect, but the air's glass
jail seals each thing in its entity:

no use to make any philosophies here:
＇ I see no
god in the holly, hear no song from
the snowbroken weeds: Hegel is not the winter
yellow in the pines: the sunlight has never
heard of trees: surrendered self among
    unwelcoming forms: stranger,
hoist your burdens, get on down the road.

Corsons Inlet

I went for a walk over the dunes again this morning
to the sea,
then turned right along
    the surf
                    rounded a naked headland
                    and returned

    along the inlet shore:

it was muggy sunny, the wind from the sea steady and high,
crisp in the running sand,
    some breakthroughs of sun
    but after a bit

continuous overcast:

the walk liberating, I was released from forms,
from the perpendiculars,
    straight lines, blocks, boxes, binds
of thought
into the hues, shadings, rises, flowing bends and blends
         of sight:

              I allow myself eddies of meaning:
yield to a direction of significance
running
like a stream through the geography of my work:
  you can find
in my sayings
         swerves of action
         like the inlet's cutting edge:
      there are dunes of motion,
organizations of grass, white sandy paths of remembrance
in the overall wandering of mirroring mind:

but Overall is beyond me: is the sum of these events
I cannot draw, the ledger I cannot keep, the accounting
beyond the account:

in nature there are few sharp lines: there are areas of
primrose
    more or less dispersed;
disorderly orders of bayberry; between the rows
of dunes,
irregular swamps of reeds,
though not reeds alone, but grass, bayberry, yarrow, all . . .
predominantly reeds:

I have reached no conclusions, have erected no boundaries,
shutting out and shutting in, separating inside
    from outside: I have
    drawn no lines:
    as

manifold events of sand
change the dune's shape that will not be the same shape
tomorrow,

so I am willing to go along, to accept
the becoming
thought, to stake off no beginnings or ends, establish
      no walls:

by transitions the land falls from grassy dunes to creek
to undercreek: but there are no lines, though
      change in that transition is clear
      as any sharpness: but "sharpness" spread out,
allowed to occur over a wider range
than mental lines can keep:

the moon was full last night: today, low tide was low:
black shoals of mussels exposed to the risk
of air
and, earlier, of sun,
waved in and out with the waterline, waterline inexact,
caught always in the event of change:
      a young mottled gull stood free on the shoals
      and ate
to vomiting: another gull, squawking possession, cracked a
      crab,
picked out the entrails, swallowed the soft-shelled legs, a
      ruddy
turnstone running in to snatch leftover bits:

risk is full: every living thing in
siege: the demand is life, to keep life: the small
white blacklegged egret, how beautiful, quietly stalks and
      spears
         the shallows, darts to shore
               to stab—what? I couldn't
    see against the black mudflats—a frightened
    fiddler crab?

      the news to my left over the dunes and
reeds and bayberry clumps was
      fall: thousands of tree swallows
      gathering for flight:
      an order held
      in constant change: a congregation

rich with entropy: nevertheless, separable, noticeable
    as one event,
           not chaos: preparations for
flight from winter,
cheet, cheet, cheet, cheet, wings rifling the green clumps,
beaks
at the bayberries
  a perception full of wind, flight, curve,
  sound:
  the possibility of rule as the sum of rulelessness:
the "field" of action
with moving, incalculable center:

in the smaller view, order tight with shape:
blue tiny flowers on a leafless weed: carapace of crab:
snail shell:
    pulsations of order
    in the bellies of minnows: orders swallowed,
broken down, transferred through membranes
to strengthen larger orders: but in the large view, no
lines or changeless shapes: the working in and out, together
    and against, of millions of events: this,
           so that I make
           no form
           formlessness:

orders as summaries, as outcomes of actions override
or in some way result, not predictably (seeing me gain
the top of a dune,
the swallows
could take flight—some other fields of bayberry
    could enter fall
    berryless) and there is serenity:

    no arranged terror: no forcing of image, plan,
or thought:
no propaganda, no humbling of reality to precept:

terror pervades but is not arranged, all possibilities
of escape open: no route shut, except in
  the sudden loss of all routes:

I see narrow orders, limited tightness, but will
not run to that easy victory:
　　　still around the looser, wider forces work:
　　　I will try
　to fasten into order enlarging grasps of disorder, widening
scope, but enjoying the freedom that
Scope eludes my grasp, that there is no finality of vision,
that I have perceived nothing completely,
　　　that tomorrow a new walk is a new walk.

Reflective

　　　　　　　　　　I found a
　　　　　　　　　　weed
　　　　　　　　　　that had a

　　　　　　　　　　mirror in it
　　　　　　　　　　and that
　　　　　　　　　　mirror

　　　　　　　　　　looked in at
　　　　　　　　　　a mirror
　　　　　　　　　　in

　　　　　　　　　　me that
　　　　　　　　　　had a
　　　　　　　　　　weed in it

Terrain

　　The soul is a region without definite boundaries:
　　　it is not certain a prairie

can exhaust it
        or a range enclose it:
it floats (self-adjusting) like the continental mass,
    where it towers most
extending its deepest mantling base
        (exactly proportional):
does not flow all one way: there is a divide:
    river systems thrown like winter tree-shadows
against the hills: branches, runs, high lakes:
            stagnant lily-marshes:

is variable, has weather: floods unbalancing
    gut it, silt altering the
distribution of weight, the nature of content:
            whirlwinds move through it
or stand spinning like separate orders: the moon comes:
    there are barren spots: bogs, rising
by self-accretion from themselves, a growth into
            destruction of growth,
change of character,
    invasion of peat by poplar and oak: semi-precious
stones and precious metals drop from muddy water into mud:

it is an area of poise, really, held from tipping,
    dark wild water, fierce eels, countercurrents:
a habitat, precise ecology of forms
            mutually to some extent
tolerable, not entirely self-destroying: a crust afloat:
    a scum, foam to the deep and other-natured:
but deeper than depth, too: a vacancy and swirl:

it may be spherical, light and knowledge merely
    the iris and opening
to the dark methods of its sight: how it comes and
            goes, ruptures and heals,
whirls and stands still: the moon comes: terrain.

The City Limits

When you consider the radiance, that it does not withhold
itself but pours its abundance without selection into every
nook and cranny not overhung or hidden; when you consider

that birds' bones make no awful noise against the light but
lie low in the light as in a high testimony; when you consider
the radiance, that it will look into the guiltiest

swervings of the weaving heart and bear itself upon them,
not flinching into disguise or darkening; when you consider
the abundance of such resource as illuminates the glow-blue

bodies and gold-skeined wings of flies swarming the dumped
guts of a natural slaughter or the coil of shit and in no
way winces from its storms of generosity; when you consider

that air or vacuum, snow or shale, squid or wolf, rose or
      lichen,
each is accepted into as much light as it will take, then
the heart moves roomier, the man stands and looks about, the

leaf does not increase itself above the grass, and the dark
work of the deepest cells is of a tune with May bushes
and fear lit by the breadth of such calmly turns to praise.

JOHN ASHBERY
(b. 1927)

"Paradigms of common experience" is John Ashbery's label for his own poems: the mind listening for its haphazard memories and unconscious desires while hearing the world's buzzing distractions. "Most of my poems are about the experience of experience . . . and the particular experience is of lesser interest to me than the way it filters through me." An Ashbery poem can sound alternately daffy or romantic, disjunctive or satiric. Its surface may seem enigmatic, but its task remains constant—to explore how we receive information and make meanings, then how those meanings are transformed. From the start of his career, Ashbery has been among the most innovative poets in the language, and he has kept his work open to both experiment (including the example of the surrealists and cubists) and tradition. Ashbery was born on a farm in Sodus, New York, studied at Harvard and Columbia, then lived for some years in Paris, where he was a translator and art critic, before returning to New York. He has taught creative writing at Brooklyn College and been honored with the Pulitzer Prize, the National Book Award, and the National Book Critics Circle Award, all in 1976; in 1985 he won the Bollingen Prize.

Glazunoviana

The man with the red hat
And the polar bear, is he here too?
The window giving on shade,
Is that here too?
And all the little helps,
My initials in the sky,
The hay of an arctic summer night?

The bear
Drops dead in sight of the window.
Lovely tribes have just moved to the north.

In the flickering evening the martins grow denser.
Rivers of wings surround us and vast tribulation.

Soonest Mended

Barely tolerated, living on the margin
In our technological society, we were always having to be
    rescued
On the brink of destruction, like heroines in *Orlando Furioso*
Before it was time to start all over again.
There would be thunder in the bushes, a rustling of coils,
And Angelica, in the Ingres painting, was considering
The colorful but small monster near her toe, as though
    wondering whether forgetting
The whole thing might not, in the end, be the only solution.
And then there always came a time when
Happy Hooligan in his rusted green automobile
Came plowing down the course, just to make sure everything
    was OK,
Only by that time we were in another chapter and confused
About how to receive this latest piece of information.
Was it information? Weren't we rather acting this out
For someone else's benefit, thoughts in a mind
With room enough and to spare for our little problems (so they
    began to seem),
Our daily quandary about food and the rent and bills to be
    paid?
To reduce all this to a small variant,
To step free at last, minuscule on the gigantic plateau—
This was our ambition: to be small and clear and free.
Alas, the summer's energy wanes quickly,
A moment and it is gone. And no longer
May we make the necessary arrangements, simple as they are.
Our star was brighter perhaps when it had water in it.

Now there is no question even of that, but only
Of holding on to the hard earth so as not to get thrown off,
With an occasional dream, a vision: a robin flies across
The upper corner of the window, you brush your hair away
And cannot quite see, or a wound will flash
Against the sweet faces of the others, something like:
This is what you wanted to hear, so why
Did you think of listening to something else? We are all talkers
It is true, but underneath the talk lies
The moving and not wanting to be moved, the loose
Meaning, untidy and simple like a threshing floor.

These then were some hazards of the course,
Yet though we knew the course *was* hazards and nothing else
It was still a shock when, almost a quarter of a century later,
The clarity of the rules dawned on you for the first time.
They were the players, and we who had struggled at the game
Were merely spectators, though subject to its vicissitudes
And moving with it out of the tearful stadium, borne on
    shoulders, at last.
Night after night this message returns, repeated
In the flickering bulbs of the sky, raised past us, taken away
    from us,
Yet ours over and over until the end that is past truth,
The being of our sentences, in the climate that fostered them,
Not ours to own, like a book, but to be with, and sometimes
To be without, alone and desperate.
But the fantasy makes it ours, a kind of fence-sitting
Raised to the level of an esthetic ideal. These were moments,
    years,
Solid with reality, faces, nameable events, kisses, heroic acts,
But like the friendly beginning of a geometrical progression
Not too reassuring, as though meaning could be cast aside
    some day
When it had been outgrown. Better, you said, to stay cowering
Like this in the early lessons, since the promise of learning
Is a delusion, and I agreed, adding that
Tomorrow would alter the sense of what had already been
    learned,

That the learning process is extended in this way, so that from
    this standpoint
None of us ever graduates from college,
For time is an emulsion, and probably thinking not to grow up
Is the brightest kind of maturity for us, right now at any rate.
And you see, both of us were right, though nothing
Has somehow come to nothing; the avatars
Of our conforming to the rules and living
Around the home have made—well, in a sense, "good citizens"
    of us,
Brushing the teeth and all that, and learning to accept
The charity of the hard moments as they are doled out,
For this is action, this not being sure, this careless
Preparing, sowing the seeds crooked in the furrow,
Making ready to forget, and always coming back
To the mooring of starting out, that day so long ago.

As One Put Drunk into the Packet-Boat

I tried each thing, only some were immortal and free.
Elsewhere we are as sitting in a place where sunlight
Filters down, a little at a time,
Waiting for someone to come. Harsh words are spoken,
As the sun yellows the green of the maple tree. . . .

So this was all, but obscurely
I felt the stirrings of new breath in the pages
Which all winter long had smelled like an old catalogue.
New sentences were starting up. But the summer
Was well along, not yet past the mid-point
But full and dark with the promise of that fullness,
That time when one can no longer wander away
And even the least attentive fall silent
To watch the thing that is prepared to happen.

A look of glass stops you
And you walk on shaken: was I the perceived?
Did they notice me, this time, as I am,
Or is it postponed again? The children
Still at their games, clouds that arise with a swift
Impatience in the afternoon sky, then dissipate
As limpid, dense twilight comes.
Only in that tooting of a horn
Down there, for a moment, I thought
The great, formal affair was beginning, orchestrated,
Its colors concentrated in a glance, a ballade
That takes in the whole world, now, but lightly,
Still lightly, but with wide authority and tact.

The prevalence of those gray flakes falling?
They are sun motes. You have slept in the sun
Longer than the sphinx, and are none the wiser for it.
Come in. And I thought a shadow fell across the door
But it was only her come to ask once more
If I was coming in, and not to hurry in case I wasn't.

The night sheen takes over. A moon of cistercian pallor
Has climbed to the center of heaven, installed,
Finally involved with the business of darkness.
And a sigh heaves from all the small things on earth,
The books, the papers, the old garters and union-suit buttons
Kept in a white cardboard box somewhere, and all the lower
Versions of cities flattened under the equalizing night.
The summer demands and takes away too much,
But night, the reserved, the reticent, gives more than it takes.

Pyrography

Out here on Cottage Grove it matters. The galloping
Wind balks at its shadow. The carriages

Are drawn forward under a sky of fumed oak.
This is America calling:
The mirroring of state to state,
Of voice to voice on the wires,
The force of colloquial greetings like golden
Pollen sinking on the afternoon breeze.
In service stairs the sweet corruption thrives;
The page of dusk turns like a creaking revolving stage in
      Warren, Ohio.

If this is the way it is let's leave,
They agree, and soon the slow boxcar journey begins,
Gradually accelerating until the gyrating fans of suburbs
Enfolding the darkness of cities are remembered
Only as a recurring tie. And midway
We meet the disappointed, returning ones, without its
Being able to stop us in the headlong night
Toward the nothing of the coast. At Bolinas
The houses doze and seem to wonder why through the
Pacific haze, and the dreams alternately glow and grow dull.
Why be hanging on here? Like kites, circling,
Slipping on a ramp of air, but always circling?

But the variable cloudiness is pouring it on,
Flooding back to you like the meaning of a joke.
The land wasn't immediately appealing; we built it
Partly over with fake ruins, in the image of ourselves:
An arch that terminates in mid-keystone, a crumbling stone
      pier
For laundresses, an open-air theater, never completed
And only partially designed. How are we to inhabit
This space from which the fourth wall is invariably missing,
As in a stage-set or dollhouse, except by staying as we are,
In lost profile, facing the stars, with dozens of as yet
Unrealized projects, and a strict sense
Of time running out, of evening presenting
The tactfully folded-over bill? And we fit
Rather too easily into it, become transparent,
Almost ghosts. One day
The birds and animals in the pasture have absorbed

The color, the density of the surroundings,
The leaves are alive, and too heavy with life.

A long period of adjustment followed.
In the cities at the turn of the century they knew about it
But were careful not to let on as the iceman and the milkman
Disappeared down the block and the postman shouted
His daily rounds. The children under the trees knew it
But all the fathers returning home
On streetcars after a satisfying day at the office undid it:
The climate was still floral and all the wallpaper
In a million homes all over the land conspired to hide it.
One day we thought of painted furniture, of how
It just slightly changes everything in the room
And in the yard outside, and how, if we were going
To be able to write the history of our time, starting with
        today,
It would be necessary to model all these unimportant details
So as to be able to include them; otherwise the narrative
Would have that flat, sandpapered look the sky gets
Out in the middle west toward the end of summer,
The look of wanting to back out before the argument
Has been resolved, and at the same time to save appearances
So that tomorrow will be pure. Therefore, since we have to do
        our business
In spite of things, why not make it in spite of everything?
That way, maybe the feeble lakes and swamps
Of the back country will get plugged into the circuit
And not just the major events but the whole incredible
Mass of everything happening simultaneously and pairing off,
Channeling itself into history, will unroll
As carefully and as casually as a conversation in the next
        room,
And the purity of today will invest us like a breeze,
Only be hard, spare, ironical: something one can
Tip one's hat to and still get some use out of.

The parade is turning into our street.
My stars, the burnished uniforms and prismatic
Features of this instant belong here. The land

Is pulling away from the magic, glittering coastal towns
To an aforementioned rendezvous with August and December.
The hunch is it will always be this way,
The look, the way things first scared you
In the night light, and later turned out to be,
Yet still capable, all the same, of a narrow fidelity
To what you and they wanted to become:
No sighs like Russian music, only a vast unravelling
Out toward the junctions and to the darkness beyond
To these bare fields, built at today's expense.

And *Ut Pictura Poesis* Is Her Name

You can't say it that way any more.
Bothered about beauty you have to
Come out into the open, into a clearing,
And rest. Certainly whatever funny happens to you
Is OK. To demand more than this would be strange
Of you, you who have so many lovers,
People who look up to you and are willing
To do things for you, but you think
It's not right, that if they really knew you . . .
So much for self-analysis. Now,
About what to put in your poem-painting:
Flowers are always nice, particularly delphinium.
Names of boys you once knew and their sleds,
Skyrockets are good—do they still exist?
There are a lot of other things of the same quality
As those I've mentioned. Now one must
Find a few important words, and a lot of low-keyed,
Dull-sounding ones. She approached me
About buying her desk. Suddenly the street was
Bananas and the clangor of Japanese instruments.
Humdrum testaments were scattered around. His head

Locked into mine. We were a seesaw. Something
Ought to be written about how this affects
You when you write poetry:
The extreme austerity of an almost empty mind
Colliding with the lush, Rousseau-like foliage of its desire to
  communicate
Something between breaths, if only for the sake
Of others and their desire to understand you and desert you
For other centers of communication, so that understanding
May begin, and in doing so be undone.

Syringa

Orpheus liked the glad personal quality
Of the things beneath the sky. Of course, Eurydice was a part
Of this. Then one day, everything changed. He rends
Rocks into fissures with lament. Gullies, hummocks
Can't withstand it. The sky shudders from one horizon
To the other, almost ready to give up wholeness.
Then Apollo quietly told him: "Leave it all on earth.
Your lute, what point? Why pick at a dull pavan few care to
Follow, except a few birds of dusty feather,
Not vivid performances of the past." But why not?
All other things must change too.
The seasons are no longer what they once were,
But it is the nature of things to be seen only once,
As they happen along, bumping into other things, getting along
Somehow. That's where Orpheus made his mistake.
Of course Eurydice vanished into the shade;
She would have even if he hadn't turned around.
No use standing there like a gray stone toga as the whole
  wheel
Of recorded history flashes past, struck dumb, unable to utter
  an intelligent

Comment on the most thought-provoking element in its train.
Only love stays on the brain, and something these people,
These other ones, call life. Singing accurately
So that the notes mount straight up out of the well of
Dim noon and rival the tiny, sparkling yellow flowers
Growing around the brink of the quarry, encapsulates
The different weights of the things.

                                          But it isn't enough
To just go on singing. Orpheus realized this
And didn't mind so much about his reward being in heaven
After the Bacchantes had torn him apart, driven
Half out of their minds by his music, what it was doing to
    them.
Some say it was for his treatment of Eurydice.
But probably the music had more to do with it, and
The way music passes, emblematic
Of life and how you cannot isolate a note of it
And say it is good or bad. You must
Wait till it's over. "The end crowns all,"
Meaning also that the "tableau"
Is wrong. For although memories, of a season, for example,
Melt into a single snapshot, one cannot guard, treasure
That stalled moment. It too is flowing, fleeting;
It is a picture of flowing scenery, though living, mortal,
Over which an abstract action is laid out in blunt,
Harsh strokes. And to ask more than this
Is to become the tossing reeds of that slow,
Powerful stream, the trailing grasses
Playfully tugged at, but to participate in the action
No more than this. Then in the lowering gentian sky
Electric twitches are faintly apparent first, then burst forth
Into a shower of fixed, cream-colored flares. The horses
Have each seen a share of the truth, though each thinks,
"I'm a maverick. Nothing of this is happening to me,
Though I can understand the language of birds, and
The itinerary of the lights caught in the storm is fully apparent
    to me.
Their jousting ends in music much
As trees move more easily in the wind after a summer storm

And is happening in lacy shadows of shore-trees, now, day
    after day."

But how late to be regretting all this, even
Bearing in mind that regrets are always late, too late!
To which Orpheus, a bluish cloud with white contours,
Replies that these are of course not regrets at all,
Merely a careful, scholarly setting down of
Unquestioned facts, a record of pebbles along the way.
And no matter how all this disappeared,
Or got where it was going, it is no longer
Material for a poem. Its subject
Matters too much, and not enough, standing there helplessly
While the poem streaked by, its tail afire, a bad
Comet screaming hate and disaster, but so turned inward
That the meaning, good or other, can never
Become known. The singer thinks
Constructively, builds up his chant in progressive stages
Like a skyscraper, but at the last minute turns away.
The song is engulfed in an instant in blackness
Which must in turn flood the whole continent
With blackness, for it cannot see. The singer
Must then pass out of sight, not even relieved
Of the evil burthen of the words. Stellification
Is for the few, and comes about much later
When all record of these people and their lives
Has disappeared into libraries, onto microfilm.
A few are still interested in them. "But what about
So-and-so?" is still asked on occasion. But they lie
Frozen and out of touch until an arbitrary chorus
Speaks of a totally different incident with a similar name
In whose tale are hidden syllables
Of what happened so long before that
In some small town, one indifferent summer.

My Erotic Double

He says he doesn't feel like working today.
It's just as well. Here in the shade
Behind the house, protected from street noises,
One can go over all kinds of old feeling,
Throw some away, keep others.
                                        The wordplay
Between us gets very intense when there are
Fewer feelings around to confuse things.
Another go-round? No, but the last things
You always find to say are charming, and rescue me
Before the night does. We are afloat
On our dreams as on a barge made of ice,
Shot through with questions and fissures of starlight
That keep us awake, thinking about the dreams
As they are happening. Some occurrence. You said it.

I said it but I can hide it. But I choose not to.
Thank you. You are a very pleasant person.
Thank you. You are too.

JAMES WRIGHT
(1927–1980)

James Wright was born in Martins Ferry, Ohio, and many of his strongest poems return to the abandoned factory towns and lonely farms of the Midwest, to "the ache and sorrow of darkened earth." His speakers and subjects are often the alienated or socially outcast, in whose desolation the poet searched for salvation. Trying, he wrote, "to make the poems say something humanly important instead of just showing off with language," Wright's first books, influenced by Thomas Hardy and Edwin Arlington Robinson, still give evidence of a practiced formal grace. After working with Robert Bly on translating the work of Georg Trakl and Latin American poets, Wright evolved a new style of the "deep image." Drawn from elusive and visionary unconscious depths, these poems' epiphanies bring word and object into startling new alignments. Wright studied at Kenyon and later at the University of Washington with Theodore Roethke. He taught for many years at Hunter College. His *Collected Poems* won the Pulitzer Prize in 1972.

At the Executed Murderer's Grave

(for J. L. D.)

Why should we do this? What good is it to us? Above all, how can we do such a thing? How can it possibly be done?

—Freud

1

My name is James A. Wright, and I was born
Twenty-five miles from this infected grave,
In Martins Ferry, Ohio, where one slave
To Hazel-Atlas Glass became my father.
He tried to teach me kindness. I return
Only in memory now, aloof, unhurried,

To dead Ohio, where I might lie buried,
Had I not run away before my time.
Ohio caught George Doty. Clean as lime,
His skull rots empty here. Dying's the best
Of all the arts men learn in a dead place.
I walked here once. I made my loud display,
Leaning for language on a dead man's voice.
Now sick of lies, I turn to face the past.
I add my easy grievance to the rest:

2

Doty, if I confess I do not love you,
Will you let me alone? I burn for my own lies.
The nights electrocute my fugitive,
My mind. I run like the bewildered mad
At St. Clair Sanitarium, who lurk,
Arch and cunning, under the maple trees,
Pleased to be playing guilty after dark.
Staring to bed, they croon self-lullabies.
Doty, you make me sick. I am not dead.
I croon my tears at fifty cents per line.

3

Idiot, he demanded love from girls,
And murdered one. Also, he was a thief.
He left two women, and a ghost with child.
The hair, foul as a dog's upon his head,
Made such revolting Ohio animals
Fitter for vomit than a kind man's grief.
I waste no pity on the dead that stink,
And no love's lost between me and the crying
Drunks of Belaire, Ohio, where police
Kick at their kidneys till they die of drink.
Christ may restore them whole, for all of me.
Alive and dead, those giggling muckers who
Saddled my nightmares thirty years ago
Can do without my widely printed sighing
Over their pains with paid sincerity.
I do not pity the dead, I pity the dying.

4

I pity myself, because a man is dead.
If Belmont County killed him, what of me?
His victims never loved him. Why should we?
And yet, nobody had to kill him either.
It does no good to woo the grass, to veil
The quicklime hole of a man's defeat and shame.
Nature-lovers are gone. To hell with them.
I kick the clods away, and speak my name.

5

This grave's gash festers. Maybe it will heal,
When all are caught with what they had to do
In fear of love, when every man stands still
By the last sea,
And the princes of the sea come down
To lay away their robes, to judge the earth
And its dead, and we dead stand undefended everywhere,
And my bodies—father and child and unskilled criminal—
Ridiculously kneel to bare my scars,
My sneaking crimes, to God's unpitying stars.

6

Staring politely, they will not mark my face
From any murderer's, buried in this place.
Why should they? We are nothing but a man.

7

Doty, the rapist and the murderer,
Sleeps in a ditch of fire, and cannot hear;
And where, in earth or hell's unholy peace,
Men's suicides will stop, God knows, not I.
Angels and pebbles mock me under trees.
Earth is a door I cannot even face.
Order be damned, I do not want to die,
Even to keep Belaire, Ohio, safe.
The hackles on my neck are fear, not grief.

(Open, dungeon! Open, roof of the ground!)
I hear the last sea in the Ohio grass,
Heaving a tide of gray disastrousness.
Wrinkles of winter ditch the rotted face
Of Doty, killer, imbecile, and thief:
Dirt of my flesh, defeated, underground.

Autumn Begins in Martins Ferry, Ohio

In the Shreve High football stadium,
I think of Polacks nursing long beers in Tiltonsville,
And gray faces of Negroes in the blast furnace at Benwood,
And the ruptured night watchman of Wheeling Steel,
Dreaming of heroes.

All the proud fathers are ashamed to go home.
Their women cluck like starved pullets,
Dying for love.

Therefore,
Their sons grow suicidally beautiful
At the beginning of October,
And gallop terribly against each other's bodies.

Lying in a Hammock at William Duffy's Farm in Pine Island, Minnesota

Over my head, I see the bronze butterfly,
Asleep on the black trunk,

Blowing like a leaf in green shadow.
Down the ravine behind the empty house,
The cowbells follow one another
Into the distances of the afternoon.
To my right,
In a field of sunlight between two pines,
The droppings of last year's horses
Blaze up into golden stones.
I lean back, as the evening darkens and comes on.
A chicken hawk floats over, looking for home.
I have wasted my life.

Beginning

The moon drops one or two feathers into the field.
The dark wheat listens.
Be still.
Now.
There they are, the moon's young, trying
Their wings.
Between trees, a slender woman lifts up the lovely shadow
Of her face, and now she steps into the air, now she is gone
Wholly, into the air.
I stand alone by an elder tree, I do not dare breathe
Or move.
I listen.
The wheat leans back toward its own darkness,
And I lean toward mine.

A Blessing

Just off the highway to Rochester, Minnesota,
Twilight bounds softly forth on the grass.

And the eyes of those two Indian ponies
Darken with kindness.
They have come gladly out of the willows
To welcome my friend and me.
We step over the barbed wire into the pasture
Where they have been grazing all day, alone.
They ripple tensely, they can hardly contain their happiness
That we have come.
They bow shyly as wet swans. They love each other.
There is no loneliness like theirs.
At home once more,
They begin munching the young tufts of spring in the
    darkness.
I would like to hold the slenderer one in my arms,
For she has walked over to me
And nuzzled my left hand.
She is black and white,
Her mane falls wild on her forehead,
And the light breeze moves me to caress her long ear
That is delicate as the skin over a girl's wrist.
Suddenly I realize
That if I stepped out of my body I would break
Into blossom.

In Response to a Rumor That the Oldest Whorehouse in Wheeling, West Virginia, Has Been Condemned

I will grieve alone,
As I strolled alone, years ago, down along
The Ohio shore.
I hid in the hobo jungle weeds

Upstream from the sewer main,
Pondering, gazing.

I saw, down river,
At Twenty-third and Water Streets
By the vinegar works,
The doors open in early evening.
Swinging their purses, the women
Poured down the long street to the river
And into the river.

I do not know how it was
They could drown every evening.
What time near dawn did they climb up the other shore,
Drying their wings?
For the river at Wheeling, West Virginia,
Has only two shores:
The one in hell, the other
In Bridgeport, Ohio.

And nobody would commit suicide, only
To find beyond death
Bridgeport, Ohio.

A Winter Daybreak Above Vence

The night's drifts
Pile up below me and behind my back,
Slide down the hill, rise again, and build
Eerie little dunes on the roof of the house.
In the valley below me,
Miles between me and the town of St.-Jeannet,
The road lamps glow.
They are so cold, they might as well be dark.
Trucks and cars

Cough and drone down there between the golden
Coffins of greenhouses, the startled squawk
Of a rooster claws heavily across
A grove, and drowns.
The gumming snarl of some grouchy dog sounds,
And a man bitterly shifts his broken gears.
True night still hands on,
Mist cluttered with a racket of its own.

Now on the mountainside,
A little way downhill among turning rocks,
A square takes form in the side of a dim wall.
I hear a bucket rattle or something, tinny,
No other stirring behind the dim face
Of the goatherd's house. I imagine
His goats are still sleeping, dreaming
Of the fresh roses
Beyond the walls of the greenhouse below them
And of lettuce leaves opening in Tunisia.

I turn, and somehow
Impossibly hovering in the air over everything,
The Mediterranean, nearer to the moon
Than this mountain is,
Shines. A voice clearly
Tells me to snap out of it. Galway

Mutters out of the house and up the stone stairs
To start the motor. The moon and the stars
Suddenly flicker out, and the whole mountain
Appears, pale as a shell.

Look, the sea has not fallen and broken
Our heads. How can I feel so warm
Here in the dead center of January? I can
Scarcely believe it, and yet I have to, this is
The only life I have. I get up from the stone.
My body mumbles something unseemly
And follows me. Now we are all sitting here strangely
On top of the sunlight.

GALWAY KINNELL
(b. 1927)

Galway Kinnell has written, "Poetry has taken on itself the task of breaking out of the closed ego. . . . The death of the self I seek, in poetry and out of poetry, is not a drying up or withering. It is a death, yes, but a death out of which one might hope to be reborn more giving, more alive, more open, more related to the natural life." Between his early, more traditional poetry of the "closed ego" and his later poetry of the domestic self, Kinnell abandoned the strictures of formal verse and sought more expressive rhythms to capture the spiritual mystery of the physical world. Sharp images and a spilling rhetoric give his poems a weighted dreaminess, and sometimes—when he strikes a political note—a vatic amplitude. Kinnell was born in Providence, Rhode Island, served in the navy during World War II, and graduated from Princeton. He has traveled widely and made his living by teaching and poetry readings. In 1983 his *Selected Poems* received the Pulitzer Prize and the American Book Award. Since 1985 he has been a professor at New York University.

Vapor Trail Reflected in the Frog Pond

1

The old watch: their
thick eyes
puff and foreclose by the moon. The young, heads
trailed by the beginnings of necks,
shiver,
in the guarantee they shall be bodies.

In the frog pond
the vapor trail of a SAC bomber creeps,

I hear its drone, drifting, high up
in immaculate ozone.

2

And I hear,
coming over the hills, America singing,
her varied carols I hear:
crack of deputies' rifles practicing their aim on stray dogs
    at night,
sput of cattleprod,
TV groaning at the smells of the human body,
curses of the soldier as he poisons, burns, grinds, and stabs
the rice of the world,
with open mouth, crying strong, hysterical curses.

3

And by rice paddies in Asia
bones
wearing a few shadows
walk down a dirt road, smashed
bloodsuckers on their heels, knowing
the flesh a man throws down in the sunshine
dogs shall eat
and the flesh that is upthrown in the air
shall be seized by birds,
shoulder blades smooth, unmarked by old feather-holes,
hands rivered
by blue, erratic wanderings of the blood,
eyes crinkled up
as they gaze up at the drifting sun that gives us our lives,
seed dazzled over the footbattered blaze of the earth.

Last Songs

1

What do they sing, the last birds
coasting down the twilight,

banking
across woods filled with darkness, their
frayed wings
curved on the world like a lover's arms
which form, night after night, in sleep,
an irremediable absence?

2

Silence. Ashes
in the grate. Whatever it is
that keeps us from heaven,
sloth, wrath, greed, fear, could we only
reinvent it on earth
as song.

The Bear

1

In late winter
I sometimes glimpse bits of steam
coming up from
some fault in the old snow
and bend close and see it is lung-colored
and put down my nose
and know
the chilly, enduring odor of bear.

2

I take a wolf's rib and whittle
it sharp at both ends
and coil it up

and freeze it in blubber and place it out
on the fairway of the bears.

And when it has vanished
I move out on the bear tracks,
roaming in circles
until I come to the first, tentative, dark
splash on the earth.

And I set out
running, following the splashes
of blood wandering over the world.
At the cut, gashed resting places
I stop and rest,
at the crawl-marks
where he lay out on his belly
to overpass some stretch of bauchy ice
I lie out
dragging myself forward with bear-knives in my fists.

3

On the third day I begin to starve,
at nightfall I bend down as I knew I would
at a turd sopped in blood,
and hesitate, and pick it up,
and thrust it in my mouth, and gnash it down,
and rise
and go on running.

4

On the seventh day,
living by now on bear blood alone,
I can see his upturned carcass far out ahead, a scraggled,
steamy hulk,
the heavy fur riffling in the wind.

I come up to him
and stare at the narrow-spaced, petty eyes,
the dismayed

face laid back on the shoulder, the nostrils
flared, catching
perhaps the first taint of me as he
died.

I hack
a ravine in his thigh, and eat and drink,
and tear him down his whole length
and open him and climb in
and close him up after me, against the wind,
and sleep.

5

And dream
of lumbering flatfooted
over the tundra,
stabbed twice from within,
splattering a trail behind me,
splattering it out no matter which way I lurch,
no matter which parabola of bear transcendence,
which dance of solitude I attempt,
which gravity-clutched leap,
which trudge, which groan.

6

Until one day I totter and fall—
fall on this
stomach that has tried so hard to keep up,
to digest the blood as it leaked in,
to break up
and digest the bone itself: and now the breeze
blows over me, blows off
the hideous belches of ill-digested bear blood
and rotted stomach
and the ordinary, wretched odor of bear,

blows across
my sore, lolled tongue a song

or screech, until I think I must rise up
and dance. And I lie still.

7

I awaken I think. Marshlights
reappear, geese
come trailing again up the flyway.
In her ravine under old snow the dam-bear
lies, licking
lumps of smeared fur
and drizzly eyes into shapes
with her tongue. And one
hairy-soled trudge stuck out before me,
the next groaned out,
the next,
the next,
the rest of my days I spend
wandering: wondering
what, anyway,
was that sticky infusion, that rank flavor of blood, that poetry,
    by which I lived?

After Making Love We Hear Footsteps

For I can snore like a bullhorn
or play loud music
or sit up talking with any reasonably sober Irishman
and Fergus will only sink deeper
into his dreamless sleep, which goes by all in one flash,
but let there be that heavy breathing
or a stifled come-cry anywhere in the house
and he will wrench himself awake
and make for it on the run—as now, we lie together,

after making love, quiet, touching along the length of our
    bodies,
familiar touch of the long-married,
and he appears—in his baseball pajamas, it happens,
the neck opening so small
he has to screw them on, which one day may make him
    wonder
about the mental capacity of baseball players—
and flops down between us and hugs us and snuggles himself
    to sleep,
his face gleaming with satisfaction at being this very child.

In the half darkness we look at each other
and smile
and touch arms across his little, startlingly muscled body—
this one whom habit of memory propels to the ground of his
    making,
sleeper only the mortal sounds can sing awake,
this blessing love gives again into our arms.

The Man Splitting Wood
in the Daybreak

The man splitting wood in the daybreak
looks strong, as though, if one weakened,
one could turn to him and he would help.
Gus Newland was strong. When he split wood
he struck hard, flashing the bright steel
through air of daybreak so fast rock maple
leapt apart—as they think marriages will
in countries about to institute divorce—
and even willow, which, though stacked
to dry a full year, on separating

actually weeps—totem wood, therefore,
to the married-until-death—miseried asunder
with many small lip-smacking gasp-noises.
But Gus is dead. We could turn to our fathers,
but they protect us only through the unperplexed
looking-back of the numerals cut into their headstones.
Or to our mothers, whose love, so devastated,
can't, even in spring, break through the hard earth.
Our spouses weaken at the same rate we do.
We have to hold our children up to lean on them.
Everyone who could help goes or hasn't arrived.
What about the man splitting wood in the daybreak,
who looked strong? That was years ago. That was me.

The Vow

When the lover
goes, the vow though
broken remains, that
trace of eternity love
brings down among us
stays, to give
dignity to the suffering
and to intensify it.

The Man on the Hotel Room Bed

He shifts on the bed carefully, so as
not to press through the first layer

into the second, which is permanently sore.
For him sleep means lying as still as possible
for as long as possible thinking the worst.
Nor does it help to outlast the night—
in seconds after the light comes
the inner darkness falls over everything.
He wonders if the left hand of the woman
in the print hanging in the dark above the bed,
who sits half turned away, her right hand
clutching her face, lies empty,
or does it move in the hair of a man
who dies, or perhaps died long ago
and sometimes comes and puts his head in her lap,
and then is gone and lies under a sign
in a field filled nearly up to the roots
holding down the hardly ever trampled grass
with mortals, the once-lovers. He goes over
the mathematics of lying awake all night alone
in a strange room: still the equations require
multiplication, by fear, of what is,
to the power of desire. He feels around—
no pillow next to his, no depression
in the pillow, no head in the depression.
Love is the religion that bereaves the bereft.
No doubt his mother's arms still waver up
somewhere reaching for him; and perhaps
his father's are now ready to gather him
there where peace and death dangerously mingle.
But the arms of prayer, which pressed his chest
in childhood—long ago, he himself, in the name of truth,
let them go slack. He lies face-down,
like something washed up. Out the window
first light pinks the glass hotel across the street.
In the religion of love to pray is to pass,
by a shining word, into the inner chamber
of the other. It is to ask the father and mother
to return and be forgiven. But in this religion
not everyone can pray—least of all

a man lying alone to avoid being abandoned,
who wants to die to escape the meeting with death.
The final second strikes. On the glass wall
the daylight grows so bright the man sees
the next darkness already forming inside it.

ANNE SEXTON
(1928–1974)

Already a suburban housewife and mother, Anne Sexton began writing poetry in 1956 at her psychiatrist's suggestion, to help her understand and recover from one of the series of mental breakdowns that stalked her. Born in Newton, Massachusetts, she stayed near Boston all her life, and from 1969 until her death she taught at Boston University. Her early confessional work and virtuosic craft yielded in later books to a more surrealistic voice, flamboyant and searing, as she continued to explore her abiding subjects—the limits of sanity and the nature and roles of womanhood. Whether writing autobiographically, transforming Grimms' fairy tales, or recasting Christian myths, Sexton's work is marked by honesty, boldness, and a comic or morbid bravado. "Her gift," said her onetime teacher Robert Lowell, "was to grip, to give words to the drama of her personality." Sexton was awarded the Pulitzer Prize in 1967. She committed suicide in 1974.

Her Kind

I have gone out, a possessed witch,
haunting the black air, braver at night;
dreaming evil, I have done my hitch
over the plain houses, light by light:
lonely thing, twelve-fingered, out of mind.
A woman like that is not a woman, quite.
I have been her kind.

I have found the warm caves in the woods,
filled them with skillets, carvings, shelves,
closets, silks, innumerable goods;
fixed the suppers for the worms and the elves:
whining, rearranging the disaligned.

A woman like that is misunderstood.
I have been her kind.

I have ridden in your cart, driver,
waved my nude arms at villages going by,
learning the last bright routes, survivor
where your flames still bite my thigh
and my ribs crack where your wheels wind.
A woman like that is not ashamed to die.
I have been her kind.

Music Swims Back to Me

Wait Mister. Which way is home?
They turned the light out
and the dark is moving in the corner.
There are no sign posts in this room,
four ladies, over eighty,
in diapers every one of them.
La la la, Oh music swims back to me
and I can feel the tune they played
the night they left me
in this private institution on a hill.

Imagine it. A radio playing
and everyone here was crazy.
I liked it and danced in a circle.
Music pours over the sense
and in a funny way
music sees more than I.
I mean it remembers better;
remembers the first night here.
It was the strangled cold of November;
even the stars were strapped in the sky
and that moon too bright

forking through the bars to stick me
with a singing in the head.
I have forgotten all the rest.

They lock me in this chair at eight a.m.
and there are no signs to tell the way,
just the radio beating to itself
and the song that remembers
more than I. Oh, la la la,
this music swims back to me.
The night I came I danced a circle
and was not afraid.
Mister?

The Truth the Dead Know

*for my mother, born March 1902, died March 1959
and my father, born February 1900, died June 1959*

Gone, I say and walk from church,
refusing the stiff procession to the grave,
letting the dead ride alone in the hearse.
It is June. I am tired of being brave.

We drive to the Cape. I cultivate
myself where the sun gutters from the sky,
where the sea swings in like an iron gate
and we touch. In another country people die.

My darling, the wind falls in like stones
from the whitehearted water and when we touch
we enter touch entirely. No one's alone.
Men kill for this, or for as much.

And what of the dead? They lie without shoes
in their stone boats. They are more like stone
than the sea would be if it stopped. They refuse
to be blessed, throat, eye and knucklebone.

The Starry Night

That does not keep me from having a terrible need of—shall I say the word—religion. Then I go out at night to paint the stars.

VINCENT VAN GOGH in a letter to his brother

The town does not exist
except where one black-haired tree slips
up like a drowned woman into the hot sky.
The town is silent. The night boils with eleven stars.
Oh starry starry night! This is how
I want to die.

It moves. They are all alive.
Even the moon bulges in its orange irons
to push children, like a god, from its eye.
The old unseen serpent swallows up the stars.
Oh starry starry night! This is how
I want to die:

into that rushing beast of the night,
sucked up by that great dragon, to split
from my life with no flag,
no belly,
no cry.

With Mercy for the Greedy

*for my friend, Ruth,
who urges me to make an appointment for the Sacrament of Confession*

Concerning your letter in which you ask
me to call a priest and in which you ask
me to wear The Cross that you enclose;
your own cross,

your dog-bitten cross,
no larger than a thumb,
small and wooden, no thorns, this rose—

I pray to its shadow,
that gray place
where it lies on your letter . . . deep, deep.
I detest my sins and I try to believe
in The Cross. I touch its tender hips, its dark jawed face,
its solid neck, its brown sleep.

True. There is
a beautiful Jesus.
He is frozen to his bones like a chunk of beef.
How desperately he wanted to pull his arms in!
How desperately I touch his vertical and horizontal axes!
But I can't. Need is not quite belief.

All morning long
I have worn
your cross, hung with package string around my throat.
It tapped me lightly as a child's heart might,
tapping secondhand, softly waiting to be born.
Ruth, I cherish the letter you wrote.

My friend, my friend, I was born
doing reference work in sin, and born
confessing it. This is what poems are:
with mercy
for the greedy,
they are the tongue's wrangle,
the world's pottage, the rat's star.

Wanting to Die

Since you ask, most days I cannot remember.
I walk in my clothing, unmarked by that voyage.
Then the almost unnameable lust returns.

Even then I have nothing against life.
I know well the grass blades you mention,
the furniture you have placed under the sun.

But suicides have a special language.
Like carpenters they want to know *which tools.*
They never ask *why build.*

Twice I have so simply declared myself,
have possessed the enemy, eaten the enemy,
have taken on his craft, his magic.

In this way, heavy and thoughtful,
warmer than oil or water,
I have rested, drooling at the mouth-hole.

I did not think of my body at needle point.
Even the cornea and the leftover urine were gone.
Suicides have already betrayed the body.

Still-born, they don't always die,
but dazzled, they can't forget a drug so sweet
that even children would look on and smile.

To thrust all that life under your tongue!—
that, all by itself, becomes a passion.
Death's a sad bone; bruised, you'd say,

and yet she waits for me, year after year,
to so delicately undo an old wound,
to empty my breath from its bad prison.

Balanced there, suicides sometimes meet,
raging at the fruit, a pumped-up moon,
leaving the bread they mistook for a kiss,

leaving the page of the book carelessly open,
something unsaid, the phone off the hook
and the love, whatever it was, an infection.

February 3, 1964

The Room of My Life

Here,
in the room of my life
the objects keep changing.
Ashtrays to cry into,
the suffering brother of the wood walls,
the forty-eight keys of the typewriter
each an eyeball that is never shut,
the books, each a contestant in a beauty contest,
the black chair, a dog coffin made of Naugahyde,
the sockets on the wall
waiting like a cave of bees,
the gold rug
a conversation of heels and toes,
the fireplace
a knife waiting for someone to pick it up,
the sofa, exhausted with the exertion of a whore,
the phone
two flowers taking root in its crotch,
the doors
opening and closing like sea clams,
the lights
poking at me,
lighting up both the soil and the laugh.
The windows,
the starving windows
that drive the trees like nails into my heart.
Each day I feed the world out there
although birds explode
right and left.
I feed the world in here too,
offering the desk puppy biscuits.
However, nothing is just what it seems to be.
My objects dream and wear new costumes,
compelled to, it seems, by all the words in my hands
and the sea that bangs in my throat.

PHILIP LEVINE
(b. 1928)

Born in Detroit, Philip Levine worked as an assembly man for Ford and as a railroad shipper in the early 1950s. He was educated at Wayne State University and at the University of Iowa; since 1958 he has taught at California State University at Fresno. He won the American Book Award in 1976 and the National Book Critics Circle Award in 1979. Levine has been called a poet of desolation. Early in his career he resolved "to find a voice for the voiceless"—for the dead souls of urban despair, the dispossessed and defeated. His concern was political as well as elegiac; the Spanish Civil War has been the focus of his assault on injustice. Pondering the fate of his emblematic cities, Detroit and Barcelona, Levine can celebrate memories of hope amidst the ruins. Written with a sure narrative command and a straightforward diction, his keening poems have an emotional intensity and control equal to the demands of his powerful subjects.

The Horse

for Ichiro Kawamoto,
humanitarian, electrician, & survivor of Hiroshima

They spoke of the horse alive
without skin, naked, hairless,
without eyes and ears, searching
for the stableboy's caress.
Shoot it, someone said, but they
let him go on colliding with
tattered walls, butting his long
skull to pulp, finding no path
where iron fences corkscrewed in
the street and bicycles turned
like question marks.
                    Some fled and

some sat down. The river burned
all that day and into the
night, the stones sighed a moment
and were still, and the shadow
of a man's hand entered
a leaf.
                    The white horse never
returned, and later they found
the stableboy, his back crushed
by a hoof, his mouth opened
around a cry that no one heard.

They spoke of the horse again
and again; their mouths opened
like the gills of a fish caught
above water.
                    Mountain flowers
burst from the red clay walls, and
they said a new life was here.
Raw grass sprouted from the cobbles
like hair from a deafened ear.
The horse would never return.

There had been no horse. I could
tell from the way they walked
testing the ground for some cold
that the rage had gone out of
their bones in one mad dance.

They Feed They Lion

Out of burlap sacks, out of bearing butter,
Out of black bean and wet slate bread,
Out of the acids of rage, the candor of tar,
Out of creosote, gasoline, drive shafts, wooden dollies,

They Lion grow.
                    Out of the gray hills
Of industrial barns, out of rain, out of bus ride,
West Virginia to Kiss My Ass, out of buried aunties,
Mothers hardening like pounded stumps, out of stumps,
Out of the bones' need to sharpen and the muscles' to stretch,
They Lion grow.
                    Earth is eating trees, fence posts,
Gutted cars, earth is calling in her little ones,
"Come home, Come home!" From pig balls,
From the ferocity of pig driven to holiness,
From the furred ear and the full jowl come
The repose of the hung belly, from the purpose
They Lion grow.
                    From the sweet glues of the trotters
Come the sweet kinks of the fist, from the full flower
Of the hams the thorax of caves,
From "Bow Down" come "Rise Up,"
Come they Lion from the reeds of shovels,
The grained arm that pulls the hands,
They Lion grow.
                    From my five arms and all my hands,
From all my white sins forgiven, they feed,
From my car passing under the stars,
They Lion, from my children inherit,
From the oak turned to a wall, they Lion,
From they sack and they belly opened
And all that was hidden burning on the oil-stained earth
They feed they Lion and he comes.

Belle Isle, 1949

We stripped in the first warm spring night
and ran down into the Detroit River

to baptize ourselves in the brine
of car parts, dead fish, stolen bicycles,
melted snow. I remember going under
hand in hand with a Polish highschool girl
I'd never seen before, and the cries
our breath made caught at the same time
on the cold, and rising through the layers
of darkness into the final moonless atmosphere
that was this world, the girl breaking
the surface after me and swimming out
on the starless waters towards the lights
of Jefferson Ave. and the stacks
of the old stove factory unwinking.
Turning at last to see no island at all
but a perfect calm dark as far
as there was sight, and then a light
and another riding low out ahead
to bring us home, ore boats maybe, or smokers
walking alone. Back panting
to the gray coarse beach we didn't dare
fall on, the damp piles of clothes,
and dressing side by side in silence
to go back where we came from.

You Can Have It

My brother comes home from work
and climbs the stairs to our room.
I can hear the bed groan and his shoes drop
one by one. You can have it, he says.

The moonlight streams in the window
and his unshaven face is whitened

like the face of the moon. He will sleep
long after noon and waken to find me gone.

Thirty years will pass before I remember
that moment when suddenly I knew each man
has one brother who dies when he sleeps
and sleeps when he rises to face this life,

and that together they are only one man
sharing a heart that always labors, hands
yellowed and cracked, a mouth that gasps
for breath and asks, Am I gonna make it?

All night at the ice plant he had fed
the chute its silvery blocks, and then I
stacked cases of orange soda for the children
of Kentucky, one gray boxcar at a time

with always two more waiting. We were twenty
for such a short time and always in
the wrong clothes, crusted with dirt
and sweat. I think now we were never twenty.

In 1948 in the city of Detroit, founded
by de la Mothe Cadillac for the distant purposes
of Henry Ford, no one wakened or died,
no one walked the streets or stoked a furnace,

for there was no such year, and now
that year has fallen off all the old newspapers,
calendars, doctors' appointments, bonds,
wedding certificates, drivers licenses.

The city slept. The snow turned to ice.
The ice to standing pools or rivers
racing in the gutters. Then bright grass rose
between the thousands of cracked squares,

and that grass died. I give you back 1948.
I give you all the years from then
to the coming one. Give me back the moon
with its frail light falling across a face.

Give me back my young brother, hard
and furious, with wide shoulders and a curse
for God and burning eyes that look upon
all creation and say, You can have it.

Rain Downriver

It has been raining now since
long before dawn, and the windows
of the Arab coffee house of Delray
are steamed over and no one looks
in or out. If I were on my way
home from the great chemical plant
on a bus of sodden men, heads rolling
with each swerve or lurch, I would get
off just here by the pale pink temple
and walk slowly the one block back
and swing open the doors on blue smoke
and that blurred language in which two
plus two means the waters of earth
have no end or beginning. I would sit
down at an empty table and open
a newspaper in which the atoms
of each meaningless lie are weighed
and I would order one bitter cup
and formally salute the ceiling,
which is blue like heaven but is
coming down in long bandages
revealing the wounds of the last rain.
In this state, which is not madness
but Michigan, here in the suburbs
of the City of God, rain brings back
the gasoline we blew in the face
of creation and sulphur which will not

soften iron or even yellow rice.
If the Messenger entered now
and called out, You are my people!
the tired waiter would waken and bring
him a coffee and an old newspaper
so that he might read in the wrong words
why the earth gives each of us
a new morning to begin the day
and later brings darkness to hide
what we did with it. Rain in winter
began first in the mind of God
as only the smallest thought,
but as the years passed quietly
into each other leaving only
the charred remains of empty hands
and the one glass that never overflowed
it came closer like the cold breath
of someone who has run through snow
to bring you news of a first birth
or to give you his abrupt, wet blessing
on the forehead. So now I go back
out into it. From a sky I can
no longer see, the fall of evening
glistens around my shoulders that
also glisten, and the world is mine.

Sweet Will

The man who stood beside me
34 years ago this night fell
on to the concrete, oily floor
of Detroit Transmission, and we
stepped carefully over him until
he wakened and went back to his press.

It was Friday night, and the others
told me that every Friday he drank
more than he could hold and fell
and he wasn't any dumber for it
so just let him get up at his
own sweet will or he'll hit you.

"At his own sweet will," was just
what the old black man said to me,
and he smiled the smile of one
who is still surprised that dawn
graying the cracked and broken windows
could start us all to singing in the cold.

Stash rose and wiped the back of his head
with a crumpled handkerchief and looked
at his own blood as though it were
dirt and puzzled as to how
it got there and then wiped the ends
of his fingers carefully one at a time

the way the mother wipes the fingers
of a sleeping child, and climbed back
on his wooden soda-pop case to
his punch press and hollered at all
of us over the oceanic roar of work,
addressing us by our names and nations—

"Nigger, Kike, Hunky, River Rat,"
but he gave it a tune, an old tune,
like "America the Beautiful." And he danced
a little two-step and smiled showing
the four stained teeth left in the front
and took another suck of cherry brandy.

In truth it was no longer Friday,
for night had turned to day as it
often does for those who are patient,
so it was Saturday in the year of '48
in the very heart of the city of man
where your Cadillac cars get manufactured.

In truth all those people are dead,
they have gone up to heaven singing
"Time on My Hands" or "Begin the Beguine,"
and the Cadillacs have all gone back
to earth, and nothing that we made
that night is worth more than me.

And in truth I'm not worth a thing
what with my feet and my two bad eyes
and my one long nose and my breath
of old lies and my sad tales of men
who let the earth break them back,
each one, to dirty blood or bloody dirt.

Not worth a thing! Just like it was said
at my magic birth when the stars
collided and fire fell from great space
into great space, and people rose one
by one from cold beds to tend a world
that runs on and on at its own sweet will.

IRVING FELDMAN
(b. 1928)

Irving Feldman was born in Coney Island, New York, and graduated from City College and Columbia. He has taught in Puerto Rico and France, at Kenyon, and since 1964 at the State University of New York at Buffalo. His work is unpredictable, veering from the visionary to the satiric. His diction and rhythms give Feldman's voice its quirky distinction, as he writes down "the slang and hot slurry of time." From Jewish fables, immigrant life, and family lore he has made wry poems, and the Holocaust has drawn passionate elegies from him. Goya and Picasso are among the artists Feldman has written of, and his long sequence "All of Us Here" takes the lifelike white-plaster figures of George Segal as its subject—images of ourselves that mirror our banalities and desires.

Family History

GENEALOGY

My family tree is mist and darkness.
Century after century,
one lay upon the other begetting me.
Then my millennium in marshes
and wandering obscurity
revealed my heritage:
monster, I lack immortality,
my race is superfluous on earth.
The last, the final generation
—after me no other, or someone else—
I lay down on top of death.
We keep our appointments with fate,
even if fate does not;
though no one came to kill me, I died.

I the ghost that I begot.
My tree is night and fog.*

MIT DEM SHPITS TSUNG AROYS†

The pink clue of mama's tongue,
the tip of it between her lips
when she concentrates, picking
at knots or threading a needle.
So she must have sat as a child,
a bit of sewing in her lap,
the tip of her tongue out showing
in imitation of her mother
or mother's mother—but I cannot
follow the clue any farther
and have nothing else to follow
into the lost domestic dark
of some small corner of the Pale.
Now she is patient but quick:
no false move, no motion wasted,
nothing that needs doing over,
nothing overdone or stinted,
everything measured *so,*
sized up by eye and no
anxiety, no pedantry.
Only now have I understood
I have no better measure for
the fitness of things than her gesture,
dreamy and alert and left-handed,
of pulling a thread to length
while the spool runs 'round in her hand.
She is proud of herself as a worker,
tireless, versatile, strong,
both craftsman and laborer.
When she aims her thread at the needle,
her wide gray eyes intensify
—in them no want, no waste, no withering—
and it pleases her to say,

*_Nacht und Nebel._ One of the Nazi extermination campaigns.
†Yiddish: With the tip of the tongue out.

*"Arbet macht dem leben ziess."**
Oh if it does, if it did
—though smeared in iron on the gate to hell—
then of hers the overflowing sweetness,
like a sugar tit touched to battered lips,
has made something of the darkness sweet.

IN THE EYE OF THE NEEDLE

Up on chairs as if they were floating
toward the kitchen ceiling, two sisters
are having hems set to the season's height,
to the middle of the knee, and no higher,
though they beg for half an inch, a quarter.
Robust and red-haired, they are two angels
beaming and grinning so they could never blow
the marvelous clarions their cheeks imply
—and I, fang still tender, venom milky,
small serpent smitten, witless with pleasure,
idling, moving my length along, spying,
summoned to Paradise by giggling
and chatter.
                    I saw this all
in the needle's eye—before time put it out—
compressed to two girls' gazes, hazel-eyed
and blue-eyed, one gentle, one imperious,
the soul at focus in its instant of sight,
expressive, shining there, revealed;
the seed of light flew down, a spark, two bits
of human seeing, and lay upon my heap
of gazes, bliss inexhaustibly blazing.

THE SINGER'S SINGER

"Vos zol ton a Yid? Epes a shneider."†

David at his harp, humming and clanking.
Fifty years of this have rounded his back,

---

*"Work makes life sweet."
†Yiddish: "What should a Jew do? [Shrugging.] A tailor."

and bending forward *looks* like prayer.
His rocking feet speed the iron treadle,
the needle fangs down faster and faster,
under the little foot, little teeth,
rising up, feed the cloth forward, male
and female together. Allegories
everywhere! A holy era for sure!
With rags, with crazy remnants he saved
—hoods and motley and mops and stars—
he pieces a garment together, cut
to no pattern, sizeless, mad, its unity
a oneness of confusion. "Old fool,"
I say, "what living man would wear your suit?
You sew for monsters, or sew for no one."
He glances up, blue eyes still squinting:
"The stone wall of terror on which you break
your head: nothing can be thought, nothing
can be done—and so, to do something,
to think nothing, you break your head.
You don't break down. You won't break through.
I, too. I sew an endless suit
to clothe the mist and keep it warm
and give it any shape I can.
My son, my son, here, please put it on."

The Dream

Once, years after your death, I dreamt
you were alive and that I'd found you
living once more in the old apartment.
But I had taken a woman up there
to make love to in the empty rooms.
I was angry at you who'd borne and loved me
and because of whom I believe in heaven.

I regretted your return from the dead
and said to myself almost bitterly,
"For godsakes, what was the big rush,
couldn't she wait one more day?"

And just so, daily somewhere Messiah
is shunned like a beggar at the door because
someone has something he wants to finish
or just something better to do, something
he prefers not to put off forever
—little pleasures so deeply wished
that Heaven's coming has to seem bad luck
or worse, God's intruding selfishness!

But you always turned Messiah away
with a penny and a cake for his trouble
—because wash had to be done, because
who could let dinner boil over and burn,
because everything had to be festive for
your husband, your daughters, your son.

F R O M All of Us Here

Simple Outlines, Human Shapes

Simple outlines, human shapes, daily acts, plain poses
—exhibits for the Museum of Humanity,
the place to take the kids on Sunday outings and show them
how it must have been to be, once upon a time,
a common man in the Century of the Common Man.
"Eternal" and homely, final but merely roughed out,
gentle and not to be budged from their perplexity,
and blanching still in the calamitous afterglow,

they're like completed destinies that are at the same time
just poor people who couldn't get out of the way,
whose names have been exalted into allegory:
Exile, Homeless, Refugee, Unknown, Mourner, Corpse.

And if we surround and see them from every side,
all the while we can't help putting ourselves in their places,
suffer for them their vulnerability to our eyes.
Life, defenseless life—with nothing left to defend!
We understand: so everything must be looking at us
with the sight that seeing too much burned from our gaze.
And if we, too, now lack inner refuge and outer force,
are the very horror your generation strolls among,
we *will* arise from these tombs of hoarfrost and ash
—if only for the children's sakes who've led us here
by the hand, and over and over touch their small faces
and crusted staring eyes to our stone fingertips—
we swear it . . .

—Surely they are saying over and over again
inside their black white silence *something* like this.
But what they suffered, they also did,
and we can't find it in our hearts to pity, or forgive.

Surely They're Just So Large

Surely they're just so large as their burdens allow,
and no smaller—yet—than the task at hand requires.
But when the light is right these figures of old earth
—the stooped pedestrian, the huddled subway rider—
are roused in their sad ghetto of anachronism
by today's untoward sun—and we see we've rolled down
the abyssal slope to a lost academy,
some dusty museum basement where plasters of
the classics have slept tumbled about cheek by jowl

in nameless peace all the minutes of these centuries:
heroes, athletes, titans in everyday clothing
who come racing in place from all the way back
to stand in no time at all—all of them, all of us
together here—at the abandoned finish line,
our fleet forerunners in prospective elegy,
champions, pioneers of the missing future:
this Laocoön braced against the supple void,
Atlas bearing up under a genocide or so,
and Sisyphus, his sleeves rolled, ready now to start
getting that apocalypse out of the cellar

—the stooped pedestrian, the huddled subway rider,
such shadows flung at speed of light across the world
by enormity, just peeping around the corner.

Of Course, We Would Wish

Of course, we would wish them angelic lookouts
on vigil to transmit—brightening and moving—
the glory still forthcoming, still pending . . .
alert geniuses of anticipation . . .
in the pure moment prior to speech. . . .

Sadly, it's the dead themselves they resemble,
no longer fussing to be served better and more,
withdrawing their demands on our attention,
and are humble suddenly and patient, keep
to their places, and make themselves smaller
to give death greater room, and hunch down farther.
It hurts to see them so decent and poor.
And it does no good to scold them for it,
to shout at these newly impoverished relations
crowding timidly in the narrow hallway,
or recall to them the old extravagance,

or tempt them back with favorite morsels
and the glowing tales that made the hearth warmer.
Not once more will they rise from the table
or come laughing out of the vestibule,
kicking the springtime's mud from their shoes.
The little and the less consume them now.
What a fever it is, to make do with nothing.
And throw off every word they ever wore,
the metaphors that made them legendary
—as if anything not literal bone, not plain
matter, was illusion, delirium, conceit,
swollenness of spirit prancing on show,
this corruption ailing in their ligaments now.
They are dying to be the letter itself:
immaculate, and perfect in form, minute,
not ever again to be read into,
and beyond whiteness white, sole, invisible.

JOHN HOLLANDER
(b. 1929)

Born in New York City, John Hollander received degrees from
Columbia and Indiana University and has spent his life in the
academic world, as teacher and versatile man of letters. He is now
professor of English at Yale. His first book—marked by wit, erudition,
and technical aplomb—was chosen by W. H. Auden for the Yale
Younger Poet series in 1958. But by the time he won the Bollingen
Prize in 1983, a more ambitious and introspective side of Hollander's
work had emerged. Having added a philosopher's rigor and a fabulist's
ingenuity to his style, he invents fictions of selfhood and of the world
as it is understood—subjectively distorted or enhanced—by the
human mind. In longer sequences that rely on subjects as diverse as
cloak-and-dagger espionage or cabalistic lore, Hollander's poetry offers
itself as a masque of interpretation. His shorter poems, kept close to
brooding patterns of speech, provide elegant, demanding
parables with a dark moral power.

The Night Mirror

What it showed was always the same—
A vertical panel with him in it,
Being a horrible bit of movement
At the edge of knowledge, overhanging
The canyons of nightmare. And when the last
Glimpse was enough—his grandmother,
Say, with a blood-red face, rising
From her Windsor chair in the warm lamplight
To tell him something—he would scramble up,
Waiting to hear himself shrieking, and gain
The ledge of the world, his bed, lit by
The pale rectangle of window, eclipsed
By a dark shape, but a shape that moved

And saw and knew and mistook its reflection
In the tall panel on the closet door
For itself. The silver corona of moonlight
That gloried his glimpsed head was enough
To send him back into silences (choosing
Fear in those chasms below), to reject
Freedom of wakeful seeing, believing
And feeling, for peace and the bondage of horrors
Welling up only from deep within
That dark planet head, spinning beyond
The rim of the night mirror's range, huge
And cold, on the pillow's dark side.

FROM **Powers of Thirteen**

3

So we came at last to meet, after the lights were out,
At someone's house or other, in a room whose ceiling
Light was accidentally switched off—and there you were
In a corner where I had not seen you just before
When I had rushed in looking for someone else. Even
Then the shadow of an earlier time deepened the
Room—and this was before I learned that in my childhood
You lived across the alley-way, the light of your room
Crept through my window-blinds, throwing ladders of light up
My ceiling in the dark (when I was four I thought that
"Shadows" meant spills of illumination from without).
Then, years later, I stumbled upon you, standing next
To an unlit floor lamp, against a mute looking-glass.

The Shadow

29

What she and I had between us once, America
And its hope had; and just as I grieve alternately
For what I know myself to have lost of what had been,
And for all that loss I was suffering all that while
I was doing, I thought, so well, so goes the nation,
Grieving for her hope, either lost, or from the very
Start, a lost cause. All our states and I are one in this.
O my America, my long-lost land lady of
The hardening ground, the house neither ancient nor in
Good repair, the brackish stream, the half-abandoned mill,
The red plastic bucket that hung in the place we kept
By the beach where, I remember, August evenings
Rang with hilarity until we trembled with cold.

An Old Song

69

Like some ill-fated butterfly, the literalists
Try to pin down—its illustrious wings extended
Not in eloquence, but unwittingly—the fragile
Spirit of doting, at all those layers of remove
From brass tacks. Yet after all, brass tacks get lost in time,
While what one was asked to get down to them from endures.
Thus: young, before sweets of doting had soured into doubt,
I made an idol of the image of her figure,
Until one soft night I found it squirming there beneath
My grateful but unbelieving body, in a bed
Borrowed but smooth with moonlight—at which the idol was
Destroyed, its shaping of desire usurped by the skill
Of remembrance, in her realm of frail-winged images.

Lepidoptery

82

"Yes, go on! This is plain talk of plainer feelings now,
Passion and pain in their imperative moods," cry the
Ninnies of experience. Fools of the omphalic
And the literal nod in comprehension. The soft
Coins stamped "STRONGLY FELT" clatter down the receptive
    slots
Of the automata of actuality, who
Start in on their dance of being deeply moved. When those
Unstrung puppets wind up their timely and mindless act,
All the ninnies buzz off to supper. Then you and I
Are finally alone, beyond the din of their ken.
Moonlight enters our unlit room and projects a bright
Shape on the wall outlined by our shadows, a figure
Of our connectedness, of what we have between us.

Twice-Told Tale

87

These two tales I tell of myself and the life I led
To its destruction, one dark, one bright: one gathered from
A few gleaming moments—a slice or two of the cake
From where it was perfectly marbled—the other one
Rising from an undersong of despair. In neither
Case is the truth of the story—or the story of
The possibility that either one could be true
Or false at all—of any interest. What matters
Is what they might be good for: the story of a lost
Joy, as a sad anchor to drop below the surface
Of where we keep on going; the other version of
What was, the tale of a hell escaped, easily sounds
Like a noisy breath of wind filling my patched old sails.

Tales of the Sea

130

After the midwinter marriages—the bride of snow
Now of one body with the black ground, the ice-heiress
Bedded with her constant rock, the far hills of one mind
With the bare sky now, and the emperor of rivers
Joined with the most recent of his flowing concubines—
After the choirs of the cold have died on the late air,
Low now as our unagitated humdrum heartbeats
Still go about their irreversible chores again,
You and I have heard the song of the long afterword:
The phrases of the moon crooning to the fields below,
The cracking language of frozen forests whose summer
Harps were long since smashed, and the profound, recurrent
      vow
This bright stream's soft echoing answer rings to the woods.

Metathalamia

Swan and Shadow

```
                            Dusk
                       Above the
                  water hang the
                       loud
                       flies
                       Here
                       O so
                       gray
                       then
            What          A pale signal will appear
            When        Soon before its shadow fades
            Where  Here in this pool of opened eye
            In us  No Upon us As at the very edges
              of where we take shape in the dark air
              this object bares its image awakening
              ripples of recognition that will
              brush darkness up into light
even after this bird this hour both drift by atop the perfect sad instant now
              already passing out of sight
              toward yet-untroubled reflection
              this image bears its object darkening
              into memorial shades Scattered bits of
            light  No of water Or something across
            water    Breaking up No Being regathered
            soon      Yet by then a swan will have
            gone         Yes out of mind into what
                       vast
                       pale
                       hush
                       of a
                       place
                       past
                  sudden dark as
                       if a swan
```

The Mad Potter

Now at the turn of the year this coil of clay
Bites its own tail: a New Year starts to choke
On the old one's ragged end. I bite my tongue
As the end of me—of my rope of stuff and nonsense
(The nonsense held, it was the stuff that broke),
Of bones and light, of levity and crime,
Of reddish clay and hope—still bides its time.

•

Each of my pots is quite unusable,
Even for contemplating as an object
Of gross unuse. In its own mode of being
Useless, though, each of them remains unique,
Subject to nothing, and themselves unseeing,
Stronger by virtue of what makes them weak.

•

I pound at all my clay. I pound the air.
This senseless lump, slapped into something like
Something, sits bound around by my despair.
For even as the great Creator's free
Hand shapes the forms of life, so—what? This pot,
Unhollowed solid, too full of itself,
Runneth over with incapacity.
I put it with the others on the shelf.

•

These tiny cups will each provide one sip
Of what's inside them, aphoristic prose
Unwilling, like full arguments, to make
Its points, then join them in extended lines
Like long draughts from the bowl of a deep lake.
The honey of knowledge, like my milky slip,
Firms slowly up against what merely flows.

•

Some of my older pieces bore inscriptions
That told a story only when you'd learned
How not to read them: LIVE reverted to EVIL,
EROS kept running backwards into SORE.
Their words, all fired up for truth, got burned.
I'll not write on weak vessels any more.

My juvenilia? I gave them names
In those days: Hans was all handles and no spout;
Bernie believed the whole world turned about
Himself alone; Sadie was close to James
(But Herman touched her bottom when he could);
Paul fell to pieces; Peter wore away
To nothing; Len was never any good;
Alf was a flat, random pancake, May
An opened blossom; Bud was an ash-tray.
Even their names break off, though: Whatsisface,
That death-mask of Desire, and—you know!—
The smaller version of that (Oh, what was it?—
You know . . .) All of my pots now have to go
By number only. Which is no disgrace.

Begin with being—in an anagram
Of unending—conclude in some dark den;
This is no matter. What I've been, I am:
What I will be is what I make of all
This clay, this moment. Now begin again . . .
Poured out of emptiness, drop by slow drop,
I start up at the quarreling sounds of water.
Pots cry out silently at me to stop.

What are we like? A barrelfull of this
Oozy wet substance, shadow-crammed, whose smudges
Of darkness lurk within but rise to kiss
The fingers that disturb the gentle edges
Of their bland world of shapelessness and bliss.

•

The half-formed cup cries out in agony,
The lump of clay suffers a silent pain.
I heard the cup, though, full of feeling, say
"O clay be true, O clay keep constant to
Your need to take, again and once again,
This pounding from your mad creator who
Only stops hurting when he's hurting you."

•

What will I then have left behind me? Over
The years I have originated some
Glazes that wear away at what they cover
And weep for what they never can become.
My Deadware, widely imitated; blue
Skyware of an amazing lightness; tired
Hopeware that I abandoned for my own
Good reasons; Hereware; Thereware; ware that grew
Weary of everything that earth desired;
Hellware that dances while it's being fired,
Noware that vanishes while being thrown.

•

Appearing to be silly, wisdom survives
Like tribes of superseded gods who go
Hiding in caves of triviality
From which they laughingly control our lives.
So with my useless pots: safe from the blow
Of carelessness, or outrage at their flaws,
They brave time's lion and his smashing paws.
—All of which tempts intelligence to call
Pure uselessness one more commodity.
The Good-for-Nothing once became our Hero,
But images of him, laid-back, carelessly
Laughing, were upright statues after all.
From straight above, each cup adds up to zero.

•

Clay to clay: Soon I shall indeed become
Dumb as these solid cups of hardened mud
(Dull *terra cruda* colored like our blood);
Meanwhile the slap and thump of palm and thumb
On wet mis-shapenness begins to hum
With meaning that was silent for so long.
The words of my wheel's turning come to ring
Truer than Truth itself does, my great *Ding*
Dong-an-sich that echoes everything
(Against it even lovely bells ring wrong):
Its whole voice gathers up the purest parts
Of all our speech, the vowels of the earth,
The aspirations of our hopeful hearts
Or the prophetic sibillance of song.

RICHARD HOWARD
(b. 1929)

Richard Howard was born in Cleveland, Ohio, and educated at
Columbia and the Sorbonne. His early work as a lexicographer and his
later career as a translator point toward the fascination with
words—from their etymologies to their overtones—that his poems
exhibit. Not merely the surfaces but the depth psychology of language
is his study: "the making of an inwardness from what is outside."
With his third book, *Untitled Subjects,* for which he was awarded the
Pulitzer Prize in 1970, Howard began a series of dramatic monologues,
closet dramas, and apostrophes that has obsessed him since and is
centered on the grand or decadent figures of nineteenth-century high
culture. Howard's portrayal of the burden and prerogatives of the
artistic sensibility is braced by a shrewd moralism, and his skeptical
but humane temperament underlies the extravagant
evocations he gives voice to.

Venetian Interior, 1889

for David Kalstone

Stand to one side. No, over here with me:
out of the light but out of darkness too,
where everything that is not odd or old
is gold and subjugates the shadows. There,
now you will be no trouble and behold none—
anything *but* trouble, at first glance,
last chance to see what I say is worth a look.

This whole palazzo is the property
of a middle-aged and penniless dilettante,
Pen Browning (Robert's son), who has made terms
—palatial terms, in fact—with towering
premises afforded by the tact

of his New York heiress, Fannie Coddington
Browning, dutiful daughter-in-law, doubtful wife.

Yet who would not be full of doubts, perplexed
at having to define Pen's talents and finance
his tastes? Their Ca' Rezzonico itself
is dubious. The ripened fruit of centuries,
rat- and roach-infested, peeling, rank,
withers with each tide that rots the piles,
though apt withal to weather these tenants as well . . .

He is painting from the model: *Dryope*,
undressed of course but draped against the draft
in a looping swathe of silver-printed stuff
that seems to move, glistening over flesh—
it *does* move! lapped in its silver mesh are coils
of a python wrapped in loving torpor round
the *contadina*'s undistracted torso.

The afternoon is numb: Dryope sleeps
in her pose, the python slips a little
down the umber slope of her thigh, and Pen,
inspired, slaps a dashing curlicue
across his canvas. "I had the Jew come by
with this brocaded velvet yesterday—
I bargained some old clothes against it, Fan,

so you needn't ask how much it cost in dollars."
To whom does Pen speak, his eyes intent, his hands
"working busily"? Beyond his "subject", look
past the unimposing *Dryope*, look through
the tufts of pampas grass extending up
to the tufa vault whose patination casts
a pall of watery splendor on the scene—

if you manage to overlook the sumptuous junk,
jasper urns, a suit of Japanese armor,
two stuffed bears, on the divan bearskins too—
there, or in this atmosphere let me say *lo!*
on that very divan Robert Browning lolls,

a short and foreshortened colossus with feet of clay
but the hardest imaginable cranium, among

his son's possessions slightly ill at ease
though well bestowed on slippery pelts, and plays
(against the wealthy Fannie—see her white shawl?)
at draughts with agate pieces, red and green,
like a page from some old parchment of kings and queens.
In approbation of his son's economies
the old man smiles now—but does she? The skull

interfering with our view of Fannie is,
I believe, or was the Mahdi's which Pen keeps
beside his easel (Victorians could make
anything into a tobacco jar). "I took
my pipe through Cannareggio on a long tramp
yesterday morning, right into the Ghetto,
looking for likely faces, which I found!

Didn't you say, Father, a satisfactory Jew
is worth a dozen Gentiles? The one who sold
that velvet to me is sure to be ready by Spring:
for *Lear,* you know, or *Lazarus* at least . . ."
Pen chatters on to charm the python, not
Dryope or Fannie who look up
only when the poet, roused, exclaims—

as rapt before himself as a child in front
of the Christmas tree: "A satisfactory Jew!
Setting mere Rothschildsplay aside, Pen,
I never saw but one in all my life:
Dizzy, I mean—the potent wizard himself,
at Hampton Court a dozen years ago,
murmuring at the Queen's ear like a wasp

who hoped to buzz his way into the diamonds . . .
With that olive cast and those glowing-coal-black eyes
and the mighty dome of his forehead (to be sure,
no Christian temple), as unlike a living man
as any waxwork at Madame Tussaud's:

354 • CONTEMPORARY AMERICAN POETRY

he had a face more mocking than a domino—
I would as soon have thought of sitting down

to tea with Hamlet or Ahasuerus . . ."
As if on cue, the poet's high voice fades,
the lights on his tree go out. Yet we have seen
enough and heard enough: the secret of losing
listeners—did Browning never learn?—
is to tell them everything. We lose details.
The Mahdi's skull and Fannie's coincide . . .

The scene blurs and the sounds become no more
than exaggerated silence. Stand with me
another moment till our presence is
sacrificed to transitions altogether.
Time will not console—at best it orders
into a kind of seasonable chaos.
Let me tell you, it will not take much

longer than a medical prescription—
I can give you ingredients, no cure . . .
Visitors to the palazzo used to speak
of the dangerous ménage—the menagerie!
Yet the Costa Rican python that cost Pen
(or Fannie) sixteen pounds was the first to go,
untempted by the rats of Rezzonico;

Dryope followed Dryope underground,
the girl carried off by a chill and buried
at San Michele, the great daub interred
in the cellars of the Metropolitan . . .
"Dear dead women, with such hair, too",
we quote, and notice that hair is the first
of ourselves to decay before—last after—death.

In a year Robert Browning too was dead, immortal;
in another, Fannie dropped her shawl and took
the veil and vows of an Episcopalian nun;
and Pen? Oh, Pen went on painting, of course—
buono di cuore, in yellow chamois gloves,

obese, oblivious, dithering into debt
and an easy death. The sale of what we saw

or saw through in Venice *realized,* as they say,
some thirty thousand pounds at Sotheby's.
I told you: first glance is last chance.
Darkness slides over the waters—oil sludge
spreading under, till even Venice dies,
immortally immerded. Earth has no other way,
our provisional earth, than to become

invisible in us and rise again.
Rezzonico . . . Disraeli . . . We realize our task.
It is to print earth so deep in memory
that a meaning reaches the surface. Nothing but
darkness abides, darkness demanding not
illumination—not from the likes of us—
but only that we yield. And we yield.

At the Monument to Pierre Louÿs

Jardin du Luxembourg

Sage nor Saint nor Soldier—these were not
the sobriquets he fastened onto Fame:
let other men indulge the mummery
endorsed by these obsequious thoroughfares

with such abandon, yard by gravelled yard—
theirs would not be the idols he adored.
What *were* the sacred semblances he chose
to traffic in? And did they cheat his trust?

Inchmeal moss has muddled the design:
a palm? a laurel? or an aureole

as futile as anathemas would be?
The cenotaph *his own estate* bequeathed

(as though forewarned no Popular Demand
would pay a sculptor, specify a plot
and meet the tariff of Perpetual Care)—
the cenotaph! obtrusive as it is,

thwarts all my efforts at decipherment.
Just as well. There is no cause to mind
whatever mutilations have occurred
as though in nothing solider than mud,

to mourn what the successive rain has made
of this "immutable" monstrosity
erected to an undermined career
beginning only when—as History does—

the tale it has to tell attains its end.
Appropriate decay: like "other men"
he lived in search of what he saw as joy,
ecstatic consolations. *There she stands!*

Balancing an urn as effortlessly
as if no more than his very ashes swelled
its brimming load, behind the stele looms
an academic Naiad rather worse

for wear but rising (the intent is clear)
gently from the reeds' enjambment—she
is cold but she is patient, waiting for
the furtive metal of her eyes to fill . . .

Glancing back in haste to catechize
her shoulders where they falter, suddenly
she catches up a hank of molten hair
and wrings it out as if it had become

another green, wet, heavy nenuphar:
she waits for the tune of little drops to fall . . .
Also appropriate: what else remains
of him but *l'odeur de la femme,* page after page?

And even that would soon evaporate
without the fickle traces of three friends
(Valéry desisted, Gide despised,
Debussy meant what he said but managed to die)

—save for such captious camaraderies,
nothing would survive a period taste
but this absurd contraption: brazen Muse
and marble slab on which all syllables

erode but APHRODITE BILITIS—
the rest is . . . silly. Who was Pierre Louÿs?
The real names of the poems in his books,
for all their happy Sapphic hoaxes, are

. . . and Other Poems. Night after night he wrote
as if there were a tide to float him on,
nacre enough to laminate his itch—
who was it called him an oyster inside a pearl?

If once and for all he could make chance into choice,
change what he had to love to what he wanted to . . .
Forever hostage to the chiding animal,
he was elided. In his will was no

peace, as he learned whenever a meal came late
or the nearest pissotière was occupied:
the change never ceases, never being complete.
There *is* a tide in the affairs of men,

but apt to strand them high and dry. You haunt
my frequentations of your great
contemporaries like a thirsty ghost . . .
I read you, *mon semblable, mon Pierre!*

ADRIENNE RICH
(b. 1929)

Adrienne Rich was born into a cultured, intellectual Baltimore family.
While she was still a precocious student at Radcliffe, her first book of
poems was chosen by W. H. Auden for the Yale Younger Poets series.
Over the next two decades her ambitions deepened as she shaped her
poems into instruments of analysis and discovery. Her involvement in
the political movements of the late 1960s eventually led to her radical
feminism, which is both an argument with the self and the effort,
personal and poetic, to recover a power prior to patriarchy. Her
lesbianism too, as Rich portrays it in her work, is less a sexual character-
istic than "the primary intensity between women" as they struggle to
fulfill themselves. More recent poems have explored her Jewish heritage,
the suicide of her husband, and the fate of women in history.
Rich continues to write provocative, even polemical prose as well,
and in all her work she has sought both the resources of change and
the "dream of a common language." Rich lived for many years
in New York City; she now lives in California,
where she teaches at Stanford.

Snapshots of a Daughter-in-Law

1

You, once a belle in Shreveport,
with henna-colored hair, skin like a peachbud,
still have your dresses copied from that time,
and play a Chopin prelude
called by Cortot: *"Delicious recollections*
float like perfume through the memory."

Your mind now, moldering like wedding-cake,
heavy with useless experience, rich
with suspicion, rumor, fantasy,
crumbling to pieces under the knife-edge
of mere fact. In the prime of your life.

Nervy, glowering, your daughter
wipes the teaspoons, grows another way.

2

Banging the coffee-pot into the sink
she hears the angels chiding, and looks out
past the raked gardens to the sloppy sky.
Only a week since They said: *Have no patience.*

The next time it was: *Be insatiable.*
Then: *Save yourself; others you cannot save.*
Sometimes she's let the tapstream scald her arm,
a match burn to her thumbnail,

or held her hand above the kettle's snout
right in the woolly steam. They are probably angels,
since nothing hurts her anymore, except
each morning's grit blowing into her eyes.

3

A thinking woman sleeps with monsters.
The beak that grips her, she becomes. And Nature,
that sprung-lidded, still commodious
steamer-trunk of *tempora* and *mores*
gets stuffed with it all: the mildewed orange-flowers,
the female pills, the terrible breasts
of Boadicea beneath flat foxes' heads and orchids.

Two handsome women, gripped in argument,
each proud, acute, subtle, I hear scream
across the cut glass and majolica
like Furies cornered from their prey:
The argument *ad feminam,* all the old knives
that have rusted in my back, I drive in yours,
ma semblable, ma soeur!

4

Knowing themselves too well in one another:
their gifts no pure fruition, but a thorn,

the prick filed sharp against a hint of scorn . . .
Reading while waiting
for the iron to heat,
writing, *My Life had stood—a Loaded Gun—*
in that Amherst pantry while the jellies boil and scum,
or, more often,
iron-eyed and beaked and purposed as a bird,
dusting everything on the whatnot every day of life.

5

Dulce ridens, dulce loquens,
she shaves her legs until they gleam
like petrified mammoth-tusk.

6

When to her lute Corinna sings
neither words nor music are her own;
only the long hair dipping
over her cheek, only the song
of silk against her knees
and these
adjusted in reflections of an eye.

Poised, trembling and unsatisfied, before
an unlocked door, that cage of cages,
tell us, you bird, you tragical machine—
is this *fertilisante douleur?* Pinned down
by love, for you the only natural action,
are you edged more keen
to prise the secrets of the vault? has Nature shown
her household books to you, daughter-in-law,
that her sons never saw?

7

*"To have in this uncertain world some stay
which cannot be undermined, is
of the utmost consequence."*

                    Thus wrote
a woman, partly brave and partly good,

who fought with what she partly understood.
Few men about her would or could do more,
hence she was labeled harpy, shrew and whore.

8

"You all die at fifteen," said Diderot,
and turn part legend, part convention.
Still, eyes inaccurately dream
behind closed windows blankening with steam.
Deliciously, all that we might have been,
all that we were—fire, tears,
wit, taste, martyred ambition—
stirs like the memory of refused adultery
the drained and flagging bosom of our middle years.

9

Not that it is done well, but
that it is done at all? Yes, think
of the odds! or shrug them off forever.
This luxury of the precocious child,
Time's precious chronic invalid,—
would we, darlings, resign it if we could?
Our blight has been our sinecure:
mere talent was enough for us—
glitter in fragments and rough drafts.

Sigh no more, ladies.
                    Time is male
and in his cups drinks to the fair.
Bemused by gallantry, we hear
our mediocrities over-praised,
indolence read as abnegation,
slattern thought styled intuition,
every lapse forgiven, our crime
only to cast too bold a shadow
or smash the mold straight off.

For that, solitary confinement,
tear gas, attrition shelling.
Few applicants for that honor.

10

                  Well,
she's long about her coming, who must be
more merciless to herself than history.
Her mind full to the wind, I see her plunge
breasted and glancing through the currents,
taking the light upon her
at least as beautiful as any boy
or helicopter,
              poised, still coming,
her fine blades making the air wince

but her cargo
no promise then:
delivered
palpable
ours.

                                    1958–1960

Planetarium

Thinking of Caroline Herschel (1750–1848)
astronomer, sister of William; and others.

                A woman in the shape of a monster
                a monster in the shape of a woman
                the skies are full of them

                a woman   'in the snow
                among the Clocks and instruments
                or measuring the ground with poles'

                in her 98 years to discover
                8 comets

                she whom the moon ruled
                like us

levitating into the night sky
riding the polished lenses

Galaxies of women, there
doing penance for impetuousness
ribs chilled
in those spaces   of the mind

An eye,

       'virile, precise and absolutely certain'
       from the mad webs of Uranusborg

               encountering the NOVA

every impulse of light exploding
from the core
as life flies out of us

       Tycho whispering at last
       'Let me not seem to have lived in vain'

What we see, we see
and seeing is changing

the light that shrivels a mountain
and leaves a man alive

Heartbeat of the pulsar
heart sweating through my body

The radio impulse
pouring in from Taurus

       I am bombarded yet I stand

I have been standing all my life in the
direct path of a battery of signals
the most accurately transmitted most
untranslatable language in the universe
I am a galactic cloud so deep   so invo-
luted that a light wave could take 15
years to travel through me   And has

taken   I am an instrument in the shape
of a woman trying to translate pulsations
into images   for the relief of the body
and the reconstruction of the mind.

                                            1968

The Burning of Paper Instead of Children

I was in danger of verbalizing my
moral impulses out of existence.
                    —Daniel Berrigan, on trial in Baltimore.

1. My neighbor, a scientist and art-collector, telephones me
in a state of violent emotion. He tells me that my son and his, aged
eleven and twelve, have on the last day of school burned a mathe-
matics textbook in the backyard. He has forbidden my son to come
to his house for a week, and has forbidden his own son to leave
the house during that time. "The burning of a book," he says,
"arouses terrible sensations in me, memories of Hitler; there are
few things that upset me so much as the idea of burning a book."

Back there: the library, walled
with green Britannicas
Looking again
in Dürer's *Complete Works*
for MELANCOLIA, the baffled woman

the crocodiles in Herodotus
the Book of the Dead
the *Trial of Jeanne d'Arc,* so blue
I think, It is her color

and they take the book away
because I dream of her too often

love and fear in a house
knowledge of the oppressor
I know it hurts to burn

2. To imagine a time of silence
or few words
a time of chemistry and music

the hollows above your buttocks
traced by my hand
or, *hair is like flesh,* you said

an age of long silence

relief

from this tongue   this slab of limestone
or reinforced concrete
fanatics and traders
dumped on this coast wildgreen clayred
that breathed once
in signals of smoke
sweep of the wind

knowledge of the oppressor
this is the oppressor's language

yet I need it to talk to you

3. *People suffer highly in poverty and it takes dignity and intelligence to overcome this suffering. Some of the suffering are: a child did not had dinner last night: a child steal because he did not have money to buy it: to hear a mother say she do not have money to buy food for her children and to see a child without cloth it will make tears in your eyes.*

(the fracture of order
the repair of speech
to overcome this suffering)

4. We lie under the sheet
after making love, speaking

of loneliness
relieved in a book
relived in a book
so on that page
the clot and fissure
of it appears
words of a man
in pain
a naked word
entering the clot
a hand grasping
through bars:

deliverance

What happens between us
has happened for centuries
we know it from literature

still it happens

sexual jealousy
outflung hand
beating bed

dryness of mouth
after panting

there are books that describe all this
and they are useless

You walk into the woods behind a house
there in that country
you find a temple
built eighteen hundred years ago
you enter without knowing
what it is you enter

so it is with us

no one knows what may happen
though the books tell everything

burn the texts   said Artaud

5. I am composing on the typewriter late at night, thinking of today. How well we all spoke. A language is a map of our failures. Frederick Douglass wrote an English purer than Milton's. People suffer highly in poverty. There are methods but we do not use them. Joan, who could not read, spoke some peasant form of French. Some of the suffering are: it is hard to tell the truth; this is America; I cannot touch you now. In America we have only the present tense. I am in danger. You are in danger. The burning of a book arouses no sensation in me. I know it hurts to burn. There are flames of napalm in Catonsville, Maryland. I know it hurts to burn. The typewriter is overheated, my mouth is burning, I cannot touch you and this is the oppressor's language.

1968

Paula Becker to Clara Westhoff

Paula Becker 1876–1907
Clara Westhoff 1878–1954

became friends at Worpswede, an artists' colony near Bremen, Germany, summer 1899. In January 1900, spent a half-year together in Paris, where Paula painted and Clara studied sculpture with Rodin. In August they returned to Worpswede, and spent the next winter together in Berlin. In 1901, Clara married the poet Rainer Maria Rilke; soon after, Paula married the painter Otto Modersohn. She died in a hemorrhage after childbirth, murmuring, *What a shame!*

The autumn feels slowed down,
summer still holds on here, even the light
seems to last longer than it should
or maybe I'm using it to the thin edge.
The moon rolls in the air. I didn't want this child.
You're the only one I've told.
I want a child maybe, someday, but not now.
Otto has a calm, complacent way
of following me with his eyes, as if to say

Soon you'll have your hands full!
And yes, I will; this child will be mine
not his, the failures, if I fail
will be all mine. We're not good, Clara,
at learning to prevent these things,
and once we have a child, it *is* ours.
But lately, I feel beyond Otto or anyone.
I know now the kind of work I have to do.
It takes such energy! I have the feeling I'm
moving somewhere, patiently, impatiently,
in my loneliness. I'm looking everywhere in nature
for new forms, old forms in new places,
the planes of an antique mouth, let's say, among the leaves.
I know and do not know
what I am searching for.
Remember those months in the studio together,
you up to your strong forearms in wet clay,
I trying to make something of the strange impressions
assailing me—the Japanese
flowers and birds on silk, the drunks
sheltering in the Louvre, that river-light,
those faces. . . . Did we know exactly
why we were there? Paris unnerved you,
you found it too much, yet you went on
with your work . . . and later we met there again,
both married then, and I thought you and Rilke
both seemed unnerved. I felt a kind of joylessness
between you. Of course he and I
have had our difficulties. Maybe I was jealous
of him, to begin with, taking you from me,
maybe I married Otto to fill up
my loneliness for you.
Rainer, of course, *knows* more than Otto knows,
he believes in women. But he feeds on us,
like all of them. His whole life, his art
is protected by women. Which of us could say that?
Which of us, Clara, hasn't had to take that leap
out beyond our being women
to save our work? or is it to save ourselves?
Marriage is lonelier than solitude.

Do you know: I was dreaming I had died
giving birth to the child.
I couldn't paint or speak or even move.
My child—I think—survived me. But what was funny
in the dream was, Rainer had written my requiem—
a long, beautiful poem, and calling me his friend.
I was *your* friend
but in the dream you didn't say a word.
In the dream his poem was like a letter
to someone who has no right
to be there but must be treated gently, like a guest
who comes on the wrong day. Clara, why don't I dream of
    you?
That photo of the two of us—I have it still,
you and I looking hard into each other
and my painting behind us. How we used to work
side by side! And how I've worked since then
trying to create according to our plan
that we'd bring, against all odds, our full power
to every subject. Hold back nothing
because we were women. Clara, our strength still lies
in the things we used to talk about:
how life and death take one another's hands,
the struggle for truth, our old pledge against guilt.
And now I feel dawn and the coming day.
I love waking in my studio, seeing my pictures
come alive in the light. Sometimes I feel
it is myself that kicks inside me,
myself I must give suck to, love . . .
I wish we could have done this for each other
all our lives, but we can't . . .
They say a pregnant woman
dreams of her own death. But life and death
take one another's hands. Clara, I feel so full
of work, the life I see ahead, and love
for you, who of all people
however badly I say this
will hear all I say and cannot say.

                                        1975–1976

For the Record

The clouds and the stars didn't wage this war
the brooks gave no information
if the mountain spewed stones of fire into the river
it was not taking sides
the raindrop faintly swaying under the leaf
had no political opinions

and if here or there a house
filled with backed-up raw sewage
or poisoned those who lived there
with slow fumes, over years
the houses were not at war
nor did the tinned-up buildings

intend to refuse shelter
to homeless old women and roaming children
they had no policy to keep them roaming
or dying, no, the cities were not the problem
the bridges were non-partisan
the freeways burned, but not with hatred

Even the miles of barbed-wire
stretched around crouching temporary huts
designed to keep the unwanted
at a safe distance, out of sight
even the boards that had to absorb
year upon year, so many human sounds

so many depths of vomit, tears
slow-soaking blood
had not offered themselves for this
The trees didn't volunteer to be cut into boards
nor the thorns for tearing flesh
Look around at all of it

and ask whose signature
is stamped on the orders, traced
in the corner of the building plans

Ask where the illiterate, big-bellied
women were, the drunks and crazies,
the ones you fear most of all: ask where you were.

1983

For an Album

Our story isn't a file of photographs
faces laughing under green leaves
or snowlit doorways, on the verge of driving
away, our story is not about women
victoriously perched on the one
sunny day of the conference,
nor lovers displaying love:

Our story is of moments
when even slow motion moved too fast
for the shutter of the camera:
words that blew our lives apart, like so,
eyes that cut and caught each other,
mime of the operating room
where gas and knives quote each other
moments before the telephone
starts ringing: our story is
how still we stood,
how fast.

1987

GARY SNYDER
(b. 1930)

"As a poet, I hold the most archaic values on earth," Gary Snyder has written. "They go back to the late Paleolithic: the fertility of the soil, the magic of animals, the power-vision in solitude, the terrifying initiation and re-birth, the love and ecstasy of the dance, the common work of the tribe. I try to hold both history and wilderness in mind, that my poems may approach the true measure of things and stand against the unbalance and ignorance of our times." Born in San Francisco and raised near Seattle, Snyder took a degree in anthropology from Reed College and later studied Oriental languages at Berkeley. He also worked as a seaman, logger, and forester; studied Buddhism in Japanese monasteries; traveled widely in Japan and India; and won the 1975 Pulitzer Prize. The rhythms of his poetry follow those of his thought and work. His Zen training helps him see "the inner world, before language, before custom, before culture." At the same time, his naturalist and ecological instincts direct Snyder's attention to the world's random and ritualized details.

Mid-August at Sourdough Mountain Lookout

Down valley a smoke haze
Three days heat, after five days rain
Pitch glows on the fir-cones
Across rocks and meadows
Swarms of new flies.

I cannot remember things I once read
A few friends, but they are in cities.
Drinking cold snow-water from a tin cup
Looking down for miles
Through high still air.

Riprap

Lay down these words
Before your mind like rocks.
            placed solid, by hands
In choice of place, set
Before the body of the mind
            in space and time:
Solidity of bark, leaf, or wall
            riprap of things:
Cobble of milky way,
            straying planets,
These poems, people,
            lost ponies with
Dragging saddles—
            and rocky sure-foot trails.
The worlds like an endless
            four-dimensional
Game of *Go*.
            ants and pebbles
In the thin loam, each rock a word
            a creek-washed stone
Granite: ingrained
            with torment of fire and weight
Crystal and sediment linked hot
            all change, in thoughts,
As well as things.

Burning Island

O Wave God   who broke through me today
    Sea Bream

374 · CONTEMPORARY AMERICAN POETRY

    massive pink and silver
    cool swimming down with me watching
             staying away from the spear

Volcano belly Keeper who lifted this island
    for our own beaded bodies adornment
    and sprinkles us all with his laugh—
          ash in the eye
    mist, or smoke,
    on the bare high limits—
          underwater lava flows easing to coral
            holes filled with striped feeding swimmers

O Sky Gods   cartwheeling
    out of   Pacific
    turning rainsqualls over like lids on us
    then shine on our sodden—
         (scanned out a rainbow today at the
           cow drinking trough
             sluicing off
       LAKHS of crystal Buddha Fields
      right on the hair of the arm!)

Who wavers right now in the bamboo:
    a half-gone waning moon.
             drank down a bowlful of shochu
               in praise of Antares
             gazing far up the lanes of Sagittarius
              richest stream of our sky—
    a cup to the center of the galaxy!
              and let the eyes stray
    right-angling the pitch of the Milky Way:
             horse-heads   rings
             clouds   too distant to *be*
             slide free.
             on the crest of the wave.

Each night
O Earth Mother
  I have wrappt my hand
  over the jut of your cobra-hood

                    sleeping;
          left my ear
All night long by your mouth.

O   All
Gods   tides   capes   currents
Flows and spirals of
          pool and powers—

As we hoe the field
     let sweet potato grow.
And as sit us all down when we may
To consider the Dharma
     bring with a flower and a glimmer.
Let us all sleep in peace   together.

Bless Masa and me as we marry
     at new moon   on the crater
This summer.

VIII. 40067

The Bath

Washing Kai in the sauna,
The kerosene lantern set on a box
     outside the ground-level window,

Lights up the edge of the iron stove and the
     washtub down on the slab
Steaming air and crackle of waterdrops
     brushed by on the pile of rocks on top
He stands in warm water
Soap all over the smooth of his thigh and stomach
     "Gary don't soap my hair!"
     —his eye-sting fear—

the soapy hand feeling
through and around the globes and curves of his body
up in the crotch,
And washing-tickling out the scrotum, little anus,
his penis curving up and getting hard
as I pull back skin and try to wash it
Laughing and jumping, flinging arms around,
I squat all naked too,

is this our body?

Sweating and panting in the stove-steam hot-stone
cedar-planking wooden bucket water-splashing
kerosene lantern-flicker wind-in-the-pines-out
sierra forest ridges night—
Masa comes in, letting fresh cool air
sweep down from the door
a deep sweet breath
And she tips him over gripping neatly, one knee down
her hair falling hiding one whole side of
shoulder, breast, and belly,
Washes deftly Kai's head-hair
as he gets mad and yells—
The body of my lady, the winding valley spine,
the space between the thighs I reach through,
cup her curving vulva arch and hold it from behind,
a soapy tickle   a hand of grail
The gates of Awe
That open back a turning double-mirror world of
wombs in wombs, in rings,
that start in music,

is this our body?

The hidden place of seed
The veins net flow across the ribs, that gathers
milk and peaks up in a nipple—fits
our mouth—
The sucking milk from this our body sends through
jolts of light; the son, the father,
sharing mother's joy

That brings a softness to the flower of the awesome
    open curling lotus gate I cup and kiss
As Kai laughs at his mother's breast he now is weaned
    from, we
    wash each other,
                    this our body

Kai's little scrotum up close to his groin,
    the seed still tucked away, that moved from us to him
In flows that lifted with the same joys forces
    as his nursing Masa later,
    playing with her breast,
Or me within her,
Or him emerging,
                    this is our body:

Clean, and rinsed, and sweating more, we stretch
    out on the redwood benches hearts all beating
Quiet to the simmer of the stove,
    the scent of cedar
And then turn over,
    murmuring gossip of the grasses,
    talking firewood,
Wondering how Gen's napping, how to bring him in
    soon wash him too—
These boys who love their mother
    who loves men, who passes on
    her sons to other women;

The cloud across the sky. The windy pines.
    the trickle gurgle in the swampy meadow

    this is our body.

Fire inside and boiling water on the stove
We sigh and slide ourselves down from the benches
    wrap the babies, step outside,

black night & all the stars.

Pour cold water on the back and thighs
Go in the house—stand steaming by the center fire

Kai scampers on the sheepskin
Gen standing hanging on and shouting,

"Bao! bao! bao! bao! bao!"

This is our body. Drawn up crosslegged by the flames
    drinking icy water
    hugging babies, kissing bellies,

Laughing on the Great Earth

Come out from the bath.

I Went into the Maverick Bar

I went into the Maverick Bar
In Farmington, New Mexico.
And drank double shots of bourbon
                    backed with beer.
My long hair was tucked up under a cap
I'd left the earring in the car.

Two cowboys did horseplay
                    by the pool tables,
A waitress asked us
                    where are you from?
a country-and-western band began to play
"We don't smoke Marijuana in Muskokie"
And with the next song,
                    a couple began to dance.

They held each other like in High School dances
                    in the fifties;
I recalled when I worked in the woods
                    and the bars of Madras, Oregon.
That short-haired joy and roughness—
                    America—your stupidity.
I could almost love you again.

We left—onto the freeway shoulders—
                    under the tough old stars—
In the shadow of bluffs
                    I came back to myself,
To the real work, to
                    "What is to be done."

Axe Handles

One afternoon the last week in April
Showing Kai how to throw a hatchet
One-half turn and it sticks in a stump.
He recalls the hatchet-head
Without a handle, in the shop
And go gets it, and wants it for his own.
A broken-off axe handle behind the door
Is long enough for a hatchet,
We cut it to length and take it
With the hatchet head
And working hatchet, to the wood block.
There I begin to shape the old handle
With the hatchet, and the phrase
First learned from Ezra Pound
Rings in my ears!
"When making an axe handle
            the pattern is not far off."
And I say this to Kai
"Look: We'll shape the handle
By checking the handle
Of the axe we cut with—"
And he sees. And I hear it again:
It's in Lu Ji's *Wên Fu,* fourth century
A.D. "Essay on Literature"—in the
Preface: "In making the handle

Of an axe
By cutting wood with an axe
The model is indeed near at hand."
My teacher Shih-hsiang Chen
Translated that and taught it years ago
And I see: Pound was an axe,
Chen was an axe, I am an axe
And my son a handle, soon
To be shaping again, model
And tool, craft of culture,
How we go on.

SYLVIA PLATH

(1932–1963)

A Boston native, Sylvia Plath graduated from Smith. While on a Fulbright Fellowship to study at Cambridge, she met and married the English poet Ted Hughes, whose subsequent influence on her work was crucial. Although her early manner was precociously studied, Plath's emphasis was autobiographical, and, because of the painful revelations in her later work, she has been grouped with Robert Lowell and Anne Sexton as a confessional poet. But gestures in her life of defiance and ecstasy, love or despair, her poems reimagine in archetypal patterns and a succession of heaped ideas and brilliant images. The voice in her mature poems is inflected with an angered or astonished irony. What Hughes called her "crackling verbal energy" is everywhere apparent in the poems' demonic rhythms, quick tonal contrasts, biting precision of word and image. The searing poems Plath wrote compulsively in the months before her suicide—about her children and her failed marriage, about death and her imagination—have seemed to readers since to be what Lowell once called them: her "appalling and triumphant fulfillment." Plath's posthumous *Collected Poems* was awarded the Pulitzer Prize in 1982.

The Colossus

I shall never get you put together entirely,
Pieced, glued, and properly jointed.
Mule-bray, pig-grunt and bawdy cackles
Proceed from your great lips.
It's worse than a barnyard.

Perhaps you consider yourself an oracle,
Mouthpiece of the dead, or of some god or other.
Thirty years now I have labored
To dredge the silt from your throat.
I am none the wiser.

Scaling little ladders with gluepots and pails of Lysol
I crawl like an ant in mourning
Over the weedy acres of your brow
To mend the immense skull-plates and clear
The bald, white tumuli of your eyes.

A blue sky out of the Oresteia
Arches above us. O father, all by yourself
You are pithy and historical as the Roman Forum.
I open my lunch on a hill of black cypress.
Your fluted bones and acanthine hair are littered

In their old anarchy to the horizon-line.
It would take more than a lightning-stroke
To create such a ruin.
Nights, I squat in the cornucopia
Of your left ear, out of the wind,

Counting the red stars and those of plum-color.
The sun rises under the pillar of your tongue.
My hours are married to shadow.
No longer do I listen for the scrape of a keel
On the blank stones of the landing.

The Hanging Man

By the roots of my hair some god got hold of me.
I sizzled in his blue volts like a desert prophet.

The nights snapped out of sight like a lizard's eyelid:
A world of bald white days in a shadeless socket.

A vulturous boredom pinned me in this tree.
If he were I, he would do what I did.

Morning Song

Love set you going like a fat gold watch.
The midwife slapped your footsoles, and your bald cry
Took its place among the elements.

Our voices echo, magnifying your arrival. New statue.
In a drafty museum, your nakedness
Shadows our safety. We stand round blankly as walls.

I'm no more your mother
Than the cloud that distills a mirror to reflect its own slow
Effacement at the wind's hand.

All night your moth-breath
Flickers among the flat pink roses. I wake to listen:
A far sea moves in my ear.

One cry, and I stumble from bed, cow-heavy and floral
In my Victorian nightgown.
Your mouth opens clean as a cat's. The window square

Whitens and swallows its dull stars. And now you try
Your handful of notes;
The clear vowels rise like balloons.

Daddy

You do not do, you do not do
Any more, black shoe
In which I have lived like a foot
For thirty years, poor and white,
Barely daring to breathe or Achoo.

Daddy, I have had to kill you.
You died before I had time——
Marble-heavy, a bag full of God,

Ghastly statue with one gray toe
Big as a Frisco seal

And a head in the freakish Atlantic
Where it pours bean green over blue
In the waters off beautiful Nauset.
I used to pray to recover you.
Ach, du.

In the German tongue, in the Polish town
Scraped flat by the roller
Of wars, wars, wars.
But the name of the town is common.
My Polack friend

Says there are a dozen or two.
So I never could tell where you
Put your foot, your root,
I never could talk to you.
The tongue stuck in my jaw.

It stuck in a barb wire snare.
Ich, ich, ich, ich,
I could hardly speak.
I thought every German was you.
And the language obscene

An engine, an engine
Chuffing me off like a Jew.
A Jew to Dachau, Auschwitz, Belsen.
I began to talk like a Jew.
I think I may well be a Jew.

The snows of the Tyrol, the clear beer of Vienna
Are not very pure or true.
With my gipsy ancestress and my weird luck
And my Taroc pack and my Taroc pack
I may be a bit of a Jew.

I have always been scared of *you*,
With your Luftwaffe, your gobbledygoo.
And your neat mustache
And your Aryan eye, bright blue.
Panzer-man, panzer-man, O You——

Not God but a swastika
So black no sky could squeak through.
Every woman adores a Fascist,
The boot in the face, the brute
Brute heart of a brute like you.

You stand at the blackboard, daddy,
In the picture I have of you,
A cleft in your chin instead of your foot
But no less a devil for that, no not
Any less the black man who

Bit my pretty red heart in two.
I was ten when they buried you.
At twenty I tried to die
And get back, back, back to you.
I thought even the bones would do.

But they pulled me out of the sack,
And they stuck me together with glue.
And then I knew what to do.
I made a model of you,
A man in black with a Meinkampf look

And a love of the rack and the screw.
And I said I do, I do.
So daddy, I'm finally through.
The black telephone's off at the root,
The voices just can't worm through.

If I've killed one man, I've killed two——
The vampire who said he was you
And drank my blood for a year,
Seven years, if you want to know.
Daddy, you can lie back now.

There's a stake in your fat black heart
And the villagers never liked you.
They are dancing and stamping on you.
They always *knew* it was you.
Daddy, daddy, you bastard, I'm through.

Fever 103°

Pure? What does it mean?
The tongues of hell
Are dull, dull as the triple

Tongues of dull, fat Cerberus
Who wheezes at the gate. Incapable
Of licking clean

The aguey tendon, the sin, the sin.
The tinder cries.
The indelible smell

Of a snuffed candle!
Love, love, the low smokes roll
From me like Isadora's scarves, I'm in a fright

One scarf will catch and anchor in the wheel.
Such yellow sullen smokes
Make their own element. They will not rise,

But trundle round the globe
Choking the aged and the meek,
The weak

Hothouse baby in its crib,
The ghastly orchid
Hanging its hanging garden in the air,

Devilish leopard!
Radiation turned it white
And killed it in an hour.

Greasing the bodies of adulterers
Like Hiroshima ash and eating in.
The sin. The sin.

Darling, all night
I have been flickering, off, on, off, on.
The sheets grow heavy as a lecher's kiss.

Three days. Three nights.
Lemon water, chicken
Water, water make me retch.

I am too pure for you or anyone.
Your body
Hurts me as the world hurts God. I am a lantern——

My head a moon
Of Japanese paper, my gold beaten skin
Infinitely delicate and infinitely expensive.

Does not my heat astound you. And my light.
All by myself I am a huge camellia
Glowing and coming and going, flush on flush.

I think I am going up,
I think I may rise——
The beads of hot metal fly, and I, love, I

Am a pure acetylene
Virgin
Attended by roses,

By kisses, by cherubim,
By whatever these pink things mean.
Not you, nor him

Not him, nor him
(My selves dissolving, old whore petticoats)——
To Paradise.

Ariel

Stasis in darkness.
Then the substanceless blue
Pour of tor and distances.

God's lioness,
How one we grow,
Pivot of heels and knees!—The furrow

Splits and passes, sister to
The brown arc
Of the neck I cannot catch,

Nigger-eye
Berries cast dark
Hooks——

Black sweet blood mouthfuls,
Shadows.
Something else

Hauls me through air——
Thighs, hair;
Flakes from my heels.

White
Godiva, I unpeel——
Dead hands, dead stringencies.

And now I
Foam to wheat, a glitter of seas.
The child's cry

Melts in the wall.
And I
Am the arrow,

The dew that flies
Suicidal, at one with the drive
Into the red

Eye, the cauldron of morning.

Lady Lazarus

I have done it again.
One year in every ten
I manage it——

A sort of walking miracle, my skin
Bright as a Nazi lampshade,
My right foot

A paperweight,
My face a featureless, fine
Jew linen.

Peel off the napkin
O my enemy.
Do I terrify?——

The nose, the eye pits, the full set of teeth?
The sour breath
Will vanish in a day.

Soon, soon the flesh
The grave cave ate will be
At home on me

And I a smiling woman.
I am only thirty.
And like the cat I have nine times to die.

This is Number Three.
What a trash
To annihilate each decade.

What a million filaments.
The peanut-crunching crowd
Shoves in to see

Them unwrap me hand and foot——
The big strip tease.
Gentlemen, ladies

These are my hands
My knees.
I may be skin and bone,

Nevertheless, I am the same, identical woman.
The first time it happened I was ten.
It was an accident.

The second time I meant
To last it out and not come back at all.
I rocked shut

As a seashell.
They had to call and call
And pick the worms off me like sticky pearls.

Dying
Is an art, like everything else.
I do it exceptionally well.

I do it so it feels like hell.
I do it so it feels real.
I guess you could say I've a call.

It's easy enough to do it in a cell.
It's easy enough to do it and stay put.
It's the theatrical

Comeback in broad day
To the same place, the same face, the same brute
Amused shout:

'A miracle!'
That knocks me out.
There is a charge

For the eyeing of my scars, there is a charge
For the hearing of my heart——
It really goes.

And there is a charge, a very large charge
For a word or a touch
Or a bit of blood

Or a piece of my hair or my clothes.
So, so, Herr Doktor.
So, Herr Enemy.

I am your opus,
I am your valuable,
The pure gold baby

That melts to a shriek.
I turn and burn.
Do not think I underestimate your great concern.

Ash, ash—
You poke and stir.
Flesh, bone, there is nothing there——

A cake of soap,
A wedding ring,
A gold filling.

Herr God, Herr Lucifer
Beware
Beware.

Out of the ash
I rise with my red hair
And I eat men like air.

Edge

The woman is perfected.
Her dead

Body wears the smile of accomplishment,
The illusion of a Greek necessity

Flows in the scrolls of her toga,
Her bare

Feet seem to be saying:
We have come so far, it is over.

Each dead child coiled, a white serpent,
One at each little

Pitcher of milk, now empty.
She has folded

Them back into her body as petals
Of a rose close when the garden

Stiffens and odors bleed
From the sweet, deep throats of the night flower.

The moon has nothing to be sad about,
Staring from her hood of bone.

She is used to this sort of thing.
Her blacks crackle and drag.

Words

Axes
After whose stroke the wood rings,
And the echoes!
Echoes traveling
Off from the center like horses.

The sap
Wells like tears, like the
Water striving
To re-establish its mirror
Over the rock

That drops and turns,
A white skull,
Eaten by weedy greens.
Years later I
Encounter them on the road——

Words dry and riderless,
The indefatigable hoof-taps.
While
From the bottom of the pool, fixed stars
Govern a life.

MARK STRAND
(b. 1934)

Born on Prince Edward Island in Canada but raised in the United States, Mark Strand graduated from Antioch, then attended both the Yale Art School and the Iowa Writers Workshop. He has spent some time teaching abroad and has translated poems from Spanish and Portuguese, in addition to writing fiction and art criticism. A frequent guest teacher at universities around the country, Strand is now professor of English at the University of Utah, and in 1990 was named the nation's fourth poet laureate. Like the paintings of Magritte, Strand's early poems manifest an eerie calm; their reticent narratives and spare, declarative tone only add to that effect. He calibrates details and moods so that they evade rather than accumulate meanings, and a disquieting element of menace slips between the gaps. Strand's meditations, for all the surreal strangeness of his material, have a decided elegance. His later work has grown broader, more overtly autobiographical and nostalgic.

Keeping Things Whole

In a field
I am the absence
of field.
This is
always the case.
Wherever I am
I am what is missing.

When I walk
I·part the air
and always
the air moves in
to fill the spaces
where my body's been.

We all have reasons
for moving.
I move
to keep things whole.

Coming to This

We have done what we wanted.
We have discarded dreams, preferring the heavy industry
of each other, and we have welcomed grief
and called ruin the impossible habit to break.

And now we are here.
The dinner is ready and we cannot eat.
The meat sits in the white lake of its dish.
The wine waits.

Coming to this
has its rewards: nothing is promised, nothing is taken away.
We have no heart or saving grace,
no place to go, no reason to remain.

The Prediction

That night the moon drifted over the pond,
turning the water to milk, and under
the boughs of the trees, the blue trees,
a young woman walked, and for an instant

the future came to her:
rain falling on her husband's grave, rain falling
on the lawns of her children, her own mouth
filling with cold air, strangers moving into her house,

a man in her room writing a poem, the moon drifting into it,
a woman strolling under its trees, thinking of death,
thinking of him thinking of her, and the wind rising
and taking the moon and leaving the paper dark.

"The Dreadful Has Already Happened"

The relatives are leaning over, staring expectantly.
They moisten their lips with their tongues. I can feel
them urging me on. I hold the baby in the air.
Heaps of broken bottles glitter in the sun.

A small band is playing old fashioned marches.
My mother is keeping time by stamping her foot.
My father is kissing a woman who keeps waving
to somebody else. There are palm trees.

The hills are spotted with orange flamboyants and tall
billowy clouds move behind them. "Go on, Boy,"
I hear somebody say, "Go on."
I keep wondering if it will rain.

The sky darkens. There is thunder.
"Break his legs," says one of my aunts,
"Now give him a kiss." I do what I'm told.
The trees bend in the bleak tropical wind.

The baby did not scream, but I remember that sigh
when I reached inside for his tiny lungs and shook them
out in the air for the flies. The relatives cheered.
It was about that time I gave up.

Now, when I answer the phone, his lips
are in the receiver; when I sleep, his hair is gathered
around a familiar face on the pillow; wherever I search
I find his feet. He is what is left of my life.

The Story of Our Lives

to Howard Moss

1

We are reading the story of our lives
which takes place in a room.
The room looks out on a street.
There is no one there,
no sound of anything.
The trees are heavy with leaves,
the parked cars never move.
We keep turning the pages,
hoping for something,
something like mercy or change,
a black line that would bind us
or keep us apart.
The way it is, it would seem
the book of our lives is empty.
The furniture in the room is never shifted,
and the rugs become darker each time
our shadows pass over them.
It is almost as if the room were the world.
We sit beside each other on the couch,
reading about the couch.
We say it is ideal.
It is ideal.

2

We are reading the story of our lives
as though we were in it,
as though we had written it.
This comes up again and again.
In one of the chapters
I lean back and push the book aside
because the book says
it is what I am doing.
I lean back and begin to write about the book.
I write that I wish to move beyond the book,

beyond my life into another life.
I put the pen down.
The book says: *He put the pen down*
and turned and watched her reading
the part about herself falling in love.
The book is more accurate than we can imagine.
I lean back and watch you read
about the man across the street.
They built a house there,
and one day a man walked out of it.
You fell in love with him
because you knew that he would never visit you,
would never know you were waiting.
Night after night you would say
that he was like me.
I lean back and watch you grow older without me.
Sunlight falls on your silver hair.
The rugs, the furniture,
seem almost imaginary now.
She continued to read.
She seemed to consider his absence
of no special importance,
as someone on a perfect day will consider
the weather a failure
because it did not change his mind.
You narrow your eyes.
You have the impulse to close the book
which describes my resistance:
how when I lean back I imagine
my life without you, imagine moving
into another life, another book.
It describes your dependence on desire,
how the momentary disclosures
of purpose make you afraid.
The book describes much more than it should.
It wants to divide us.

3
This morning I woke and believed
there was no more to our lives

than the story of our lives.
When you disagreed, I pointed
to the place in the book where you disagreed.
You fell back to sleep and I began to read
those mysterious parts you used to guess at
while they were being written
and lose interest in after they became
part of the story.
In one of them cold dresses of moonlight
are draped over the chairs in a man's room.
He dreams of a woman whose dresses are lost,
who sits in a garden and waits.
She believes that love is a sacrifice.
The part describes her death
and she is never named,
which is one of the things
you could not stand about her.
A little later we learn
that the dreaming man lives
in the new house across the street.
This morning after you fell back to sleep
I began to turn pages early in the book:
it was like dreaming of childhood,
so much seemed to vanish,
so much seemed to come to life again.
I did not know what to do.
The book said: *In those moments it was his book.*
A bleak crown rested uneasily on his head.
He was the brief ruler of inner and outer discord,
anxious in his own kingdom.

4

Before you woke
I read another part that described your absence
and told how you sleep to reverse
the progress of your life.
I was touched by my own loneliness as I read,
knowing that what I feel is often the crude
and unsuccessful form of a story
that may never be told.

I read and was moved by a desire to offer myself
to the house of your sleep.
He wanted to see her naked and vulnerable,
to see her in the refuse, the discarded
plots of old dreams, the costumes and masks
of unattainable states.
It was as if he were drawn
irresistibly to failure.
It was hard to keep reading.
I was tired and wanted to give up.
The book seemed aware of this.
It hinted at changing the subject.
I waited for you to wake not knowing
how long I waited,
and it seemed that I was no longer reading.
I heard the wind passing
like a stream of sighs
and I heard the shiver of leaves
in the trees outside the window.
It would be in the book.
Everything would be there.
I looked at your face
and I read the eyes, the nose, the mouth . . .

5

If only there were a perfect moment in the book;
if only we could live in that moment,
we could begin the book again
as if we had not written it,
as if we were not in it.
But the dark approaches
to any page are too numerous
and the escapes are too narrow.
We read through the day.
Each page turning is like a candle
moving through the mind.
Each moment is like a hopeless cause.
If only we could stop reading.
He never wanted to read another book

and she kept staring into the street.
The cars were still there,
the deep shade of trees covered them.
The shades were drawn in the new house.
Maybe the man who lived there,
the man she loved, was reading
the story of another life.
She imagined a bare parlor,
a cold fireplace, a man sitting
writing a letter to a woman
who has sacrificed her life for love.
If there were a perfect moment in the book,
it would be the last.
The book never discusses the causes of love.
It claims confusion is a necessary good.
It never explains. It only reveals.

6

The day goes on.
We study what we remember.
We look into the mirror across the room.
We cannot bear to be alone.
The book goes on.
They became silent and did not know how to begin
the dialogue which was necessary.
It was words that created divisions in the first place,
that created loneliness.
They waited.
They would turn the pages, hoping
something would happen.
They would patch up their lives in secret:
each defeat forgiven because it could not be tested,
each pain rewarded because it was unreal.
They did nothing.

7

The book will not survive.
We are the living proof of that.
It is dark outside, in the room it is darker.

I hear your breathing.
You are asking me if I am tired,
if I want to keep reading.
Yes, I am tired.
Yes, I want to keep reading.
I say yes to everything.
You cannot hear me.
They sat beside each other on the couch.
They were the copies, the tired phantoms
of something they had been before.
The attitudes they took were jaded.
They stared into the book
and were horrified by their innocence,
their reluctance to give up.
They sat beside each other on the couch.
They were determined to accept the truth.
Whatever it was they would accept it.
The book would have to be written
and would have to be read.
They are the book and they are
nothing else.

Where Are the Waters of Childhood?

See where the windows are boarded up,
where the gray siding shines in the sun and salt air
and the asphalt shingles on the roof have peeled or fallen off,
where tiers of oxeye daisies float on a sea of grass?
That's the place to begin.

Enter the kingdom of rot,
smell the damp plaster, step over the shattered glass,
the pockets of dust, the rags, the soiled remains of a mattress,
look at the rusted stove and sink, at the rectangular stain
on the wall where Winslow Homer's *Gulf Stream* hung.

Go to the room where your father and mother
would let themselves go in the drift and pitch of love,
and hear, if you can, the creak of their bed,
then go to the place where you hid.

Go to your room, to all the rooms whose cold, damp air you
    breathed,
to all the unwanted places where summer, fall, winter, spring,
seem the same unwanted season, where the trees you knew
    have died
and other trees have risen. Visit that other place
you barely recall, that other house half hidden.

See the two dogs burst into sight. When you leave,
they will cease, snuffed out in the glare of an earlier light.
Visit the neighbors down the block; he waters his lawn,
she sits on her porch, but not for long.
When you look again they are gone.

Keep going back, back to the field, flat and sealed in mist.
On the other side, a man and a woman are waiting;
they have come back, your mother before she was gray,
your father before he was white.

Now look at the North West Arm, how it glows a deep
    cerulean blue.
See the light on the grass, the one leaf burning, the cloud
that flares. You're almost there, in a moment your parents
will disappear, leaving you under the light of a vanished star,
under the dark of a star newly born. Now is the time.

Now you invent the boat of your flesh and set it upon the
    waters
and drift in the gradual swell, in the laboring salt.
Now you look down. The waters of childhood are there.

CHARLES WRIGHT
(b. 1935)

Born in Pickwick Dam, Tennessee, Charles Wright took degrees from
Davidson College and the University of Iowa. During army service in
Italy, he first read the work of Ezra Pound and pledged himself to a
career in poetry. He taught for many years at the University of
California at Irvine and is now poet-in-residence at the University of
Virginia. He received the American Book Award in 1983. The
surrealism of Wright's early work was refined to an elegant, nearly
Symbolist obliquity with which he wrote about his own past in
several long sequences. Recent poems are even more ambitious in their
combinations of nostalgic detail and rhetorical ascents to the sublime.
The luxuriant textures and rhythms of Wright's work point to his
conviction that language itself, like certain landscapes, is a "sacred
place," a repository of images charged with mystery and possibility.
Rather than by argument or narrative, his poems move by "linkages,"
assembled emotions and memories.

Stone Canyon Nocturne

Ancient of Days, old friend, no one believes you'll come back.
No one believes in his own life anymore.

The moon, like a dead heart, cold and unstartable, hangs by a
    thread
At the earth's edge,
Unfaithful at last, splotching the ferns and the pink shrubs.

In the other world, children undo the knots in their tally
    strings.
They sing songs, and their fingers blear.

And here, where the swan hums in his socket, where bloodroot
And belladonna insist on our comforting,
Where the fox in the canyon wall empties our hands, ecstatic
    for more,

Like a bead of clear oil the Healer revolves through the night
  wind,
Part eye, part tear, unwilling to recognize us.

Spider Crystal Ascension

The spider, juiced crystal and Milky Way, drifts on his web
  through the night sky
And looks down, waiting for us to ascend . . .

At dawn he is still there, invisible, short of breath, mending
  his net.

All morning we look for the white face to rise from the lake
  like a tiny star.
And when it does, we lie back in our watery hair and rock.

Clear Night

Clear night, thumb-top of a moon, a back-lit sky.
Moon-fingers lay down their same routine
On the side deck and the threshold, the white keys and the
  black keys.
Bird hush and bird song. A cassia flower falls.

I want to be bruised by God.
I want to be strung up in a strong light and singled out.
I wanted to be stretched, like music wrung from a dropped
  seed.
I want to be entered and picked clean.

And the wind says "What?" to me.
And the castor beans, with their little earrings of death, say
  "What?" to me.

And the stars start out on their cold slide through the dark.
And the gears notch and the engines wheel.

Homage to Paul Cézanne

At night, in the fish-light of the moon, the dead wear our
    white shirts
To stay warm, and litter the fields.
We pick them up in the mornings, dewy pieces of paper and
    scraps of cloth.
Like us, they refract themselves. Like us,
They keep on saying the same thing, trying to get it right.
Like us, the water unsettles their names.

Sometimes they lie like leaves in their little arks, and curl up at
    the edges.
Sometimes they come inside, wearing our shoes, and walk
From mirror to mirror.
Or lie in our beds with their gloves off
And touch our bodies. Or talk
In a corner. Or wait like envelopes on a desk.

They reach up from the ice plant.
They shuttle their messengers through the oat grass.
Their answers rise like rust on the stalks and the spidery
    leaves.

We rub them off our hands.

•

Each year the dead grow less dead, and nudge
Close to the surface of all things.
They start to remember the silence that brought them there.
They start to recount the gain in their soiled hands.

Their glasses let loose, and grain by grain return to the river
    bank.
They point to their favorite words
Growing around them, revealed as themselves for the first
    time:
They stand close to the meanings and take them in.

They stand there, vague and without pain,
Under their fingernails an unreturnable dirt.
They stand there and it comes back,
The music of everything, syllable after syllable

Out of the burning chair, out of the beings of light.
It all comes back.
And what they repeat to themselves, and what they repeat to
    themselves,
Is the song that our fathers sing.

•

In steeps and sighs,
The ocean explains itself, backing and filling
What spaces it can't avoid, spaces
In black shoes, their hands clasped, their eyes teared at the
    edges:
We watch from the high hillside,
The ocean swelling and flattening, the spaces
Filling and emptying, horizon blade
Flashing the early afternoon sun.

The dead are constant in
The white lips of the sea.
Over and over, through clenched teeth, they tell
their story, the story each knows by heart:
Remember me, speak my name.
When the moon tugs at my sleeve,
When the body of water is raised and becomes the body of light,
Remember me, speak my name.

•

The dead are a cadmium blue.
We spread them with palette knives in broad blocks and
    planes.

We layer them stroke by stroke
In steps and ascending mass, in verticals raised from the earth.

We choose, and layer them in,
Blue and a blue and a breath,

Circle and smudge, cross-beak and buttonhook,
We layer them in. We squint hard and terrace them line by
    line.

And so we are come between, and cry out,
And stare up at the sky and its cloudy panes,

And finger the cypress twists.
The dead understand all this, and keep in touch,

Rustle of hand to hand in the lemon trees,
Flags, and the great sifts of anger

To powder and nothingness.
The dead are a cadmium blue, and they understand.

•

The dead are with us to stay.
Their shadows rock in the back yard, so pure, so black,
Between the oak tree and the porch.

Over our heads they're huge in the night sky.
In the tall grass they turn with the zodiac.
Under our feet they're white with the snows of a thousand
    years.

They carry their colored threads and baskets of silk
To mend our clothes, making us look right,
Altering, stitching, replacing a button, closing a tear.
They lie like tucks in our loose sleeves, they hold us together.

They blow the last leaves away.
They slide like an overflow into the river of heaven.
Everywhere they are flying.

The dead are a sleight and a fade
We fall for, like flowering plums, like white coins from the
    rain
Their sighs are gaps in the wind.

•

The dead are waiting for us in our rooms,
Little globules of light
In one of the far corners, and close to the ceiling, hovering,
    thinking our thoughts.

Often they'll reach a hand down,
Or offer a word, and ease us out of our bodies to join them in
    theirs.
We look back at our other selves on the bed.

We look back and we don't care and we go.

And thus we become what we've longed for,
                              past tense and otherwise,
A BB, a disc of light,
                    song without words.
And refer to ourselves
In the third person, seeing that other arm
Still raised from the bed, fingers like licks and flames in the
    boned air.

Only to hear that it's not time.
Only to hear that we must re-enter and lie still, our arms at
    rest at our sides,
The voices rising around us like mist

And dew, *it's all right, it's all right, it's all right* . . .

•

The dead fall around us like rain.
They come down from the last clouds in the late light for the
    last time
And slip through the sod.

They lean uphill and face north.
                        Like grass,
They bend toward the sea, they break toward the setting sun.

We filigree and we baste.
But what do the dead care for the fringe of words,
Safe in their suits of milk?
What do they care for the honk and flash of a new style?

And who is to say if the inch of snow in our hearts
Is rectitude enough?

Spring picks the locks of the wind.
High in the night sky the mirror is hauled up and unsheeted.
In it we twist like stars.

Ahead of us, through the dark, the dead
Are beating their drums and stirring the yellow leaves.

•

We're out here, our feet in the soil, our heads craned up at the
    sky,
The stars streaming and bursting behind the trees.

At dawn, as the clouds gather, we watch
The mountain glide from the east on the valley floor,
Coming together in starts and jumps.
Behind their curtain, the bears
Amble across the heavens, serene as black coffee . . .

Whose unction can intercede for the dead?
Whose tongue is toothless enough to speak their piece?

What we are given in dreams we write as blue paint,
Or messages to the clouds.
At evening we wait for the rain to fall and the sky to clear.
Our words are words for the clay, uttered in undertones,
Our gestures salve for the wind.

We sit out on the earth and stretch our limbs,
Hoarding the little mounds of sorrow laid up in our hearts.

The Other Side of the River

Easter again, and a small rain falls
On the mockingbird and the housefly,
                                    on the Chevrolet
In its purple joy
And the TV antennas huddled across the hillside—

Easter again, and the palm trees hunch
Deeper beneath their burden,
                              the dark puddles take in

Whatever is given them,
And nothing rises more than halfway out of itself—

Easter with all its little mouths open into the rain.

                                •

There is no metaphor for the spring's disgrace,
No matter how much the rose leaves look like bronze dove
    hearts,
No matter how much the plum trees preen in the wind.

For weeks I've thought about the Savannah River,
For no reason,
            and the winter fields around Garnett, South Carolina
My brother and I used to hunt
At Christmas,
                Princess and Buddy working the millet stands
And the vine-lipped face of the pine woods
In their languorous zig-zags,
The quail, when they flushed, bursting like shrapnel points
Between the trees and the leggy shrubs
                                        into the undergrowth,
Everything else in motion as though under water,
My brother and I, the guns, their reports tolling from far away
Through the aqueous, limb-filtered light,
December sun like a single tropical fish
Uninterested anyway,

suspended and holding still
In the coral stems of the pearl-dusked and distant trees . . .

There is no metaphor for any of this,
Or the meta-weather of April,
The vinca blossoms like deep bruises among the green.

●

It's linkage I'm talking about,
                    and harmonies and structures
And all the various things that lock our wrists to the past.

Something infinite behind everything appears,
                                    and then disappears.

It's all a matter of how
                    you narrow the surfaces.
It's all a matter of how you fit in the sky.

●

Often, at night, when the stars seem as close as they do now,
    and as full,
And the trees balloon and subside in the way they do
                                    when the wind is right,
As they do now after the rain,
                    the sea way off with its false sheen,
And the sky that slick black of wet rubber,
I'm 15 again, and back on Mt. Anne in North Carolina
Repairing the fire tower,
Nobody else around but the horse I packed in with,
                    and five days to finish the job.
Those nights were the longest nights I ever remember,
The lake and pavilion 3,000 feet below
                                    as though modeled in tinfoil,
And even more distant than that,
The last fire out, the after-reflection of Lake Llewellyn
Aluminum glare in the sponged dark,
Lightning bugs everywhere,
                    the plump stars
Dangling and falling near on their black strings.

These nights are like that,
The silvery alphabet of the sea
                                   increasingly difficult to transcribe,
And larger each year, everything farther away, and less clear,
Than I want it to be,
                    not enough time to do the job,
And faint thunks in the earth,
As though somewhere nearby a horse was nervously pawing
    the ground.

                                        •

I want to sit by the bank of the river,
                    in the shade of the evergreen tree,
And look in the face of whatever,
                    the whatever that's waiting for me.

                                        •

There comes a point when everything starts to dust away
More quickly than it appears,
                    when what we have to comfort the dark
Is just that dust, and just its going away.

25 years ago I used to sit on this jut of rocks
As the sun went down like an offering through the glaze
And backfires of Monterey Bay,
And anything I could think of was mine because it was there
                    in front of me, numinously everywhere,
Appearing and piling up . . .

So to have come to this,
                    remembering what I did do, and what I
                    didn't do,
The gulls whimpering over the boathouse,
                                        the monarch butterflies

Cruising the flower beds,
And all the soft hairs of spring thrusting up through the wind,
And the sun, as it always does,
                    dropping into its slot without a click,
Is a short life of trouble.

AUDRE LORDE
(b. 1934)

"I am," Audre Lorde has written, "Black, Woman, and Poet—all three
are facts outside the realm of choice. . . . But what is in my blood and
kin of richness, of brown earth and noon sun and the strength to love
them, comes the roundabout way from Africa through sun islands to a
stony coast; and these are the gifts through which I sing, through
which I see." Born in New York City to West Indian parents, Lorde
graduated from Hunter College and Columbia, and worked as a
librarian and teacher. Since 1981 she has been professor of English at
Hunter. Her earlier introspective style was later pitched higher, and
her anger at injustice and oppression grew more vivid. Although she
has written about her personal life and about African peoples and
culture (particularly those of Dahomey), Lorde's portraits of American
inner-city life are central to her vision of pain and struggle.

Coal

I
is the total black, being spoken
from the earth's inside.
There are many kinds of open
how a diamond comes into a knot of flame
how sound comes into a word, colored
by who pays what for speaking.
Some words are open like a diamond
on glass windows
singing out within the passing crash of sun
Then there are words like stapled wagers
in a perforated book—buy and sign and tear apart—
and come whatever wills all chances
the stub remains
an ill-pulled tooth with a ragged edge.

Some words live in my throat
breeding like adders. Others know sun
seeking like gypsies over my tongue
to explode through my lips
like young sparrows bursting from shell.
Some words
bedevil me.

Love is a word, another kind of open.
As the diamond comes into a knot of flame
I am Black because I come from the earth's inside
now take my word for jewel in the open light.

Movement Song

I have studied the tight curls on the back of your neck
moving away from me
beyond anger or failure
your face in the evening schools of longing
through mornings of wish and ripen
we were always saying goodbye
in the blood in the bone over coffee
before dashing for elevators going
in opposite directions
without goodbyes.

Do not remember me as a bridge nor a roof
as the maker of legends
nor as a trap
door to that world
where black and white clericals
hang on the edge of beauty in five o'clock elevators
twitching their shoulders to avoid other flesh
and now
there is someone to speak for them

moving away from me into tomorrows
morning of wish and ripen
your goodbye is a promise of lightning
in the last angels hand
unwelcome and warning
the sands have run out against us
we were rewarded by journeys
away from each other
into desire
into mornings alone
where excuse and endurance mingle
conceiving decision.

Do not remember me
as disaster
nor as the keeper of secrets
I am the fellow rider in the cattle cars
watching
you move
slowly out of my bed
saying we cannot waste time
only ourselves.

Afterimages

I

However the image enters
its force remains within
my eyes
rockstrewn caves where dragonfish evolve
wild for life, relentless and acquisitive
learning to survive
where there is no food
my eyes are always hungry

and remembering
however the image enters
its force remains.
A white woman stands bereft and empty
a black boy hacked into a murderous lesson
recalled in me forever
like a lurch of earth on the edge of sleep
etched into my visions
food for dragonfish that learn
to live upon whatever they must eat
fused images beneath my pain.

I I

The Pearl River floods through the streets of Jackson
A Mississippi summer televised.
Trapped houses kneel like sinners in the rain
a white woman climbs from her roof to a passing boat
her fingers tarry for a moment on the chimney
now awash
tearless and no longer young, she holds
a tattered baby's blanket in her arms.
In a flickering afterimage of the nightmare rain
a microphone
thrust up against her flat bewildered words
  "we jest come from the bank yestiddy
        borrowing money to pay the income tax
        now everything's gone. I never knew
        it could be so hard."
Despair weighs down her voice like Pearl River mud
caked around the edges
her pale eyes scanning the camera for help or explanation
unanswered
she shifts her search across the watered street, dry-eyed
        "hard, but not this hard."
Two tow-headed children hurl themselves against her
hanging upon her coat like mirrors
until a man with ham-like hands pulls her aside

snarling "She ain't got nothing more to say!"
and that lie hangs in his mouth
like a shred of rotting meat.

III

I inherited Jackson, Mississippi.
For my majority it gave me Emmett Till
his 15 years puffed out like bruises
on plump boy-cheeks
his only Mississippi summer
whistling a 21 gun salute to Dixie
as a white girl passed him in the street
and he was baptized my son forever
in the midnight waters of the Pearl.

His broken body is the afterimage of my 21st year
when I walked through a northern summer
my eyes averted
from each corner's photographies
newspapers protest posters magazines
Police Story, Confidential, True
the avid insistence of detail
pretending insight or information
the length of gash across the dead boy's loins
his grieving mother's lamentation
the severed lips, how many burns
his gouged out eyes
sewed shut upon the screaming covers
louder than life
all over
the veiled warning, the secret relish
of a black child's mutilated body
fingered by street-corner eyes
bruise upon livid bruise
and wherever I looked that summer
I learned to be at home with children's blood
with savored violence
with pictures of black broken flesh

used, crumpled, and discarded
lying amid the sidewalk refuse
like a raped woman's face.

A black boy from Chicago
whistled on the streets of Jackson, Mississippi
testing what he'd been taught was a manly thing to do
his teachers
ripped his eyes out his sex his tongue
and flung him to the Pearl weighted with stone
in the name of white womanhood
they took their aroused honor
back to Jackson
and celebrated in a whorehouse
the double ritual of white manhood
confirmed.

IV

"If earth and air and water do not judge them who are we to refuse a crust of
bread?"

Emmett Till rides the crest of the Pearl, whistling
24 years his ghost lay like the shade of a raped woman
and a white girl has grown older in costly honor
(what did she pay to never know its price?)
now the Pearl River speaks its muddy judgment
and I can withhold my pity and my bread.

"Hard, but not this hard."
Her face is flat with resignation and despair
with ancient and familiar sorrows
a woman surveying her crumpled future
as the white girl besmirched by Emmett's whistle
never allowed her own tongue
without power or conclusion
unvoiced
she stands adrift in the ruins of her honor
and a man with an executioner's face
pulls her away.

Within my eyes
the flickering afterimages of a nightmare rain
a woman wrings her hands
beneath the weight of agonies remembered
I wade through summer ghosts
betrayed by vision
hers and my own
becoming dragonfish to survive
the horrors we are living
with tortured lungs
adapting to breathe blood.

A woman measures her life's damage
my eyes are caves, chunks of etched rock
tied to the ghost of a black boy
whistling
crying and frightened
her tow-headed children cluster
like little mirrors of despair
their father's hands upon them
and soundlessly
a woman begins to weep.

JAY WRIGHT
(b. 1935)

Born in Albuquerque, New Mexico, Jay Wright graduated from
Berkeley and studied comparative literature at Rutgers. He has worked
as a playwright and teacher and now lives in New Hampshire.
Describing his poetry as the effort "to uncover the weave," Wright
has envisioned black culture as woven of strands from sources as
diverse as anthropology and symbolism, the Mexican landscape and
Dante's *Commedia,* Navajo cosmologies, Dogon and Bambara tribal
religions, gospel and jazz. His is an erudite as well as a spiritual quest.
In his work historic and mythic voices cross with his own; one of
them is that of Benjamin Banneker, the self-taught eighteenth-century
black scientist, surveyor, and almanac maker. Poetry, says Wright,
undertakes "the discovery, explication, interpretation, exploration, and
transformation of experience," and he has claimed the
broadest possible heritage for his task.

The Homecoming Singer

The plane tilts in to Nashville,
coming over the green lights
like a toy train skipping past
the signals on a track.
The city is livid with lights,
as if the weight of all the people
shooting down her arteries
had inflamed them.
It's Friday night,
and people are home for the homecomings.
As I come into the terminal,
a young black man, in a vested gray suit,
paces in the florid Tennessee air,
breaks into a run like a halfback

in open field, going past the delirious faces,
past the poster of Molly Bee,
in her shiny chaps, her hips tilted forward
where the guns would be, her legs set,
as if she would run, as if she were
a cheerleader who doffs her guns
on Saturday afternoon and careens
down the sidelines after some broken field runner,
who carries it in, for now,
for all the state of Tennessee
with its nut smelling trees,
its stolid little stone walls
set out under thick blankets of leaves,
its crisp lights dangling on the porches
of homes that top the graveled driveways,
where people who cannot yodel or yell
putter in the grave October afternoons,
waiting for Saturday night and the lights
that spatter on Molly Bee's silver chaps.
I don't want to think of them,
or even of the broken field runner in the terminal,
still looking for his girl, his pocket
full of dates and parties, as I come
into this Friday night of homecomings
and hobble over the highway in a taxi
that has its radio tuned to country music.
I come up to the campus,
with a large wreath jutting up
under the elegant dormitories,
where one girl sits looking down at the shrieking cars,
as the lights go out, one by one, around her
and the laughter drifts off, rising, rising,
as if it would take flight away
from the livid arteries of Nashville.
Now, in sleep, I leave my brass-headed bed,
and see her enter with tall singers,
they in African shirts, she in a robe.
She sits, among them, as a golden lance
catches her, suddenly chubby, with soft lips

and unhurried eyes, quite still in the movement
around her, waiting, as the other voices fade,
as the movement stops, and starts to sing,
her voice moving up from its tart entrance
until it swings as freely
as an ecstatic dancer's foot,
rises and plays among the windows
as it would with angels and falls,
almost visible, to return to her,
and leave her shaking with the tears
I'm ashamed to release, and leave her
twisting there on that stool with my shame
for the livid arteries, the flat Saturdays,
the inhuman homecomings of Nashville.
I kneel before her. She strokes my hair,
as softly as she would a cat's head
and goes on singing, her voice shifting
and bringing up the Carolina calls,
the waterboy, the railroad cutter, the jailed,
the condemned, all that had been forgotten
on this night of homecomings, all
that had been misplaced in those livid arteries.
She finishes, and leaves,
her shy head tilted and wrinkled,
in the green-tinged lights of the still campus.
I close my eyes and listen,
as she goes out to sing this city home.

Benjamin Banneker Sends His *Almanac* to Thomas Jefferson

Old now,
your eyes nearly blank

from plotting the light's
movement over the years,
you clean your *Almanac,*
and place it next
to the heart of this letter.
I have you in mind,
giving a final brush and twist
to the difficult pages,
staring down the shape of the numbers
as though you would find a flaw
in their forms.
Solid, these calculations
verify your body on God's earth.
At night,
the stars submit themselves
to the remembered way you turn them;
the moon gloats under your attention.
I, who know so little of stars,
whose only acquaintance with the moon
is to read a myth, or to listen
to the surge
of songs the women know,
sit in your marvelous reading
of all movement,
of all relations.

So you look into what we see
yet cannot see,
and shape and take a language
to give form to one or the other,
believing no form will escape,
no movement appear, nor stop,
without explanation,
believing no reason is only reason,
nor without reason.
I read all of this into your task,
all of this into the uneasy
reproof of your letter.

Surely, there must be a flaw.
These perfect calculations fall apart.
There are silences
that no perfect number can retrieve,
omissions no perfect line could catch.
How could a man but challenge God's
impartial distributions?
How could a man sit among
the free and ordered movements
of stars, and waters, beasts and birds,
each movement seen or accounted for,
and not know God jealous,
and not know that he himself must be?

So you go over the pages again,
looking for the one thing
that will not reveal itself,
judging what you have received,
what you have shaped,
believing it cannot be strange
to the man you address.
But you are strange to him
—your skin, your tongue,
the movement of your body,
even your mysterious ways with stars.
You argue here with the man and God,
and know that no man can be right,
and know that no God will argue right.
Your letter turns on what the man knows,
on what God, you think, would have us know.
All stars will forever move under your gaze,
truthfully, leading you from line to line,
from number to number, from truth to truth,
while the man will read your soul's desire,
searcher, searching yourself,
losing the relations.

Journey to the Place of Ghosts

Wölbe dich, Welt:
Wenn die Totenmuschel heranschwimmt,
will es hier läuten.

Vault over, world:
when the seashell of death washes up
there will be a knelling.
                    Paul Celan, *Stimmen* (Voices)

          Death knocks all night at my door.
          The soul answers,
          and runs from the water in my throat.
          Water will sustain me when I climb
                              the steep hill
          that leads to a now familiar place.
          I began, even as a child, to learn water's order,
          and, as I grew intact, the feel of its warmth
          in a new sponge, of its weight in a virgin towel.
          I have earned my wine in another's misery,
          when rum bathed a sealed throat
          and cast its seal on the ground.
          I will be bound, to the one who leads me away,
          by the ornaments on my wrists, the gold dust
          in my ears, below my eye and tied to my
                              loin cloth in a leather pouch.
          They dress me now in my best cloth,
          and fold my hands, adorned with silk,
                              against my left cheek.

          Gold lies with me on my left side.
          Gold has become the color of distance,
                              and of your sorrow.

          Sorrow lies, red clay on my brow.
          Red pepper caresses my temples.
          I am adorned in the russet-brown message
          the soul brings from its coming-to-be.

There is a silken despair in my body
that grief shakes from it,
a cat's voice, controlled by palm-wine
               and a widow's passion.
It is time to feed the soul
  —a hen, eggs, mashed yams—
and encourage the thirst resting
near the right hand I see before me.
          Always I think of death.
           I cannot eat.
          I walk in sadness, and I die.
Yet life is the invocation sealed in the coffin,
and will walk through our wall,
passing and passing and passing,
           until it is set down,
to be lifted from this body's habitation.
I now assume the widow's pot,
the lamp that will lead me through solitude,
to the edge of my husband's journey.
I hold three stones upon my head,
darkness I will release when I run
from the dead,
with my eyes turned away
             toward another light.

This is the day of rising.
A hut sits in the bush, sheltered by summe,
standing on four forked ends.

We have prepared for the soul's feast
with pestle, mortar, a strainer, three
hearthstones, a new pot and new spoon.
Someone has stripped the hut's body
and dressed it with the edowa.
Now, when the wine speaks
and the fire has lifted its voice,
the dead will be clothed in hair,
            the signs of our grief.
Sun closes down on an intensity of ghosts.
It is time to close the path.

It is time for the snail's pace
of coming again into life,
       with the world swept clean,
       the crying done,
and our ordinary garments decent in the dead one's eyes.

C . K . WILLIAMS
(b. 1936)

Born in Newark, New Jersey, Charles Kenneth Williams studied at
Bucknell and the University of Pennsylvania. He has worked as a
group therapist for disturbed adolescents and as an editor, speech
writer, and translator. He has since taught creative writing at several
universities and now lives in Paris. The 1987 National Book Critics
Circle Award was given to his fifth book of poems, *Flesh and Blood.* His
first two books, with an angry, hurtling voice that deals in lurid
details, examine the lower depths of society and the psyche, its
hopeless mess of wounds and absences. Subsequent books shifted to
long, loping lines in the manner of Walt Whitman, and Williams's
poems grew more inclusive and elevated, although his subjects
remained downbeat—vulnerable or victimized members of society. His
stories consistently move back to Williams's own baffled yearnings
and out toward sympathy and moral enlightenment.

It Is This Way with Men

They are pounded into the earth
like nails; move an inch,
they are driven down again.
The earth is sore with them.
It is a spiny fruit
that has lost hope
of being raised and eaten.
It can only ripen and ripen.
And men, they too are wounded.
They too are sifted from their loss
and are without hope. The core
softens. The pure flesh softens
and melts. There are thorns, there
are the dark seeds, and they end.

The Gas Station

This is before I'd read Nietzsche. Before Kant or Kierkegaard,
   even before Whitman and Yeats.
I don't think there were three words in my head yet. I knew,
   perhaps, that I should suffer,
I can remember I almost cried for this or for that, nothing
   special, nothing to speak of.
Probably I was mad with grief for the loss of my childhood,
   but I wouldn't have known that.
It's dawn. A gas station. Route twenty-two. I remember
   exactly: route twenty-two curved,
there was a squat, striped concrete divider they'd put in after a
   plague of collisions.
The gas station? Texaco, Esso—I don't know. They were just
   words anyway then, just what their signs said.
I wouldn't have understood the first thing about monopoly or
   imperialist or oppression.
It's dawn. It's so late. Even then, when I was never tired, I'm
   just holding on.
Slumped on my friend's shoulder, I watch the relentless,
   wordless misery of the route twenty-two sky
that seems to be filming my face with a grainy oil I keep trying
   to rub off or in.
Why are we here? Because one of my friends, in the men's
   room over there, has blue balls.
He has to jerk off. I don't know what that means, "blue balls,"
   or why he has to do that—
it must be important to have to stop here after this long night,
   but I don't ask.
I'm just trying, I think, to keep my head as empty as I can for
   as long as I can.
One of my other friends is asleep. He's so ugly, his mouth
   hanging, slack and wet.
Another—I'll never see this one again—stares from the window
   as though he were frightened.

Here's what we've done. We were in Times Square, a pimp
    found us, corralled us, led us somewhere,
down a dark street, another dark street, up dark stairs, dark
    hall, dark apartment,
where his whore, his girl or his wife or his mother for all I
    know dragged herself from her sleep,
propped herself on an elbow, gazed into the dark hall, and
    agreed, for two dollars each, to take care of us.
Take care of us. Some of the words that come through me now
    seem to stay, to hook in.
My friend in the bathroom is taking so long. The filthy sky
    must be starting to lighten.
It took me a long time, too, with the woman, I mean. Did I
    mention that she, the woman, the whore or mother,
was having her time and all she would deign do was to blow
    us? Did I say that? Deign? Blow?
What a joy, though, the idea was in those days. Blown! What
    a thing to tell the next day.
She only deigned, though, no more. She was like a machine.
    When I lift her back to me now,
there's nothing there but that dark, curly head, working, a
    machine, up and down, and now,
Freud, Marx, Fathers, tell me, what am I, doing this, telling
    this, on her, on myself,
hammering it down, cementing it, sealing it in, but a machine,
    too? *Why am I doing this?*
I still haven't read Augustine. I don't understand Chomsky that
    well. Should I?
My friend at last comes back. Maybe the right words were
    there all along. *Complicity. Wonder.*
How pure we were then, before Rimbaud, before Blake. *Grace.*
    Love. Take care of us. Please.

Tar

The first morning of Three Mile Island: those first disquieting,
   uncertain, mystifying hours.
All morning a crew of workmen have been tearing the old
   decrepit roof off our building,
and all morning, trying to distract myself, I've been wandering
   out to watch them
as they hack away the leaden layers of asbestos paper and
   disassemble the disintegrating drains.
After half a night of listening to the news, wondering how to
   know a hundred miles downwind
if and when to make a run for it and where, then a coming
   bolt awake at seven
when the roofers we've been waiting for since winter sent their
   ladders shrieking up our wall,
we still know less than nothing: the utility company continues
   making little of the accident,
the slick federal spokesmen still have their evasions in some
   semblance of order.
Surely we suspect now we're being lied to, but in the
   meantime, there are the roofers,
setting winch-frames, sledging rounds of tar apart, and there I
   am, on the curb across, gawking.

I never realized what brutal work it is, how matter-of-factly
   and harrowingly dangerous.
The ladders flex and quiver, things skid from the edge, the
   materials are bulky and recalcitrant.
When the rusty, antique nails are levered out, their heads pull
   off; the underroofing crumbles.
Even the battered little furnace, roaring along as patient as a
   donkey, chokes and clogs,
a dense, malignant smoke shoots up, and someone has to fiddle
   with a cock, then hammer it,

before the gush and stench will deintensify, the dark, Dantean
broth wearily subside.
In its crucible, the stuff looks bland, like licorice, spill it,
though, on your boots or coveralls,
it sears, and everything is permeated with it, the furnace
gunked with burst and half-burst bubbles,
the men themselves so completely slashed and mucked they
seem almost from another realm, like trolls.
When they take their break, they leave their brooms standing
at attention in the asphalt pails,
work gloves clinging like Br'er Rabbit to the bitten shafts, and
they slouch along the precipitous lip,
the enormous sky behind them, the heavy noontime air alive
with shimmers and mirages.

Sometime in the afternoon I had to go inside: the advent of
our vigil was upon us.
However much we didn't want to, however little we would do
about it, we'd understood:
we were going to perish of all this, if not now, then soon, if
not soon, then someday.
Someday, some final generation, hysterically aswarm beneath
an atmosphere as unrelenting as rock,
would rue us all, anathematize our earthly comforts, curse our
surfeits and submissions.
I think I know, though I might rather not, why my roofers
stay so clear to me and why the rest,
the terror of that time, the reflexive disbelief and distancing, all
we should hold on to, dims so.
I remember the president in his absurd protective booties,
looking absolutely unafraid, the fool.
I remember a woman on the front page glaring across the misty
Susquehanna at those looming stacks.
But, more vividly, the men, silvered with glitter from the
shingles, clinging like starlings beneath the eaves.
Even the leftover carats of tar in the gutter, so black they
seemed to suck the light out of the air.
By nightfall kids had come across them: every sidewalk on the
block was scribbled with obscenities and hearts.

Alzheimer's: The Wife

for Renée Mauger

She answers the bothersome telephone, takes the message,
    forgets the message, forgets who called.
One of their daughters, her husband guesses: the one with the
    dogs, the babies, the boy Jed?
Yes, perhaps, but how tell which, how tell anything when all
    the name tags have been lost or switched,
when all the lonely flowers of sense and memory bloom and
    die now in adjacent bites of time?
Sometimes her own face will suddenly appear with terrifying
    inappropriateness before her in a mirror.
She knows that if she's patient, its gaze will break, demurely,
    decorously, like a well-taught child's,
it will turn from her as though it were embarrassed by the
    secrets of this awful hide-and-seek.
If she forgets, though, and glances back again, it will still be in
    there, furtively watching, crying.

MARVIN BELL
(b. 1937)

Born in New York City and raised on Long Island, Marvin Bell
studied at Alfred University, then did graduate work at the University
of Chicago and at the Iowa Writers Workshop. After a hitch in the
army, he returned to teach at Iowa in 1965 and has remained there. "I
would like to write poetry," he says, "which finds salvation in the
physical world and the here and now, which redefines the soul, if you
will, in terms of emotional depth, and that emotional depth in terms
of the physical world and the world of human relationships." Bell can
combine a witty intelligence with forlorn feelings, and he writes
modest poems alert to the mutations of identity, the mysteries
of the self, and the vicissitudes of middle-class,
second-generation-American family life.

The Self and the Mulberry

I wanted to see the self, so I looked at the mulberry.
It had no trouble accepting its limits,
yet defining and redefining a small area
so that any shape was possible, any movement.
It stayed put, but was part of all the air.
I wanted to learn to be there and not there
like the continually changing, slightly moving
mulberry, wild cherry and particularly the willow.
Like the willow, I tried to weep without tears.
Like the cherry tree, I tried to be sturdy and productive.
Like the mulberry, I tried to keep moving.
I couldn't cry right, couldn't stay or go.
I kept losing parts of myself like a soft maple.
I fell ill like the elm. That was the end
of looking in nature to find a natural self.
Let nature think itself not manly enough!

Let nature wonder at the mystery of laughter.
Let nature hypothesize man's indifference to it.
Let nature take a turn at saying what love is!

To Dorothy

You are not beautiful, exactly.
You are beautiful, inexactly.
You let a weed grow by the mulberry
and a mulberry grow by the house.
So close, in the personal quiet
of a windy night, it brushes the wall
and sweeps away the day till we sleep.

A child said it, and it seemed true:
"Things that are lost are all equal."
But it isn't true. If I lost you,
the air wouldn't move, nor the tree grow.
Someone would pull the weed, my flower.
The quiet wouldn't be yours. If I lost you,
I'd have to ask the grass to let me sleep.

White Clover

Once when the moon was out about three-quarters
and the fireflies who are the stars
of backyards
were out about three-quarters
and about three-fourths of all the lights

in the neighborhood
were on because people can be at home,
I took a not so innocent walk
out among the lawns,
navigating by the light of lights,
and there there were many hundreds of moons
on the lawns
where before there was only polite grass.
These were moons on long stems,
their long stems giving their greenness
to the center of each flower
and the light giving its whiteness to the tops
of the petals. I could say
it was light from stars
touched the tops of flowers and no doubt
something heavenly reaches what grows outdoors
and the heads of men who go hatless,
but I like to think we have a world
right here, and a life
that isn't death. So I don't say it's better
to be right here. I say this is where
many hundreds of core-green moons
gigantic to my eye
rose because men and women had sown green grass,
and flowered to my eye in man-made light,
and to some would be as fire in the body
and to others a light in the mind
over all their property.

Drawn by Stones, by Earth, by Things that Have Been in the Fire

I can tell you about this because I have held in my hand
the little potter's sponge called an "elephant ear."
Naturally, it's only a tiny version of an ear,

but it's the thing you want to pick up out of the toolbox
when you wander into the deserted ceramics shop
down the street from the cave where the fortune-teller works.
Drawn by stones, by earth, by things that have been in the
    fire.

The elephant ear listens to the side of the vase
as it is pulled upwards from a dome of muddy clay.
The ear listens to the outside wall of the pot
and the hand listens to the inside wall of the pot,
and between them a city rises out of dirt and water.
Inside this city live the remains of animals,
animals who prepared for two hundred years to be clay.

Rodents make clay, and men wearing spectacles make clay,
though the papers they were signing go up in flames
and nothing more is known of these long documents
except by those angels who divine in our ashes.
Kings and queens of the jungle make clay
and royalty and politicians make clay although
their innocence stays with their clothes until unravelled.

There is a lost soldier in every ceramic bowl.
The face on the dinner plate breaks when the dish does
and lies for centuries unassembled in the soil.
These things that have the right substance to begin with,
put into the fire at temperatures that melt glass,
keep their fingerprints forever, it is said,
like inky sponges that walk away in the deep water.

Wednesday

Gray rainwater lay on the grass in the late afternoon.
The carp lay on the bottom, resting, while dusk took shape

in the form of the first stirrings of his hunger,
and the trees, shorter and heavier, breathed heavily upwards.
Into this sodden, nourishing afternoon I emerged,
partway toward a paycheck, halfway toward the weekend,
carrying the last mail and holding above still puddles
the books of noble ideas. Through the fervent branches,
carried by momentary breezes of local origin,
the palpable Sublime flickered as motes on broad leaves,
while the Higher Good and the Greater Good contended
as sap on the bark of the maples, and even I
was enabled to witness the truly Existential where it loitered
famously in the shadows as if waiting for the moon.
All this I saw in the late afternoon in the company of no one.

And of course I went back to work the next morning. Like
     you,
like anyone, like the rumored angels of high office,
like the demon foremen, the bedeviled janitors, like you,
I returned to my job—but now there was a match-head in my
     thoughts.
In its light, the morning increasingly flamed through the
     window
and, lit by nothing but mind-light, I saw that the horizon
was an idea of the eye, gilded from within, and the sun
the fiery consolation of our nighttimes, coming far.
Within this expectant air, which had waited the night indoors,
carried by—who knows?—the rhythmic jarring of brain tissue
by footsteps, by colors visible to closed eyes, by a music
in my head, knowledge gathered that could not last the day,
love and error were shaken as if by the eye of a storm,
and it would not be until quitting that such a man
might drop his arms, that he had held up all day since the
     dew.

CHARLES SIMIC
(b. 1938)

Charles Simic was born in Yugoslavia, and memories of war-torn Europe haunt his imagination. He emigrated to the United States with his family in 1949, later served in the army, and graduated from New York University. Since 1974 he has taught at the University of New Hampshire and in 1990 was awarded the Pulitzer Prize. His poems seem to have emerged from the dark forest of folklore; their deceptive simplicity is the medium for Simic's unnerving attention to objects, his dream images and cognitive traps. Simic's darkly gnomic poems have made a world for themselves—a world, he says, "where magic is possible, where chance reigns, where metaphors have their supreme logic." His surrealistic technique demands that "meaning is a function of proximity. An archangel is much more interesting in the company of a pig than a saint in prayer." Angel and pig, the fabulous and the familiar—Simic's startling juxtapositions offer new definitions of reality.

Tapestry

It hangs from heaven to earth.
There are trees in it, cities, rivers,
small pigs and moons. In one corner
snow is falling over a charging cavalry,
in another women are planting rice.

You can also see:
a chicken carried off by a fox,
a naked couple on their wedding night,
a column of smoke,
an evil-eyed woman spitting into a pail of milk.

What is behind it?
—Space, plenty of empty space.

And who is talking now?
—A man asleep under a hat.

And when he wakes up?
—He'll go into the barbershop.
They'll shave his beard, nose, ears and hair
To look like everyone else.

My Shoes

Shoes, secret face of my inner life:
Two gaping toothless mouths,
Two partly decomposed animal skins
Smelling of mice-nests.

My brother and sister who died at birth
Continuing their existence in you,
Guiding my life
Toward their incomprehensible innocence.

What use are books to me
When in you it is possible to read
The Gospel of my life on earth
And still beyond, of things to come?

I want to proclaim the religion
I have devised for your perfect humility
And the strange church I am building
With you as the altar.

Ascetic and maternal, you endure:
Kin to oxen, to Saints, to condemned men,
With your mute patience, forming
The only true likeness of myself.

Concerning My Neighbors, the Hittites

Great are the Hittites.
Their ears have mice and mice have holes.
Their dogs bury themselves and leave the bones
To guard the house. A single weed holds all their storms
Until the spiderwebs spread over the heavens.
There are bits of straw in their lakes and rivers
Looking for drowned men. When a camel won't pass
Through the eye of one of their needles,
They tie a house to its tail. Great are the Hittites.
Their fathers are in cradles, their newborn make war.
To them lead floats, a leaf sinks. Their god is the size
Of a mustard seed so that he can be quickly eaten.

They also piss against the wind,
Pour water in a leaky bucket,
Strike two tears to make fire,
And have tongues with bones in them,
Bones of a wolf gnawed by lambs.

•

They are also called mound-builders,
They are called Asiatic horses
That will drink on the Rhine, they are called
My grandmother's fortune telling, they are called
You can't take it to the grave with you.

It's that hum in your left ear,
A sigh coming from deep within you,
A dream in which you keep falling forever,
The hour in which you sit up in bed
As though someone has shouted your name.
No one knows why the Hittites exist,
Still, when two are whispering
One of them is listening.

Did they catch the falling knife?
They caught it like a fly with closed mouths.

Did they balance the last egg?
They struck the egg with a bone so it won't howl.
Did they wait for dead man's shoes?
The shoes went in at one ear and out the other.
Did they wipe the blood from their mousetraps?
They burnt the blood to warm themselves.
Are they cold with no pockets in their shrouds?
If the sky falls they shall have clouds for supper.

What do they have for us
To put in our pipes and smoke?
They have the braid of a beautiful girl
That drew a team of cattle
And the engraving of him who slept
With dogs and rose with fleas
Searching for its trace in the sky.

·

And so there are fewer and fewer of them now.
Who wrote their name on paper
And burnt the paper? Who put snake-bones
In their pillows? Who threw nail-parings
In their soup? Who made them walk
Under the ladder? Who stuck pins
In their snapshots?

The wart of warts and his brother evil-eye.
Bone-lazy and her sister rabbit's-foot.
Cross-your-fingers and their father dogstar.
Knock-on-wood and his mother hell-fire.

Because the tail can't wag the cow.
Because the woods can't fly to the dove.
Because the stones haven't said their last word.
Because dunghills rise and empires fall.

·

They are leaving behind
All the silver spoons
Found inside their throats at birth,

A hand they bit because it fed them,
Two rats from a ship that is still sinking,
A collection of various split hairs,
The leaf they turned over too late.

•

All that salt cast over the shoulder,
All that bloody meat travelling under the saddles
    of nomads . . .

Here comes a forest in wolf's clothing,
The wise hen bows to the umbrella.

When the bloodshot evening meets the bloodshot night,
They tell each other bloodshot tales.

That bare branch over them speaks louder than words.
The moon is worn threadbare.

I repeat: lean days don't come singly,
It takes all kinds to make the sun rise.

The night is each man's castle.
Don't let the castle out of the bag.

Wind in the valley, wind in the high hills,
Practice will make this body fit this bed.

•

May all roads lead
Out of a sow's ear
To what's worth
Two in the bush.

Watermelons

Green Buddhas
On the fruit stand.
We eat the smile
And spit out the teeth.

Eyes Fastened with Pins

How much death works,
No one knows what a long
Day he puts in. The little
Wife always alone
Ironing death's laundry.
The beautiful daughters
Setting death's supper table.
The neighbors playing
Pinochle in the backyard
Or just sitting on the steps
Drinking beer. Death,
Meanwhile, in a strange
Part of town looking for
Someone with a bad cough,
But the address somehow wrong,
Even death can't figure it out
Among all the locked doors . . .
And the rain beginning to fall.
Long windy night ahead.
Death with not even a newspaper
To cover his head, not even
A dime to call the one pining away,
Undressing slowly, sleepily,
And stretching naked
On death's side of the bed.

Empire of Dreams

On the first page of my dreambook
It's always evening
In an occupied country.
Hour before the curfew.
A small provincial city.
The houses all dark.
The store-fronts gutted.

I am on a street corner
Where I shouldn't be.
Alone and coatless
I have gone out to look
For a black dog who answers to my whistle.
I have a kind of halloween mask
Which I am afraid to put on.

Prodigy

I grew up bent over
a chessboard.

I loved the word *endgame*.

All my cousins looked worried.

It was a small house
near a Roman graveyard.
Planes and tanks
shook its windowpanes.

A retired professor of astronomy
taught me how to play.

That must have been in 1944.

In the set we were using,
the paint had almost chipped off
the black pieces.

The white King was missing
and had to be substituted for.

I'm told but do not believe
that that summer I witnessed
men hung from telephone poles.

I remember my mother
blindfolding me a lot.
She had a way of tucking my head
suddenly under her overcoat.

In chess, too, the professor told me,
the masters play blindfolded,
the great ones on several boards
at the same time.

F R O M The World Doesn't End

We were so poor I had to take the place of the
bait in the mousetrap. All alone in the cellar, I
could hear them pacing upstairs, tossing and turn-
ing in their beds. "These are dark and evil days,"
the mouse told me as he nibbled my ear. Years
passed. My mother wore a cat-fur collar which
she stroked until its sparks lit up the cellar.

•

The stone is a mirror which works poorly.
Nothing in it but dimness. Your dimness or its dim-
ness, who's to say? In the hush your heart sounds
like a black cricket.

MICHAEL S. HARPER

(b. 1938)

"Being a Black poet and an American poet," Michael Harper has written, "are two aspects of the same story, two ways of telling the same story. I'm both/and, not either/or." Harper has been more interested in history than in polemics, and he seeks to combine myth and autobiography along with African-American traditions and idioms. His goal has been "to speak about time and place and my own people as a kind of metaphor which can be extended and applied to everybody." Although the literary influences on his work range from Theodore Roethke to Sterling Brown, the primary influence on Harper was musical—the syncopations of jazz, the sweet and sour of blues. Born in Brooklyn, New York, he was educated at California State University and the University of Iowa. Subsequent travels forced him to see "the tension between stated moral idealism and brutal historical realities, and I investigated the inner reality of those struggles to find the lyrical expression of their secrets in my own voice." Since 1970 Harper has taught at Brown.

Dear John, Dear Coltrane

a love supreme, a love supreme
a love supreme, a love supreme

> Sex fingers toes
> in the marketplace
> near your father's church
> in Hamlet, North Carolina—
> witness to this love
> in this calm fallow
> of these minds,
> there is no substitute for pain:

genitals gone or going,
seed burned out,
you tuck the roots in the earth,
turn back, and move
by river through the swamps,
singing: *a love supreme, a love supreme;*
what does it all mean?
Loss, so great each black
woman expects your failure
in mute change, the seed gone.
You plod up into the electric city—
your song now crystal and
the blues. You pick up the horn
with some will and blow
into the freezing night:
a love supreme, a love supreme—

Dawn comes and you cook
up the thick sin 'tween
impotence and death, fuel
the tenor sax cannibal
heart, genitals and sweat
that makes you clean—
a love supreme, a love supreme—

Why you so black?
cause I am
why you so funky?
cause I am
why you so black?
cause I am
why you so sweet?
cause I am
why you so black?
cause I am
a love supreme, a love supreme:

So sick
you couldn't play *Naima,*
so flat we ached

for song you'd concealed
with your own blood,
your diseased liver gave
out its purity,
the inflated heart
pumps out, the tenor kiss,
tenor love:
a love supreme, a love supreme—
a love supreme, a love supreme—

Grandfather

In 1915 my grandfather's
neighbors surrounded his house
near the dayline he ran
on the Hudson
in Catskill, NY
and thought they'd burn
his family out
in a movie they'd just seen
and be rid of his kind:
the death of a lone black
family is *the Birth*
of a Nation,
or so they thought.
His 5'4" waiter gait
quenched the white jacket smile
he'd brought back from watered
polish of my father
on the turning seats,
and he asked his neighbors
up on his thatched porch
for the first blossom of fire
that would burn him down.

They went away, his nation,
spittooning their torched necks
in the shadows of the riverboat
they'd seen, posse decomposing;
and I see him on Sutter
with white bag from your
restaurant, challenged by his first
grandson to a foot-race
he will win in white clothes.

I see him as he buys galoshes
for his railed yard near Mineo's
metal shop, where roses jump
as the el circles his house
toward Brooklyn, where his rain fell;
and I see cigar smoke in his eyes,
chocolate Madison Square Garden chews
he breaks on his set teeth,
stitched up after cancer,
the great white nation immovable
as his weight wilts
and he is on a porch
that won't hold my arms,
or the legs of the race run
forwards, or the film
played backwards on his grandson's eyes.

Nightmare Begins Responsibility

I place these numbed wrists to the pane
watching white uniforms whisk over
him in the tube-kept
prison
fear what they will do in experiment

watch my gloved stickshifting gasolined hands
breathe *boxcar-information-please* infirmary tubes
distrusting white/pink mending paperthin
silkened end hairs, distrusting tubes
shrunk in his *trunk-skincapped*
shaven head, in thighs
distrusting-white-hands-picking-baboon-light
on this son who will not make his second night
of this wardstrewn intensive airpocket
where his father's asthmatic
hymns of *night-train,* train done gone
his mother can only know that he has flown
up into essential calm unseen corridor
going boxscarred home, *mamaborn, sweetsonchild
gonedowntown* into *researchtestingwarehousebatteryacid
mama-son-done-gone* / me telling her 'nother
train tonight, no music, no breathstroked
heartbeat in my infinite distrust of them:

and of my distrusting self
white-doctor-who-breathed-for-him-all-night
say it for two sons gone,
say nightmare, say it loud
panebreaking heartmadness:
nightmare begins responsibility.

The Militance of a Photograph in the Passbook of a Bantu under Detention

Peace is the active presence of Justice.

The wrinkles on the brown face
of the carrying case
conform to the buttocks,

on which the streaks of water
from a five-gallon can
dribble on the tailfront
of the borrowed shirt
he would wear if he could
drain the pus from his swaddling
bandages, striations of skin
tunneling into the photograph.

This is no simple mug shot
of a runaway boy in a training
film, Soweto's pummeled wire,
though the turrets of light
glisten in smoke, the soft
coal hooding his platform
entrance, dull and quiet.

His father's miner's shoes
stand in puddles of polish,
the black soot baked
into images of brittle torso,
an inferno of bullets laid
out in a letter bomb,
the frontispiece of one sergeant-
major blackening his mustache.

On the drive to Evaton
a blank pass away from Sharpeville
where the freehold morgans
were bought by a black bishop
from Ontario, Canada, on a trek
northward from the Cape in 1908,
I speak to myself as the woman
riding in the backseat talks
of this day, her husband's
death, twenty-three years ago,
run over by an Afrikaner in the wrong
passing lane; the passbook on the shoulder
of the road leading to Evaton
is not the one I have in my hand,

and the photograph is not of my great-
grandfather, who set sail for Philadelphia
in the war year of 1916.
He did not want a reception, his letters
embarking on a platform at Queenstown
where his eloquence struck two Zulu warriors
pledged to die in the homelands
because they could not spin their own gold.

These threaded heads weigh down the ears
in design of the warrior, Shaka,
indifferent to the ruthless offerings
over the dead bodies of his wives,
childless in his campaigns with the British,
who sit on the ships of the Indian Ocean
each kraal shuddering near the borders;

her lips turn in profile
to the dust rising over a road
where his house once stood;
one could think of the women
carrying firewood as an etching
in remembrance to the silence,
commencing at Sharpeville,
but this is Evaton, where he would come
from across the galleyship of spears
turning in his robes to a bookmark;
it is a good book, the picture of words
in the gloss of a photograph,
the burned image of the man who wears
this image on the tongue of a child,
who might hold my hand
as we walk in late afternoon
into the predestined sun.

The press of wrinkles on the blanketed
voice of the man who took the train
from Johannesburg
is flattened in Cape Town,
and the history of this book

is on a trestle where Gandhi
worshipped in Natal,
and the Zulu lullaby
I cannot sing in Bantu
is this song in the body
of a passbook
and the book passes
into a shirt
and the back that wears it.

FRANK BIDART
(b. 1939)

Frank Bidart was born in Bakersfield, California, the son of a farmer. He graduated from the University of California at Riverside, then went to Harvard, where he studied with Robert Lowell. Although he has returned briefly to California as visiting professor at Berkeley, he has stayed in Boston and teaches at Wellesley. At the start of his career, Bidart says he realized that he "needed a way to embody the mind moving through the elements of its world, actively contending with and organizing them, while they somehow retain the illusion of their independence and nature, are felt as 'out there' or 'other.'" Drawn to extreme, sometimes psychotic states (two of his longest, most chilling dramatic monologues focus on Ellen West and Vaslav Nijinsky), Bidart achieves the voice in his poems by cinematic montage and layout on the page—syntax, punctuation, and typography reflecting the mind's unconscious strategies.

Another Life

Peut-être n'es-tu pas suffisamment mort.
C'est ici la limite de notre domaine. Devant
toi coule un fleuve.

                                    Valéry.

"—In a dream I never *exactly* dreamed,
but that is, somehow, the quintessence
of what I *might* have dreamed,

                            Kennedy is in Paris

again; it's '61; once again
some new national life seems possible,
though desperately, I try to remain unduped,
even cynical . . .

                    He's standing in an open car,

brilliantly lit, bright orange
next to a grey de Gaulle, and they stand
not far from me, slowly moving up the Champs-Elysées . . .

Bareheaded in the rain, he gives a short
choppy wave, smiling like a sun god.

—I stand and
look, suddenly at peace; once again mindlessly
moved,
            as they bear up the fields of Elysium

the possibility of Atlantic peace,

reconciliation between all that power, energy,
optimism,—
            and an older wisdom, without
illusions, without force, the austere source
of nihilism, corrupted only by its dream of Glory . . .

But no—; as I
watch, the style is

                    not quite right—;

                    Kennedy is *too* orange . . .

And de Gaulle, white, dead
white, ghost white, not even grey . . .

                            As my heart
began to grieve for my own awkwardness and
ignorance, which would never be
soothed by the informing energies
                            of whatever

wisdom saves,—

                    I saw a young man, almost
my twin, who had written
                    'MONSTER'
in awkward lettering with a crayon across
the front of his sweat shirt.
                    He was gnawing on his arm,

in rage and anger gouging up
pieces of flesh—; but as I moved to stop him, somehow
help him,
      suddenly he looked up,

and began, as I had, to look at Kennedy and de Gaulle:

and then abruptly, almost as if I were seeing him
through a camera lens, his figure
split in two,—
      or doubled,—

and all the fury
      drained from his stunned, exhausted face . . .

But only for a moment. Soon his eyes turned down
to the word on his chest. The two figures
again became one,

and with fresh energy he attacked the mutilated arm . . .

—Fascinated, I watched as this
pattern, this cycle,
      repeated several times.

Then he reached out and touched me.

—Repelled,
      I pulled back . . . But he became
frantic, demanding that I become
the body he split into:
      'It's harder
to manage *each* time! Please,
give me your energy;—*help me!*'

      —I said it was impossible,
there was *no part* of us the same:
we were just watching a parade together:
(and then, as he reached for my face)
      leave me *alone!*

He smirked, and said
I was never alone.

                I told him to go to hell.

He said that this was hell.

                  —I said it was impossible,
there was *no part* of us the same:
we were just watching a parade together:
                     when I saw

Grief, avenging Care, pale
Disease, Insanity, Age, and Fear,
                 —all the raging desolations

which I had come to learn were my patrimony;
the true progeny of my parents' marriage;
the gifts hidden within the mirror;

—standing guard at the gate of this place,
triumphant,
           striking poses
               eloquent of the disasters they embodied . . .

—I took several steps to the right, and saw
Kennedy was paper-thin,
               as was de Gaulle;
mere cardboard figures
whose possible real existence
lay buried beneath a million tumbling newspaper
                     photographs . . .

—I turned, and turned, but now all that was left
was an enormous
             fresco;—on each side, the unreadable
                  fresco of my life . . ."

Happy Birthday

Thirty-three, goodbye—
the awe I feel

is not that you won't come again, or why—

or even that after
a time, we think of those who are dead

with a sweetness that cannot be explained—

but that I've read the trading-cards:
RALPH TEMPLE CYCLIST CHAMPION TRICK RIDER

WILLIE HARRADON CYCLIST
THE YOUTHFUL PHENOMENON

F. F. IVES CYCLIST
100 MILES 6 H. 25 MIN. 30 SEC.

—as the fragile metal of their
wheels stopped turning, as they

took on wives, children, accomplishments, all those
predilections which also insisted on ending,

they could not tell themselves from what they had done.

Terrible to dress in the clothes
of a period that must end.

They didn't plan it that way—
they didn't plan it that way.

The Sacrifice

When Judas writes the history of SOLITUDE,—
. . . let him celebrate

Miss Mary Kenwood; who, without
help, placed her head in a plastic bag,

then locked herself
in a refrigerator.

•

—Six months earlier, after thirty years
teaching piano, she had watched

her mother slowly die of throat cancer.
Watched her *want* to die . . .

What once had given Mary life
in the end didn't want it.

Awake, her mother screamed for help to die.
—She felt

GUILTY . . . She knew that *all* men in these situations felt
innocent—; helpless—; yet guilty.

•

Christ knew the Secret. Betrayal
is necessary; as is woe for the betrayer.

The solution, Mary realized at last,
must be brought out of my own body.

Wiping away our sins, Christ stained us with his blood—;
to offer yourself, yet need *betrayal,* by *Judas,* before
SHOULDERING

THE GUILT OF THE WORLD—;
. . . *Give me the courage not to need Judas.*

•

When Judas writes the history of solitude,
let him record

that to the friend who opened
the refrigerator, it seemed

death fought; before giving in.

ROBERT PINSKY
(b. 1940)

Born in Long Branch, New Jersey, Robert Pinsky studied at Rutgers
and Stanford, where he came under the influence of Yvor Winters,
who advocated prosodic rigor and a discursive clarity of thought.
Those are qualities in Pinsky's own poems, which seek to reveal the
hidden emotional dimensions of ordinary activities and the communal
life. "I am interested," he has written, "in the truth of such things not
symbolically, but actually." His book-length poem, *An Explanation of
America,* explores national myths and realities without shying away
from either pungent detail or abstract meditation. His later poems turn
more boldly to fabular and autobiographical sources. All of them are
written in a balanced, pulsing style that mixes the colloquial and the
elevated, the suburban and the spiritual. Pinsky is also a forceful
critic; he has taught at Wellesley and Berkeley and is now
a professor at Boston University.

Poem about People

The jaunty crop-haired graying
Women in grocery stores,
Their clothes boyish and neat,
New mittens or clean sneakers,

Clean hands, hips not bad still,
Buying ice cream, steaks, soda,
Fresh melons and soap—or the big
Balding young men in work shoes

And green work pants, beer belly
And white T-shirt, the porky walk
Back to the truck, polite; possible
To feel briefly like Jesus,

A gust of diffuse tenderness
Crossing the dark spaces
To where the dry self burrows
Or nests, something that stirs,

Watching the kinds of people
On the street for a while—
But how love falters and flags
When anyone's difficult eyes come

Into focus, terrible gaze of a unique
Soul, its need unlovable: my friend
In his divorced schoolteacher
Apartment, his own unsuspected

Paintings hung everywhere,
Which his wife kept in a closet—
Not, he says, that she wasn't
Perfectly right; or me, mis-hearing

My rock radio sing my self-pity:
"The Angels Wished Him Dead"—all
The hideous, sudden stare of self,
Soul showing through like the lizard

Ancestry showing in the frontal gaze
Of a robin busy on the lawn.
In the movies, when the sensitive
Young Jewish soldier nearly drowns

Trying to rescue the thrashing
Anti-semitic bully, swimming across
The river raked by nazi fire,
The awful part is the part truth:

Hate my whole kind, but me,
Love me for myself. The weather
Changes in the black of night,
And the dream-wind, bowling across

The sopping open spaces
Of roads, golf-courses, parking lots,
Flails a commotion
In the dripping treetops,

Tries a half-rotten shingle
Or a down-hung branch, and we
All dream it, the dark wind crossing
The wide spaces between us.

Ralegh's Prizes

And Summer turns her head with its dark tangle
All the way toward us; and the trees are heavy,
With little sprays of limp green maple and linden
Adhering after a rainstorm to the sidewalk
Where yellow pollen dries in pools and runnels.

Along the oceanfront, pink neon at dusk:
The long, late dusk, a light wind from the water
Lifting a girl's hair forward against her cheek
And swaying a chain of bulbs.
                                        In luminous booths,
The bright, traditional wheel is on its ratchet,
And ticking gaily at its little pawl;
And the surf revolves; and passing cars and people,
Their brilliant colors—all strange and hopeful as Ralegh's
Trophies: the balsam, the prizes of untried virtue,
Bananas and armadillos that a Captain
Carries his Monarch from another world.

Dying

Nothing to be said about it, and everything—
The change of changes, closer or further away:
The Golden Retriever next door, Gussie, is dead,

Like Sandy, the Cocker Spaniel from three doors down
Who died when I was small; and every day
Things that were in my memory fade and die.

Phrases die out: first, everyone forgets
What doornails are; then after certain decades
As a dead metaphor, *"dead as a doornail"* flickers

And fades away. But someone I know is dying—
And though one might say glibly, "everyone is,"
The different pace makes the difference absolute.

The tiny invisible spores in the air we breathe,
That settle harmlessly on our drinking water
And on our skin, happen to come together

With certain conditions on the forest floor,
Or even a shady corner of the lawn—
And overnight the fleshy, pale stalks gather,

The colorless growth without a leaf or flower;
And around the stalks, the summer grass keeps growing
With steady pressure, like the insistent whiskers

That grow between shaves on a face, the nails
Growing and dying from the toes and fingers
At their own humble pace, oblivious

As the nerveless moths, that live their night or two—
Though like a moth a bright soul keeps on beating,
Bored and impatient in the monster's mouth.

The Hearts

The legendary muscle that wants and grieves,
The organ of attachment, the pump of thrills
And troubles, clinging in stubborn colonies

Like pulpy shore-life battened on a jetty.
Slashed by the little deaths of sleep and pleasure,
They swell in the nurturing spasms of the waves,

Sucking to cling; and even in death itself—
Baked, frozen—they shrink to grip the granite harder.
"Rid yourself of attachments and aversions"—

But in her father's orchard, already, he says
He'd like to be her bird, and she says: Sweet, yes,
Yet I should kill thee with much cherishing,

Showing that she knows already—as Art Pepper,
That first time he takes heroin, already knows
That he will go to prison, and that he'll suffer

And knows he needs to have it, or die; and the one
Who makes the General lose the world for love
Lets him say, *Would I had never seen her,* but Oh!

Says Enobarbus, Then you would have missed
A wonderful piece of work, which left unseen
Would bring less glory to your travels. Among

The creatures in the rock-torn surf, a wave
Of agitation, a gasp. A scholar quips,
Shakespeare was almost certainly homosexual,

Bisexual, or heterosexual, the sonnets
Provide no evidence on the matter. He writes
Romeo an extravagant speech on tears,

In the Italian manner, his teardrops cover
His chamber window, says the boy, he calls them crystals,
Inanely, and sings them to Juliet with his heart:

The almost certainly invented heart
Which Buddha denounces, in its endless changes
Forever jumping and moving, like an ape.

Over the poor beast's head the crystal fountain
Crashes illusions, the cold salt spume of pain
And meaningless distinction, as Buddha says,

But here in the crystal shower mouths are open
To sing, it is Lee Andrews and The Hearts
In 1957, singing *I sit in my room*

Looking out at the rain. My teardrops are
Like crystals, they cover my windowpane, the turns
Of these illusions we make become their glory:

To Buddha every distinct thing is illusion
And becoming is destruction, but still we sing
In the shower. I do. In the beginning God drenched

The Emptiness with images: the potter
Crosslegged at his wheel in Benares market
Making mud cups, another cup each second

Tapering up between his fingers, one more
To sell the tea-seller at a penny a dozen,
And tea a penny a cup. The customers smash

The empties, and waves of traffic grind the shards
To mud for new cups, in turn; and I keep one here
Next to me: holding it a while from out of the cloud

Of dust that rises from the shattered pieces,
The risen dust alive with fire, then settled
And soaked and whirling again on the wheel that turns

And looks on the world as on another cloud,
On everything the heart can grasp and throw away
As a passing cloud, with even Enlightenment

Itself another image, another cloud
To break and churn a salt foam over the heart
Like an anemone that sucks at clouds and makes

Itself with clouds and sings in clouds and covers
Its windowpane with clouds that blur and melt,
Until one clings and holds—as once in the Temple

In the time before the Temple was destroyed
A young priest saw the seraphim of the Lord:
Each had six wings, with two they covered their faces,

With two they covered their legs and feet, with two
They darted and hovered like dragonflies or perched
Like griffins in the shadows near the ceiling—

These are the visions, too barbarous for heaven
And too preposterous for belief on earth,
God sends to taunt his prophet with the truth

No one can see, that leads to who knows where.
A seraph took a live coal from the altar
And seared the prophet's lips, and so he spoke.

As the record ends, a coda in retard:
The Hearts in a shifting velvety *ah,* and *ah*
Prolonged again, and again as Lee Andrews

Reaches *ah* high for *I have to gain Faith, Hope*
And Charity, God only knows the girl
Who will love me—Oh! if we only could

Start over again! Then The Hearts chant the chords
Again a final time, *ah* and the record turns
Through all the music, and on into silence again.

ROBERT HASS
(b. 1941)

Robert Hass was born in San Francisco, graduated from St. Mary's
College, and took his Ph.D. from Stanford in 1971. Also a critic,
translator, and editor, he teaches at Berkeley. He was the 1972 Yale
Younger Poet and in 1985 won the National Book Critics Circle
Award for criticism. The California coast—the rugged, exquisite
landscape of Robinson Jeffers—dominates Hass's first book, but his
subsequent work moved from description to meditation. While still
colloquial and vigorous, his style has grown more intellectually
complex. In it an instinctive, sometimes erotic, wonder at the world is
combined with a skeptical imagination. He acknowledges William
Wordsworth and Ezra Pound as important influences; the poetic
sensibility of the Orient is also apparent in Hass's explorations of
the nature of desire and the limits of language as it crosses with
and seeks to capture experience.

Heroic Simile

When the swordsman fell in Kurosawa's *Seven Samurai*
in the gray rain,
in Cinemascope and the Tokugawa dynasty,
he fell straight as a pine, he fell
as Ajax fell in Homer
in chanted dactyls and the tree was so huge
the woodsman returned for two days
to that lucky place before he was done with the sawing
and on the third day he brought his uncle.

They stacked logs in the resinous air,
hacking the small limbs off,
tying those bundles separately.
The slabs near the root
were quartered and still they were awkwardly large;

the logs from midtree they halved:
ten bundles and four great piles of fragrant wood,
moons and quarter moons and half moons
ridged by the saw's tooth.

The woodsman and the old man his uncle
are standing in midforest
on a floor of pine silt and spring mud.
They have stopped working
because they are tired and because
I have imagined no pack animal
or primitive wagon. They are too canny
to call in neighbors and come home
with a few logs after three days' work.
They are waiting for me to do something
or for the overseer of the Great Lord
to come and arrest them.

How patient they are!
The old man smokes a pipe and spits.
The young man is thinking he would be rich
if he were already rich and had a mule.
Ten days of hauling
and on the seventh day they'll probably
be caught, go home empty-handed
or worse. I don't know
whether they're Japanese or Mycenaean
and there's nothing I can do.
The path from here to that village
is not translated. A hero, dying,
gives off stillness to the air.
A man and a woman walk from the movies
to the house in the silence of separate fidelities.
There are limits to imagination.

Meditation at Lagunitas

All the new thinking is about loss.
In this it resembles all the old thinking.
The idea, for example, that each particular erases
the luminous clarity of a general idea. That the clown-
faced woodpecker probing the dead sculpted trunk
of that black birch is, by his presence,
some tragic falling off from a first world
of undivided light. Or the other notion that,
because there is in this world no one thing
to which the bramble of *blackberry* corresponds,
a word is elegy to what it signifies.
We talked about it late last night and in the voice
of my friend, there was a thin wire of grief, a tone
almost querulous. After a while I understood that,
talking this way, everything dissolves: *justice,*
pine, hair, woman, you and *I.* There was a woman
I made love to and I remembered how, holding
her small shoulders in my hands sometimes,
I felt a violent wonder at her presence
like a thirst for salt, for my childhood river
with its island willows, silly music from the pleasure boat,
muddy places where we caught the little orange-silver fish
called *pumpkinseed.* It hardly had to do with her.
Longing, we say, because desire is full
of endless distances. I must have been the same to her.
But I remember so much, the way her hands dismantled bread,
the thing her father said that hurt her, what
she dreamed. There are moments when the body is as
        numinous
as words, days that are the good flesh continuing.
Such tenderness, those afternoons and evenings,
saying *blackberry, blackberry, blackberry.*

Between the Wars

When I ran, it rained. Late in the afternoon—
midsummer, upstate New York, mornings I wrote,
read Polish history, and there was a woman
whom I thought about; outside the moody, humid
American sublime—late in the afternoon,
toward sundown, just as the sky was darkening,
the light came up and redwings settled in the cattails.
They were death's idea of twilight, the whole notes
of a requiem the massed clouds croaked
above the somber fields. *Lady of eyelashes,*
do you hear me? Whiteness, otter's body,
coolness of the morning, rubbed amber
and the skin's salt, do you hear me? This is Poland speaking,
"era of the dawn of freedom," nineteen twenty-two.
When I ran, it rained. The blackbirds settled
their clannish squabbles in the reeds, and light came up.
First darkening, then light. And then pure fire.
Where does it come from? out of the impure
shining that rises from the soaked odor of the grass,
the levitating, Congregational, meadow-light-at-twilight
light that darkens the heavy-headed blossoms
of wild carrot, out of that, out of nothing
it boils up, pools on the horizon, fissures up,
igniting the undersides of clouds: pink flame,
red flame, vermilion, purple, deeper purple, dark.
You could wring the sourness of the sumac from the air,
the fescue sweetness from the grass, the slightly
maniacal cicadas tuning up to tear the fabric
of the silence into tatters, so that night,
if it wants to, comes as a beggar to the door
at which, if you do not offer milk and barley
to the maimed figure of the god, your well will foul,
your crops will wither in the fields. In the eastern marches
children know the story that the aspen quivers
because it failed to hide the Virgin and the Child

when Herod's hunters were abroad. Think: night is the god
dressed as the beggar drinking the sweet milk.
Gray beard, thin shanks, the look in the eyes
idiot, unbearable, the wizened mouth agape,
like an infant's that has cried and sucked and cried
and paused to catch its breath. The pink nubbin
of the nipple glistens. I'll suckle at that breast,
the one in the song of the muttering illumination
of the fields before the sun goes down, before
the black train crosses the frontier from Prussia
into Poland in the age of the dawn of freedom.
Fifty freight cars from America, full of medicine
and the latest miracle, canned food.
The war is over. There are unburied bones
in the fields at sun-up, skylarks singing,
starved children begging chocolate on the tracks.

Misery and Splendor

Summoned by conscious recollection, she
would be smiling, they might be in a kitchen talking,
before or after dinner. But they are in this other room,
the window has many small panes, and they are on a couch
embracing. He holds her as tightly
as he can, she buries herself in his body.
Morning, maybe it is evening, light
is flowing through the room. Outside,
the day is slowly succeeded by night,
succeeded by day. The process wobbles wildly
and accelerates: weeks, months, years. The light in the room
does not change, so it is plain what is happening.
They are trying to become one creature,
and something will not have it. They are tender
with each other, afraid

their brief, sharp cries will reconcile them to the moment
when they fall away again. So they rub against each other,
their mouths dry, then wet, then dry.
They feel themselves at the center of a powerful
and baffled will. They feel
they are an almost animal,
washed up on the shore of a world—
or huddled against the gate of a garden—
to which they can't admit they can never be admitted.

AMY CLAMPITT
(b. 1920)

Although she had been writing for years, Amy Clampitt's first commercial book was not published until she was sixty-three. During her long apprenticeship, while she worked as a librarian for the National Audubon Society in New York City and as a free-lance researcher and editor, Clampitt wrote novels as well as poems; her narrative scaffoldings and erudite fascination with details from the natural world can be traced to this background. The longer perspectives of her background—Clampitt was born in New Providence, Iowa, and educated at Grinnell—are also evident in her choice of subjects. A tourist's curiosity, a reader's speculative passions, and a citizen's moral quandaries are among her concerns. Her style, marked by a volute syntax and rich rhetorical gestures, does not obscure the traditional themes—mortality chief among them—that structure and sustain the dramatic shape and force of her verse.

Beach Glass

While you walk the water's edge,
turning over concepts
I can't envision, the honking buoy
serves notice that at any time
the wind may change,
the reef-bell clatters
its treble monotone, deaf as Cassandra
to any note but warning. The ocean,
cumbered by no business more urgent
than keeping open old accounts
that never balanced,
goes on shuffling its millenniums
of quartz, granite, and basalt.
                              It behaves

toward the permutations of novelty—
driftwood and shipwreck, last night's
beer cans, spilt oil, the coughed-up
residue of plastic—with random
impartiality, playing catch or tag
or touch-last like a terrier,
turning the same thing over and over,
over and over. For the ocean, nothing
is beneath consideration.
                        The houses
of so many mussels and periwinkles
have been abandoned here, it's hopeless
to know which to salvage. Instead
I keep a lookout for beach glass—
amber of Budweiser, chrysoprase
of Almadén and Gallo, lapis
by way of (no getting around it,
I'm afraid) Phillips'
Milk of Magnesia, with now and then a rare
translucent turquoise or blurred amethyst
of no known origin.
                        The process
goes on forever: they came from sand,
they go back to gravel,
along with the treasuries
of Murano, the buttressed
astonishments of Chartres,
which even now are readying
for being turned over and over as gravely
and gradually as an intellect
engaged in the hazardous
redefinition of structures
no one has yet looked at.

Imago

Sometimes, she remembers, a chipped flint
would turn up in a furrow,
pink as a peony (from the iron in it)
or as the flared throat of a seashell:
a nomad's artifact fished from the broth,
half sea half land—hard evidence
of an unfathomed state of mind.

Nomads. The wagon train that camped
and left its name on Mormon Ridge.
The settlers who moved on to California,
bequeathing a laprobe pieced from the hide
of a dead buffalo, the frail sleigh
that sleeps under the haymow, and a headstone
so small it might be playing house,
for the infant daughter, aged two days,
no name, they also left behind.

Half sea half land: the shirker propped
above her book in a farmhouse parlor
lolls with the merfolk who revert to foam,
eyeing at a distance the lit pavilions
that seduced her, their tailed child,
into the palaces of metamorphosis. She pays
now (though they do not know this)
by treading, at every step she takes,
on a parterre of tomahawks.

A thirst for something definite so dense
it feels like drowning. Grant Wood
turned everything to cauliflower,
the rounded contours of a thunderhead,
flint-hard. He made us proud:
though all those edges might not be quite
the way it was, at least he'd tried.

"But it has no form!" they'd say to
the scribbler whose floundering fragments
kept getting out of hand—and who, either
fed up with or starved out of
her native sloughs, would, stowed aboard
the usual nomadic moving van, trundle her
dismantled sensibility elsewhere.

Europe, that hodgepodge of ancestral
calamities, was hard and handsome, its rubble
confident, not shriveling on the vine,
as here, like an infertile melon—the Virgin
jejune in her grotto of cold plaster, half sick
of that sidelong enclave, the whispered "Cathlick."

Antiquity unshrouds on wimpling canvas,
adjunct of schoolhouse make-believe: the Italy
of urns and cypresses, of stairways
evolving toward a state of mind
not to be found except backstage
among hunchbacks and the miscreants
who control the scenery, flanked
by a pair of masks whose look, at even
this remove, could drill through bone:
the tragic howl, the comic rictus,
eyeholes that stare out of the crypt
of what no grownup is ever heard to speak of
but in the strangled tone whose lexicon
is summed up in one word: *Bankrupt.*

Bankrupt: the abysm of history,
a slough to be pulled out of
any way you could. Antiquity, the backward
suction of the dark, amounted to a knothole
you plugged with straw, old rags, pages
ripped from last year's Sears Roebuck catalog,
anything, to ward off the blizzard.

Not so, for the born-again, the
shuddering orifices of summer.

On prayer-meeting night, outside
the vestibule among multiple
bell-pulls of Virginia creeper,
the terrible clepsydra of becoming
distils its drop: a luna moth, the emblem
of the born-again, furred like an orchid
behind the ferned antennae, a totem-
garden of lascivious pheromones,
hangs, its glimmering streamers
pierced by the dripstone burin of the eons
with the predatory stare out of the burrow,
those same eyeholes. Imago
of unfathomable evolvings, living
only to copulate and drop its litter,
does it know what it is, what it has been,
what it may or must become?

Stacking the Straw

In those days the oatfields'
fenced-in vats of running platinum,
the yellower alloy of wheat and barley,
whose end, however gorgeous all that trammeled
rippling in the wind, came down
to toaster-fodder, cereal
as a commodity, were a rebuke
to permanence—to bronze or any metal
less utilitarian than the barbed braids
that marked off a farmer's property,
or the stoked dinosaur of a steam engine
that made its rounds from farm to farm,
after the grain was cut and bundled,
and powered the machine that did the threshing.

Strawstacks' beveled loaves, a shape
that's now extinct, in those days were
the nearest thing the region had
to monumental sculpture. While hayracks
and wagons came and went, delivering bundles,
carting the winnowed ore off to the granary,

a lone man with a pitchfork stood aloft
beside the hot mouth of the blower,
building about himself, forkful
by delicately maneuvered forkful,
a kind of mountain, the golden
stuff of mulch, bedding for animals.
I always thought of him with awe—
a craftsman whose evolving altitude
gave him the aura of a hero. He'd come down
from the summit of the season's effort
black with the baser residues of that
discarded gold. Saint Thomas of Aquino
also came down from the summit
of a lifetime's effort, and declared
that everything he'd ever done was straw.

Medusa

The tentacles, the brazen phiz whose glare
stands every fibril of the mind on end—
lust looked at backward as it were,
an antique scare tactic, either self-protection
or a libel on the sex whose periodic
blossom hangs its ungathered garland
from the horned clockwork of the moon:
as cause or consequence, or both, hysteric
symptoms no doubt figure here. She'd been

a beauty till Poseidon, in a flagrant
trespass, closed with her on Athena's temple floor.

The tide-rip torrents in the blood, the dark
gods not to be denied—or a mere indiscretion?
Athena had no time at all for talk like this.
The sea-god might be her old rival, but the woman
he'd gone to bed with was the one who paid.
A virginal revenge at one remove—there's none more
sordid or more apt to ramify, as this one did:
the fulgent tresses roiled to water-snake-
like writhe, and for long lashes'
come-hither flutterings, the stare
that hardens the psyche's soft parts to rock.

The female ogre, for the Puritan
revisionists who took her over, had a new
and siren sliminess. John Milton
put her at the gate of hell, *a woman to
the waist, and fair; but ended foul, in
many a scaly fold, voluminous and vast—*
whose name indeed was Sin. And in the den
of doctrine run amok, the armored glister
of a plodding Holiness revealed her
as likewise divided but, all told, *most
loathsome, filthy, foul, and full of vile disdain.*

The Gorgon, though, is no such Manichean tease,
no mantrap caterer of forbidden dishes,
whose lewd stews keep transgression warm.
The stinging jellyfish, the tubeworm,
the tunicate, the sea anemone's
whorled comb are privier to her mysteries:
her salts are cold, her home-
land Hyperborean (the realm that gave us
the Snow Queen and the English gentleman),
her mask the ravening aspect of the moon,
her theater a threshing floor that terror froze.

Terror of origins: the sea's heave, the cold mother
of us all; disdain of the allure that draws us in,

that stifles as it nurtures, that feeds on
what it feeds, on what it comforts, whether male
or female: ay, in the very tissue of desire
lodge viscid barbs that turn the blood to coral,
the heartbeat to a bed of silicates. What surgeon
can unthread those multiplicities of cause
of hurt from its effect; dislodge, spicule by spicule,
the fearful armories within; unclench the airless
petrifaction toward the core, the geode's rigor?

DAVE SMITH
(b. 1942)

David Jeddie Smith was born in Portsmouth, Virginia, and educated at
the University of Virginia, Southern Illinois University, and Ohio
University. He has taught at many universities, including those of
Utah and Florida, and is now professor of English at Virginia
Commonwealth University. Heir to the expansive southern rhetoric,
mythic imagination, and narrative energies of Robert Penn Warren
and James Dickey, Smith writes in a husky, bardic manner of human
rituals and rural tragedies, as well as of the quieter recesses of
memory. His earlier poems were often dramatic monologues and
haunted testimonies; since then Smith has developed his voice into
what he calls a "second self." The settings of his poems—from
tidewater Virginia to the Utah mountains—
are charged, symbolic landscapes.

Elegy in an Abandoned Boatyard

. . . mindful of the unhonored dead
                    —Thomas Gray

Here they stood, whom the Kecoughtan first believed
gods from another world, one pair of longjohns
each, bad-yellow, knotted with lice,
the godless bandy-legged runts
with ear bit off, or eye gouged,
                              who killed and prayed
over whatever flew, squatted, or swam.

In huts hacked from mulberry, pine, and swamp cypress,
they huddled ripe as hounds.
At cockcrow scratched, shuffled paths,
took skiffs and ferried to dead-rise scows,
twenty-footers of local design and right draft

for oysters, crabs, and croakers.
                              They were seaworthy.

According to diaries hand-scrawled, and terse court records,
our ancestors: barbarous, habitual, Virginians.

Some would not sail, came ashore, walked on the land,
kept faces clenched, lay seed and family,
moved often, and are gone. Of them
this harbor says nothing.
                              Of the sea's workmen, not much,
no brass plate of honor, no monument in the square,
no square, merely the wreckage of a place.
                              But they stood,
proud, surly in mist at the hovel of the boatwright,
the arm pointed: *Build me one like that yonder!*
Meaning the hull I see bottom up in ashen water—

nameless now as themselves, except to the squat one
known to crush clams in his palms, our kin,
the boatwright. He gave credit to each son,
barring feud, and took stick in hand
to dig from earth the grave first line of a keel,

who often would lift his brow seaward, but nothing said,
while a shape buried in air hove up
and he made it become what they wanted,
                              Like that one yonder!

And this was all the image for tomorrow he would give,
each reimagined, the best guess changing
to meet the sea's habitual story
of rot and stink and silence.
To make the hulls he knew
would riddle to nothing, he came
into this world as I have now entered his place
and sit at his charred and flood-finished log.

Only when I begin to hear the lies
he allowed each to invent
can I feel the hugeness of his belief, when I take up
a cap left as worthless, hung on a cypress stump, or feel

the plain cast of a stick pulse down my arm like the current
of conception—
                    then I see it,
                            an immense shadow
on water.
                My eyes harden,
                        and there it is,
                                the wind cradle
of the Eagle's wings. As it might be for men,
even the least, riding the rising funnel
of air, dreaming change,
                        until I think of chicks screeching,
and the unborn who need us
to honor the places and the names of their passage
as we sit and try to dream back
the first wreckage, the last hope. I see
                        the one brother
become many floating and sinking,
lovely shadows all over the earth, and put my back
against the trunk they left me here, and pull
the stick to shape the dirt.
                        The line grows
quick with hunger, not perfect
but man-shaped and flight-worthy, a kind
of speech I take
for the unfinished country
the boatwright must have
dreamed, looking for his image
to rise and loom clearer
out of the water that beats in,
out of the water that bore us all here.

The Roundhouse Voices

In full glare of sunlight I came here, man-tall but thin
as a pinstripe, and stood outside the rusted fence

with its crown of iron thorns while
the soot cut into our lungs with tiny diamonds.
I walked through houses with my grain-lovely slugger
from Louisville that my uncle bought and stood
in the sun that made its glove soft on my hand
until I saw my chance to crawl under and get past
anyone who would demand a badge and a name.

The guard hollered that I could get the hell from there quick
when I popped in his face like a thief. All I ever wanted
to steal was life and you can't get that easy
in the grind of a railyard. *You can't catch me,*
lardass, I can go left or right good as the Mick,
I hummed to him, holding my slugger by the neck
for a bunt laid smooth where the coal cars
jerked and let me pass between tracks
until, in a slide on ash, I fell safe and heard
the wheeze of his words: *Who the hell are you, kid?*

I hear them again tonight, Uncle, hard as big brakeshoes,
when I lean over your face in the box of silk. The years
you spent hobbling from room to room alone crawl
up my legs and turn this house to another
house, round and black as defeat, where slugging
comes easy when you whip the gray softball over
the glass diesel globe. Footsteps thump on the stairs
like that fat ball against bricks and when I miss
I hear you warn me to watch the timing, to keep
my eyes on your hand and forget the fence,
hearing also that other voice that keeps me out and away
from you on a day worth playing good ball. Hearing
Who the hell . . . I see myself like a burning speck
of cinder come down the hill and through a tunnel
of porches like stands, running on deep ash,
and I give him the finger, whose face still gleams
clear as a B&O headlight, just to make him get up
and chase me into a dream of scoring at your feet.
At Christmas that guard staggered home sobbing,
the thing in his chest tight as a torque wrench.
In the summer I did not have to run and now

who is the one who dreams of a drink as he leans over
tools you kept bright as a first-girl's promise? I
have no one to run from or to, nobody to give
my finger to as I steal his peace. Uncle, the light
bleeds on your gray face like the high barbed-wire
shadows I had to get through and maybe you don't remember
you said to come back, to wait and you'd show me
the right way to take a hard pitch
in the sun that shudders on the ready man. I'm here

though this is a day I did not want to see. In the roundhouse
the rasp and heel-click of compressors is still,
soot lies deep in every greasy fingerprint.
I called you from the pits and you did not come up
and I felt the fear when I stood on the tracks
that are like stars which never lead us
into any kind of light and I don't know who'll
tell me now when the guard sticks his blind snoot
between us: take off and beat the bastard out.
Can you hear him over the yard, grabbing his chest,
cry out, *Who the goddamn hell are you, kid?*

I gave him every name in the book, Uncle, but he caught us
and what good did all those hours of coaching do?
You lie on your back, eyeless forever, and I think
how once I climbed to the top of a diesel and stared
into that gray roundhouse glass where, in anger,
you threw up the ball and made a star
to swear at greater than the Mick ever dreamed.
It has been years but now I know what followed there
every morning the sun came up, not light
but the puffing bad-bellied light of words.

All day I have held your hand, trying to say back that life,
to get under that fence with words I lined
and linked up and steamed into a cold room
where the illusion of hope means skin torn in boxes
of tools. The footsteps come pounding into words
and even the finger I give death is words
that won't let us be what we wanted, each one

chasing and being chased by dreams in the dark.
Words are all we ever were and they did us
no damn good. Do you hear that?

Do you hear the words that, in oiled gravel, you gave me
when you set my feet in the right stance to swing?
They are coal-hard and they come in wings
and loops like despair not even the Mick
could knock out of this room, words softer
than the centers of hearts in guards or uncles,
words skinned and numbed by too many bricks.
I have had enough of them and bring them back here
where the tick and creak of everything dies
in your tiny starlight and I stand down
on my knees to cry, *Who the hell are you, kid?*

Lake Drummond Dream

"For we are not pans and barrows . . ."
      —Ralph Waldo Emerson

Reading Emerson. Cottonmouths are moving mildly
in swamp midden, the whip
of nerve-spurred flesh
going down, glints

incidental in the rolling fume of darkness
where the moon fingers like thought
and eases around the rib cage
of beauty. To find life

in the eye's cleavage: a spread spiralling water
gone still, sudden. Puddle in back yard,
the standing scum. Depth unexpected
in all things, the striking

quickness of the afternoon overhead, remembered,
and not to be able to confess the name,
the nature of what marries all.
Then, the self sitting

stiller than the sparrowhawk inside his glance,
already owning, without awareness,
small wings. Dreaming of home,
the lake, spine-sliders,

not expecting to touch, across the library desk,
a woman's hand, finding it dry, cool,
eyes shocked open, all
the darkness around

uncurled from deep texts of matter. Know it comes,
hear, touch time's announcement. Plant
the feet on the floor's waterskin.
Try to know the unavoidable

thing, meeting its depth.

MARILYN HACKER

(b. 1942)

Marilyn Hacker was born in New York City on Thanksgiving Day.
She was educated at New York University and the Art Students
League. Having worked as an antiquarian bookseller, she is now a
teacher and magazine editor, living with her daughter part of each
year in New York and part in Paris. Her first book won both the 1973
Lamont Prize and the 1975 National Book Award. Prosodic virtuosity
and a rakish tone have been hallmarks of her verse from the start.
Each of Hacker's books has been an installment of the chronicle of
her own history, often filled with erotic intrigues, political struggles,
and exotic locales and characters. She dredges her romantic impulses
with irony, and her candid, self-knowing, generous manner deals
effectively with both the lesbian affairs she recounts and the pointed
feminist attitudes she maintains.

FROM **Taking Notice**

7

If we talk, we're too tired to make love; if we
make love, these days, there's hardly time to talk.
We sit to share supper once, twice a week.
You're red and white with cold; we're brusque, scared, shy.
Difficult speech curdles the café au lait
next morning. In the short twelve hours between
we rubbed, laughed, tongued, exhorted, listened, came,
slept like packed spoons. Wrapped up against the day
we trudge through slush as far as the downtown
subway, brush cold-tattered lips. You're gone
to hunch sock-shod over your camera, while

I stare a spiral notebook down six miles
north, indulging some rich weave of weeks where
we'd work, play, not cross-reference calendars.

11

In the Public Theater lobby, I wait for Marie.
Black overcoat, brown plait: two people waltz
close, through the crowd's buzz. I watch, finding fault
with the dance's hierarchic He and She.
They weave past; Tall leads, Short follows. I see
they're women. I love them. I stand near
them, grin, wish I wore a lavender star.
Marie's here, blinking, owlish. We hug. We
go upstairs. The two women sit one row
ahead, kissing. I look at them, look away.
They are more edifying than the play
(will they laugh at woman-made misogyny?
Yes . . .) but I shouldn't stare, and when I do
I flush above the belt and throb below.

14

And I shout at Iva, whine at you. Easily
we choose up for nuclear family,
with me the indirect, snivelling, put-upon
mother/wife, child's villain, feminist heroine,
bore. On thick white plates the failed communion
congeals. Iva bawls in her room. You're on
edge, worked out, fed up, could leave. Shakily
we stop. You wash dishes, drop one; it breaks. We
should laugh. We don't. A potted plant crashed too.
Frowning, I salvage the crushed shoots, while you
deflect my scowl with yours. You leave a phone
message for your friend, while I read one
last picture book, permit a bedtime drink
to a nude child, who's forgiven me—I think.

25

We work, play, don't cross-reference calendars
here. Sun gilds a scrub-oak hill; the fig tree
drops purple dry first fruit on the cement
terrace that's, for the rest of August, ours,
where you project perspectives, blond head bent
to big papers. I chart stratigraphy
of my desk, glimpse, in a pitcher, flowers
you brought, for our year, though we're both diffident
to celebrate. I start letters, can't write
what it's like, face to face, learning to live
through four A.M. eruptions, when we fight
like bruised children we were. Can I believe
persistent love demands change, not forgive-
ness, accept the hard gift of your different sight?

Ballad of Ladies Lost and Found

for Julia Alvarez

Where are the women who, *entre deux guerres,*
came out on college-graduation trips,
came to New York on football scholarships,
came to town meeting in a decorous pair?
Where are the expatriate *salonnières,*
the gym teacher, the math-department head?
Do nieces follow where their odd aunts led?
The elephants die off in Cagnes-sur-Mer.
H.D., whose "nature was bisexual,"
and plain old Margaret Fuller died as well.

Where are the single-combat champions:
the Chevalier d'Eon with curled peruke,
Big Sweet who ran with Zora in the jook,
open-handed Winifred Ellerman,
Colette, who hedged her bets and always won?
Sojourner's sojourned where she need not pack

decades of whitegirl conscience on her back.
The spirit gave up Zora; she lay down
under a weed-field miles from Eatonville,
and plain old Margaret Fuller died as well.

Where's Stevie, with her pleated schoolgirl dresses,
and Rosa, with her permit to wear pants?
Who snuffed Clara's *mestiza* flamboyance
and bled Frida onto her canvases?
Where are the Niggerati hostesses,
the kohl-eyed ivory poets with severe
chignons, the rebels who grew out their hair,
the bulldaggers with marcelled processes?
Conglomerates co-opted Sugar Hill,
and plain old Margaret Fuller died as well.

Anne Hutchinson, called witch, termagant, whore,
fell to the long knives, having tricked the noose.
Carolina María de Jesús'
tale from the slagheaps of the landless poor
ended on a straw mat on a dirt floor.
In action thirteen years after fifteen
in prison, Eleanor of Aquitaine
accomplished half of Europe and fourscore
anniversaries for good or ill,
and plain old Margaret Fuller died as well.

Has Ida B. persuaded Susan B.
to pool resources for a joint campaign?
(Two Harriets act a pageant by Lorraine,
cheered by the butch drunk on the IRT
who used to watch me watch her watching me;
We've notes by Angelina Grimké Weld
for choral settings drawn from the *Compiled
Poems* of Angelina Weld Grimké.)
There's no such tense as Past Conditional,
and plain old Margaret Fuller died as well.

Who was Sappho's protégée, and when did
we lose Hrotsvitha, dramaturge and nun?

What did bibulous Suzanne Valadon
think about Artemisia, who tended
to make a life-size murderess look splendid?
Where's Aphra, fond of dalliance and the pun?
Where's Jane, who didn't indulge in either one?
Whoever knows how Ende, Pintrix, ended
is not teaching Art History at Yale,
and plain old Margaret Fuller died as well.

Is Beruliah upstairs behind the curtain
debating Juana Inés de la Cruz?
Where's *savante* Anabella, Augusta-Goose,
Fanny, Maude, Lidian, Freda and Caitlin,
"without whom this could never have been written"?
Louisa who wrote, scrimped, saved, sewed, and nursed,
Malinche, who's, like all translators, cursed,
Bessie, whose voice was hemp and steel and satin,
outside a segregated hospital,
and plain old Margaret Fuller died as well.

Where's Amy, who kept Ada in cigars
and love, requited, both country and courtly,
although quinquagenarian and portly?
Where's Emily? It's very still upstairs.
Where's Billie, whose strange fruit ripened in bars?
Where's the street-scavenging Little Sparrow?
Too poor, too mean, too weird, too wide, too narrow:
Marie Curie, examining her scars,
was not particularly beautiful;
and plain old Margaret Fuller died as well.

Who was the grandmother of Frankenstein?
The Vindicatrix of the Rights of Woman.
Madame de Sévigné said prayers to summon
the postman just as eloquent as mine,
though my Madame de Grignan's only nine.
But Mary Wollstonecraft had never known
that daughter, nor did Paula Modersohn.
The three-day infants blinked in the sunshine.

The mothers turned their faces to the wall;
and plain old Margaret Fuller died as well.

Tomorrow night the harvest moon will wane
that's floodlighting the silhouetted wood.
Make your own footnotes; it will do you good.
Emeritae have nothing to explain.
She wasn't very old, or really plain—
my age exactly, volumes incomplete.
"The life, the life, will it never be sweet?"
She wrote it once; I quote it once again
midlife at midnight when the moon is full
and I can almost hear the warning bell
offshore, sounding through starlight like a stain
on waves that heaved over what she began
and truncated a woman's chronicle,
and plain old Margaret Fuller died as well.

Nights of 1964–66: The Old Reliable

The laughing soldiers fought to their defeat
        JAMES FENTON, "In a Notebook"

White decorators interested in art,
Black file clerks with theatrical ambitions,
kids making pharmaceutical revisions
in journals Comp. instructors urged they start,
the part-Cherokee teenage genius (maybe)
the secretary who hung out with fairies,
the copywriter wanting to know, where is
my husband? the soprano with the baby,
all drank draft beer or lethal sweet Manhattans
or improvised concoctions with tequila
in summer, when, from Third Street, we could feel a
night breeze waft in whose fragrances were Latin.

The place was run by Polish refugees:
squat Margie, gaunt Speedy (whose sobriquet
transliterated what?) He'd brought his play
from Łódź. After a while, we guessed Margie's
illiteracy was why *he* cashed checks
and *she* perched near the threshold to ban pros,
the underage, the fugitive, and those
arrayed impertinently to their sex.
The bar was talk and cruising; in the back
room, we danced: Martha and the Vandellas,
Smokey and the Miracles; while sellers
and buyers changed crisp tens for smoke and smack.
Some came in after work, some after supper,
plumage replenished to meet who knew who.
Behind the bar, Margie dished up beef stew.
On weeknights, you could always find an upper
to speed you to your desk, and drink till four.
Loosened by booze, we drifted, on the ripples
of Motown, home in new couples, or triples,
were back at dusk, with ID's, at the door.
Bill was my roommate, Russell drank with me,
although they were a dozen years my seniors.
I walked off with the eighteen-year-old genius
—an Older Woman, barely twenty-three.
Link was new as Rimbaud, and better looking,
North Beach bar *paideon* of doomed Jack Spicer,
like Russell, our two-meter artificer,
a Corvo whose *ecclesia* was cooking.
Bill and Russell were painters. Bill had been
a monk in Kyoto. Stoned, we sketched together,
till he discovered poppers and black leather
and Zen consented to new discipline.
We shared my Sixth Street flat with a morose
cat, an arch cat, and pot-plants we pruned daily.
His boyfriend had left him for an Israeli
dancer; my husband was on Mykonos.
Russell loved Harold who was Black and bad,
and lavished on him dinners "meant for men"
like Escoffier and Brillat-Savarin.

Staunch blond Dora made rice. When she had
tucked in the twins, six flights of tenement
stairs they'd descend, elevenish, and stroll
down Third Street, desultory night patrol
gone mauve and green under the virulent
streetlights, to the bar, where Bill and I
(if we'd not come to dinner), Link, and Lew,
and Betty had already had a few.
One sweatsoaked night in pitiless July,
wedged on booth-benches of cracked Naugahyde,
we planned a literary magazine
where North Beach met the Lower East Side scene.
We could have called it *When Worlds Collide*.
Dora was gone, "In case the children wake up."
Link lightly had decamped with someone else
(the German engineer? Or was he Bill's?).
Russell's stooped *vale* brushed my absent makeup.
Armed children spared us home, our good-night hugs
laisser-passer. We railed against the war.
Soon, some of us bussed South with SNCC and CORE.
Soon, some of us got busted dealing drugs.
The file clerks took exams and forged ahead.
The decorators' kitchens blazed persimmon.
The secretary started kissing women,
and so did I, and my three friends are dead.

LOUISE GLÜCK
(b. 1943)

Born in New York City, Louise Glück studied at Sarah Lawrence and
Columbia. She has taught at Goddard and at Warren Wilson College
and lives in Vermont. Her work is intermittently, and blisteringly,
autobiographical. For the most part, though, Glück's poems are
composed, reflective, often plangent disclosures. Spare, exact, but
enigmatic, her work has mythic dimensions, concerned to trace the
outlines and gauge the power of those large psychic forces at work in
a life: the "thrust and ache" of men and women in their bodies, the
"dying orders" of nature, the "ancient repetitions" of family life.
Glück's books ask difficult questions about gender and generation, and
seek out crepuscular moments of change with a dark, exalted
imagination, a gravity of phrasing and unearthly tone. She won the
National Book Critics Circle Award in 1985.

Messengers

You have only to wait, they will find you.
The geese flying low over the marsh,
glittering in black water.
They find you.

And the deer—
how beautiful they are,
as though their bodies did not impede them.
Slowly they drift into the open
through bronze panels of sunlight.

Why would they stand so still
if they were not waiting?
Almost motionless, until their cages rust,
the shrubs shiver in the wind,
squat and leafless.

You have only to let it happen:
that cry—*release, release*—like the moon
wrenched out of earth and rising
full in its circle of arrows

until they come before you
like dead things, saddled with flesh,
and you above them, wounded and dominant.

The Drowned Children

You see, they have no judgment.
So it is natural that they should drown,
first the ice taking them in
and then, all winter, their wool scarves
floating behind them as they sink
until at last they are quiet.
And the pond lifts them in its manifold dark arms.

But death must come to them differently,
so close to the beginning.
As though they had always been
blind and weightless. Therefore
the rest is dreamed, the lamp,
the good white cloth that covered the table,
their bodies.

And yet they hear the names they used
like lures slipping over the pond:
What are you waiting for
come home, come home, lost
in the waters, blue and permanent.

The Garden

1   THE FEAR OF BIRTH

One sound. Then the hiss and whir
of houses gliding into their places.
And the wind
leafs through the bodies of animals—

But my body that could not content itself
with health—why should it be sprung back
into the chord of sunlight?

It will be the same again.
This fear, this inwardness,
until I am forced into a field
without immunity
even to the least shrub that walks
stiffly out of the dirt, trailing
the twisted signature of its root,
even to a tulip, a red claw.

And then the losses,
one after another,
all supportable.

2   THE GARDEN

The garden admires you.
For your sake it smears itself with green pigment,
the ecstatic reds of the roses,
so that you will come to it with your lovers.

And the willows—
see how it has shaped these green
tents of silence. Yet
there is still something you need,
your body so soft, so alive, among the stone animals.

Admit that it is terrible to be like them,
beyond harm.

3 THE FEAR OF LOVE

That body lying beside me like obedient stone—
once its eyes seemed to be opening,
we could have spoken.

At that time it was winter already.
By day the sun rose in its helmet of fire
and at night also, mirrored in the moon.
Its light passed over us freely,
as though we had lain down
in order to leave no shadows,
only these two shallow dents in the snow.
And the past, as always, stretched before us,
still, complex, impenetrable.

How long did we lie there
as, arm in arm in their cloaks of feathers,
the gods walked down
from the mountain we built for them?

4 ORIGINS

As though a voice were saying
You should be asleep by now—
But there was no one. Nor
had the air darkened,
though the moon was there,
already filled in with marble.

As though, in a garden crowded with flowers,
a voice had said
How dull they are, these golds,
so sonorous, so repetitious
until you closed your eyes,
lying among them, all
stammering flame:

And yet you could not sleep,
poor body, the earth
still clinging to you—

5 THE FEAR OF BURIAL

In the empty field, in the morning,
the body waits to be claimed.
The spirit sits beside it, on a small rock—
nothing comes to give it form again.

Think of the body's loneliness.
At night pacing the sheared field,
its shadow buckled tightly around.
Such a long journey.
And already the remote, trembling lights of the village
not pausing for it as they scan the rows.
How far away they seem,
the wooden doors, the bread and milk
laid like weights on the table.

Palais des Arts

Love long dormant showing itself:
the large expected gods
caged really, the columns
sitting on the lawn, as though perfection
were not timeless but stationary—that
is the comedy, she thinks,
that they are paralyzed. Or like the matching swans,
insular, circling the pond: restraint so passionate
implies possession. They hardly speak.
On the other bank, a small boy throws bits of bread
into the water. The reflected monument
is stirred, briefly, stricken with light—
She can't touch his arm in innocence again.
They have to give that up and begin
as male and female, thrust and ache.

Lamentations

1 THE LOGOS

They were both still,
the woman mournful, the man
branching into her body.

But god was watching.
They felt his gold eye
projecting flowers on the landscape.

Who knew what he wanted?
He was god, and a monster.
So they waited. And the world
filled with his radiance,
as though he wanted to be understood.

Far away, in the void that he had shaped,
he turned to his angels.

2 NOCTURNE

A forest rose from the earth.
O pitiful, so needing
God's furious love—

Together they were beasts.
They lay in the fixed
dusk of his negligence;
from the hills, wolves came, mechanically
drawn to their human warmth,
their panic.

Then the angels saw
how He divided them:
the man, the woman, and the woman's body.

Above the churned reeds, the leaves let go
a slow moan of silver.

3   THE COVENANT

Out of fear, they built a dwelling place.
But a child grew between them
as they slept, as they tried
to feed themselves.

They set it on a pile of leaves,
the small discarded body
wrapped in the clean skin
of an animal. Against the black sky
they saw the massive argument of light.

Sometimes it woke. As it reached its hands
they understood they were the mother and father,
there was no authority above them.

4   THE CLEARING

Gradually, over many years,
the fur disappeared from their bodies
until they stood in the bright light
strange to one another.
Nothing was as before.
Their hands trembled, seeking
the familiar.

Nor could they keep their eyes
from the white flesh
on which wounds would show clearly
like words on a page.

And from the meaningless browns and greens
at last God arose, His great shadow
darkening the sleeping bodies of His children,
and leapt into heaven.

How beautiful it must have been,
the earth, that first time
seen from the air.

Mock Orange

It is not the moon, I tell you.
It is these flowers
lighting the yard.

I hate them.
I hate them as I hate sex,
the man's mouth
sealing my mouth, the man's
paralyzing body—

and the cry that always escapes,
the low, humiliating
premise of union—

In my mind tonight
I hear the question and pursuing answer
fused in one sound
that mounts and mounts and then
is split into the old selves,
the tired antagonisms. Do you see?
We were made fools of.
And the scent of mock orange
drifts through the window.

How can I rest?
How can I be content
when there is still
that odor in the world?

S A N D R A
M c P H E R S O N
(b. 1943)

Sandra McPherson was born in San Jose, California, studied at San Jose State College, and went on to do graduate work at the University of Washington. She has taught at several universities, including Iowa, and is currently professor of English at the University of California at Davis. Describing McPherson's early work, Elizabeth Bishop wrote, "it's like turning the light switch off, and there in the dark—reality: all kinds of likely and unlikely things, incandescent on their own, beginning to stir and breathe." McPherson's imagination is wry and alert. Likely and unlikely things, precisely observed, are transformed into ideas. She is not embarrassed by elegance or sentiment and has written affectingly about her family, her birth parents, her divorce; about relationships between mother and daughter, past and present. Her poems pulse with real speech but have a surprising, luxuriant lexicon.

Black Soap

1

White lather on black soap—
Maria's gift. It reminds me
Of when a woman died
And they handed me her ring.

Then they left to divide the roots for her.
Daylight went down there shining.
By accident, cleaning the hearth
Of a house to leave it for good,
I learned how to see
A star come out: work
My hand into the ashes.

2

"You've thrown a chestnut hull into the fireplace again,"
Said Colette's mother, "My clean ashes!"
Naughty Colette had soiled the washing ashes
Of applewood, poplar, and elm.
Stretched over the big cauldron
In the washhouse, hemp cloth held the ashes
The washwoman poured a jug of boiling water on.
They smelled almost sweet as the lye
Filtered into the mass of linen.
The air darkened with blue clouds.
In the smoking lava layer of ashes,
A few cinders of chestnut hulls,
The tannin's yellow stain.

3

Look for something
You've been every day of your life.
You said it was "lonely."
I'm certain it is also "clean."
My body's big years diminish soap.
My grandmother, whose diamond it was,
Had a stone in her tub.
I rubbed it on my feet
As later I walked,
Building little hoofs,
All summer shoeless on creek gravel.

That black bar of stone
In the widow's clean house,
That volcanic pumice skips
Over most hard places
But softens at least one.

4

Once there was a downpour of rain
They took as a judgment.

It confused her billowing, steaming skirts.
Another time—those times were hard—
The executioner let go the twisted hemp
From her neck sooner than he should
Because the flames reached his hands.
Nor would I, if I'd had to live then,
Put my hands into the fire
Those three hours it took to reduce her.
But after, I'd scrub all over
With the ashes of the still warm
Black heart of the witch.

The Microscope in Winter

Caught in my mittens' mohair barbs—
goosedown like thrown boas of a chorus line,
evergreen needles with pitch stitches,
some wavy unshaven seeds of virgin's bower.
My eye looks down the funnel: under the light
the crooked finger of a pervert in a car;
dew in the golf-tee goblet of a lichen—
a lone crystal of glamour in a darkened theatre.
Such quiet bodies, gathered in the dusk,
thalluses and plumose fruits, silvery everything.

I bought this for a woman in crisis
so her outlook could rise
to the height of a burr
and leap the distance through a quill.
But she says, *Not yet,* feet the size
of catkin stamens. For she will study
her sleep, she says, she'll diet her curiosity,
blind to this charming mouse-food, blind

except to nightmares. She focuses on children
and we are terror. We are all too big.

Yet precisely because of your monster, dearest,
we require technology for you.
A good spider must have more eyes
than two: She needs a camera,
telescope for undomesticated space,
binoculars to hoop the faster birds.
Through these prescription lenses, face
beings who do not care you're there.
Then, to your relief, neither will you.

Boodee—dew in its eye—reflects the light,
a flashbulb in a mirror; green tastebuds
bulge all over, nappy as a rug and knotted.
Or see this red oak leaf like our mother-flesh.
Shiny. Like jerky. Or potato-chip skins
where insects chewed us for another hour of life.

It is chilly when I wrest the sweater from the tree.
Dial it in clear: There is your monster,
saying to all the larger world that scares it,
I grow kinked but not mad,
so rest on me, liverwort-haired maenad,
scientific muddy shepherdess. Look into this,
how, scintillating under battery light,
I am a greater power of moss.
My microscopic cushion shows its claws.

Streamers

All the women who leave tell me they're happy.
But my friend, kneeling with me, is the only

one who goes on living by herself
and owns five houses,
one of them on land sloping to an "arm of the sea,"

silver and indigo, young salmon worrying,
stealing anchovies schooled up.

The sea which dangles, this August forenoon,
from the thumb of a dock
a stunning swimmer, leaning against plush

sea-fans and kicking
her warp of tentacles
slowly out across the current.

We've dropped to our elbows.

> I remember winters here,
> frost on the wharf
> so long you could mow it;
> a consumptive ship,

> the Barbarossa,
> pumping out basements-worth of water
> all day, all dark,

> water that made it
> sink inside
> outside buoying it light.

> You could touch its rope
> and draw the huge ship near.

And this *cyanea* is as big
as our daughters,
as long as my friend's old bridal veil

(I wore a scarf)
perishing under woolens in a steamer trunk
on an attic voyage.

The rest of its ensemble imports
from Spain: tiered flounces, bunched bodice,

and bolero, mostly
of a salmon-watermelon-shrimp

or peach-ginger pastel; lips
and gonads tucked into a skirt
scalloped into eight notched lappets

weighted with a crystalline rhopalium.
Such is the fashion.

> "Women have so seldom
> been an attraction to me,"
> said Sherlock Holmes in "Lion's Mane,"
> "for my brain has always governed my heart,

> "but I could not look upon
> her perfect clear-cut face,
> with all the soft freshness of downlands
> in her delicate colouring,

> "without realizing
> no young man would cross her path unscathed."

Ah, friend,
not only must we scathe,
we must also know the remedies:

> Ammonia, vinegar, or meat tenderizer,
> papaya juice, gasoline, olive oil,
> ocean water (never fresh).

> Remove tentacles with a gloved hand,
> apply flour, baking powder,
> shaving soap.

> Come to the sea with these.
> Then scrape.

And yet her clear head
of flawless Orrefors . . .

Dilation, contraction.

Do you recall the day
of our equal depressions?

My husband telephoned back and forth,
listened to you then to me,
unable to synchronize our calls.

He described us to each other.
Then he went fishing.
He navigated through the Lions' Manes,

obnoxious, cursed—
one cannot touch them, tear them
off a line—

and ran his boat elsewhere,
to other animals,
seals, puffins, dogfish

nipping away at bait and catch,
skill, success, and hunger.

You and I were in some depth together,
miles apart, he said

and it helped.

      Now, perhaps, we've begun the migration
      (if only our third friend were here,
      and our fourth . . .).

The woman in the Marine Science Center welcomes
these medusae every August warmth,
holds out her arms to show

how big she's witnessed them.
But for now our arms and knees support

not any frozenness
but our still undistraction,
a concentration on the pulse

that is not stone
and turns no one to stone
who really stays to see her.

And she leans there, greeting, in her door,
all current, streamers, tired and toxic

but striating, ruffling,
armlessly herding eggs
like transparent hotcross buns.

Our hair hangs over the dock,
her tentacles eight-hundred, nine-,
pulling us out of the rock,

relaxing, flexing.
She is unparalyzing,

no hard parts at all,
and she is all alone.

ALFRED CORN
(b. 1943)

Raised in Georgia, and long a resident of New York City; a student of
the refined nuances of French literature, and an admirer of the
visionary line of American poets from Walt Whitman to Hart Crane;
the author of two book-length autobiographical poems, alternating
with collections of briefer lyrics—Alfred Corn resolves his contending
impulses in a style that matches rhetorical authority with subtlety of
blended image and idea. The landscapes of history—past settings and
the current "scene"—concern him; his long poem "A Call in the Midst
of the Crowd" juxtaposes archetypal fragments of New York history
with an account of his own life in the city. But Corn's poems
also seek—in art and nature, memory and religious belief—the
sources of transcendence. He has taught at Yale, Columbia, and
UCLA, and received many awards, including a fellowship from the
Academy of American Poets.

Darkening Hotel Room

I

The glass on the picture from the Bible
Has gone pale and reflective, the mirror dull.
A room of rectangles, dark door moldings,

Gray windows; mind itself turning corners
From sleep to awareness to attention
To notions. Up and down the hallway doors

Open to boom shut. And always less light.
The porcelain lamp exists in silver
Outline, drawn something like those solemn curls

On the pillar capital silhouetted
Outside. Ninety winters this room has housed
Other selves—young women in long dresses,

Men like walruses bearded. Bibles, crochet,
Ointment. They would be gathering for warmth
Around the fireplace that now stands empty,

Dark, cold. Others fell asleep in this hour,
That ornate pillar the last image formed
In closing eyes, the curtain descending.

I I

Something between dream and not-dream that goes
Back thirty years and a thousand miles
Away: I almost see her standing
At the sink, wearing . . . a cotton blouse, slacks;
A little thin, what with rationing,
A husband in the Pacific, three children.
She glances at the turk's-caps and lantana
Outside—no, that was a later house.

Afternoon light models her face into
Fatigue, kindness, a worry wrinkle
Between dark brows. Curly hair,
Short and not well arranged. In another
Room someone misses a note of the scale;
And she bends down to me, a mound
Of not much more than self. She smiles,
Her head turning this way, that way. . . .

This is possible, but of course not
Real; unless every picture held in
Thought silently is real. An uncommon radiance
Attaches itself, like the candle's,
To the strain and flicker of recall,
Small incandescence, halo at night.
It appears as a gift, second sight
With the power to transport in safe conduct
To lost houses, forbidden rooms,
To when she still—. But it can't be
Memory. I remember nothing. Absence.

Which came grotesquely, with toys
And birthday cake, they told me later.
To reach in confidence for efficient,
Bony arms and only find—.
Puzzling; and it still is, how
A bereavement, immaterially, goes on,
An asceticism, for a lifetime.
As you might choose caution, and, what,
Thoughtfulness—in order to survive.
Survive! The blunt desire to endure,
Imagining what might be restored.
I don't remember, nonetheless see
Light, afternoon, as she bends down
In large outline, like a cloud approaching.

I I I

The man wrapped in darkness is free to dream:
All those I invite may inform this space,
My company until the darkened room
Rises to the surface—coming back like
Someone's biography, summoned up whole,
To be relived and almost understood.

The bearded man may have done as much—
Suddenly reaching out for the young woman
Banked next to him in the loose braid of sleep.
At night's lowest point he divides and numbers
His consolations. She stirs, yawns, neither
Understanding nor minding his rough hug.

But I won't wake you. Sleep, love, rooms that
Shelter us, for how long? The speed of night,
Of thought. Older than my grandparents . . .
Worlds later, gray light restores a picture
Of the Master teaching his disciples,
Indifferent to, unaware of us.

Fire: The People

Toplight hammered down by shadowless noon,
A palindrome of midnight, retrograde
From last month's solstice in smoke and flame,
In molten glares from chrome or glass. I feel
Fever from the cars I pass, delirium
Trembling out from the radiators.
The dog-day romance seems to be physical,
As young free lances come into their own,
Sunbrowned, imperial in few clothes,
Heat-struck adulthood a subject to youth
And fitful as traffic, the mind pure jumble
But for that secret overriding voice
Advising and persuading at each crossroads;
The struggle toward freedom to forge a day.

Smoke; flame; oiled, gray-brown air.
Jackhammers and first gear on the avenues;
Stuntmen driving taxicabs; patient, blue,
Hippo aggressiveness of a bus, nudging
Aside the sedans. And the peculiar
Fascination of a row of workshops—
The dark interiors with skylight sunstripes;
A figure walking in slow motion among
Pistons; rough justice of a die cutter;
A helmeted diver, wielding acetylene,
Crouched over some work of sunken treasure
That sparkles gold at a probe from his torch. . . .
Seismic shocks interrupt this dream—a stampede
Of transports flat out to make the light,
Mack truck, Diamond Reo, a nameless tanker,
Iil International, a Seatrain destined
For the Port Authority docks—one more
Corrugated block to pile on the rest,
Red, green, gray, and blue, waiting for a ship
In the Grancolombiana line. . . .

The seagoing city radiates invisibly
Over the world, a documentary sublime.

Lunch hour, even the foods are fast, potluck
In the melting pot: the Italian girl
With a carton of chicken; Puerto Rican folding
A pizza; the black woman with an egg roll;
A crop-headed secretary in round,
Metal spectacles eats plain yogurt (she's
Already mantis thin) and devours glamour
Mags. . . . Our crowd scene, a moving fresco:
But is it really there? The adversary
Today is named Random. How capture all this
Without being taken captive in turn,
Install it as something more than backdrop,
As a necessity, not a sundry?
Suppose just an awareness of the way
Living details might be felt as vision
Is vision, full, all there ever was—this
Instant palindromic noon, the joined hands
Of the clock, end and beginning. . . . Surely
The first to consider imagining stars
Constellations had already done as much,
Just by making some brilliant connections;
Mind crowned itself in a round of leaps from point
To point across the empty stage of night. . . .

•

Now as a pigeon banks, descends, hovers,
And drops on asphalt with back-thrust wings,
Comes a desire to be lifted in the balance,
Rise to some highest point and then be met
By a fierce new light haloing lashes shatter
Into spears of aurora, naked eye become
Prismatic at last and given to see in kind
All the transformed inhabitants forever go
About their errands, on a new scale: the rainbow
Is the emblem for this moment filtering through

The body's meshwork nerves, and a heartbeat impulse
All around puts troops of feet in step with music,
Persistent, availing, that disregards the frayed
Years, vagaries, downfall among trash, accident,
Loss; or because it knows these rushes upward
On something like heartbreak into the only sky,
Air aspirant with fractioned voices, feverfew
Of the sensed illusion, higher ground, progressions
Sounded in the spheres—so each step takes them further,
Sceptered, into daytime, saluting the outcome.
There is a fire that surpasses the known burning,
Its phoenix center a couple that must be there,
Blast furnace, dynamo, engendering a city,
Phosphor spines that bend and meet to weld, to fuse
As a divining rod—sluicings, spillway, braid,
Chorded basses that set myriad threads afire,
Newborn limbs and reach of the proven tendon now
Let go into empowered brilliance, rayed showers,
The garden regained. In this light the place appears:
Hands that rise or fall, muted gestures of welcome
And good-bye, face that turns and comes forward to claim
A smile latent in the afternoon air, vague crowds
Falling down streets without character toward
An offered covenant—love that gives them each a name.

Naskeag

Once a day the rocks, with little warning—
not much looked for even by the spruce
and fir ever at attention above—
fetch up on these tidal flats and bars.
Large, cratelike rocks, wrapped in kelp;
layer on imprinted layer,
umber to claret to olivegreen,

of scalloped marbling. . . .
Not far along the path of obstacles
and steppingstones considered,
fluid skeins of bladder wrack
lie tufted over the mussel shoals—
the seabed black as a shag's neck,
a half-acre coalfield, but alive.
Recklessly multiple, myriads compact,
the small airtight coffers (in chipped enamel)
are starred over with bonelike barnacles
that crackle and simmer throughout the trek,
gravel-crepitant underfoot.

Evening comes now not with the Evening
Star, but with a breathing fog.
And fog is the element here,
a new term, vast by indefinition,
a vagrant damping of the deep tones
of skies and bars and sea.
Sand, mud, sand, rock: one jagged pool
basining a water invisible
except as quick trembles
over algal weed—itself
half-absent, a virid gel.
Walking means to lose the way
in fog, the eye drawn out to a farther point,
a dark graph on the faint blue inlet watershine;
out to where a heron stands,
stationing its sharp silhouette
against the fogbright dusk.
Then, not to be approached,
lifts off and rows upward, *up, up,*
a flexible embracing-forward on the air,
rising out of view
behind an opaque expanse of calcium flame.

The great kelp-dripping rocks,
at random positions,
lost in thought and dematerializing
with the gray hour,

release, indelibly, their pent-up contents.
—Even the scattered feathers here
are petrified, limewhite blades and stony down.
The sky, from eastward, deepens
with the dawning insight
as the seas begin to rise, the flats
slide away, the hulls bear off the ground,
and the eye alien to so self-sufficing
a tidal system turns and takes up how to
retrace the steps that brought it there.

EDWARD HIRSCH
(b. 1950)

Edward Hirsch was born in Chicago, graduated from Grinnell College, and received his Ph.D. from the University of Pennsylvania. His poetry has been honored with a National Book Critics Circle Award (1986) and the Rome Prize from the American Academy and Institute of Arts and Letters. He teaches now at the University of Houston. Hirsch believes, with Ezra Pound, that "only emotion endures," and his inventive poems ring with urgent, outsize feelings about human suffering, the toils of family and urban life, the redemptive possibilities of art and love. The loneliness of the passionate soul is his study, and the pitch of Hirsch's poems rises toward the recognition that "losing itself becomes a kind / of song."

Fast Break

In memory of Dennis Turner, 1946–1984

A hook shot kisses the rim and
hangs there, helplessly, but doesn't drop,

and for once our gangly starting center
boxes out his man and times his jump

perfectly, gathering the orange leather
from the air like a cherished possession

and spinning around to throw a strike
to the outlet who is already shoveling

an underhand pass toward the other guard
scissoring past a flat-footed defender

who looks stunned and nailed to the floor
in the wrong direction, trying to catch sight

of a high, gliding dribble and a man
letting the play develop in front of him

in slow motion, almost exactly
like a coach's drawing on the blackboard,

both forwards racing down the court
the way that forwards should, fanning out

and filling the lanes in tandem, moving
together as brothers passing the ball

between them without a dribble, without
a single bounce hitting the hardwood

until the guard finally lunges out
and commits to the wrong man

while the power-forward explodes past them
in a fury, taking the ball into the air

by himself now and laying it gently
against the glass for a lay-up,

but losing his balance in the process,
inexplicably falling, hitting the floor

with a wild, headlong motion
for the game he loved like a country

and swiveling back to see an orange blur
floating perfectly through the net.

A Short Lexicon of Torture
in the Eighties

That's not a man in pain
                    but *a Brazilian phone*—
It won't be making any outgoing calls.

That's not a woman sprawling on the floor
But *an old-fashioned dance,*
                     like the tango.

Pull up a chair with a knotted rope.
Let's have *a tea party with toast*
                  and *hors d'oeuvres.*

Let's take a seat
           on *the parrot's perch.*
Let's rock to *the motorola* with headphones.

Do you want to bathe
              in the porcelain tub?
Do you want to sing to *the little hare?*

Let's stroll over to *the guest room.*
Let's take a bus ride
            to *the San Juanica bridge.*

Forget the ovens and smokestacks.
Forge *the rack and screw,*
              the tiger's cage.

We're celebrating *a birthday party*
                   in your honor.
We're lighting candles on your favorite cake.

We're taking you to *a parade*
               on a sandy beach.
You're going down in *a submarine.*

My Father's Back

There's an early memory that I carry around
In my mind
        like an old photograph in my wallet,
A little graying and faded, a picture
That I don't much like
            but nonetheless keep,

Fingering it now and then like a sore tooth,
Knowing it's there,
                        not needing to see it anymore. . . .

The sun slants down on the shingled roof.
The wind breathes in the needled pines.
And I am lying in the grass on my third birthday,
Red-faced and watchful
                        but not squalling yet,
Not yet rashed or hived up
                        from eating the wrong food
Or touching the wrong plant,
                        my father's leaving.

A moment before he was holding me up
Like a new trophy, and I was a toddler
With my face in the clouds,
                        spinning around
With a head full of stars,
                        getting so dizzy.
A moment before I was squealing with joy
In the tilt-a-whirl of his arms,
Drifting asleep in the cavern of his chest. . . .

I remember waking up to the twin peaks
Of his shoulders moving away, a shirt clinging
To his massive body,
                        a mountain receding.
I remember the giant distance between us:
A drop or two of rain, a sheen on the lawn,
And then I was sitting up
                        in the grainy half-light
Of a man walking away from his family.

I don't know why we go over the old hurts
Again and again in our minds, the false starts
And true beginnings
                        of a world we call the past,
As if it could tell us who we are now,
Or were, or might have been. . . .
                                    It's drizzling.
A car door slams, just once, and he's gone.
Tiny pools of water glisten on the street.

JORIE GRAHAM
(b. 1951)

Born in New York City, the daughter of a journalist and a sculptor, Jorie Graham was raised in Italy, studied at the Sorbonne, graduated in film studies from New York University, and then attended the Iowa Writers Workshop, where she now teaches. Her poems have large ambitions and a reckless music. She is attracted to ecstatics, saints and artists, and tries to push a poem past its conventional limits so that it becomes a kind of energized field within which her subjects—herself, really, projected into ceremonial occasions—can be both condensed and exploded. Risking a privacy of purpose, Graham wants "to catch the world / at pure idea," and the results of her efforts can seem like freshly minted sensations or thoughts.

Over and Over Stitch

Late in the season the world digs in, the fat blossoms
hold still for just a moment longer.
Nothing looks satisfied,
but there is no real reason to move on much further:
this isn't a bad place;
why not pretend

we wished for it?
The bushes have learned to live with their haunches.
The hydrangea is resigned
to its pale and inconclusive utterances.
Towards the end of the season
it is not bad

to have the body. To have experienced joy
as the mere lifting of hunger
is not to have known it
less. The tobacco leaves

don't mind being removed
to the long racks—all uses are astounding

to the used.
There are moments in our lives which, threaded, give us
    heaven—
noon, for instance, or all the single victories
of gravity, or the kudzu vine,
most delicate of manias,
which has pressed its luck

this far this season.
It shines a gloating green.
Its edges darken with impatience, a kind of wind.
Nothing again will ever be this easy, lives
being snatched up like dropped stitches, the dry stalks of
    daylilies
marking a stillness we can't keep.

San Sepolcro

In this blue light
    I can take you there,
snow having made me
    a world of bone
seen through to. This
    is my house,

my section of Etruscan
    wall, my neighbor's
lemontrees, and, just below
    the lower church,
the airplane factory.
    A rooster

crows all day from mist
    outside the walls.
There's milk on the air,
    ice on the oily
lemonskins. How clean
    the mind is,

holy grave. It is this girl
    by Piero
della Francesca, unbuttoning
    her blue dress,
her mantle of weather,
    to go into

labor. Come, we can go in.
    It is before
the birth of god. No-one
    has risen yet
to the museums, to the assembly
    line—bodies

and wings—to the open air
    market. This is
what the living do: go in.
    It's a long way.
And the dress keeps opening
    from eternity

to privacy, quickening.
    Inside, at the heart,
is tragedy, the present moment
    forever stillborn,
but going in, each breath
    is a button

coming undone, something terribly
    nimble-fingered
finding all of the stops.

Orpheus and Eurydice

Up ahead, I know, he felt it stirring in himself already, the
    glance,
the darting thing in the pile of rocks,

already in him, there, shiny in the rubble, hissing Did you
    want to remain
completely unharmed?—

the point-of-view darting in him, shiny head in the ash-heap,

hissing Once upon a time, and then Turn now darling give me
    that look,

that perfect shot, give me that place where I'm erased. . . .

The thing, he must have wondered, could it be put to rest,
    there, in the glance,
could it lie back down into the dustyness, giving its outline
    up?

When we turn to them—limbs, fields, expanses of
    dust called meadow and avenue—
will they be freed then to slip back in?

Because you see he could not be married to it anymore,
    this field with minutes in it
called woman, its presence in him the thing called

future—could not be married to it anymore, expanse tugging
    his mind out into it,
tugging the wanting-to-finish out.

What he dreamed of was this road (as he walked on it), this
    dustyness,
but without their steps on it, their prints, without
song—

What she dreamed, as she watched him turning with the bend
    in the road (can you
understand this?)—what she dreamed

was of disappearing into the seen

not of disappearing, lord, into the real—

And yes she could feel it in him already, up ahead, that
      wanting-to-turn-and-
cast-the-outline-over-her

by his glance,

sealing the edges down,

saying I know you from somewhere darling, don't I,
saying You're the kind of woman who etcetera—

(Now the cypress are swaying) (Now the lake in the distance)
(Now the view-from-above, the aerial attack of *do you
remember?*)—

now the glance reaching her shoreline wanting only to be
      recalled,
now the glance reaching her shoreline wanting only to be
      taken in,

(somewhere the castle above the river)

(somewhere you holding this piece of paper)

(what will you do next?) (—feel it beginning?)

now she's raising her eyes, as if pulled from above,

now she's looking back into it, into the poison the beginning,

giving herself to it, looking back into the eyes,

feeling the dry soft grass beneath her feet for the first time
      now the mind

looking into that which sets the _____ in motion and seeing
      in there

a doorway open nothing on either side
(a slight wind now around them, three notes from up the hill)

through which morning creeps and the first true notes—

For they were deep in the earth and what is possible swiftly
      took hold.

RITA DOVE
(b. 1952)

Rita Dove was born in Akron, Ohio and studied at Miami University
of Ohio, the University of Tübingen, and the University of Iowa. She
has taught at Arizona State University and is now professor of English
at the University of Virginia. Dove has written that the goal of all her
work is "to combine historical occurrence with the epiphanal quality
of the lyric poem." Her twice-told narrative sequence, *Thomas and
Beulah,* which won the 1987 Pulitzer Prize, uses vignettes from the
lives of her grandparents to chronicle the experience of a generation of
black Americans. Her earlier work too displays
imaginative range and dramatic skill.

Adolescence—II

Although it is night, I sit in the bathroom, waiting.
Sweat prickles behind my knees, the baby-breasts are alert.
Venetian blinds slice up the moon; the tiles quiver in pale
    strips.

Then they come, the three seal men with eyes as round
As dinner plates and eyelashes like sharpened tines.
They bring the scent of licorice. One sits in the washbowl,

One on the bathtub edge; one leans against the door.
"Can you feel it yet?" they whisper.
I don't know what to say, again. They chuckle,

Patting their sleek bodies with their hands.
"Well, maybe next time." And they rise,
Glittering like pools of ink under moonlight,

And vanish. I clutch at the ragged holes
They leave behind, here at the edge of darkness.
Night rests like a ball of fur on my tongue.

Parsley*

1 THE CANE FIELDS

There is a parrot imitating spring
in the palace, its feathers parsley green.
Out of the swamp the cane appears

to haunt us, and we cut it down. El General
searches for a word; he is all the world
there is. Like a parrot imitating spring,

we lie down screaming as rain punches through
and we come up green. We cannot speak an R—
out of the swamp, the cane appears

and then the mountain we call in whispers *Katalina.*
The children gnaw their teeth to arrowheads.
There is a parrot imitating spring.

El General has found his word: *perejil.*
Who says it, lives. He laughs, teeth shining
out of the swamp. The cane appears

in our dreams, lashed by wind and streaming.
And we lie down. For every drop of blood
there is a parrot imitating spring.
Out of the swamp the cane appears.

2 THE PALACE

The word the general's chosen is parsley.
It is fall, when thoughts turn
to love and death; the general thinks
of his mother, how she died in the fall
and he planted her walking cane at the grave
and it flowered, each spring stolidly forming
four-star blossoms. The general

---

*On October 2, 1957, Rafael Trujillo (1891–1961), dictator of the Dominican
Republic, ordered 20,000 blacks killed because they could not pronounce the
letter "r" in *perejil,* the Spanish word for parsley.

pulls on his boots, he stomps to
her room in the palace, the one without
curtains, the one with a parrot
in a brass ring. As he paces he wonders
Who can I kill today. And for a moment
the little knot of screams
is still. The parrot, who has traveled

all the way from Australia in an ivory
cage, is, coy as a widow, practising
spring. Ever since the morning
his mother collapsed in the kitchen
while baking skull-shaped candies
for the Day of the Dead, the general
has hated sweets. He orders pastries
brought up for the bird; they arrive

dusted with sugar on a bed of lace.
The knot in his throat starts to twitch;
he sees his boots the first day in battle
splashed with mud and urine
as a soldier falls at his feet amazed—
how stupid he looked!—at the sound
of artillery. *I never thought it would sing*
the soldier said, and died. Now

the general sees the fields of sugar
cane, lashed by rain and streaming.
He sees his mother's smile, the teeth
gnawed to arrowheads. He hears
the Haitians sing without R's
as they swing the great machetes:
Katalina, they sing, *Katalina,*

mi madle, mi amol en muelte. God knows
his mother was no stupid woman; she
could roll an R like a queen. Even
a parrot can roll an R! In the bare room
the bright feathers arch in a parody
of greenery, as the last pale crumbs
disappear under the blackened tongue. Someone

calls out his name in a voice
so like his mother's, a startled tear
splashes the tip of his right boot.
My mother, my love in death.
The general remembers the tiny green sprigs
men of his village wore in their capes
to honor the birth of a son. He will
order many, this time, to be killed

for a single, beautiful word.

Canary

for Michael S. Harper

Billie Holiday's burned voice
had as many shadows as lights,
a mournful candelabra against a sleek piano,
the gardenia her signature under that ruined face.

(Now you're cooking, drummer to bass,
magic spoon, magic needle.
Take all day if you have to
with your mirror and your bracelet of song.)

Fact is, the invention of women under siege
has been to sharpen love in the service of myth.

If you can't be free, be a mystery.

GJERTRUD
SCHNACKENBERG
(b. 1953)

A graduate of Mount Holyoke College, Gjertrud Schnackenberg was born in Tacoma, Washington. Her first book, with its long elegy for her father (who was a professor of history), account of her house over the centuries, and portrait of Darwin, established Schnackenberg as a sort of naturalist of her own past. Her elegiac imagination, in fact, is obsessed with history, the way the past inhabits or haunts the present. The formality of her verse contains the life of the emotions in measures that are strict but delicate. Schnackenberg's best work is modeled with an elegant gravity and offers a wise, reflective sense of culture and its claims on human feeling.

The Paperweight

The scene within the paperweight is calm,
A small white house, a laughing man and wife,
Deep snow. I turn it over in my palm
And watch it snowing in another life,

Another world, and from this scene learn what
It is to stand apart: she serves him tea
Once and forever, dressed from head to foot
As she is always dressed. In this toy, history

Sifts down through the glass like snow, and we
Wonder if her single deed tells much
Or little of the way she loves, and whether he
Sees shadows in the sky. Beyond our touch,

Beyond our lives, they laugh, and drink their tea.
We look at them just as the winter night

With its vast empty spaces bends to see
Our isolated little world of light,

Covered with snow, and snow in clouds above it,
And drifts and swirls too deep to understand.
Still, I must try to think a little of it,
With so much winter in my head and hand.

Signs

Threading the palm, a web of little lines
Spells out the lost money, the heart, the head,
The wagging tongues, the sudden deaths, in signs
We would smooth out, like imprints on a bed,

In signs that can't be helped, geese heading south,
In signs read anxiously, like breath that clouds
A mirror held to a barely open mouth,
Like telegrams, the gathering of crowds—

The plane's X in the sky, spelling disaster:
Before the whistle and hit, a tracer flare;
Before rubble, a hairline crack in plaster
And a housefly's panicked scribbling on the air.

Supernatural Love

My father at the dictionary-stand
Touches the page to fully understand
The lamplit answer, tilting in his hand

His slowly scanning magnifying lens,
A blurry, glistening circle he suspends
Above the word "Carnation." Then he bends

So near his eyes are magnified and blurred,
One finger on the miniature word,
As if he touched a single key and heard

A distant, plucked, infinitesimal string,
"The obligation due to every thing
That's smaller than the universe." I bring

My sewing needle close enough that I
Can watch my father through the needle's eye,
As through a lens ground for a butterfly

Who peers down flower-hallways toward a room
Shadowed and fathomed as this study's gloom
Where, as a scholar bends above a tomb

To read what's buried there, he bends to pore
Over the Latin blossom. I am four,
I spill my pins and needles on the floor

Trying to stitch "Beloved" X by X.
My dangerous, bright needle's point connects
Myself illiterate to this perfect text

I cannot read. My father puzzles why
It is my habit to identify
Carnations as "Christ's flowers," knowing I

Can give no explanation but "Because."
Word-roots blossom in speechless messages
The way the thread behind my sampler does

Where following each X I awkward move
My needle through the word whose root is love.
He reads, "A pink variety of Clove,

Carnatio, the Latin, meaning flesh."
As if the bud's essential oils brush
Christ's fragrance through the room, the iron-fresh

Odor carnations have floats up to me,
A drifted, secret, bitter ecstasy,
The stems squeak in my scissors, *Child, it's me,*

He turns the page to "Clove" and reads aloud:
"The clove, a spice, dried from a flower-bud."
Then twice, as if he hasn't understood,

He reads, "From French, for *clou,* meaning a nail."
He gazes, motionless. "Meaning a nail."
The incarnation blossoms, flesh and nail,

I twist my threads like stems into a knot
And smooth "Beloved," but my needle caught
Within the threads, *Thy blood so dearly bought,*

The needle strikes my finger to the bone.
I lift my hand, it is myself I've sewn,
The flesh laid bare, the threads of blood my own,

I lift my hand in startled agony
And call upon his name, "Daddy daddy"—
My father's hand touches the injury

As lightly as he touched the page before,
Where incarnation bloomed from roots that bore
The flowers I called Christ's when I was four.

SELECTED
BIBLIOGRAPHY

A. R. AMMONS

Ommateum (1955), *Expressions of Sea Level* (1964), *Corsons Inlet* (1965), *Tape for the Turn of the Year* (1965), *Northfield Poems* (1966), *Uplands* (1970), *Briefings* (1971), *Collected Poems 1951–1971* (1972), *Sphere: The Form of a Motion* (1974), *Diversifications* (1975), *The Snow Poems* (1977), *A Coast of Trees* (1981), *Worldly Hopes* (1983), *Lake Effect Country* (1983), *Selected Poems: Expanded Edition* (1986), *Sumerian Vistas* (1987).

JOHN ASHBERY

Some Trees (1956), *The Tennis Court Oath* (1962), *Rivers and Mountains* (1966), *The Double Dream of Spring* (1970), *Three Poems* (1972), *Self-Portrait in a Convex Mirror* (1975), *Houseboat Days* (1977), *As We Know* (1979), *Shadow Train* (1981), *A Wave* (1984), *Selected Poems* (1985), *April Galleons* (1987).

A Nest of Ninnies (novel, with James Schuyler; 1969), *Three Plays* (1978), *Reported Sightings* (art criticism; 1989).

MARVIN BELL

A Probable Volume of Dreams (1969), *The Escape into You* (1971), *Residue of Song* (1974), *Stars Which See, Stars Which Do Not See* (1977), *These Green-Going-to-Yellow* (1981), *Segues* (with William Stafford; 1983), *Drawn by Stones, by Earth, by Things that Have Been in the Fire* (1984), *New and Selected Poems* (1987).

Old Snow Just Melting (essays and interviews; 1983).

JOHN BERRYMAN

The Dispossessed (1948), *Homage to Mistress Bradstreet* (1956), *77 Dream Songs* (1964), *Short Poems* (1967), *Berryman's Sonnets* (1967), *His Toy, His Dream, His Rest* (1968), *The Dream Songs* (1969), *Love & Fame* (1970), *Delusions, Etc.* (1972), *Henry's Fate* (1977), *Collected Poems, 1937–1971* (1989).

Stephen Crane (biography; 1950), *Recovery* (novel; 1973), *The Freedom of the Poet* (essays and stories; 1976).

FRANK BIDART

Golden State (1973), *The Book of the Body* (1977), *The Sacrifice* (1983), *In the Western Night: Collected Poems, 1965–1990* (1990).

ELIZABETH BISHOP

North & South (1946), *Poems: North & South—A Cold Spring* (1955), *Questions of Travel* (1965), *The Complete Poems* (1969), *Geography III* (1976), *Complete Poems, 1927–1979* (1983).

Collected Prose (1984).

EDGAR BOWERS

The Form of Loss (1956), *The Astronomers* (1965), *Living Together: New and Selected Poems* (1973), *For Louis Pasteur* (1989).

AMY CLAMPITT

The Kingfisher (1983), *What the Light Was Like* (1985), *Archaic Figure* (1987), *Westward* (1990).

ALFRED CORN

All Roads at Once (1976), *A Call in the Midst of the Crowd* (1978), *The Various Light* (1980), *Notes from a Child of Paradise* (1984), *The West Door* (1988).

The Metamorphoses of Metaphor (essays; 1987).

ROBERT CREELEY

For Love: Poems, 1950–1960 (1962), *Words* (1967), *Pieces* (1969), *A Day Book* (1972), *Selected Poems* (1976), *Presences* (1976), *Hello* (1978), *Later* (1979), *Collected Poems, 1945–1975* (1982), *Mirrors* (1983), *Memory Gardens* (1986), *Windows* (1990).

The Island (novel; 1963), *The Gold Diggers* (stories; 1965), *A Quick Graph* (essays; 1970), *Contexts of Poetry* (interviews; 1973), *Was That a Real Poem* (essays; 1979), *Collected Prose* (1984).

J. V. CUNNINGHAM

The Helmsman (1942), *The Judge Is Fury* (1947), *Doctor Drink* (1950), *To What Strangers, What Welcome* (1964), *Collected Poems and Epigrams* (1971).

Collected Essays (1974).

JAMES DICKEY

Drowning with Others (1962), *Helmets* (1964), *Buckdancer's Choice* (1965), *Poems, 1957–1967* (1967), *The Eye-Beaters, Blood, Victory, Madness, Buckhead and Mercy* (1970), *The Zodiac* (1976), *The Strength of Fields* (1979), *Puella* (1982).

Babel to Byzantium (criticism; 1968), *Self-Interviews* (1970), *Deliverance* (novel; 1970), *Sorties* (essays; 1971), *Night Hurdling* (miscellaneous prose; 1983), *Alnilam* (novel; 1987).

RITA DOVE

The Yellow House on the Corner (1980), *Museum* (1983), *Thomas and Beulah* (1986), *Grace Notes* (1989).

Fifth Sunday (stories; 1985).

ROBERT DUNCAN

Caesar's Gate (1956), *Selected Poems* (1959), *The Opening of the Field* (1960), *Roots and Branches* (1964), *Bending the Bow* (1968), *Ground Work* (1984), *Ground Work II* (1987).

Fictive Certainties (essays; 1985).

IRVING FELDMAN

Works and Days (1961), *The Pripet Marshes* (1965), *Magic Papers* (1970), *Lost Originals* (1972), *Leaping Clear* (1976), *New and Selected Poems* (1979), *Teach Me, Dear Sister* (1983), *All of Us Here* (1986).

JEAN GARRIGUE

The Ego and the Centaur (1947), *The Monument Rose* (1953), *A Water Walk by Villa d'Este* (1959), *Country Without Maps* (1964), *New and Selected Poems* (1967), *Studies for an Actress* (1973).

Marianne Moore (criticism; 1965), *The Animal House* (novella; 1966).

ALLEN GINSBERG

Howl (1956), *Kaddish* (1961), *Empty Mirror: Early Poems* (1961), *Reality Sandwiches* (1963), *Angkor Wat* (1968), *Planet News* (1968), *Airplane Dreams* (1968), *The Gates of Wrath* (1972), *The Fall of America* (1973), *Iron Horse* (1973), *First Blues* (1975), *Mind Breaths* (1977), *Plutonian Ode* (1981), *Collected Poems* (1984), *White Shroud* (1986).

The Yage Letters (with William Burroughs; 1963), *Indian Journals* (1969), *Allen Verbatim* (lectures; 1974), *Journals: Early Fifties Early Sixties* (1977), *Composed on the Tongue* (conversations; 1980), *Straight Hearts' Delight* (letters; 1980).

LOUISE GLÜCK

Firstborn (1968), *The House on Marshland* (1975), *Descending Figure* (1980), *The Triumph of Achilles* (1985), *Ararat* (1990).

JORIE GRAHAM

Hybrids of Plants and of Ghosts (1980), *Erosion* (1983), *The End of Beauty* (1987).

MARILYN HACKER

Presentation Piece (1974), *Separations* (1976), *Taking Notice* (1980), *Assumptions* (1985), *Love, Death, and the Changing of the Seasons* (1986), *Going Back to the River* (1990).

MICHAEL S. HARPER

Dear John, Dear Coltrane (1970), *History Is Your Own Heartbeat* (1971), *Song: I Want a Witness* (1972), *Debridement* (1973), *Nightmare Begins Responsibility* (1975), *Images of Kin: New and Selected Poems* (1977), *Healing Song for the Inner Ear* (1984).

ROBERT HASS

Field Guide (1973), *Praise* (1979), *Human Wishes* (1989).

Twentieth Century Pleasures (essays; 1984).

ROBERT HAYDEN

Heart-Shape in the Dust (1940), *The Lion and the Archer* (1948), *Figure of Time* (1955), *A Ballad of Remembrance* (1962), *Selected Poems* (1966), *Words in the Mourning Time* (1970), *The Night-Blooming Cereus* (1972), *Angle of Ascent* (1975), *American Journal* (1978), *Collected Poems* (1985).

Collected Prose (1984).

ANTHONY HECHT

A Summoning of Stones (1954), *The Hard Hours* (1967), *Millions of Strange Shadows* (1977), *The Venetian Vespers* (1979), *The Transparent Man* (1990), *Collected Earlier Poems* (1990).

Obbligati (essays; 1986).

EDWARD HIRSCH

For the Sleepwalkers (1981), *Wild Gratitude* (1986), *The Night Parade* (1989).

JOHN HOLLANDER

A Crackling of Thorns (1958), *Movie-Going* (1962), *Visions from the Ramble* (1965), *Types of Shape* (1969), *The Night Mirror* (1971), *Town and Country Matters* (1972), *The Head of the Bed* (1974), *Tales Told of the Fathers* (1975), *Reflections on Espionage* (1976), *Spectral Emanations: New and Selected Poems* (1978), *Blue Wine* (1979), *Powers of Thirteen* (1983), *In Time and Place* (1986), *Harp Lake* (1988).

The Untuning of the Sky (criticism; 1961), *Vision and Resonance* (criticism; 1975), *The Figure of Echo* (criticism; 1981), *Rhyme's Reason: A Guide to English Verse* (1981), *Melodious Guile* (criticism; 1988).

RICHARD HOWARD

Quantities (1962), *The Damages* (1967), *Untitled Subjects* (1969), *Findings* (1971), *Two-Part Inventions* (1974), *Fellow Feelings* (1976), *Misgivings* (1979), *Lining Up* (1983), *No Traveller* (1989).

Alone with America (criticism; 1969), *Preferences* (criticism; 1974).

RICHARD HUGO

A Run of Jacks (1961), *Death of the Kapowsin Tavern* (1965), *Good Luck in Cracked Italian* (1969), *The Lady in Kicking Horse Reservoir* (1973), *What Thou Lovest Well, Remains American* (1975), *31 Letters and 13 Dreams* (1977), *White Center* (1980), *The Right Madness on Skye* (1980), *Making Certain It Goes On: Collected Poems* (1984).

The Triggering Town (essays; 1979), *Death and the Good Life* (novel; 1981), *The Real West Marginal Way* (autobiography; 1986).

RANDALL JARRELL

Blood for a Stranger (1942), *Little Friend, Little Friend* (1945), *Losses* (1948), *The Seven-League Crutches* (1951), *Selected Poems* (1955), *The Woman at the Washington Zoo* (1960), *The Lost World* (1965), *Complete Poems* (1969).

Poetry and the Age (essays; 1953), *Pictures from an Institution* (novel; 1954), *A Sad Heart at the Supermarket* (essays; 1962), *The Third Book of Criticism* (essays; 1969), *Kipling, Auden & Co.* (essays; 1980).

DONALD JUSTICE

The Summer Anniversaries (1960), *Night Light* (1967), *Departures* (1973), *Selected Poems* (1979), *The Sunset Maker* (1987).

Platonic Scripts (essays; 1984).

GALWAY KINNELL

What a Kingdom It Was (1960), *Flower Herding on Mount Monadnock* (1964), *Body Rags* (1968), *The Book of Nightmares* (1971), *The Avenue Bearing the Initial of Christ into the New World* (1974), *Mortal Acts, Mortal Words* (1980), *Selected Poems* (1982), *The Past* (1985), *When One Has Lived a Long Time Alone* (1990).

Black Light (novel; 1966), *Walking Down the Stairs* (interviews; 1978).

CAROLYN KIZER

The Ungrateful Garden (1961), *Knock Upon the Silence* (1965), *Midnight Was My Cry* (1971), *Mermaids in the Basement* (1984), *Yin* (1984), *The Nearness of You* (1986).

DENISE LEVERTOV

The Double Image (1946), *Here and Now* (1957), *With Eyes at the Back of Our Heads* (1959), *The Jacob's Ladder* (1961), *O Taste and See* (1964), *The Sorrow Dance* (1967), *Relearning the Alphabet* (1970), *To Stay Alive* (1971), *Footprints* (1972), *The Freeing of the Dust* (1975), *Life in the Forest* (1978), *Collected Earlier Poems, 1940–1960* (1979), *Candles in Babylon* (1982), *Poems, 1960–1967* (1983), *Oblique Prayers* (1984), *Poems, 1968–1972* (1987), *Breathing the Water* (1987), *A Door in the Hive* (1989).

The Poet in the World (essays; 1973), *Light Up the Cave* (essays; 1981).

PHILIP LEVINE

On the Edge (1963), *Not This Pig* (1968), *Red Dust* (1971), *They Feed They Lion* (1972), *1933* (1974), *The Names of the Lost* (1976), *Ashes* (1979), *7 Years from Somewhere* (1979), *One for the Rose* (1981), *Selected Poems* (1984), *Sweet Will* (1985), *A Walk with Tom Jefferson* (1988).

Don't Ask (interviews; 1981).

AUDRE LORDE

The First Cities (1968), *Cables to Rage* (1970), *From a Land Where Other People Live* (1973), *New York Head Shop and Museum* (1974), *Coal* (1976), *The Black Unicorn* (1978), *Chosen Poems, Old and New* (1982), *Our Dead Behind Us* (1986).

The Cancer Journals (prose; 1980), *Zami: A New Spelling of My Name* (prose; 1982), *Sister Outsider* (essays; 1984), *A Burst of Light* (essays; 1988).

ROBERT LOWELL

Lord Weary's Castle (1946), *The Mills of the Kavanaughs* (1951), *Life Studies* (1959), *Imitations* (1961), *For the Union Dead* (1964), *Near the Ocean* (1967), *Notebook, 1967–68* (1969), *History* (1973), *For Lizzie and Harriet* (1973), *The Dolphin* (1973), *Selected Poems* (1976), *Day by Day* (1977).

The Old Glory (plays; 1965), *Collected Prose* (1987).

SANDRA McPHERSON

Elegies for the Hot Season (1970), *Radiation* (1973), *The Year of Our Birth* (1978), *Patron Happiness* (1983), *Streamers* (1988).

WILLIAM MEREDITH

Love Letter from an Impossible Land (1944), *Ships and Other Figures* (1948), *The Open Sea* (1958), *The Wreck of the Thresher* (1964), *Earth Walk: New and Selected Poems* (1970), *Hazard, the Painter* (1975), *The Cheer* (1980), *Partial Accounts: New and Selected Poems* (1987).

JAMES MERRILL

First Poems (1951), *The Country of a Thousand Years of Peace* (1959), *Water Street* (1962), *Nights and Days* (1966), *The Fire Screen* (1969), *Braving the Elements* (1972), *The Yellow Pages* (1974), *Divine Comedies* (1976), *Mirabell: Books of*

Number (1978), *Scripts for the Pageant* (1980), *The Changing Light at Sandover* (1982), *From the First Nine: Poems, 1946–1976* (1982), *Late Settings* (1985), *The Inner Room* (1988).

The Seraglio (novel; 1957), *The (Diblos) Notebook* (novel; 1965), *Recitative* (essays; 1986).

W. S. MERWIN

A Mask for Janus (1952), *The Dancing Bears* (1954), *Green with Beasts* (1956), *The Drunk in the Furnace* (1960), *The Moving Target* (1963), *The Lice* (1967), *The Carrier of Ladders* (1970), *Writings to an Unfinished Accompaniment* (1973), *The Compass Flower* (1975), *Finding the Islands* (1982), *Opening the Hand* (1983), *The Rain in the Trees* (1988), *Selected Poems* (1988).

The Miner's Pale Children (prose; 1970), *Houses and Travellers* (prose; 1977), *Unframed Originals* (autobiography; 1982).

HOWARD MOSS

The Wound and the Weather (1946), *The Toy Fair* (1954), *A Swimmer in the Air* (1957), *A Winter Come, a Summer Gone* (1960), *Finding Them Lost* (1965), *Second Nature* (1968), *Selected Poems* (1971), *Buried City* (1975), *A Swim off the Rocks* (1976), *Notes from the Castle* (1980), *Rules of Sleep* (1984), *New Selected Poems* (1985).

The Magic Lantern of Marcel Proust (criticism; 1962), *Instant Lives* (satire; 1974), *Minor Monuments: Selected Essays* (1986).

HOWARD NEMEROV

The Image and the Law (1947), *Guide to the Ruins* (1950), *The Salt Garden* (1955), *Mirrors and Windows* (1958), *The Next Room of the Dream* (1962), *The Blue Swallows* (1967), *Gnomes and Occasions* (1973), *The Western Approaches* (1975), *Collected Poems* (1977), *Sentences* (1980), *Inside the Onion* (1984), *War Stories* (1987).

The Melodramatists (novel; 1949), *Federigo* (novel; 1954), *The Homecoming Game* (novel; 1957), *A Commodity of Dreams* (stories; 1959), *Poetry and Fiction* (essays; 1963), *Journal of the Fictive Life* (autobiography; 1965), *Stories, Fables, and Other Diversions* (1971), *Reflexions on Poetry and Poetics* (essays; 1972), *Figures of Thought* (essays; 1978), *The Oak in the Acorn* (criticism; 1987).

FRANK O'HARA

Meditations in an Emergency (1957), *Odes* (1960), *Lunch Poems* (1964), *Love Poems (Tentative Title)* (1965), *In Memory of My Feelings* (1967), *Collected Poems* (1971), *Poems Retrieved* (1977), *Early Writing* (1977).

Art Chronicles, 1954–1966 (1975), *Standing Still and Walking in New York* (essays and interview; 1975), *Selected Plays* (1978).

CHARLES OLSON

The Maximus Poems (1960), *The Distances* (1960), *Archeologist of Morning* (1971), *The Maximus Poems* (1983), *Collected Poems (Excluding the* Maximus *Poems)* (1987).

Call Me Ishmael (criticism; 1947), *The Mayan Letters* (1953), *The Human Universe* (essays; 1967), *Letters for Origin* (1970), *Poetry and Truth* (lectures; 1971), *Additional Prose* (1974), *The Fiery Hunt* (plays; 1977), *Muthologos: The Collected Lectures & Interviews* (Vol. I, 1978; Vol. II, 1979).

ROBERT PINSKY

Sadness and Happiness (1975), *An Explanation of America* (1979), *History of My Heart* (1984), *The Want Bone* (1990).

Landor's Poetry (criticism; 1968), *The Situation of Poetry* (criticism; 1976), *Poetry and the World* (essays; 1988).

SYLVIA PLATH

The Colossus (1962), *Ariel* (1966), *Crossing the Water* (1971), *Winter Trees* (1972), *Collected Poems* (1981).

The Bell Jar (novel; 1963), *Letters Home* (1975), *Johnny Panic and the Bible of Dreams* (stories; 1979), *The Journals of Sylvia Plath* (1982).

ADRIENNE RICH

A Change of World (1951), *The Diamond Cutters* (1955), *Snapshots of a Daughter-in-Law* (1963), *Necessities of Life* (1966), *Leaflets* (1969), *The Will to Change* (1971), *Diving into the Wreck* (1973), *The Dream of a Common Language* (1978), *A Wild Patience Has Taken Me This Far* (1981), *The Fact of a Doorframe: Poems Selected and New* (1985), *Your Native Land, Your Life* (1986), *Time's Power* (1989).

Of Woman Born: Motherhood as Experience and Institution (prose; 1976), *On Lies, Secrets, and Silence* (essays; 1979), *Blood, Bread, and Poetry* (essays; 1986).

THEODORE ROETHKE

Open House (1941), *The Lost Son* (1948), *Praise to the End!* (1951), *The Waking* (1953), *Words for the Wind* (1958), *The Far Field* (1964), *Collected Poems* (1966).

On the Poet and His Craft (essays; 1965), *Selected Letters* (1968), *Straw for the Fire* (notebooks; 1972).

GJERTRUD SCHNACKENBERG

Portraits and Elegies (1982), *The Lamplit Answer* (1985).

JAMES SCHUYLER

Freely Espousing (1969), *The Crystal Lithium* (1972), *Hymn to Life* (1974), *The Morning of the Poem* (1980), *A Few Days* (1985), *Selected Poems* (1988).

Alfred and Guinevere (novel; 1958), *A Nest of Ninnies* (novel, with John Ashbery; 1969), *The Home Book* (prose; 1977), *What's for Dinner?* (novel; 1978).

ANNE SEXTON

To Bedlam and Part Way Back (1960), *All My Pretty Ones* (1962), *Live or Die* (1966), *Love Poems* (1969), *Transformations* (1971), *The Book of Folly* (1972), *The Death Notebooks* (1974), *The Awful Rowing Toward God* (1975), *45 Mercy Street* (1976), *Words for Dr. Y* (1978), *The Complete Poems* (1981).

Anne Sexton: A Self-Portrait in Letters (1977), *No Evil Star* (essays and interviews; 1985).

CHARLES SIMIC

Dismantling the Silence (1971), *Return to a Place Lit by a Glass of Milk* (1974), *Charon's Cosmology* (1977), *Classic Ballroom Dances* (1980), *Austerities* (1982), *Selected Poems* (1985), *Unending Blues* (1986), *The World Doesn't End* (1989).

The Uncertain Certainty (essays and interviews; 1985).

DAVE SMITH

Mean Rufus Throw Down (1973), *The Fisherman's Whore* (1974), *Cumberland Station* (1977), *Goshawk, Antelope* (1979), *Homage to Edgar Allan Poe* (1981),

Dream Flights (1981), *In the House of the Judge* (1983), *Gray Soldiers* (1983), *The Roundhouse Voices: Selected and New Poems* (1985), *Cuba Night* (1990).

Onliness (novel; 1981), *Southern Delights* (stories; 1984), *Local Assays* (essays; 1985).

W. D. SNODGRASS

Heart's Needle (1959), *After Experience* (1968), *The Fuehrer Bunker* (1977), *Selected Poems, 1957–1987* (1987).

In Radical Pursuit (essays; 1975).

GARY SNYDER

Riprap (1959), *Myths and Texts* (1960), *The Back Country* (1968), *Regarding Wave* (1970), *Turtle Island* (1974), *Axe Handles* (1983), *Left Out in the Rain* (1986).

Earth House Hold (essays; 1969), *The Old Ways* (essays; 1977), *The Real Work* (interviews and talks; 1980), *The Practice of the Wild* (essays; 1990).

MARK STRAND

Sleeping with One Eye Open (1964), *Reasons for Moving* (1968), *Darker* (1970), *The Story of Our Lives* (1973), *The Late Hour* (1978), *Selected Poems* (1980), *The Continuous Life* (1990).

The Monument (prose; 1978), *Mr. and Mrs. Baby* (stories; 1985).

MAY SWENSON

Another Animal (1954), *A Cage of Spines* (1958), *To Mix with Time* (1963), *Half Sun Half Sleep* (1967), *Iconographs* (1970), *New and Selected Things Taking Place* (1978), *In Other Words* (1987).

MONA VAN DUYN

Valentines to the Wide World (1959), *A Time of Bees* (1964), *To See, to Take* (1970), *Bedtime Stories* (1972), *Merciful Disguises* (1973), *Letters from a Father* (1982), *Near Changes* (1990).

DAVID WAGONER

Dry Sun, Dry Wind (1953), *A Place to Stand* (1958), *The Nesting Ground* (1963), *Staying Alive* (1966), *New and Selected Poems* (1969), *Riverbed* (1972), *Sleeping in the Woods* (1974), *Travelling Light* (1976), *Collected Poems, 1956–1976* (1976), *Who Shall Be the Sun?* (1978), *In Broken Country* (1979), *Landfall* (1981), *First Light* (1983), *Through the Forest: New and Selected Poems* (1987).

The Man in the Middle (novel; 1954), *Money Money Money* (novel; 1955), *Rock* (novel; 1958), *The Escape Artist* (novel; 1965), *Baby, Come on Inside* (novel; 1968), *Where Is My Wandering Boy Tonight?* (novel; 1970), *The Road to Many a Wonder* (novel; 1974), *Tracker* (novel; 1975), *Whole Hog* (novel; 1976), *The Hanging Garden* (novel; 1980).

ROBERT PENN WARREN

Selected Poems, 1923–1943 (1944), *Brother to Dragons* (1953), *Promises* (1957), *You, Emperor and Others* (1960), *Incarnations* (1968), *Audubon: A Vision* (1969), *Or Else* (1974), *Now and Then* (1978), *Being Here* (1980), *Rumor Verified* (1981), *Chief Joseph of the Nez Perce* (1983), *New and Selected Poems: 1923–1985* (1985).

Night Rider (novel; 1939), *At Heaven's Gate* (novel; 1943), *All the King's Men* (novel; 1946), *The Circus in the Attic* (stories; 1947), *World Enough and Time* (novel; 1950), *Band of Angels* (novel; 1955), *The Cave* (novel; 1959), *Flood* (novel; 1964), *Meet Me in the Green Glen* (novel; 1971), *A Place to Come To* (novel; 1977), *New and Selected Essays* (1989).

RICHARD WILBUR

The Beautiful Changes (1947), *Ceremony* (1950), *Things of This World* (1956), *Advice to a Prophet* (1961), *Walking to Sleep* (1969), *The Mind-Reader* (1976), *New and Collected Poems* (1988).

Responses (essays; 1976).

C. K. WILLIAMS

Lies (1969), *I Am the Bitter Name* (1972), *With Ignorance* (1977), *Tar* (1983), *Flesh and Blood* (1987), *Poems, 1963–1983* (1988).

CHARLES WRIGHT

The Grave of the Right Hand (1970), *Hard Freight* (1973), *Bloodlines* (1975), *China Trace* (1977), *The Southern Cross* (1981), *Country Music: Selected Early*

Poems (1982), *The Other Side of the River* (1984), *Zone Journals* (1988), *The World of the Ten Thousand Things* (1990).

Halflife (essays and interviews; 1988).

JAMES WRIGHT

The Green Wall (1957), *Saint Judas* (1959), *The Branch Will Not Break* (1963), *Collected Poems* (1971), *Two Citizens* (1973), *To a Blossoming Pear Tree* (1977), *This Journey* (1982), *Above the River: The Complete Poems* (1990).

Collected Prose (1982).

JAY WRIGHT

The Homecoming Singer (1971), *Soothsayers and Omens* (1976), *Dimensions of History* (1976), *The Double Invention of Komo* (1980), *Explication/Interpretation* (1984), *Selected Poems* (1987), *Elaine's Book* (1988).

The West Door. Originally appeared in *The New Yorker.* Copyright © 1988 by Alfred Corn. All rights reserved. Reprinted by permission of Viking Penguin, a division of Penguin Books USA, Inc.

Robert Creeley: "I Know a Man," "The Rescue," "Air: The Love of a Woman," "For Friendship," "For Love," "Again," and "The World" from *Collected Poems of Robert Creeley, 1945–1975.* Copyright © 1983 by The Regents of the University of California. Reprinted by permission of the University of California Press.

J.V. Cunningham: "For My Contemporaries," "For My Wife," and excerpts from "A Century of Epigrams" (29, 53, 55, 62 and 76) from *The Collected Poems and Epigrams of J.V. Cunningham,* Swallow Press, 1971. Reprinted by permission of Ohio University Press.

James Dickey: "The Heaven of Animals" (originally appeared in *The New Yorker*), "The Hospital Window," and "The Sheep Child" from *Poems.* Copyright © 1967 by James Dickey. "The Strength of Fields" from *The Central Motion.* Copyright © 1983 by James Dickey. Reprinted by permission of Wesleyan University Press.

Rita Dove: "Parsley" and "Adolescence—II" from *Museum* and *The Yellow House on the Corner.* Copyright © 1980, 1983 by Rita Dove. Reprinted by permission of Carnegie–Mellon University Press. "Canary" from *Grace Notes.* Copyright © 1989 by Rita Dove. Reprinted by permission of W.W. Norton and Company, Inc.

Robert Duncan: "A Poem Beginning with a Line by Pindar" from *The Opening of the Field.* Copyright © 1960 by Robert Duncan. "Styx" from *Ground Work II.* Copyright © 1987 by Robert Duncan. Reprinted by permission of New Directions Publishing Corporation.

Irving Feldman: "Family History" from *New and Selected Poems.* Copyright © 1979 by Irving Feldman. "The Dream" is reprinted by permission of the author. Excerpts from "All Of Us Here" from *All of Us Here.* Copyright © 1983, 1984, 1985, 1986 by Irving Feldman. All rights reserved. Reprinted by permission of Viking Penguin, a division of Penguin Books USA, Inc.

Jean Garrigue: "Amsterdam Letter" (originally appeared in *The New Yorker*) and "Cracked Looking Glass" from *New and Selected Poems*; and "After Reading *The Country of the Pointed Firs*" from *Studies for an Actress.* Copyright © 1964, 1973 by The Estate of Jean Garrigue. Reprinted by permission of the Eakins Press Foundation Publishers.

Allen Ginsberg: "Wales Visitation" (originally appeared in *The New Yorker*), excerpt from "Howl," "Sunflower Sutra," and "My Sad Self" from *Collected Poems 1947–1980.* Copyright © 1955, 1958, 1968 by Allen Ginsberg. Reprinted by permission of Harper & Row Publishers, Inc.

Louise Glück: "Messengers" from *The House on Marshland,* The Ecco Press, 1975. Copyright © 1971, 1972, 1973, 1974, 1975 by Louise Glück. "The Drowned Children" (originally appeared in *The New Yorker*), "The Garden," "Palais des Arts," and "Lamentations" from *Descending Figure,* The Ecco Press, 1980. Copyright © 1976, 1977, 1978, 1979, 1980 by Louise Glück. "Mock Orange" from *Triumph of Achilles,* The Ecco Press, 1985. Copyright © 1985 by Louise Glück. Reprinted by permission of The Ecco Press.

Jorie Graham: "Over and Over Stitch" from *Erosion.* Copyright © 1982 by Princeton University Press. "San Sepolcro" from *Hybrids of Plants and of Ghosts.* Copyright © 1980 by Princeton University Press. Reprinted by permission of Princeton

1965 by Maureen Granville-Smith, executrix for the Estate of Frank O'Hara. Reprinted by permission of Alfred A. Knopf, Inc. "To the Harbormaster" and "Meditations in an Emergency" from *Meditations in an Emergency.* Copyright © 1957 by Frank O'Hara. Reprinted by permission of Grove Weidenfeld. "A Step Away from Them," "The Day Lady Died," and "Ave Maria" from *Lunch Poems.* Copyright © 1964 by Frank O'Hara. Reprinted by permission of City Lights Books.

Charles Olson: "The Kingfishers" from *Collected Poetry of Charles Olson,* edited by George Butterick. Copyright © 1987 by the Estate of Charles Olson. Reprinted by permission of the University of California Press.

Robert Pinsky: "The Hearts" from *The Want Bone.* Copyright 1990 by Robert Pinsky. Reprinted by permission of the author. "Ralegh's Prizes" (originally appeared in *The New Yorker*) and "Dying" from *History of My Heart,* first published by The Ecco Press in 1984. Copyright © 1984 by Robert Pinsky. Reprinted by permission of The Ecco Press. "Poem About People" from *Sadness and Happiness.* Copyright © 1975 by Princeton University Press. Reprinted by permission of Princeton University Press.

Sylvia Plath: "The Colossus" from *The Colossus and Other Poems.* Copyright © 1961 by Sylvia Plath. Reprinted by permission of Alfred A. Knopf, Inc. "The Hanging Man," Copyright © 1960 by Ted Hughes; "Morning Song," Copyright © 1961 by Ted Hughes; "Daddy," Copyright © 1963 by Ted Hughes; "Fever 103°," Copyright © 1963 by Ted Hughes; "Ariel," Copyright © 1965 by Ted Hughes; "Lady Lazarus," Copyright © 1963 by Ted Hughes; "Edge," Copyright © 1963 by Ted Hughes; "Words," Copyright © 1965 by Ted Hughes from *The Collected Poems of Sylvia Plath,* Harper and Row Publishers, Inc. and *Collected Poems,* Faber & Faber, Ltd. Reprinted by permission of Harper and Row Publishers, Inc. and Olwyn Hughes, London.

Adrienne Rich: "For the Record" from *Your Native Land, Your Life.* Copyright © 1986 by Adrienne Rich. "For An Album" from *Time's Power, 1985–1988.* Copyright © 1989 by Adrienne Rich. "Snapshots of a Daughter-in-Law," "Planetarium," "The Burning of Paper Instead of Children," and "Paula Becker to Clara Westhoff" from *The Fact of a Doorframe, Poems Selected and New 1950–1984.* Copyright © 1981, 1984 by Adrienne Rich, Copyright © 1975, 1978 by W.W. Norton and Company, Inc. Reprinted by permission of W.W. Norton and Company, Inc.

Theodore Roethke: "Cuttings (later)," Copyright 1948 by Theodore Roethke; "Root Cellar," Copyright 1943 by Modern Poetry Association, Inc.; "The Shape of the Fire," Copyright 1947 by Theodore Roethke, "The Waking," Copyright 1953 by Theodore Roethke; "I Knew a Woman," Copyright 1954 by Theodore Roethke; "In a Dark Time," Copyright © 1960 by Beatrice Roethke, administratrix of the Estate of Theodore Roethke. All from *The Collected Poems of Theodore Roethke.* Used by permission of Doubleday, a division of Bantam, Doubleday, Dell Publishing Group, Inc.

Gjertrud Schnackenberg: "Signs" and "Supernatural Love" from *The Lamplit Answer.* Copyright © 1982, 1985 by Gjertrud Schnackenberg. "The Paperweight" from *Portraits and Elegies.* Copyright © 1982, 1986 by Gjertrud Schnackenberg. Reprinted by permission of Farrar, Straus & Giroux, Inc.

James Schuyler: "The Crystal Lithium," "Shimmer," and "Korean Mums" from *Selected Poems.* Copyright © 1969, 1972, 1974, 1980, 1981, 1982, 1984, 1985, 1988 by James Schuyler. Reprinted by permission of Farrar, Straus & Giroux, Inc

Anne Sexton: "Her Kind" and "Music Swims Back To Me" from *To Bedlam and Part Way Back*. Copyright © 1960 by Anne Sexton. "The Truth the Dead Know," "The Starry Night," and "With Mercy for the Greedy" from *All My Pretty Ones*. Copyright © 1962 by Anne Sexton. "Wanting to Die" from *Live or Die*. Copyright © 1966 by Anne Sexton. "The Room of My Life" from *The Awful Rowing Toward God*. Copyright © 1975 by Loring Conant, Jr., executor of the Estate of Anne Sexton. Reprinted by permission of Houghton Mifflin Co.

Charles Simic: excerpts from *The World Doesn't End*. Copyright © 1989 by Charles Simic. Reprinted by permission of Harcourt Brace Jovanovich, Inc. "Eyes Fastened With Pins" from *Charon's Cosmology*. Copyright © 1977 by Charles Simic. "Empire of Dreams" and "Prodigy" from *Classic Ballroom Dances*. Copyright © 1980 by Charles Simic. "Watermelons" from *Return to a Place Lit by a Glass of Milk*. Copyright © 1974 by Charles Simic. "Tapestry," "My Shoes," and "Concerning My Neighbors, the Hittites" from *Dismantling the Silence*. Copyright © 1971 by Charles Simic. Reprinted by permission of George Braziller, Inc.

Dave Smith: "Lake Drummond Dream" from *Cuba Night*. Copyright 1990 by Dave Smith. Reprinted by permission of William Morrow & Company, Inc. "Elegy in an Abandoned Boatyard" and "The Roundhouse Voices" from *The Roundhouse Voices*. Copyright © 1985 by Dave Smith. Both originally appeared in *The New Yorker*. Reprinted by permission of the University of Illinois Press.

W.D. Snodgrass: "April Inventory," "Mementos, 1," "A Locked House," and parts 2 and 6 of "Heart's Needle" from *Selected Poems 1957–1987*. Copyright 1959, 1986, 1987 by W.D. Snodgrass. Reprinted by permission of Soho Press.

Gary Snyder: "Riprap" and "Mid-August at Sourdough Mountain Lookout." Copyright © 1965 by Gary Snyder. Reprinted by permission of the author. "Axe Handles" from *Axe Handles*. Copyright © 1983 by Gary Snyder. Published by North Point Press and reprinted with their permission. "Burning Island" from *Regarding Wave*. Copyright © 1970 by Gary Snyder. "The Bath" and "I Went Into the Maverick Bar" from *Turtle Island*. Copyright © 1974 by Gary Snyder. Reprinted by permission of New Directions Publishing Corporation.

Mark Strand: "Keeping Things Whole" from *Reasons for Moving*. Copyright © 1964 by Mark Strand. "Coming to This," "The Prediction," and " 'The Dreadful Has Already Happened' " from *Darker*. Copyright © 1968, 1969, 1970 by Mark Strand. "The Story of Our Lives" from *The Story of Our Lives*. Copyright © 1972 by Mark Strand. Originally appeared in *The New Yorker*. "Where Are The Waters of Childhood?" from *Late Hours*. Copyright © 1973, 1975, 1976, 1977, 1978 by Mark Strand. Originally appeared in *The New Yorker*. All currently from *Selected Poems*. Reprinted by permission of Atheneum Publishers, an imprint of Macmillan Publishing Company.

May Swenson: "Teleology." Copyright © 1971 by May Swenson. "Stone Gullets." Copyright © 1978 by May Swenson. "Unconscious Came a Beauty." Copyright © 1968 by May Swenson. Originally appeared in *The New Yorker*. "Staying at Ed's Place." Copyright © 1975 by May Swenson. Originally appeared in *The New Yorker*. Reprinted by permission of the author. "Strawberrying" from *In Other Words*. Copyright © 1987 by May Swenson. Reprinted by permission of Alfred A. Knopf, Inc.

Mona Van Duyn: "Homework." Copyright © 1969 by Mona Van Duyn. Originally appeared in *Poetry*. "Into Mexico" and "The Twins" from *To See, To Take*.

ABOUT THE EDITOR

J. D. McClatchy is the author of three collections of poems, *Scenes From Another Life* (1981), *Stars Principal* (1986), and *The Rest of the Way* (1990), and a book of criticism, *White Paper* (1989). He has edited several other books as well, and his essays and reviews appear regularly in the leading journals. A recipient of awards and fellowships from the American Academy and Institute of Arts and Letters, the National Endowment for the Arts, and the Guggenheim Foundation, he has taught at Princeton, Yale, UCLA, and other universities, and has served as poetry editor of *The Yale Review.* He lives in New York City.